I0483474

BiteSize Python for Intermediate Learners

This book is an introduction to Python for intermediate learners. It allows readers to take a slow and steady approach to building upon their understanding of Python code. While there are many books, websites, and online courses about the topic, Python programming is broken down here into easily digestible lessons of less than 5 minutes each, following a tried and tested BiteSize approach.

Each lesson begins with a clear and concise introduction to the topic, giving the reader a strong base to start from and gets them ready for deeper learning. This is followed by coding demonstrations that further explore the ideas discussed. The book offers practice tasks in different difficulty levels, so readers can test their knowledge and grow their confidence. The reader will also play with case studies to solve real-world problems. Tips on how to incorporate Generative AI into a learning toolkit are provided, for purposes like feedback, practice exercises, code reviews, and exploring advanced topics. Recommended AI prompts can help readers identify areas for improvement, review key concepts, and track progress.

This book is designed for intermediate learners with a basic understanding of Python. It is ideal for individuals with busy schedules or limited time for studying.

Chapman & Hall/CRC
The Python Series

About the Series

Python has been ranked as the most popular programming language, and it is widely used in education and industry. This book series will offer a wide range of books on Python for students and professionals. Titles in the series will help users learn the language at an introductory and advanced level, and explore its many applications in data science, AI, and machine learning. Series titles can also be supplemented with Jupyter notebooks.

Introduction to Python for Humanists
William J.B. Mattingly

Python for Scientific Computation and Artificial Intelligence
Stephen Lynch

Learning Professional Python Volume 1: The Basics
Usharani Bhimavarapu and Jude D. Hemanth

Learning Professional Python Volume 2: Advanced
Usharani Bhimavarapu and Jude D. Hemanth

Learning Advanced Python from Open Source Projects
Rongpeng Li

Foundations of Data Science with Python
John Mark Shea

Data Mining with Python: Theory, Applications, and Case Studies
Di Wu

A Simple Introduction to Python
Stephen Lynch

Introduction to Python: with Applications in Optimization, Image and Video Processing, and Machine Learning
David Baez-Lopez and David Alfredo Báez Villegas

Tidy Finance with Python
Christoph Frey, Christoph Scheuch, Stefan Voigt and Patrick Weiss

Introduction to Quantitative Social Science with Python
Weiqi Zhang and Dmitry Zinoviev

Python Programming for Mathematics
Julien Guillod

Geocomputation with Python
Michael Dorman, Anita Graser, Jakub Nowosad and Robin Lovelace

BiteSize Python for Absolute Beginners: With Practice Labs, Real-World Examples, and Generative AI Assistance
Di Wu

Data Clustering with Python: From Theory to Implementation
Guojun Gan

Linear Algebra for Data Science with Python
John M. Shea

BiteSize Python for Intermediate Learners: With Practice Labs, Real-World Examples, and ChatGPT
Di Wu

For more information about this series please visit: https://www.routledge.com/Chapman--HallCRC-The-Python-Series/book-series/PYTH

BiteSize Python for Intermediate Learners

With Practice Labs, Real-World Examples, and Generative AI Assistance

Di Wu

CRC Press
Taylor & Francis Group
Boca Raton London New York

CRC Press is an imprint of the
Taylor & Francis Group, an **informa** business

A CHAPMAN & HALL BOOK

Designed Cover Image: ShutterStock ID 1387214564

First edition published 2026
by CRC Press
2385 NW Executive Center Drive, Suite 320, Boca Raton FL 33431

and by CRC Press
4 Park Square, Milton Park, Abingdon, Oxon, OX14 4RN

CRC Press is an imprint of Taylor & Francis Group, LLC

© 2026 Di Wu

ISBN: 978-1-041-03684-5 (hbk)
ISBN: 978-1-041-03682-1 (pbk)
ISBN: 978-1-003-62486-8 (ebk)

DOI: 10.1201/9781003624868

Typeset in Latin Modern font
by KnowledgeWorks Global Ltd.

To my parents.

Contents

List of Figures

List of Tables

Foreword

WHY WE NEED THIS BOOK

Start your journey into the exciting world of Python programming with this book! Built upon the first book: *BiteSize Python for Absolute Beginners*, as the second book in the *BiteSize Python* series, this book is designed for intermediate learners with basic understanding of Python and still introduces advanced Python topics in a refreshingly accessible way.

Forget overwhelming textbooks and long lectures, *BiteSize Python* breaks down the learning process into short, manageable lessons, each around 5 to 10 minutes. Whether you're busy or have trouble focusing for long periods, this approach makes it easy to fit learning Python into your daily routine.

You will learn essential Python concepts effortlessly through engaging lessons, practice labs, and real-world examples. From grasping basic syntax to writing your own programs, this book gives you the skills and confidence to become a capable Python programmer.

What makes *BiteSize Python* unique is its adaptability to your learning style. Whether you enjoy hands-on practice, self-reflection exercises, reviewing solutions, or interacting with generative AI, this book has something for everyone.

Discover the joy of learning Python at your own pace and unlock endless possibilities in the programming world. With this book, start your journey toward empowerment, efficiency, and practical skills that will quickly transform you from a beginner to a confident Python programmer.

Preface

WHY THIS BOOK IS DIFFERENT

While there are many books, websites, and online courses about the topic, we differentiate our book in multiple ways:

- BiteSize Approach: Breaks down Python programming into easily digestible lessons of less than 5 minutes each.

- Beginner-Friendly: Designed for absolute beginners with no prior programming experience.

- Practical Learning: Offers hands-on practice labs and real-world examples to reinforce learning.

- Time-Efficient: Ideal for individuals with busy schedules or limited time for studying.

- Comprehensive Coverage: Covers essential Python concepts and skills necessary for writing basic programs.

- Interactive Learning: Includes self-reflection exercises and solutions review to enhance understanding and retention.

SPECIFIC AIMS

As an introduction to Python, this book allows readers to take a slow and steady approach to understanding Python code, explaining concepts, connecting programming with real-life examples, writing Python programs, and completing case studies. The aims of this book are as follows:

- Give a simple and easy-to-understand introduction to Python programming for people who are complete beginners.

- Break down the learning process into bite-sized lessons to accommodate readers' limited time and attention spans.

- Help readers understand Python code and develop the skills to write their own programs.

- Provide a range of learning formats, including concept overviews, practice labs, and self-reflection exercises, to fit different learning styles.

- Showcase many interesting case studies and provide readers with a solid understanding of how to apply the knowledge to our real world.

HOW TO USE THIS BOOK

This book is made to give you a rich and engaging learning experience. Our method focuses on *BiteSize* learning, making hard topics easy by breaking them down into simple, understandable parts:

- Each lesson begins with a clear and short *introduction* to the topic. This gives you a strong base to start from and gets you ready for deeper learning.

- After the introduction, you will see *coding demonstrations* that show the ideas discussed. These examples are simple and useful, helping you really understand the concepts.

- After the introduction and demo, it is time to practice! The *practice* tasks come in different difficulty levels, so you can test your knowledge and grow your confidence. Make sure you try hard before checking the solutions!

- To help you learn better, we suggest using *Generative AI* tools like ChatGPT for feedback, practice exercises, code reviews, and finding advanced topics. These prompts can help you see where to improve, review main ideas, and think about your progress. We actually adopted some of the prompts that are created by AI in this book! Generative AI as a tool is great, but only we should use it wisely.

- Apply Python to make a difference! *Case studies* combine all the small ideas to show how you can use them to solve real-world problems.

- Most coding demos, practice tasks, and case studies come with *Jupyter Notebooks*. This format allows you to look at, change, and run the code, giving you a hands-on experience that makes learning more fun.

We believe this book will guide you step by step to learn Python and use it confidently in real life. No matter whether you are new to coding or just want to improve your Python skills, this book will help you reach your learning goals through these little fun *Bites*!

INTERACT WITH AI

To get the most out of your interaction with a generative AI tool like ChatGPT, always begin your conversation with the following prompt:

```
You are an expert in Python programming. Act as a tutor helping a
student who is learning Python programming.
```

This prompt sets the tone for the conversation and ensures the AI will provide helpful and detailed guidance tailored to your learning. Here are some general suggestions and prompts for effective interaction:

- Can you explain how [concept] works?
- What's the difference between [concept 1] and [concept 2]?
- Can you provide an example of a function that does [specific task]?
- Show me how to use a [specific structure or method] to achieve [goal].
- I don't understand why [specific method] isn't working. Can you help me troubleshoot it?
- My code: [Your Python Code] is not running. What is wrong? Can you correct it?
- Review my code: [Your Python Code]. Can you improve my code to make it more professional?
- Can you explain why [specific aspect] works this way?

In each Interact with GenAI section, we prepared specific suggestions and prompts for the specific topic as well. We hope you can utilize generative AI as a great tool to enhance and assist your learning.

ACKNOWLEDGMENT

The author has utilized various Generative AI models, including ChatGPT (4o-mini), Gemini (2.0), Claude (3.5 Haiku), Gemma (1.1:7b, 2:9b), Llama (3.1:8b, 3.2:3b), Apple Intelligence (Beta), and DeepSeek (R1:671b), to improve the language, proofread code comments, and come up with some ideas for the "Interact with GenAI" section. All the text generated by generative AI has been carefully reviewed and revised to meet academic standards.

I would also like to acknowledge the reviewers, editors, and publishers making the book happen.

Author Biographies

Dr. Di Wu is an Assistant Professor of Finance, Information Systems, and Economics Department of Business School, Lehman College. He obtained a Ph.D. in computer science from the Graduate Center, CUNY. His research interests are (1) temporal extensions to RDF and semantic web, (2) applied data science, and (3) experiential learning and pedagogy in business education. He developed and taught courses including Strategic Management, Databases, Business Statistics, Management Decision Making, Programming Languages (C++, Java, and Python), Data Structures and Algorithms, Data Mining, Big Data, and Machine Learning.

I

Object-Oriented Programming

S ECTION I: OBJECT-ORIENTED PROGRAMMING introduces a powerful programming approach that organizes code into classes and objects, to help manage and
scale complex systems more effectively. In this section, you'll learn about the core
concepts of OOP, including classes and objects, which serve as the blueprint and
instances of your code, respectively. The section also explores the four fundamental
principles of OOP: inheritance, polymorphism, abstraction, and encapsulation,
which help create flexible and reusable code. Additionally, you'll learn how to write
clear class documentation, making your code easier to read and work with. Even if
you don't plan to create your own packages, understanding how OOP plays a key
role in how they're built will help you use popular libraries like NumPy, Pandas, and
Matplotlib more effectively. This knowledge prepares you to work confidently with
the tools covered in this book.

By the end of this section, you will be able to:

- Understand the foundational concepts of object-oriented programming, including classes and objects.

- Apply inheritance to create hierarchical relationships between classes.

- Utilize polymorphism to design flexible and interchangeable code components.

- Implement abstraction and encapsulation to hide complexity and protect data
  within your programs.

- Professionally document class definitions to improve code clarity and user efficiency.

CHAPTER 1

Introduction to OOP

OBJECT-ORIENTED PROGRAMMING (OOP) is a programming concept centered around the concept of objects. These objects are instances of classes, which can be thought of as blueprints for creating individual instances. OOP emphasizes the organization of code into reusable, modular units, making it easier to manage, maintain, and understand complex software systems. You might have noticed that all strings have the same basic functions, and different instances of the same data structure, like a `list`, can behave in similar ways. In this chapter, we are going to learn the concept of OOP in detail, including the four aspects: inheritance, polymorphism, encapsulation, and abstraction. We'll also learn how to prepare clear and professional documentation, so other people can use our defined classes effectively.

Are you ready? Let's get started!

1.1 THE IDEA

1.1.1 Explanation

The key idea of OOP is about classes, objects, and their relationships. Let's summarize them here:

- A class is a blueprint for creating objects. It defines a set of attributes and methods that the created object (instances) will have. Think of a class as a template.
- An object is an instance of a class. It is a self-contained entity that contains both data (attributes, properties, fields) and functions (methods) that operate on the data.
- The class defines the structure and behavior (in the form of attributes and methods), while objects are the concrete instances of the class. Multiple objects can be created from a single class, each with its own unique set of values for the attributes.

DOI: 10.1201/9781003624868-1

1.1.2   Real-life Examples

For example, a class `Car` may have attributes, which are the data points that define a car, such as `make`, `model`, `year`, and `color`. The class `Car` may have functions, which are the actions a car can perform, such as `start()`, `stop()`, and `drive()`. The objects of `Car` are individual cars. Each car (object) will have specific values for the attributes defined in the `Car` class. For example, one object might represent a red 2020 Toyota Corolla, while another object might represent a blue 2019 Honda Civic.

Let's look at another example. A class `Employee` may have attributes that define an employee, such as `name`, `id`, `department`, and `salary`. The class may also have actions an employee can perform, such as `promote()`, `transfer()`, and `give_raise()`. The objects of `Employee` are individual employees in the company, and each employee (object) will have specific values for the attributes defined in the `Employee` class. For example, one object might represent an employee named John Doe in the IT department, while another object might represent an employee named Jane Smith in the HR department.

We may have a class `Smartphone` that represents all smartphones. The class `Smartphone` may have attributes, such as `brand`, `model`, `storage`, `color`, and `price`. It may have methods that a smartphone can perform, such as `make_call()`, `send_message()`, and `apply_discount()`. The objects of `Smartphone` represent each smartphone, which has specific values for the attributes defined in the `Smartphone` class. For example, one object might represent an iPhone 16 with 256GB storage, while another object might represent a Samsung Galaxy S23 with 512GB storage.

1.1.3   Practice

Task: Think about a class `Student` and its objects. Can you describe this class with its possible attributes and methods, and make up some objects of this class?

Possible answer: The class `Student` should have attributes that define a student, such as `name`, `student_id`, `major`, `gpa`, and `year`. It should have methods that a student may perform, such as `enroll_course()`, `update_gpa()`, and `graduate()`. The objects of the class `Student` will have specific values for the attributes defined in the `Student` class. For example, one object might represent a student Alice in Computer Science, while another object might represent a student Bob in Mathematics.

Task: Think about a class `Animal` and its objects. Can you describe this class with its possible attributes and methods, and make up some objects of this class?

Possible answer: The class `Animal` should have attributes that define an animal, such as `species`, `name`, `age`, `habitat`, and `diet`. It should have methods that an animal can perform, such as `make_sound()`, `eat()`, and `move()`. The objects of the class `Animal` will have specific values for the attributes defined in the `Animal` class. For example, one object might represent a lion named Leo, while another object might represent an elephant named Ella.

1.2 CREATE A CLASS

1.2.1 Demonstration

In Python, defining a class starts with the `class` keyword followed by the class name and a colon `:`. The class name should follow the convention of being a meaningful noun, written in PascalCase (each word starts with an uppercase letter).

Inside the class, you can define attributes and methods to describe its behavior. Attributes are variables to store data. They can be instance attributes (specific to each object) or class attributes (shared across all objects of the class). For example, `self.name` in a class stores information specific to an instance. Methods are functions to define behaviors or actions that objects of the class can perform. Methods often use `self` to access instance attributes or other methods.

The `self` is a reference to the instance of the class currently being used. Think of `self` as the way a method knows which object its working with. Together, attributes represent what an object is and methods represent what an object can do. This structure allows you to create reusable and organized blueprints for objects.

For example, we can define a `Car` class and add attributes and methods. The `__init__()` method initializes the car's attributes: `make`, `model`, `year`, and `color`. The `self` refers to the object that this method is creating.

We also define three methods: `start()`, `stop()`, and `drive()`, which represent actions the car can perform. The `self` refers to the object that calls the methods. We also define a special method: `__repr__()`. It returns a `str` that represents the object.

```python
# Defining the class Car
class Car:
  # Initialize the Car object with make, model, year, and color
  def __init__(self, make, model, year, color):
    self.make = make     # Assign the make of the car
    self.model = model   # Assign the model of the car
    self.year = year     # Assign the year of the car
    self.color = color   # Assign the color of the car

  # Method to start the car
  def start(self):
    print(f'The {self.color} {self.make} {self.model} is starting.')

  # Method to stop the car
  def stop(self):
    print(f'The {self.color} {self.make} {self.model} is stopping.')

  # Method to drive the car
  def drive(self):
    print(f'The {self.color} {self.make} {self.model} is driving.')

  # Method to return a string representation of the Car object
  def __repr__(self):
    return f'I am a {self.color} {self.make} {self.model} car!'
```

We create three objects, `car1`, `car2`, and `car3`, each with specific attributes.

```
# Creating objects (instances of the Car class)
car1 = Car('Toyota', 'Corolla', 2020, 'red')

car1
```

I am a red Toyota Corolla car!

```
# Creating objects (instances of the Car class)
car2 = Car('Honda', 'Civic', 2019, 'blue')

car2
```

I am a blue Honda Civic car!

```
# Creating objects (instances of the Car class)
car3 = Car('Tesla', 'Model S', 2024, 'silver')

car3
```

I am a silver Tesla Model S car!

We call the `start()` method on `car1`, the `drive()` method on `car2`, and `stop()` method on `car3`, demonstrating how each object can perform actions defined by the class.

```
# Using the methods on the objects
car1.start()
car2.drive()
car3.stop()
```

The red Toyota Corolla is starting.
The blue Honda Civic is driving.
The silver Tesla Model S is stopping.

Recall that we discussed the `Employee` class example previously. Here, we demonstrate the class definition and object creation for it.

```
# Define a class to represent an Employee
class Employee:
  # Initialize an Employee object
  def __init__(self, name, employee_id, department, salary):
    self.name = name
    self.employee_id = employee_id
    self.department = department
    self.salary = salary

  # Method to promote an employee
  def promote(self):
    print(f'{self.name} has been promoted.')

  # Method to transfer an employee to a new department
  def transfer(self, new_department):
    self.department = new_department
    print(f'{self.name} has been transferred to {self.department}.')
```

```
# Method to give an employee a raise
def give_raise(self, amount):
  self.salary += amount
  print(f'New salary of {self.name} is ${self.salary}.')

# Create two Employee objects
employee1 = Employee('John Doe', 'E123', 'IT', 60000)
employee2 = Employee('Jane Smith', 'E124', 'HR', 55000)

# Use the methods on the Employee objects
employee1.promote()
employee2.transfer('Marketing')
employee1.give_raise(5000)
```

```
John Doe has been promoted.
Jane Smith has been transferred to Marketing.
New salary of John Doe is $65000.
```

Recall we have discussed the **Smartphone** class previously. Here is the demonstration of defining the class and creating objects.

```
# Define a class to represent a Smartphone
class Smartphone:
  # Initialize a Smartphone object
  def __init__(self, brand, model, storage, color, price):
    self.brand = brand
    self.model = model
    self.storage = storage
    self.color = color
    self.price = price

  # Method to simulate making a call on the smartphone
  def make_call(self, phone_number):
    print(f'{self.brand} {self.model} is calling {phone_number}.')

# Create two Smartphone objects
phone1 = Smartphone('Apple', 'iPhone 16', 256, 'black', 999)
phone2 = Smartphone('Samsung', 'Galaxy S23', 512, 'white', 849)

# Use the make_call method on the Smartphone objects
phone1.make_call('123-456-7890')
phone2.make_call('987-654-3210')
```

```
Apple iPhone 16 is calling 123-456-7890.
Samsung Galaxy S23 is calling 987-654-3210.
```

1.2.2 Practice

Task: Define the class **Student** and create some objects. Recall that we discussed the class **Student** as:

- *Attributes:* These are the data points that define a student, such as name, student_id, major, gpa, and year.

- *Methods:* These are the actions a student can perform, such as enroll_course(), update_gpa(), and graduate().

```python
# Define a class to represent a Student
class Student:
  # Initialize a Student object with name, student_id, major, gpa, and year
  def __init__(self, name, student_id, major, gpa, year):
    self.name = name
    self.student_id = student_id
    self.major = major
    self.gpa = gpa
    self.year = year

  # Method to enroll a student in a course
  def enroll_course(self, course):
    print(f'{self.name} has enrolled in {course}.')

  # Method to update a student's GPA
  def update_gpa(self, new_gpa):
    self.gpa = new_gpa
    print(f'{self.name}\'s new GPA is {self.gpa}.')

  # Method to check if a student has met the graduation requirements
  def graduate(self):
    if self.year == 'Senior' and self.gpa >= 2.0:
      print(f'{self.name} has graduated!')
    else:
      print(f'{self.name} has not met the graduation requirements.')

# Create two Student objects
student1 = Student('Alice', 'S1001', 'Computer Science', 3.8, 'Junior')
student2 = Student('Bob', 'S1002', 'Mathematics', 3.4, 'Senior')

# Use the methods on the Student objects
student1.enroll_course('Data Structures')
student2.update_gpa(3.6)
student2.graduate()
```

```
Alice has enrolled in Data Structures.
Bob's new GPA is 3.6.
Bob has graduated!
```

Task: Define the class Animal and create some objects. Recall that we have discussed the class Animal as:

- *Attributes:* These are the data points that define an animal, such as species, name, age, habitat, and diet.
- *Methods:* These are the actions an animal can perform, such as make_sound(), eat(), and move().

```python
# Define a class to represent an Animal
class Animal:
  # Initialize an Animal object with species, name, age, habitat, and diet
  def __init__(self, species, name, age, habitat, diet):
```

```
    self.species = species
    self.name = name
    self.age = age
    self.habitat = habitat
    self.diet = diet

  # Method to simulate an animal making a sound
  def make_sound(self):
    print(f'{self.name} the {self.species} makes a sound.')

  # Method to simulate an animal eating
  def eat(self, food):
    print(f'{self.name} the {self.species} is eating {food}.')

  # Method to simulate an animal moving
  def move(self):
    print(f'{self.name} the {self.species} is moving.')

# Create two Animal objects
animal1 = Animal('Lion', 'Leo', 5, 'Savannah', 'Carnivore')
animal2 = Animal('Elephant', 'Ella', 10, 'Grasslands', 'Herbivore')

# Use the methods on the Animal objects
animal1.make_sound()
animal2.eat('grass')
animal1.move()
```

```
Leo the Lion makes a sound.
Ella the Elephant is eating grass.
Leo the Lion is moving.
```

Here we summarize the examples in the demonstration and practice in Table 1.1.

TABLE 1.1 Examples of Classes, Attributes, and Instances

Class	Attributes	Instances
Car	make, model, year, color	Toyota Corolla (2020, red), Honda Civic (2019, blue), Tesla Model S (2024, silver)
Employee	name, employee_id, department, salary	John Doe (IT, E123, $60,000), Jane Smith (HR, E124, $55,000)
Smartphone	brand, model, storage, color, price	iPhone 16 (256GB, black), Galaxy S23 (512GB, white)
Student	name, student_id, major, gpa, year	Alice (Computer Science, Junior, 3.8), Bob (Mathematics, Senior, 3.4)
Animal	species, name, age, habitat, diet	Leo (Lion, 5 years, Savannah, Carnivore), Ella (Elephant, 10 years, Grasslands, Herbivore)

Here we summarize the special functions, for their purpose and examples, in Table 1.2 for readers' convenience.

TABLE 1.2 Important Functions in Class Definition

Function	Explanation	Examples
`__init__`	Initializes the object with given attributes.	`__init__(self, make, model, year, color)`
`__repr__`	Returns a string representation of the object, often for developers.	`__repr__(self)`
`__str__`	Returns a user-friendly string representation of the object.	`__str__(self)`
`__eq__`	Compares two objects for equality.	`__eq__(self, obj)`
`__lt__`	Compares if one object is less than another.	`__lt__(self, obj)`
`__gt__`	Compares if one object is greater than another.	`__gt__(self, obj)`
Other methods	Define actions the object can perform (e.g., start, drive, promote).	`start(self), give_raise(self, amount), make_call(self, phone_number)`

1.3 FOUR ASPECTS

OOP is a powerful concept in software development that helps in organizing and structuring code. There are four main OOP concepts: inheritance, polymorphism, encapsulation, and abstraction:

- Inheritance allows a new class (child or subclass) to inherit the attributes and methods of an existing class (parent or superclass). This promotes code reuse and establishes a natural hierarchy between classes. We introduce inheritance in detail in Chapter 2.
- Polymorphism allows objects of different classes to be treated as objects of a common superclass. The most common use of polymorphism in OOP is when a parent class reference is used to refer to a child class object and the method call is resolved at runtime. We introduce polymorphism in detail in Chapter 3.
- Encapsulation is the practice of bundling the data and the methods that operate on the data into a single unit or class, and restricting access to some of the object's components. This means that the internal state of an object is hidden from the outside world, and access is controlled via public methods (getters and setters). We introduce encapsulation in detail in Chapter 4.
- Abstraction is the concept of hiding the complex implementation details and showing only the essential features of the object. It allows focusing on the object's functionality without worrying about the intricate inner workings. We introduce abstraction in detail in Chapter 5.

In summary, encapsulation protects data, inheritance promotes code reuse and establishes relationships between classes, polymorphism allows for flexibility and dynamic method resolution, and abstraction simplifies interactions with complex systems by hiding unnecessary details. Together, these concepts form the foundation of OOP, enabling developers to write code that is modular, scalable, and easier to understand and maintain.

1.4 INTERACT WITH GENAI

To get the most out of your interaction with a generative AI tool like ChatGPT, always begin your conversation with the following prompt:

You are an expert in Python programming. Act as a tutor helping a student who is learning Python programming.

This prompt sets the tone for the conversation and ensures the AI will provide helpful and detailed guidance tailored to your learning. Here are some general suggestions and prompts for effective interaction:

- Can you explain how [concept] works?
- What's the difference between [concept 1] and [concept 2]?
- Can you provide an example of a function that does [specific task]?
- Show me how to use a [specific structure or method] to achieve [goal].
- I don't understand why [specific method] isn't working. Can you help me troubleshoot it?
- My code: [Your Python Code] is not running. What is wrong?
- Review my code: [Your Python Code]. Can you improve my code to make it more professional?
- Can you explain why [specific aspect] works this way?

We also prepared specific suggestions and prompts for the general concept, OOP, as well.

- Define OOP and its distinction from procedural programming.
- Explain classes and objects in Python, highlighting their relationship.
- Discuss OOP's benefits in organizing and managing complex code.
- Differentiate a class from an object in OOP.
- Explore how a class can have multiple independent objects.
- Explain the four aspects of OOP: inheritance, encapsulation, polymorphism, and abstraction.
- Model real-world entities using OOP.
- Demonstrate OOP's role in project scalability.
- Explain OOP's contribution to modular software design.
- Address common challenges when learning OOP.
- Analyze how poor OOP design leads to unnecessary complexity.
- Guide on choosing between classes and functions in Python.

CHAPTER 2

Inheritance

INHERITANCE IS A FUNDAMENTAL concept in object-oriented programming that enables a subclass (child class) to inherit attributes and methods from a superclass (parent class). Inheritance improves code reuse by allowing subclasses to have existing functionalities without duplication, while also creating a structured hierarchy that organizes classes logically. Central to inheritance is the *is-a* relationship, where a subclass represents a specialized version of its parent (e.g., a Dog class is a specific type of the more general Animal class). This relationship ensures clarity in design, promotes modularity, and aligns real-world categorization with code structure. Are you ready? Let's get started!

2.1 WHAT IS INHERITANCE?

Let's read the definition of four classes, A, B, C, and D, and observe how subclasses inherit the attributes and methods from their superclasses.

2.1.1 Demonstration

```python
# Defining a class A, and two subclasses B and C of A
class A:
  # Initialize an object of class A with attributes att1 and att2
  def __init__(self, att1, att2):
    self.att1, self.att2 = att1, att2

  # Method act defined in class A
  def act(self):
    print('The act defined in Class A')

# Defining subclass B of A
class B(A):
  # Initialize an object of class B with att1, att2, and att3
  def __init__(self, att1, att2, att3):
    super().__init__(att1, att2)  # Call the constructor of class A
    self.att3 = att3
```

DOI: 10.1201/9781003624868-2

```
# Defining subclass C of A
class C(A):
  # Initialize an object of class C with  att1, att2, and att4
  def __init__(self, att1, att2, att4):
    super().__init__(att1, att2)  # Call the constructor of class A
    self.att4 = att4

# Defining subclass D of C
class D(C):
  # Initialize an object of class D with att1, att2, att4, and att5
  def __init__(self, att1, att2, att4, att5):
    super().__init__(att1, att2, att4)  # Call the constructor of class C
    self.att5 = att5
```

The super() before __init__() is most used in the constructors. It is a convenient way to call methods defined in super classes without repeating the definition of constructor. Now, let's create some objects to test the defined classes.

```
a = A('Class A', 'SuperClass')
print(a.att1, a.att2)
a.act()
```

```
Class A SuperClass
The act defined in Class A
```

```
b = B('Class B', 'subclass', 'Bat')
print(b.att1, b.att2, b.att3)
b.act()
```

```
Class B subclass Bat
The act defined in Class A
```

```
c = C('Class C', 'subclass', 'Cat')
print(c.att1, c.att2, c.att4)
c.act()
```

```
Class C subclass Cat
The act defined in Class A
```

Note that although both class B and class A inherit the att1 and att2 from their superclass A, the att3 belongs to class B only, and the att4 belongs to class C only. Calling att4 from B class objects or calling att3 from C class objects may lead to errors.

```
b.att4
```

```
---------------------------------------------------------------------
AttributeError                          Traceback (most recent call last)
<ipython-input-11-6c8f52bf73ce> in <cell line: 1>()
----> 1 b.att4

AttributeError: 'B' object has no attribute 'att4'
```

```
c.att3
```

```
---------------------------------------------------------------------
AttributeError                          Traceback (most recent call last)
```

```
<ipython-input-12-de6a77231cb6> in <cell line: 1>()
----> 1 c.att3

AttributeError: 'C' object has no attribute 'att3'
```

```
d = D('Class D', 'subsubclass', 'Camel', 'Desert')
print(d.att1, d.att2, d.att4, d.att5)
d.act()
```

```
Class D subsubclass Camel Desert
The act defined in Class A
```

Note that d as an object of the class D, it inherits the attributes att1, att2, and att4. It won't have the attribute att3 either. Also, the superclass won't have the attributes defined in their subclasses. The inheritance happens from superclass to subclasses.

2.2 ANIMAL CLASS REVISIT

Let's revisit the Animal class we discussed earlier and define some subclasses of it.

```python
# Define a base class Animal
class Animal:
  # Initialize an Animal object with name and species
  def __init__(self, name, species):
    self.name = name
    self.species = species

  # Method to simulate making a sound
  def make_sound(self):
    print(f'This {self.species} {self.name} makes a sound.')

# Define a subclass Dog of Animal
class Dog(Animal):
  # Initialize a Dog object with name and breed
  def __init__(self, name, breed):
    super().__init__(name, 'Dog')  # Call the constructor of Animal
    self.breed = breed

# Define a subclass Cat of Animal
class Cat(Animal):
  # Initialize a Cat object with name and breed
  def __init__(self, name, breed):
    super().__init__(name, 'Cat')  # Call the constructor of Animal
    self.breed = breed

# Define a subclass Shorthair of Cat
class Shorthair(Cat):
  # Initialize a Shorthair object with name and age
  def __init__(self, name, age):
    super().__init__(name, 'Shorthair')  # Call the constructor of Cat
    self.age = age
```

Now, we can initiate some instances of these classes to observe the inheritances.

```
# Create objects of the classes
animal1 = Animal('Abby', 'Animal')
animal1.make_sound()   # Output: This Animal Abby makes a sound.

dog1 = Dog('Buddy', 'Golden Retriever')
dog1.make_sound()   # Output: This Dog Buddy makes a sound.
print(dog1.breed)   # Output: Golden Retriever

cat1 = Cat('Cathy', 'Shorthair')
cat1.make_sound()   # Output: This Cat Cathy makes a sound.
print(cat1.breed)   # Output: Shorthair

cat2 = Shorthair('Conner', '10')
cat2.make_sound()   # Output: This Cat Conner makes a sound.
print(cat2.breed)   # Output: Shorthair
print(cat2.age)   # Output: 10
```

```
This Animal Abby makes a sound.
This Dog Buddy makes a sound.
Golden Retriever
This Cat Cathy makes a sound.
Shorthair
This Cat Conner makes a sound.
Shorthair
10
```

Note that all instances created from Dog class are having the species as Dog. This default value has been assigned by the constructor def __init__(self, name, breed) in Dog class. Also, all instances created from Cat class are having the species as Cat. This default value has been given by the constructor def __init__(self, name, breed) in Cat class. Furthermore, all instances created from all subclasses of Cat class are having the species as default Cat too.

2.3 CASE STUDIES

Task: You are given a Person class with attributes for name and age as below:

```
# Define the Person class
class Person:
    def __init__(self, name, age):
        self.name = name
        self.age = age
```

Your task is to:

1. Define a Student class that inherits from Person. The Student class should have an additional attribute student_id.
2. Create a Person object person.
3. Create a Student object student.
4. Print the name and age of the person.
5. Print the name, age, and student_id of the student.

```
# Define the Person class
class Person:
    # Initialize a Person object with name and age
    def __init__(self, name, age):
        self.name = name
        self.age = age

# Define the Student class inheriting from Person
class Student(Person):
    # Initialize a Student object with name, age, and student_id
    def __init__(self, name, age, student_id):
        super().__init__(name, age)   # Call the constructor of Person
        self.student_id = student_id

# Create a Person object
person = Person('John Doe', 40)
print(f'Person Name: {person.name}, Age: {person.age}')

# Create a Student object
student = Student('Alice Smith', 20, 'S12345')
print(f'''Student Name: {student.name},
          Age: {student.age},
          Student ID: {student.student_id}''')
```

```
Person Name: John Doe, Age: 40
Student Name: Alice Smith,
          Age: 20,
          Student ID: S12345
```

In this solution, the Person class is a given simple class with two attributes, name and age. The Student class inherits from Person and adds a new attribute, student_id. The super().__init__(name, age) call in the Student class ensures that the name and age attributes are initialized using the constructor of the Person class.

Task: Create an inheritance hierarchy for animals. Start with a base class Animal that has attributes for species and diet as below:

```
# Define the Animal class
class Animal:
    def __init__(self, species, diet):
        self.species = species
        self.diet = diet
```

Your task is to:

1. Create two subclasses, Mammal and Bird, each with an additional attribute: fur_color for Mammal and wing_span for Bird.
2. Create an Animal object animal.
3. Create a Mammal object mammal.
4. Create a Bird object bird.
5. Print the details of each object.

```
# Define the Animal class
class Animal:
  # Initialize an Animal object with species and diet
  def __init__(self, species, diet):
    self.species = species
    self.diet = diet

# Define the Mammal class inheriting from Animal
class Mammal(Animal):
  # Initialize a Mammal object with species, diet, and fur_color
  def __init__(self, species, diet, fur_color):
    super().__init__(species, diet)  # Call the constructor of Animal
    self.fur_color = fur_color

# Define the Bird class inheriting from Animal
class Bird(Animal):
  # Initialize a Bird object with species, diet, and wing_span
  def __init__(self, species, diet, wing_span):
    super().__init__(species, diet)  # Call the constructor of Animal
    self.wing_span = wing_span

# Create an Animal object
animal = Animal('Generic Animal', 'Omnivore')
print(f'Species: {animal.species}, Diet: {animal.diet}')

# Create a Mammal object
mammal = Mammal('Tiger', 'Carnivore', 'Orange')
print(f'''Species: {mammal.species},
  Diet: {mammal.diet},
  Fur Color: {mammal.fur_color}''')

# Create a Bird object
bird = Bird('Eagle', 'Carnivore', '7 feet')
print(f'''Species: {bird.species},
  Diet: {bird.diet},
  Wing Span: {bird.wing_span}''')
```

```
Species: Generic Animal, Diet: Omnivore
Species: Tiger,
  Diet: Carnivore,
  Fur Color: Orange
Species: Eagle,
  Diet: Carnivore,
  Wing Span: 7 feet
```

In this solution, the `Animal` is the base class with `species` and `diet` attributes. The `Mammal` and `Bird` are classes inherit from `Animal` and add their own unique attributes, `fur_color` for `Mammal` and `wing_span` for `Bird`.

Task: Design an inheritance structure for vehicles. Start with a base class `Vehicle` that has attributes for `make` and `model` as:

```python
# Define the Vehicle class
class Vehicle:
    def __init__(self, make, model):
        self.make = make
        self.model = model
```

Your task is to:

1. Create two subclasses, Car and Truck, each with an additional attribute: number_of_doors for Car and cargo_capacity for Truck.
2. Create a Vehicle object vehicle.
3. Create a Car object car.
4. Create a Truck object truck.
5. Print the details of each object.

```python
# Define the Vehicle class
class Vehicle:
    # Initialize a Vehicle object with make and model
    def __init__(self, make, model):
        self.make = make
        self.model = model

# Define the Car class inheriting from Vehicle
class Car(Vehicle):
    # Initialize a Car object with make, model, and number_of_doors
    def __init__(self, make, model, number_of_doors):
        super().__init__(make, model)  # Call the constructor of Vehicle
        self.number_of_doors = number_of_doors

# Define the Truck class inheriting from Vehicle
class Truck(Vehicle):
    # Initialize a Truck object with make, model, and cargo_capacity
    def __init__(self, make, model, cargo_capacity):
        super().__init__(make, model)  # Call the constructor of Vehicle
        self.cargo_capacity = cargo_capacity

# Create a Vehicle object
vehicle = Vehicle('Generic Make', 'Generic Model')
print(f'Make: {vehicle.make}, Model: {vehicle.model}')

# Create a Car object
car = Car('Honda', 'Civic', 4)
print(f'''Make: {car.make}, Model: {car.model},
  Number of Doors: {car.number_of_doors}''')

# Create a Truck object
truck = Truck('Ford', 'F-150', '1000 lbs')
print(f'''Make: {truck.make}, Model: {truck.model},
  Cargo Capacity: {truck.cargo_capacity}''')
```

```
Make: Generic Make, Model: Generic Model
Make: Honda, Model: Civic,
  Number of Doors: 4
Make: Ford, Model: F-150,
  Cargo Capacity: 1000 lbs
```

Again, in this solution, `Vehicle` is the base class with `make` and `model` attributes. The `Car` and `Truck` are classes inherit from `Vehicle` and add their own unique attributes, `number_of_doors` for `Car` and `cargo_capacity` for `Truck`.

2.4 INTERACT WITH GENAI

Here are some questions and prompts you can interact with generative AI tools, including ChatGPT.

- Define inheritance in OOP and its implementation in Python.
- Explain inheritance's role in creating reusable, maintainable code.
- Describe the relationship between parent and child classes.
- Analyze benefits and potential drawbacks of inheritance.
- Create a parent class and demonstrate inheritance.
- Show method overriding in a child class.
- Use `super()` to call a parent class method.
- Simplify code using inheritance (e.g., vehicle modeling).
- Share attributes and methods across multiple classes.
- Explain what happens when a child class doesn't override a parent method.
- Describe the `super()` function in class hierarchy.
- Explore a child class's ability to add unique methods and attributes.
- Differentiate between extending and overriding a class.
- Explain multiple inheritance in Python and its potential issues.
- Discuss Python's handling of method conflicts in multiple inheritance.
- Design a class hierarchy for an e-commerce platform.
- Manage different data types using inheritance.
- Apply inheritance to manage similar business processes.
- Identify common inheritance mistakes.
- Explain the 'is-a' relationship in inheritance.

## CHAPTER 3

Polymorphism

POLYMORPHISM IS A CORE concept in object-oriented programming (OOP) that allows objects of different classes to be treated as objects of a common superclass. It enables a single interface to represent different types, which can be particularly powerful when working with inheritance.

In simpler terms, polymorphism allows you to define methods in a base class and have those methods be overridden by subclasses to provide specific behavior. This allows for flexibility and extensibility in code, where the same method can behave differently depending on the object calling it.

Are you ready? Let's get started!

3.1 WHAT IS POLYMORPHISM

3.1.1 Demonstration

Let's define some classes to demonstrate how the general action `speak()` of all `Animal` objects behaves differently in the specific objects of the subclasses: `Cat`, `Lion`, `LionBaby`.

```python
# Base class Animal
class Animal:
  # Method speak for the Animal class
  def speak(self):
    # Default behavior for speak method in Animal class
    print('Make some noise and I don't know what it sounds like...')

# Derived class Cat inheriting from Animal
class Cat(Animal):
  # Method speak overridden in Cat class
  def speak(self):
    # Specific behavior for speak method in Cat class
    print('Meo')

# Derived class Lion inheriting from Cat
```

DOI: 10.1201/9781003624868-3

```
class Lion(Cat):
  # Method speak overridden in Lion class
  def speak(self):
    # Specific behavior for speak method in Lion class
    print('AHHHHHH!')

# Derived class LionBaby inheriting from Lion
class LionBaby(Lion):
  # Method speak overridden in LionBaby class
  def speak(self):
    # Specific behavior for speak method in LionBaby class
    print('I\'m the king of the world!')

# Create objects of each class
a = Animal()
c = Cat()
l = Lion()
lb = LionBaby()

# Call the speak method on each object
a.speak()
c.speak()
l.speak()
lb.speak()
```

```
Make some noise and I don't know what it sounds like...
Meo
AHHHHHH!
I'm the king of the world!
```

In this example, defined in the `Animal` class, the `speak()` method provides a generic implementation that does not know the specific sound an animal makes. Then, the class `Cat` inherits from `Animal` and overrides the `speak()` method to provide the sound that a cat makes (`Meo`). Furthermore, the class `Lion` inherits from `Cat` and further overrides the `speak()` method to represent the roar of a lion (`AHHHHHH!`). At last, the class `LionBaby` inherits from `Lion` and overrides the `speak()` method to express a unique phrase (`I'm the king of the world!`). Each subclass provides a more specific implementation of the `speak()` method, demonstrating polymorphism.

3.2 FAMILY TREE REVISITED

Let's revisit our family tree example to understand polymorphism.

```
# Define the Grandparent class
class Grandparent:
  # Method speak for the Grandparent class
  def speak(self):
    print('Grandparent says, "Back in my day..."')

# Define the Parent class inheriting from Grandparent
class Parent(Grandparent):
  # Method speak overridden in Parent class
```

```python
  def speak(self):
    print('Parent says, "When I was your age..."')

# Define the Child class inheriting from Parent
class Child(Parent):
  # Method speak overridden in Child class
  def speak(self):
    print('Child says, "Can I have some money?"')

# Define the Grandchild class inheriting from Child
class Grandchild(Child):
  # Method speak overridden in Grandchild class
  def speak(self):
    print('Grandchild says, "I love my Lego set!"')

# Create instances of each class
grandparent = Grandparent()
parent = Parent()
child = Child()
grandchild = Grandchild()

# Demonstrating polymorphism
for person in (grandparent, parent, child, grandchild):
  person.speak()
```

```
Grandparent says, "Back in my day..."
Parent says, "When I was your age..."
Child says, "Can I have some money?"
Grandchild says, "I love my Lego set!"
```

In this example, the class `Grandparent` has a method `speak()`. Then, the class `Parent` inherits from `Grandparent` and overrides `speak()`. Next, the class `Child` inherits from `Parent` and overrides `speak()`. At last, the class `Grandchild` inherits from `Child` and overrides `speak()`. Each of these classes has its version of the `speak()` method, demonstrating polymorphism. Even though the method has the same name across different classes, it behaves differently depending on the class of the object that invokes it. In particular, each class overrides the `speak()` method to provide a message specific to that generation. So, when the `speak()` method is called on different objects (`grandparent`, `parent`, `child`, and `grandchild`), each object responds according to its own implementation of the method.

3.3 ANIMALS REVISIT

Let's use the animals example to demonstrate polymorphism once again.

```python
# Define the Animal class
class Animal:
  # Method sound for the Animal class
  def sound(self):
    print('Some generic animal sound')

# Define the Mammal class inheriting from Animal
```

```
class Mammal(Animal):
  # Method sound overridden in Mammal class
  def sound(self):
    print('Mammal makes a sound')

# Define the Bird class inheriting from Animal
class Bird(Animal):
  # Method sound overridden in Bird class
  def sound(self):
    print('Bird chirps')

# Create instances of each class
animal = Animal()
mammal = Mammal()
bird = Bird()

# Demonstrating polymorphism
for creature in (animal, mammal, bird):
  # Call the sound method on each object
  creature.sound()
```

```
Some generic animal sound
Mammal makes a sound
Bird chirps
```

In this example, the class `Animal` has a method `sound()`. Then, the class `Mammal` inherits from `Animal` and overrides `sound()` and the class `Bird` inherits from `Animal` and overrides `sound()` too.

3.4 VEHICLES REVISIT

Let's use the vehicles example to demonstrate polymorphism.

```
# Define the Vehicle class
class Vehicle:
  # Method start_engine for the Vehicle class
  def start_engine(self):
    print('The vehicle engine starts')

# Define the Car class inheriting from Vehicle
class Car(Vehicle):
  # Method start_engine overridden in Car class
  def start_engine(self):
    print('The car engine starts with a roar')

# Define the Truck class inheriting from Vehicle
class Truck(Vehicle):
  # Method start_engine overridden in Truck class
  def start_engine(self):
    print('The truck engine starts with a rumble')

# Create instances of each class
vehicle = Vehicle()
car = Car()
```

```
truck = Truck()

# Demonstrating polymorphism
for auto in (vehicle, car, truck):
    # Call the start_engine method on each object
    auto.start_engine()
```

```
The vehicle engine starts
The car engine starts with a roar
The truck engine starts with a rumble
```

In this example, the class `Vehicle` defines the general method `start_engine()`. The class `Car` inherits from `Vehicle` and overrides `start_engine()`, and the class `Truck` inherits from `Vehicle` and overrides `start_engine()` too.

3.5   CASE STUDIES

Polymorphism is a powerful concept in OOP that enhances the flexibility and reusability of code. By allowing objects of different types to be treated as objects of a common superclass, polymorphism enables methods to be written in a more general way. The practice problems provided here should help solidify your understanding of how polymorphism works and how it can be implemented in Python.

Task: Given a base class `Employee` with a method `get_pay()` as below:

```
# Define the Employee class
class Employee:
    def get_pay(self):
        return 'Generic employee pay'
```

Your task is to:

1. Create subclasses `FullTimeEmployee` and `PartTimeEmployee` that override the `get_pay()` method.
2. Create an `Employee` object.
3. Create a `FullTimeEmployee` object.
4. Create a `PartTimeEmployee` object.
5. Call the `get_pay()` method on each object and print the results.

```
# Define the Employee class
class Employee:
  # Method get_pay for the Employee class
  def get_pay(self):
    return 'Generic employee pay'

# Define the FullTimeEmployee class inheriting from Employee
class FullTimeEmployee(Employee):
  # Method get_pay overridden in FullTimeEmployee class
  def get_pay(self):
    return 'Full-time employee pay'

# Define the PartTimeEmployee class inheriting from Employee
```

```
class PartTimeEmployee(Employee):
  # Method get_pay overridden in PartTimeEmployee class
  def get_pay(self):
    return 'Part-time employee pay'

# Create instances of each class
employee = Employee()
full_time = FullTimeEmployee()
part_time = PartTimeEmployee()

# Demonstrating polymorphism
for worker in (employee, full_time, part_time):
  # Call the get_pay method on each object
  print(worker.get_pay())
```

```
Generic employee pay
Full-time employee pay
Part-time employee pay
```

In this solution, `FullTimeEmployee` and `PartTimeEmployee` override the `get_pay()` method to provide specific pay information. Thus, when the `get_pay()` method is called on different objects, each object returns its own implementation of the method.

Task: Given a base class `Shape` with a method `area()` as below:

```
import math

# Define the Shape class
class Shape:
    def area(self):
        return 'Undefined area'
```

Your task is to:

1. Create subclasses `Circle`, `Rectangle`, and `Triangle` that override the `area()` method to calculate the area of the respective shapes.
2. Create a `Shape` object.
3. Create a `Circle` object with a radius of 3.
4. Create a `Rectangle` object with width 4 and height 5.
5. Create a `Triangle` object with base 6 and height 7.
6. Call the `area()` method on each object and print the results.

```
import math

# Define the Shape class
class Shape:
  # Method area for the Shape class
  def area(self):
    return 'Undefined area'

# Define the Circle class inheriting from Shape
class Circle(Shape):
  # Constructor for Circle class
  def __init__(self, radius):
```

```
    self.radius = radius

    # Method area overridden in Circle class
    def area(self):
      return math.pi * self.radius ** 2

# Define the Rectangle class inheriting from Shape
class Rectangle(Shape):
  # Constructor for Rectangle class
  def __init__(self, width, height):
    self.width = width
    self.height = height

  # Method area overridden in Rectangle class
  def area(self):
    return self.width * self.height

# Define the Triangle class inheriting from Shape
class Triangle(Shape):
  # Constructor for Triangle class
  def __init__(self, base, height):
    self.base = base
    self.height = height

  # Method area overridden in Triangle class
  def area(self):
    return 0.5 * self.base * self.height

# Create instances of each class
shape = Shape()
circle = Circle(3)
rectangle = Rectangle(4, 5)
triangle = Triangle(6, 7)

# Demonstrating polymorphism
for shape_obj in (shape, circle, rectangle, triangle):
  # Call the area method on each object
  print(f'Area: {shape_obj.area()}')
```

```
Area: Undefined area
Area: 28.274333882308138
Area: 20
Area: 21.0
```

This is a classic example to practice polymorphism. In this solution, the `Circle`, `Rectangle`, and `Triangle` override the `area()` method to calculate the area based on their specific formulas. Thus, when the `area()` method is called on different objects, each object returns the correct area based on its specific shape.

Task: Given a base class `Appliance` with a method `turn_on()` as below:

```
# Define the Appliance class
class Appliance:
    def turn_on(self):
        return 'Appliance is now on'
```

Your task is to:

1. Create subclasses `WashingMachine`, `Refrigerator`, and `Microwave` that override the `turn_on()` method.
2. Create an `Appliance` object.
3. Create a `WashingMachine` object.
4. Create a `Refrigerator` object.
5. Create a `Microwave` object.
6. Call the `turn_on()` method on each object and print the results.

```python
# Define the Appliance class
class Appliance:
  # Method turn_on for the Appliance class
  def turn_on(self):
    return 'Appliance is now on'

# Define the WashingMachine class inheriting from Appliance
class WashingMachine(Appliance):
  # Method turn_on overridden in WashingMachine class
  def turn_on(self):
    return 'Washing machine starts spinning'

# Define the Refrigerator class inheriting from Appliance
class Refrigerator(Appliance):
  # Method turn_on overridden in Refrigerator class
  def turn_on(self):
    return 'Refrigerator starts cooling'

# Define the Microwave class inheriting from Appliance
class Microwave(Appliance):
  # Method turn_on overridden in Microwave class
  def turn_on(self):
    return 'Microwave starts heating'

# Create instances of each class
appliance = Appliance()
washing_machine = WashingMachine()
refrigerator = Refrigerator()
microwave = Microwave()

# Demonstrating polymorphism
for appliance_obj in (appliance, washing_machine, refrigerator, microwave):
  # Call the turn_on method on each object
  print(appliance_obj.turn_on())
```

```
Appliance is now on
Washing machine starts spinning
Refrigerator starts cooling
Microwave starts heating
```

Do you like this case study? In the solution, the superclass `Appliance` defines a generic method `turn_on()`. The subclasses, `WashingMachine`, `Refrigerator`, and `Microwave`, inherit the `Appliance` method and override `turn_on()` to provide specific behavior for each appliance. When the `turn_on()` method is called on different objects, each object executes its own version of the method.

3.6 INTERACT WITH GENAI

Here are some questions and prompts you can interact with generative AI tools, including ChatGPT.

- Define polymorphism in OOP and its key significance.
- Identify polymorphism types supported in Python.
- Explain why polymorphism is crucial for code flexibility.
- Demonstrate method overriding in parent and child classes.
- Show polymorphism with a common method across different object types.
- Create a simplified shape management example using polymorphism.
- Illustrate polymorphism in Python's built-in functions like `len()`.
- Demonstrate operator overloading with + for strings and numbers.
- Compare polymorphism and inheritance.
- Define a polymorphic method.
- Explore if polymorphism can exist without inheritance.
- Discuss polymorphism and interfaces in Python.
- Design a polymorphic payment processing system.
- Identify and address polymorphism implementation challenges.
- Ensure type safety in Python polymorphism.
- Explain potential unexpected behaviors in method overrides.

## CHAPTER 4

Encapsulation

ENCAPSULATION IS ONE of the fundamental principles of object-oriented programming (OOP). Encapsulation involves restricting direct access to some of an object's components, which is a way of preventing accidental interference and misuse of the data. In simpler terms, encapsulation helps to hide the internal state of an object from the outside world and only expose a controlled interface. This can be achieved through the use of access modifiers like protected (_) and private (__).

Are you ready? Let's get started!

4.1 INTRODUCTION TO ENCAPSULATION

4.1.1 Demonstration

Let's define a class E to demonstrate how to use the protected (_) and private (__) modifiers.

```python
# Class E definition
class E:
  def __init__(self):
    # Public attribute
    self.att1 = 1

    # Protected attribute (indicated by a single underscore)
    self._att2 = 2

    # Private attribute (indicated by double underscores)
    self.__att3 = 3

# Create an instance of class E
e = E()

# Accessing public attribute
print(e.att1)   # Output: 1

# Accessing protected attribute
```

DOI: 10.1201/9781003624868-4

```
print(e._att2)    # Output: 2

# Attempting to access private attribute directly
print(e.__att3)   # Raises: AttributeError
```

```
1
2
```

```
------------------------------------------------------------------------
AttributeError                          Traceback (most recent call last)
<ipython-input-3-619045af17e5> in <cell line: 18>()
     16
     17 # Attempting to access private attribute directly (will raise an
     AttributeError)
---> 18 print(e.__att3)

AttributeError: 'E' object has no attribute '__att3'
```

In this demonstration, att1 is a public attribute that can be accessed and modified directly without any restrictions. _att2 is a protected attribute indicated by a single underscore. It can be accessed directly but is intended to be accessed only within the class or its subclasses. __att3 is a private attribute indicated by double underscores. It cannot be accessed directly outside the class.

In order to provide access to protected and private attributes, we can add getters and setters. Getters and setters are methods used to control access to an object's attributes. They hide the internal representation of an attribute from direct external access, allow you to add validations before setting or getting attribute values, and can return calculated or transformed values. The modern approach in Python is using property decorators, like @property and @<attribute>.setter. Let's modify the class E by adding getter and setter methods.

```
# Class E definition
class E:
  def __init__(self):
    # Public attribute
    self.att1 = 1

    # Protected attribute (indicated by a single underscore)
    self._att2 = 2

    # Private attribute (indicated by double underscores)
    self.__att3 = 3

  # Getter method for the protected attribute _att2
  @property
  def att2(self):
    return self._att2

  # Setter method for the protected attribute _att2
  @att2.setter
  def att2(self, v):
    print(f'''You are out of your mind!
        The original value {self._att2} will be changed to {v}''')
```

```
    self._att2 = v

    # Getter method for the private attribute __att3
    @property
    def att3(self):
      print('I am a private attribute!')
      return self.__att3

    # Method to set the private attribute __att3 (provides controlled access)
    def set_att3(self, v):
      print(f'''You are out of your mind!
          The original value {self.__att3} will be changed to {v}''')
      self.__att3 = v

    # Setter method for the private attribute __att3
    @att3.setter
    def att3(self, v):
      print(f'''You are out of your mind!
          The original value {self.__att3} will be changed to {v}''')
      self.__att3 = v

# Create an instance of class E
e = E()

# Print original values
print('Original values')
print(e.att1)
print(e.att2)
print(e.att3)

# Change values
print('We are changing the values')
e.att1 = 4
e.att2 = 5
e.att3 = 6

# Print changed values
print(e.att1)
print(e.att2)
print(e.att3)
```

```
Original values
1
2
I am a private attribute!
3
We are changing the values
You are out of your mind!
          The original value 2 will be changed to 5
You are out of your mind!
          The original value 3 will be changed to 6
4
5
I am a private attribute!
6
```

In this modified demonstration, the `@property` and `@att2.setter` decorators provide controlled access and modification. The `@property`, `@att3.setter`, and `set_att3()` methods provide controlled access and modification, with warning messages printed whenever the value is changed.

4.2 BANK ACCOUNT

Let's consider a real-life example of a bank account to understand encapsulation. In a bank account, your balance is not something that anyone can just change. There are strict rules (methods) in place to manage how money is deposited or withdrawn, and the balance is kept hidden from direct access. The `__balance` attribute is private and cannot be accessed directly from outside the class. This is enforced by prefixing the attribute name with double underscores (`__`). The `deposit()`, `withdraw()`, and `get_balance()` methods are public and provide controlled access to modify or view the balance. Thus, the internal state (`__balance`) of the `BankAccount` object is protected from unauthorized changes, ensuring that only the defined methods can modify it.

```python
# Define the BankAccount class
class BankAccount:
  def __init__(self, owner, balance=0):
    # Public attribute: owner
    self.owner = owner

    # Private attribute: balance (indicated by double underscores)
    self.__balance = balance

  # Method to deposit money
  def deposit(self, amount):
    if amount > 0:
      self.__balance += amount
      print(f'{amount} deposited. New balance: {self.__balance}')
    else:
      print('Deposit amount must be positive')

  # Method to withdraw money
  def withdraw(self, amount):
    if 0 < amount <= self.__balance:
      self.__balance -= amount
      print(f'{amount} withdrawn. New balance: {self.__balance}')
    else:
      print('Insufficient balance or invalid withdrawal amount')

  # Method to get the current balance
  def get_balance(self):
    return self.__balance

# Create a BankAccount object
account = BankAccount('Alice', 1000)

# Accessing public attribute
```

```
print(account.owner)   # Output: Alice

# Attempting to access private attribute directly (raises AttributeError)
# print(account.__balance)

# Using public methods to interact with private attribute
account.deposit(500)   # Output: 500 deposited. New balance: 1500
account.withdraw(200)   # Output: 200 withdrawn. New balance: 1300

# Getting the balance using a public method
print(f'Current balance: {account.get_balance()}')   # Output: 1300
```

```
Alice
500 deposited. New balance: 1500
200 withdrawn. New balance: 1300
Current balance: 1300
```

4.3 STUDENT GRADES

In this example, we'll encapsulate a student's grades to prevent them from being modified directly.

```python
# Define the Student class
class Student:
  def __init__(self, name, grades=[]):
    # Public attribute: name
    self.name = name

    # Private attribute: grades (indicated by double underscores)
    self.__grades = grades

  # Method to add a grade
  def add_grade(self, grade):
    if 0 <= grade <= 100:
      self.__grades.append(grade)
      print(f'Grade {grade} added.')
    else:
      print('Invalid grade')

  # Method to get the grades
  def get_grades(self):
    return self.__grades

  # Method to calculate the average grade
  def get_average_grade(self):
    return sum(self.__grades) / len(self.__grades) if self.__grades else 0

# Create a Student object
student = Student('John')

# Adding grades using public method
student.add_grade(85)
student.add_grade(92)
```

```
# Attempting to access private attribute directly (raises AttributeError)
# print(student.__grades)

# Using public methods to interact with private attribute
print(f'Grades: {student.get_grades()}')      # Output: [85, 92]
print(f'Average Grade: {student.get_average_grade()}')   # Output: 88.5
```

```
Grade 85 added.
Grade 92 added.
Grades: [85, 92]
Average Grade: 88.5
```

4.4 CAR ENGINE

In this example, we'll encapsulate the state of a car's engine to ensure its only started or stopped through controlled methods.

```python
# Define the Car class
class Car:
  def __init__(self, make, model):
    # Public attributes: make and model
    self.make = make
    self.model = model

    # Private attribute: engine_running (indicated by double underscores)
    self.__engine_running = False

  # Method to start the engine
  def start_engine(self):
    if not self.__engine_running:
      self.__engine_running = True
      print(f'{self.make} {self.model} engine started.')
    else:
      print(f'{self.make} {self.model} engine is already running.')

  # Method to stop the engine
  def stop_engine(self):
    if self.__engine_running:
      self.__engine_running = False
      print(f'{self.make} {self.model} engine stopped.')
    else:
      print(f'{self.make} {self.model} engine is not running.')

  # Method to check if the engine is running
  def is_engine_running(self):
    return self.__engine_running

# Create a Car object
car = Car('Toyota', 'Camry')

# Starting the engine using public method
car.start_engine()  # Output: Toyota Camry engine started.

# Checking engine state
```

```
print(f'Is engine running? {car.is_engine_running()}')   # Output: True

# Stopping the engine using public method
car.stop_engine()   # Output: Toyota Camry engine stopped.

# Attempting to access private attribute directly (raises AttributeError)
# print(car.__engine_running)
```

```
Toyota Camry engine started.
Is engine running? True
Toyota Camry engine stopped.
```

4.5   CASE STUDIES

Encapsulation is a key principle in object-oriented programming that helps protect an object's internal state and ensures that it is only modified in controlled ways. By restricting access to an object's attributes and providing public methods to interact with them, encapsulation enhances security, reduces bugs, and makes the code more maintainable.

Task: Create a class `Employee` that encapsulates the employee's salary. The salary should not be accessible directly but can be updated or retrieved through methods.

Your task is to:

1. Create an `Employee` object with a given name and salary.
2. Provide methods to give a raise and retrieve the current salary.
3. Prevent direct access to the salary attribute.

```python
# Define the Employee class
class Employee:
  def __init__(self, name, salary):
    # Public attribute: name
    self.name = name

    # Private attribute: salary (indicated by double underscores)
    self.__salary = salary

  # Method to give a raise
  def give_raise(self, amount):
    if amount > 0:
      self.__salary += amount
      print(f'{self.name} got a raise of {amount}. New salary: {self.__salary}')
    else:
      print('Raise amount must be positive')

  # Method to get the salary
  def get_salary(self):
    return self.__salary

# Create an Employee object
employee = Employee('Jane', 50000)
```

```
# Giving a raise using public method
employee.give_raise(5000)   # Output: Jane got a raise of 5000. New salary: 55000

# Attempting to access private attribute directly (raises AttributeError)
# print(employee.__salary)

# Getting the salary using a public method
print(f'Current salary: {employee.get_salary()}')   # Output: 55000
```

```
Jane got a raise of 5000. New salary: 55000
Current salary: 55000
```

In the solution, the `__salary` attribute is private and cannot be accessed directly. Methods like `give_raise()` and `get_salary()` provide controlled access to this attribute.

Task: Create a class `Book` that encapsulates the number of pages. The number of pages should not be modified directly but can be read using a method. Additionally, provide a method to add more pages.

Your task is to:

1. Create a `Book` object with a title and a number of pages.
2. Provide methods to add more pages and retrieve the current number of pages.
3. Prevent direct modification of the pages attribute.

```
# Define the Book class
class Book:
    def __init__(self, title, pages):
        # Public attribute: title
        self.title = title

        # Private attribute: pages (indicated by double underscores)
        self.__pages = pages

    # Method to add pages
    def add_pages(self, extra_pages):
        if extra_pages > 0:
            self.__pages += extra_pages
            print(f'{extra_pages} pages added. Total pages: {self.__pages}')
        else:
            print('Page count must be positive')

    # Method to get the number of pages
    def get_pages(self):
        return self.__pages

# Create a Book object
book = Book('Python Programming', 300)

# Adding pages using public method
book.add_pages(50)   # Output: 50 pages added. Total pages: 350

# Attempting to access private attribute directly (raises AttributeError)
```

```
# print(book.__pages)

# Getting the number of pages using a public method
print(f'Number of pages: {book.get_pages()}')   # Output: 350
```

```
50 pages added. Total pages: 350
Number of pages: 350
```

In this solution, the `__pages` attribute is private and cannot be modified directly. Methods like `add_pages()` and `get_pages()` provide controlled access to this attribute.

Task: Create a class `Movie` that encapsulates the rating of the movie. The rating should only be updated through a method, ensuring that the rating remains within a valid range (0 to 10).

Your task is to:

1. Create a `Movie` object with a title and an initial rating.
2. Provide methods to update the rating and retrieve the current rating.
3. Ensure the rating remains within a valid range.

```python
# Define the Movie class
class Movie:
  def __init__(self, title, rating):
    # Public attribute: title
    self.title = title

    # Private attribute: rating (indicated by double underscores)
    # Ensure rating is within the range [0, 10]
    self.__rating = max(0, min(rating, 10))

  # Method to set a new rating
  def set_rating(self, new_rating):
    if 0 <= new_rating <= 10:
      self.__rating = new_rating
      print(f'New rating for {self.title}: {self.__rating}')
    else:
      print('Rating must be between 0 and 10')

  # Method to get the current rating
  def get_rating(self):
    return self.__rating

# Create a Movie object
movie = Movie('Inception', 9)

# Updating the rating using public method
movie.set_rating(10)   # Output: New rating for Inception: 10

# Attempting to access private attribute directly (raises AttributeError)
# print(movie.__rating)
```

```
# Getting the rating using a public method
print(f'Current rating: {movie.get_rating()}')    # Output: 10
```

Clearly, the `__rating` attribute is private and can only be modified through the `set_rating()` method, which ensures the rating stays within the 0 to 10 range.

4.6   INTERACT WITH GENAI

Here are some questions and prompts you can interact with generative AI tools, including ChatGPT.

- Define encapsulation in OOP and its core importance.
- Explain how encapsulation protects data integrity in a class.
- Distinguish between public, protected, and private attributes in Python.
- Describe how getter and setter methods support encapsulation.
- Demonstrate creating a class with encapsulated attributes.
- Show getter and setter methods for controlling private data access.
- Create an example protecting sensitive information using encapsulation.
- Justify why class attributes should be private or protected.
- Compare getter/setter methods with direct attribute access.
- Explore encapsulation without private attributes.
- Identify risks of bypassing encapsulation in Python.
- Explain how encapsulation facilitates class refactoring and extension.
- Analyze the trade-off between encapsulation and flexibility in Python.
- Demonstrate preventing accidental data modification through encapsulation.
- Identify common encapsulation implementation mistakes.
- Discuss Python's encapsulation limitations compared to other languages.
- Explore encapsulation challenges in Python's dynamic typing.

## CHAPTER 5

Abstraction

A BSTRACTION is another fundamental concept in object-oriented programming (OOP). It refers to the process of hiding the internal implementation details of an object and only exposing the necessary functionality. It allows you to break down complex logic into manageable, understandable parts, define a blueprint that derived classes must follow, and hide unnecessary details from the user of the class. In simpler terms, abstraction helps to reduce complexity by allowing programmers to focus on what an object does rather than how it does it.

Are you excited? Let's get started!

5.1   INTRODUCTION TO ABSTRACTION

5.1.1   Demonstration

Let's create a series of classes, `Idea`, `G1`, `G2`, and `G3`, to demonstrate the idea of abstraction.

```python
# Import the abstract base class module
import abc
from abc import ABC

# Define an abstract base class 'Idea' using inheritance from 'ABC' class
class Idea(ABC):
  # Abstract method 'done', which must be implemented by any subclass
  @abc.abstractmethod
  def done(self):
    pass

# Class 'G1' inherits from 'Idea', but does not implement the 'done' method
class G1(Idea):
  def work(self):
    print("I'm working on it!")

# Class 'G2' inherits from 'G1', overriding the 'work' method
class G2(G1):
```

DOI: 10.1201/9781003624868-5

```
  def work(self):
    print("I'm still working on it!")

# Class 'G3' inherits from 'G2' and implements the abstract 'done' method
class G3(G2):
  # 'done' method implementation
  def done(self):
    print("I got it done!")

# Instances of G1 and G2 cannot be created because they are abstract
# Attempting to create an instance of G1 or G2 would raise an error

# Cannot create g1
# g1 = G1()  # Uncommenting this would raise an error

# Cannot create g2
# g2 = G2()  # Uncommenting this would raise an error

# Instance of G3 can be created since it implements the 'done' method
g3 = G3()
g3.work()   # Calls the 'work' method from G2
g3.done()   # Calls the 'done' method from G3
```

```
I'm still working on it!
I got it done!
```

In this demonstration, the ABC (Abstract Base Class) is a base class that helps you create abstract classes, and the abstractmethod is a decorator used to declare abstract methods. The Idea class is an abstract class that declares the done method as an abstract method. Any subclass of Idea must implement the done method to be instantiated. G1 inherits from Idea but doesn't implement the done method, making it abstract and non-instantiable. G2 inherits from G1 and overrides the work method. G3 inherits from G2 and implements the done method, making it a concrete class that can be instantiated.

Because G1 and G2 don't implement the abstract done method, they remain as abstract classes. Instances of G1 and G2 cannot be created. Only G3 can be instantiated because it provides a concrete implementation of done.

This example demonstrates the use of abstract base classes, method overriding, and inheritance in Python OOP.

5.2 VEHICLES

Let's demonstrate abstraction using a classic example involving vehicles. When you drive a car, you don't need to know how the engine works, how fuel is converted into energy, or how the braking system functions internally. All you need to do is use the interface provided: the steering wheel, accelerator, brake pedals, and gear shift. The complex operations are hidden, and you're only exposed to the essential functionality required to drive the car.

```python
# Import ABC and abstractmethod from the abc module
from abc import ABC, abstractmethod

# Define an abstract base class Vehicle
class Vehicle(ABC):
  # Abstract method start_engine, which must be implemented by any subclass
  @abstractmethod
  def start_engine(self):
    pass

  # Abstract method stop_engine, which must be implemented by any subclass
  @abstractmethod
  def stop_engine(self):
    pass

  # Concrete method honk with a default implementation
  def honk(self):
    print('Honking!')

# Define a concrete class Car inheriting from Vehicle
class Car(Vehicle):
  # Implementation of the start_engine abstract method
  def start_engine(self):
    print('Car engine started.')

  # Implementation of the stop_engine abstract method
  def stop_engine(self):
    print('Car engine stopped.')

# Define a concrete class Motorcycle inheriting from Vehicle
class Motorcycle(Vehicle):
  # Implementation of the start_engine abstract method
  def start_engine(self):
    print('Motorcycle engine started.')

  # Implementation of the stop_engine abstract method
  def stop_engine(self):
    print('Motorcycle engine stopped.')

# Instantiate objects and use abstract methods
my_car = Car()
my_car.start_engine()    # Output: Car engine started.
my_car.honk()            # Output: Honking!
my_car.stop_engine()     # Output: Car engine stopped.

my_motorcycle = Motorcycle()
my_motorcycle.start_engine()    # Output: Motorcycle engine started.
my_motorcycle.honk()            # Output: Honking!
my_motorcycle.stop_engine()     # Output: Motorcycle engine stopped.
```

```
Car engine started.
Honking!
Car engine stopped.
Motorcycle engine started.
Honking!
```

```
Motorcycle engine stopped.
```

In this example, the `Vehicle` class is an abstract class. It contains abstract methods (`start_engine()` and `stop_engine()`), which are methods without any implementation. Subclasses are required to provide concrete implementations for these methods. These methods are defined using the `@abstractmethod` decorator. They serve as a template for subclasses, ensuring that certain methods are implemented. The `honk()` method in the `Vehicle` class is a concrete method with implementation. It can be used directly by subclasses or overridden if needed. `Car` and `Motorcycle` inherit from `Vehicle`. They provide specific implementations for the abstract methods, so they are concrete classes.

5.3 PAYMENT

Let's consider another classic example, which is a payment system where different types of payments (like credit card and PayPal) need to be processed. We'll use abstraction to define a common interface for all payment types.

```python
# Import ABC and abstractmethod from the abc module
from abc import ABC, abstractmethod

# Define an abstract base class Payment
class Payment(ABC):
  # Abstract method must be implemented by any subclass
  @abstractmethod
  def process_payment(self, amount):
    pass

# Define a concrete class CreditCardPayment inheriting from Payment
class CreditCardPayment(Payment):
  # Implementation of the process_payment abstract method
  def process_payment(self, amount):
    print(f'Processing credit card payment of {amount} dollars.')

# Define a concrete class PayPalPayment inheriting from Payment
class PayPalPayment(Payment):
  # Implementation of the process_payment abstract method
  def process_payment(self, amount):
    print(f'Processing PayPal payment of {amount} dollars.')

# Using the abstract interface
# Create an instance of CreditCardPayment and call process_payment
payment_method = CreditCardPayment()
payment_method.process_payment(100)

# Create an instance of PayPalPayment and call process_payment
payment_method = PayPalPayment()
payment_method.process_payment(150)
```

```
Processing credit card payment of 100 dollars.
Processing PayPal payment of 150 dollars.
```

5.4 CASE STUDIES

Task: Remember our class `Animal`? Let's create an abstract class `Animal` that defines a common interface for all animals with an abstract method `make_sound()`. Create concrete subclasses `Dog` and `Bird` that implement the `make_sound()` method.

Your task is to:

1. Define an abstract class `Animal`.
2. Implement the `make_sound()` method in `Dog` and `Bird` subclasses.
3. Create instances of `Dog` and `Bird` and call the `make_sound()` method on them.

```python
# Import ABC and abstractmethod from the abc module
from abc import ABC, abstractmethod

# Define an abstract base class Animal
class Animal(ABC):
    # Abstract method make_sound, which must be implemented by any subclass
    @abstractmethod
    def make_sound(self):
        pass

# Define a concrete class Dog inheriting from Animal
class Dog(Animal):
    # Implementation of the make_sound abstract method
    def make_sound(self):
        print('Woof! Woof!')

# Define a concrete class Bird inheriting from Animal
class Bird(Animal):
    # Implementation of the make_sound abstract method
    def make_sound(self):
        print('Chirp! Chirp!')

# Using the abstract interface
# Create an instance of Dog and call make_sound
dog = Dog()
dog.make_sound()   # Output: Woof! Woof!

# Create an instance of Bird and call make_sound
bird = Bird()
bird.make_sound()   # Output: Chirp! Chirp!
```

```
Woof! Woof!
Chirp! Chirp!
```

In this example, the `Animal` class defines the abstract method `make_sound()` that must be implemented by any subclass. The `Dog` and `Bird` classes provide their specific implementations of the `make_sound()` method.

Task: Let's revisit the `Shape` class. You should create an abstract class `Shape` that defines a common interface for all shapes with an abstract method `area()`. Create concrete subclasses `Circle` and `Rectangle` that implement the `area()` method.

Your task is to:

1. Define an abstract class Shape.
2. Implement the area() method in Circle and Rectangle subclasses.
3. Create instances of Circle and Rectangle and call the area() method on them.

```python
# Import ABC, abstractmethod from abc module, and math module
from abc import ABC, abstractmethod
import math

# Define an abstract base class Shape
class Shape(ABC):
  # Abstract method area, which must be implemented by any subclass
  @abstractmethod
  def area(self):
    pass

# Define a concrete class Circle inheriting from Shape
class Circle(Shape):
  # Constructor to initialize the radius
  def __init__(self, radius):
    self.radius = radius

  # Implementation of the area abstract method
  def area(self):
    return math.pi * (self.radius ** 2)

# Define a concrete class Rectangle inheriting from Shape
class Rectangle(Shape):
  # Constructor to initialize the width and height
  def __init__(self, width, height):
    self.width = width
    self.height = height

  # Implementation of the area abstract method
  def area(self):
    return self.width * self.height

# Using the abstract interface
# Create an instance of Circle and call area
circle = Circle(5)
print(f'Area of the circle: {circle.area()}')

# Create an instance of Rectangle and call area
rectangle = Rectangle(4, 6)
print(f'Area of the rectangle: {rectangle.area()}')
```

```
Area of the circle: 78.53981633974483
Area of the rectangle: 24
```

In this solution, the Shape class defines the abstract method area() that must be implemented by any subclass. The Circle and Rectangle classes provide their specific implementations of the area() method.

5.5   INTERACT WITH GENAI

Here are some questions and prompts you can interact with generative AI tools, including ChatGPT.

- Define abstraction in OOP and its significance.
- Explain how abstraction simplifies complex systems.
- Describe the relationship between abstraction and implementation hiding.
- Show a concrete class implementing abstract methods.
- Demonstrate abstraction simplifying a class interface.
- Differentiate abstraction from encapsulation.
- Explore abstraction's possibility without inheritance.
- Explain abstraction's role in modular design.
- Discuss separating high-level design from implementation.
- Analyze trade-offs between abstraction and direct implementation.
- Design a user authentication system using abstraction.
- Create a plugin architecture with abstraction.
- Address common challenges with abstraction in Python.
- Explain how abstract classes improve team collaboration.
- Discuss consequences of incomplete abstract method implementation.
- Integrate abstraction with other OOP principles.

## CHAPTER 6

Documentation

DOCUMENTING YOUR CODE, especially when defining classes, is crucial for ensuring that other developers (and your future self) can understand how your code works. Proper documentation should describe the purpose of the class, its methods, and its attributes. In Python, this is typically done using docstrings, which are string literals that appear right after the class or function definition. We use `'''documentation'''` in the class definition to automatically generate DocStrings, which are similar to javadoc. The docstrings we used will be reflected in `help()` function.

Are you ready? Let's get started!

6.1 INTRODUCTION

6.1.1 Demonstration

Let's compare the definition of two classes, `NoDoc` and `Doc`, and compare the result of `help()` function applied to them.

```python
class NoDoc():
  def __init__(self, att1):
    self.att1 = att1

  def method1(p1, p2, p3):
    return f'{p1} {p2} {p3} are something'
```

```python
help(NoDoc)
```

```
Help on class NoDoc in module __main__:

class NoDoc(builtins.object)
 |  NoDoc(att1)
 |
 |  Methods defined here:
 |
 |  __init__(self, att1)
```

DOI: 10.1201/9781003624868-6

```
|       Initialize self.  See help(type(self)) for accurate signature.
|
|   method1(p1, p2, p3)
|
|   ----------------------------------------------------------------------
|   Data descriptors defined here:
|
|   __dict__
|       dictionary for instance variables (if defined)
|
|   __weakref__
|       list of weak references to the object (if defined)
```

```python
class Doc():
    '''This is a class with documentation'''

    def __init__(self, att1):
        ''' The constructor takes value for att1

        keyargument:
        att1(str)   -- the name of the doc
        '''
        self.att1 = att1

    def method(p1, p2, p3):
        '''The method that combines three substrings together

        keyarguments:
        p1(str)  -- a substring
        p2(str)  -- a substring
        p3(str)  -- a substring

        return(str) -- the concatenated string
        '''
        return f'{p1} {p2} {p3} are something'
```

```python
help(Doc)
```

```
Help on class Doc in module __main__:

class Doc(builtins.object)
 |  Doc(att1)
 |
 |  This is a class with documentation
 |
 |  Methods defined here:
 |
 |  __init__(self, att1)
 |      The constructor takes value for att1
 |
 |      keyargument:
 |      att1(str)   -- the name of the doc
 |
 |  method(p1, p2, p3)
```

```
|       The method that combines three substrings together
|
|       keyarguments:
|       p1(str)  -- a substring
|       p2(str)  -- a substring
|       p3(str)  -- a substring
|
|       return(str) -- the concatenated string
|
|   ----------------------------------------------------------------------
|   Data descriptors defined here:
|
|   __dict__
|       dictionary for instance variables (if defined)
|
|   __weakref__
|       list of weak references to the object (if defined)
```

In this demonstration, the class Doc provides a comprehensive explanation of its purpose, outlining the functions' objectives, anticipated inputs, and outputs. This helps readers and users in comprehending the class's functionality, enabling them to utilize it effectively.

6.2 BOOK

Let's define and document a simple Book class.

```
# Define a class Book to represent a book
class Book:
    '''
    A class to represent a book.

    Attributes
    ----------
    title : str
        The title of the book.
    author : str
        The author of the book.
    pages : int
        The number of pages in the book.
    '''

    # Constructor to initialize the Book class with title, author, and pages
    def __init__(self, title, author, pages):
        '''
        Initialize the Book class with title, author, and pages.

        Parameters
        ----------
        title : str
            The title of the book.
        author : str
```

```
        The author of the book.
    pages : int
        The number of pages in the book.
    '''

    self.title = title
    self.author = author
    self.pages = pages

# Method to provide a brief description of the book
def description(self):
    '''
    Provides a brief description of the book.

    Returns
    -------
    str
        A formatted string describing the book.
    '''

    return f'\'{self.title}\' by {self.author}, {self.pages} pages.'

# Method to simulate reading a number of pages
def read_pages(self, num_pages):
    '''
    Simulate reading a number of pages.

    Parameters
    ----------
    num_pages : int
        The number of pages to read.

    Returns
    -------
    str
        A message indicating how many pages have been read.
    '''

    if num_pages > self.pages:
        return f'You can\'t read more than ({self.pages}) pages.'
    return f'You have read {num_pages} pages of \'{self.title}\'.'
```

In this demonstration, the first part of the class docstring provides a brief description of what the class represents.

The `Attributes` section lists and describes the class's attributes, including their types and roles. The docstring for the `__init__` method explains how to initialize the class, describing the parameters needed to create an instance of the class. Each parameter is listed with its type and a brief explanation of its role.

In addition, each method in the class has its own docstring. These docstrings provide a brief description of what the method does. If the method takes any parameters, they are listed with their types and descriptions in the `Parameters` section. The `Returns` section describes what the method returns, including the type and a brief explanation.

6.3 INTERACT WITH GENAI

Here are some questions and prompts you can interact with generative AI tools, including ChatGPT.

- Explain the importance of documentation in class definitions.
- Describe how documentation improves code maintainability.
- Highlight the significance of consistent documentation style.
- Create a well-documented Python class using docstrings.
- Write a method docstring with parameter and return type details.
- Demonstrate attribute documentation in class docstrings.
- Compare docstrings with inline comments.
- Explain the value of usage examples in docstrings.
- Compare docstring styles and selection criteria.
- Explain documentation's role in understanding class hierarchies.
- Describe how documentation improves open-source project accessibility.
- Explain documentation's role in debugging class methods.
- Demonstrate documentation for inheritable classes.
- Identify and prevent common class documentation mistakes.
- Ensure documentation remains current with class evolution.
- Outline best practices for documenting complex methods.

## CHAPTER 7

Case Studies

W E HAVE LEARNED the core aspects of object-oriented programming concepts— encapsulation, inheritance, polymorphism, and abstraction. We also learned how to properly document the class definition. Let's play with some case studies to have a comprehensive understanding of how these principles are applied in real-life scenarios. To save space, readers should call the `help()` function to observe the documentation of the defined classes.

Are you excited? Let's get started!

7.1 IPHONE

7.1.1 Background

Since the first iPhone was introduced to us, we have changed how we live everyday. Let's make a case study about iPhones and show a little appreciation of this great invention. (Don't be serious, I made this up) Let's put iPhone family into three categories:

- Original one: with 1 camera, 1 sensor,
- Old one: with 2 or more cameras (user-input), and 2 sensor and
- Recent one: with 2 or more cameras (user-input), and 2 or more sensors (user-input).

7.1.2 Implementation

```
import abc
from abc import ABC

# Abstract base class for all iPhones
class iphone(ABC):
    '''The wrapper class of all iphones'''

    def __init__(self, series, camera, sensor):
```

```python
        '''The initiator of all iphones

        Keyword arguments:
        series (str)  -- the series name of the iphone
        camera (int)  -- the number of cameras
        sensor (int)  -- the number of sensors
        '''
        self.family = 'iPhone'
        self.series = series
        self.camera = camera
        self.sensor = sensor

    # Abstract method to be implemented by subclasses
    @abc.abstractmethod
    def __repr__(self):
        '''
        Abstract method
        '''
        pass

# Concrete subclass for Original iPhones
class OriginaliPhone(iphone):
    '''The class for Original iphones'''

    def __init__(self, series):
        '''The initiator of original iphones

        Keyword arguments:
        series (str)  -- the series name of the iphone
        # of camera is 1
        # of sensors is 1
        '''
        super().__init__(series, 1, 1)

    def __repr__(self):
        '''The string of the iphone'''
        return f'''{self.family} family member,
          Series {self.series},
          with {self.camera} camera'''

# Concrete subclass for Old iPhones
class OldiPhone(iphone):
    def __init__(self, series, camera):
        '''The initiator of original iphones

        Keyword arguments:
        series (str)  -- the series name of the iphone
        camera (int)  -- the number of cameras
        # of sensors is 2
        '''
        super().__init__(series, camera, 2)

    def __repr__(self):
        '''The string of the iphone'''
        return f'''{self.family} family member,
```

```
            Series {self.series},
            with {self.camera} cameras and {self.sensor} sensors'''

# Concrete subclass for Recent iPhones
class RecentiPhone(iphone):
    def __init__(self, series, camera, sensor):
        '''The initiator of all iphones

        Keyword arguments:
        series (str)  -- the series name of the iphone
        camera (int)  -- the number of cameras
        sensor (int)  -- the number of sensors
        '''

        super().__init__(series, camera, sensor)

    def __repr__(self):
        '''The string of the iphone'''
        return f'''{self.family} family member,
            Series {self.series},
            with {self.camera} cameras and {self.sensor} sensors'''

    # Additional method for Recent iPhones
    def new_feature(self):
        '''The new feature of the iphone'''
        print('I can report a car-crash!')
```

7.1.3 Usage

```
# Raise TypeError
#i = iphone()

ori_iphone = OriginaliPhone('4s')
print(ori_iphone)

old_iphone = OldiPhone('10ProMax', 3)
print(old_iphone)

recent_iphone = RecentiPhone('14ProMax', 5, 5)
print(recent_iphone)

recent_iphone.new_feature()
```

```
iPhone family member,
        Series 4s,
        with 1 camera
iPhone family member,
        Series 10ProMax,
        with 3 cameras and 2 sensors
iPhone family member,
        Series 14ProMax,
        with 5 cameras and 5 sensors
I can report a car-crash!
```

7.2 EMPLOYEE

7.2.1 Background

A college hires hundreds students for various works, so students can get financial support and learning experience. To manage the system, you are asked to write a Python program to manage the record.

You are going to create five classes:

1. Student, Student_Not_Working, Student_Working, Student_Working_FT, Student_Working_PT.
2. Student and Student_Working are abstract classes.

7.2.2 Implementation

```python
# Importing libraries
import abc
from abc import ABC

# Defining student class
class Student(ABC):
    '''The abstract base class for all students'''

    def __init__(self, first_name, last_name, stu_ID):
        '''Create a student based on the first name, last name, and student ID

        Keyword arguments:
        first_name (str)  -- the first name of the student
        last_name (str)   -- the last name of the student
        stu_ID (str)      -- the string ID of the student
        '''
        self.first_name = first_name
        self.last_name = last_name
        self.stu_ID = stu_ID

    def intro(self):
        '''Introduction of Student using argument in format function'''
        return f'My name is {self.first_name} {self.last_name} ({self.stu_ID}).'

    @abc.abstractmethod
    def pay(self):
        '''Abstract method to be implemented by subclasses'''
        pass

# Defining Student Not working class
class Student_Not_Working(Student):
    '''The class for students not working'''

    def pay(self):
        return f'Payment will be {0}'

# Defining Student working class
```

```python
class Student_Working(Student):
  def __init__(self, first_name, last_name, stu_ID,
               department, supervisor_full_name):
    '''The abstract class for students working'''

    super().__init__(first_name, last_name, stu_ID)

    if isinstance(department, str) and isinstance(supervisor_full_name, str):
      self.department = department
      self.supervisor_full_name = supervisor_full_name
    else:
      raise TypeError("Enter string as value")

  @abc.abstractmethod
  def pay(self):
    '''Abstract method to be implemented by subclasses'''
    pass

# Defining Student Working fulltime class
class Student_Working_FT(Student_Working):
  def __init__(self, first_name, last_name, stu_ID,
               department, supervisor_full_name, annual_rate):
    '''Create a student working fulltime'''

    super().__init__(first_name, last_name, stu_ID,
                     department, supervisor_full_name)

    if isinstance(annual_rate, int):
      self.annual_rate = annual_rate
    else:
      raise TypeError("Enter integer as value")

  def pay(self):
    '''Calculate biweekly payment'''
    return f'Payment will be {(self.annual_rate/365)*14:.2f}'

# Defining student working part time class
class Student_Working_PT(Student_Working):
  '''The class for students working part time'''
  def __init__(self, first_name, last_name, stu_ID,
               department, supervisor_full_name, hourly_rate):
    '''Create a student working part time'''

    super().__init__(first_name, last_name, stu_ID,
                     department, supervisor_full_name)

    if isinstance(hourly_rate, int):
      self.hourly_rate = hourly_rate
    else:
      raise TypeError("Enter integer as value")

  def pay(self):
    '''Calculate payment based on hours worked'''
    hours = int(input("Please Enter the hours worked: "))
```

```
    if isinstance(hours, int):
      return f'Payment will be {float(self.hourly_rate * hours):.2f}'
    else:
      raise TypeError("Enter integer as value")
```

7.2.3 Usage

```
# Establishing an instance of Student class should raise an error
#stu0 = Student('Abby', 'Bolt', '0000')

# Establishing an instance of Student_Not_Working class
stu1 = Student_Not_Working('Abby', 'Bolt', '0001')
print(stu1.intro())
print(stu1.pay())

# Establishing an instance of Student_Working class should raise an error
#stu2 = Student_Working('Abby', 'Bolt', '0002', 'CS', 'Alan')

# Establishing an instance of Student_Working_FT class
stu3 = Student_Working_FT('Abby', 'Bolt', '0003', 'CS', 'Alan Turing', 50000)
print(stu3.intro())
print(stu3.pay())

# Establishing an instance of Student_Working_PT class
stu4 = Student_Working_PT('Abby', 'Bolt', '0004', 'CS', 'Alan Turing', 20)
print(stu4.intro())
print(stu4.pay())
```

```
My name is Abby Bolt (0001).
Payment will be 0
My name is Abby Bolt (0003).
Payment will be 1917.81
My name is Abby Bolt (0004).
Please Enter the hours worked: 28
Payment will be 560.00
```

7.3 UNIVERSITY SYSTEM

7.3.1 Overview

We'll design a university system that manages different types of people associated with the university: students, professors, and staff. This system will demonstrate how these roles share common attributes and behaviors while also having unique characteristics. The system should protect the personal information of each individual (e.g., social security number), share common attributes like name and age across different roles (students, professors, staff), allow different roles to implement aget_role() method differently, and provide a general Person class that defines the common interface for all roles.

7.3.2 Implementation

```python
# Import ABC and abstractmethod from the abc module
from abc import ABC, abstractmethod

# Define an abstract class Person
class Person(ABC):
  """
  Abstract class representing a person at the university.

  Attributes
  ----------
  name : str
    The person's name.
  age : int
    The person's age.
  """

  # Constructor to initialize the Person class
  def __init__(self, name, age):
    self._name = name
    self._age = age
    self.__ssn = None   # Encapsulated attribute

  # Abstract method to return the role of the person
  @abstractmethod
  def get_role(self):
    """
    Abstract method to return the role of the person.
    """
    pass

  # Method to set the Social Security Number
  def set_ssn(self, ssn):
    """
    Sets the Social Security Number.

    Parameters
    ----------
    ssn : str
      The social security number.
    """
    self.__ssn = ssn

  # Method to get the Social Security Number
  def get_ssn(self):
    """
    Gets the Social Security Number.

    Returns
    -------
    str
      The social security number.
    """
    return f'SSN: {self.__ssn}'
```

```python
# Define a concrete class Student inheriting from Person
class Student(Person):
  """
  Represents a student at the university.
  """

  # Constructor to initialize the Student class
  def __init__(self, name, age, major):
    super().__init__(name, age)
    self.major = major

  # Implementation of the get_role abstract method
  def get_role(self):
    return f'Student majoring in {self.major}'

# Define a concrete class Professor inheriting from Person
class Professor(Person):
  """
  Represents a professor at the university.
  """

  # Constructor to initialize the Professor class
  def __init__(self, name, age, department):
    super().__init__(name, age)
    self.department = department

  # Implementation of the get_role abstract method
  def get_role(self):
    return f'Professor in the {self.department} department'

# Define a concrete class Staff inheriting from Person
class Staff(Person):
  """
  Represents a staff member at the university.
  """

  # Constructor to initialize the Staff class
  def __init__(self, name, age, position):
    super().__init__(name, age)
    self.position = position

  # Implementation of the get_role abstract method
  def get_role(self):
    return f'Staff member working as {self.position}'
```

7.3.3 Usage

```python
# Usage
john = Student('John Doe', 20, 'Computer Science')
john.set_ssn('123-45-6789')
print(john.get_role())   # Polymorphism
print(john.get_ssn())    # Encapsulation
```

```
dr_smith = Professor('Dr. Smith', 45, 'Mathematics')
print(dr_smith.get_role())  # Polymorphism

jane = Staff('Jane Doe', 35, 'Administrator')
print(jane.get_role())  # Polymorphism
```

```
Student majoring in Computer Science
SSN: 123-45-6789
Professor in the Mathematics department
Staff member working as Administrator
```

In this implementation, the __ssn attribute in the Person class is private and can only be accessed or modified through getter and setter methods. Student, Professor, and Staff inherit from the Person class, sharing common attributes like name and age. Each subclass (Student, Professor, and Staff) implements the get_role() method differently. The Person class is an abstract class that defines the common interface (get_role()) for all subclasses.

7.4 VEHICLE RENTAL SYSTEM

7.4.1 Overview

We can design a vehicle rental system where different types of vehicles (cars, trucks, motorcycles) can be rented. This system will demonstrate how different vehicles share common functionalities while also implementing their own specific behaviors. The system protects sensitive vehicle data, such as engine number, shares common attributes like make, model, and year across different vehicle types, allows different vehicle types to implement a rent() method differently, and provides a general Vehicle class that defines the common interface for all vehicles.

7.4.2 Implementation

```python
# Import ABC and abstractmethod from the abc module
from abc import ABC, abstractmethod

# Define an abstract class Vehicle
class Vehicle(ABC):
    """
    Abstract class representing a vehicle.

    Attributes
    ----------
    make : str
        The vehicle's make.
    model : str
        The vehicle's model.
    year : int
        The vehicle's manufacturing year.
    """

    # Constructor to initialize the Vehicle class
```

```python
  def __init__(self, make, model, year):
    self.make = make
    self.model = model
    self.year = year
    self.__engine_number = None   # Encapsulated attribute

  # Abstract method to rent the vehicle
  @abstractmethod
  def rent(self):
    """
    Abstract method to rent the vehicle.
    """
    pass

  # Method to set the engine number
  def set_engine_number(self, engine_number):
    """
    Sets the engine number.

    Parameters
    -----------
    engine_number : str
      The engine number.
    """
    self.__engine_number = engine_number

  # Method to get the engine number
  def get_engine_number(self):
    """
    Gets the engine number.

    Returns
    --------
    str
      The engine number.
    """
    return f'Engine Number: {self.__engine_number}'

# Define a concrete class Car inheriting from Vehicle
class Car(Vehicle):
  """
  Represents a car.
  """

  # Implementation of the rent abstract method
  def rent(self):
    return f'Renting a car: {self.make} {self.model}, {self.year}'

# Define a concrete class Truck inheriting from Vehicle
class Truck(Vehicle):
  """
  Represents a truck.
  """

  # Implementation of the rent abstract method
```

```
  def rent(self):
    return f'Renting a truck: {self.make} {self.model}, {self.year}'

# Define a concrete class Motorcycle inheriting from Vehicle
class Motorcycle(Vehicle):
    """
    Represents a motorcycle.
    """

    # Implementation of the rent abstract method
    def rent(self):
      return f'Renting a motorcycle: {self.make} {self.model}, {self.year}'
```

7.4.3 Usage

```
# Usage
toyota_car = Car('Toyota', 'Corolla', 2020)
toyota_car.set_engine_number('ENG12345')
print(toyota_car.rent())    # Polymorphism
print(toyota_car.get_engine_number())    # Encapsulation

ford_truck = Truck('Ford', 'F-150', 2019)
print(ford_truck.rent())    # Polymorphism

harley_motorcycle = Motorcycle('Harley-Davidson', 'Street 750
```

```
Renting a car: Toyota Corolla, 2020
Engine Number: ENG12345
Renting a truck: Ford F-150, 2019
Renting a motorcycle: Harley-Davidson Street 750, 2018
```

In this implementation, the `__engine_number` attribute in the `Vehicle` class is private and can only be accessed or modified through getter and setter methods. `Car`, `Truck`, and `Motorcycle` inherit from the `Vehicle` class, sharing common attributes like `make`, `model`, and `year`. Each subclass (`Car`, `Truck`, and `Motorcycle`) implements the `rent()` method differently. The `Vehicle` class is an abstract class that defines the common interface (`rent()`) for all subclasses.

7.5 ONLINE MARKETPLACE

7.5.1 Overview

The online marketplace allows sellers to list products, and buyers to purchase them. Different types of products (like electronics, clothing, and groceries) have their own specific attributes and discount policies. The system manages product listings, customer shopping carts, and checkouts. The marketplace system protects sensitive data like product IDs and user IDs, shares common features between different product types and user roles, allows actions like calculating discounts to behave differently depending on the product type, and provides a generalized `Product` and `User` class that defines common behaviors and attributes.

7.5.2   Implementation

```python
from abc import ABC, abstractmethod

# Abstract base class representing a product in the marketplace
class Product(ABC):
    """
    Abstract class representing a product in the marketplace.

    Attributes
    ----------
    name : str
        The name of the product.
    price : float
        The price of the product.
    """

    def __init__(self, name, price):
        self.name = name
        self.price = price
        self.__product_id = None   # Encapsulated attribute

    # Method to set the product ID
    def set_product_id(self, product_id):
        self.__product_id = product_id

    # Method to get the product ID
    def get_product_id(self):
        return f'Product ID: {self.__product_id}'

    # Abstract method to calculate the discount
    @abstractmethod
    def calculate_discount(self):
        """
        Abstract method to calculate the discount.
        """
        pass

# Class representing an electronic product
class Electronics(Product):
    """
    Represents an electronic product.
    """

    def __init__(self, name, price, warranty_years):
        super().__init__(name, price)
        self.warranty_years = warranty_years

    # Implementation of the calculate_discount abstract method
    def calculate_discount(self):
        return self.price * 0.90   # 10% discount

# Class representing a clothing product
class Clothing(Product):
    """
```

```python
    Represents a clothing product.
    """

    def __init__(self, name, price, size):
        super().__init__(name, price)
        self.size = size

    # Implementation of the calculate_discount abstract method
    def calculate_discount(self):
        return self.price * 0.80  # 20% discount

# Class representing a grocery item
class Grocery(Product):
    """
    Represents a grocery item.
    """

    def __init__(self, name, price, expiration_date):
        super().__init__(name, price)
        self.expiration_date = expiration_date

    # Implementation of the calculate_discount abstract method
    def calculate_discount(self):
        return self.price * 0.95  # 5% discount

# Abstract base class representing a user in the marketplace
class User(ABC):
    """
    Abstract class representing a user in the marketplace.

    Attributes
    -----------
    name : str
        The name of the user.
    """

    def __init__(self, name):
        self.name = name
        self._user_id = None  # Encapsulated attribute

    # Method to set the user ID
    def set_user_id(self, user_id):
        self._user_id = user_id

    # Method to get the user ID
    def get_user_id(self):
        return f'User ID: {self._user_id}'

    # Abstract method to purchase a product
    @abstractmethod
    def purchase(self, product):
        """
        Abstract method to purchase a product.
        """
        pass
```

```python
# Class representing a seller in the marketplace
class Seller(User):
    """
    Represents a seller in the marketplace.
    """

    def __init__(self, name):
        super().__init__(name)
        self.products = []  # List to store seller's products

    # Method to add a product to the seller's inventory
    def add_product(self, product):
        self.products.append(product)
        return f'Product {product.name} added to the seller\'s inventory.'

    # Method to remove a product from the seller's inventory
    def remove_product(self, product):
        if product in self.products:
            self.products.remove(product)
            return f'Product {product.name} removed from the seller\'s inventory.'
        return f'Product {product.name} not found in inventory.'

    # Implementation of the purchase abstract method
    def purchase(self, product):
        return f'Sellers cannot purchase products.'

# Class representing a buyer in the marketplace
class Buyer(User):
    """
    Represents a buyer in the marketplace.
    """

    def __init__(self, name):
        super().__init__(name)
        self.shopping_cart = []  # List to store buyer's shopping cart

    # Implementation of the purchase abstract method
    def purchase(self, product):
        self.shopping_cart.append(product)
        return f'Product {product.name} added to shopping cart.'

    # Method to complete checkout
    def checkout(self):
        total = sum([item.calculate_discount() for item in self.shopping_cart])
        self.shopping_cart.clear()
        return f'Checkout complete. Total amount: ${total:.2f}'
```

7.5.3 Usage

```
# Seller adds products
seller = Seller('Alice')
laptop = Electronics('Laptop', 1200, 2)
jeans = Clothing('Jeans', 50, 'L')
apple = Grocery('Apple', 1, '2024-09-01')

seller.add_product(laptop)
seller.add_product(jeans)
seller.add_product(apple)

# Buyer purchases products
buyer = Buyer('Bob')
buyer.set_user_id('B001')

print(buyer.purchase(laptop))   # Buyer adds laptop to the shopping cart
print(buyer.purchase(jeans))    # Buyer adds jeans to the shopping cart

# Buyer checks out
print(buyer.checkout())  # Buyer completes checkout with discounts applied
```

```
Product Laptop added to shopping cart.
Product Jeans added to shopping cart.
Checkout complete. Total amount: $1120.00
```

In this implementation, __product_id and _user_id are private and can only be accessed via their getter methods. This ensures that sensitive data remains secure. Electronics, Clothing, and Grocery classes inherit from the abstract Product class, sharing the common attributes and methods. Seller and Buyer classes inherit from the abstract User class, allowing common behavior among users while still enabling specific differences. The calculate_discount() method is overridden in each subclass of Product. This method calculates a discount based on the type of product. For instance, electronics get a 10% discount, clothing items get a 20% discount, and groceries get a 5% discount. Both Product and User classes are abstract, which means they cannot be instantiated directly. They define the interfaces that their subclasses must implement. This structure allows you to enforce consistent behaviors across all types of products and users.

II

Data Manipulation

S ECTION II: DATA MANIPULATION introduces advanced data structures that are essential for efficient data manipulation in Python. The section focuses on the ndarray provided by the NumPy package, and the Series and DataFrame structures from the Pandas package. You will learn how to leverage these powerful tools to retrieve, manipulate, and analyze data. Through hands-on practice, you'll gain a deeper understanding of how these packages can be used to transform raw data into actionable insights, making them indispensable in data science and analytics.

By the end of this section, you will be able to:

- Understand and use the ndarray structure in NumPy for advanced numerical operations.

- Work with Pandas Series to handle one-dimensional labeled data efficiently.

- Utilize Pandas DataFrame to manage and analyze two-dimensional tabular data.

- Retrieve and manipulate data using NumPy and Pandas for effective data analysis.

- Develop a solid understanding of how these packages contribute to data science workflows.

## CHAPTER 8

N-dimensional Arrays

I N Python, basic data structures like `list` and `tuple` can store collections of items, making them similar to arrays. These structures are flexible because they can hold mixed data types, but they aren't optimized for numerical or scientific operations. The `ndarray`, provided by the Numpy package, is a more efficient alternative for handling large datasets and numerical computations. Unlike lists or tuples, ndarrays are specialized for numerical data and support multidimensional arrays, like matrices. While lists and tuples are more general-purpose, ndarrays trade that generality for efficiency, especially when performing mathematical calculations on large amounts of data.

Are you ready? Let's get started!

8.1 WHAT IS A N-DIMENSIONAL ARRAY

8.1.1 Explanation

In Python's NumPy package, an N-dimensional array, often called `ndarray`, is a powerful and flexible structure for handling large datasets and performing complex mathematical operations efficiently.

NumPy N-dimensional Array (`ndarray`) has following major features:

- **Performance**: Generally faster for numerical operations compared to Python lists, especially for large datasets.
- **Homogeneity**: All elements in an ndarray are of the same data type, which allows for efficient computation and memory usage.
- **Indexing/Slicing**: Allows for advanced indexing and slicing, making it easy to access and manipulate subarrays.
- **Structure**: An ndarray can have multiple dimensions (axes). For example, a 2D array is like a matrix with rows and columns, while a 3D array could be thought of as a stack of matrices.
- **Operations**: Supports a wide range of mathematical operations (e.g., addition,

DOI: 10.1201/9781003624868-8

multiplication) that are optimized for performance and can be applied element-wise.

8.2 LESSON: COMPARE NDARRAY WITH LIST

Comparing to `ndarray`, Python list differs in following ways:

- **Performance**: Generally slower for numerical tasks compared to NumPy arrays due to the overhead of Python's dynamic typing and the lack of optimized numerical operations.
- **Homogeneity**: Lists can contain elements of different data types, which may lead to inefficiencies in computations and require additional handling for mathematical operations.
- **Indexing/Slicing**: Supports basic indexing and slicing, but lacks the advanced capabilities of NumPy arrays.
- **Structure**: A Python list is a one-dimensional collection of items. While lists can contain nested lists (e.g., lists of lists) to simulate multidimensional arrays, this approach is less intuitive and less efficient for numerical computations.
- **Operations**: Basic operations are available, but they are not optimized for mathematical computations. Lists lack built-in support for element-wise operations.

8.2.1 Test Your Understanding

We discussed `ndarray` and `list` separately above. Now Let's compare them side by side regarding the structure, operations, homogeneity, indexing/slicing, and performance.

A possible solution is shown in Table 8.1.

8.3 PERFORMANCE COMPARISON

8.3.1 Demonstration

To compare the efficiency between `ndarray` and `list`, we use the `%timeit` function. The `%timeit` function in Python is a magic command provided by IPython (commonly used in Jupyter notebooks) to measure the execution time of code snippets. It is used for benchmarking and optimizing code performance. `%timeit` runs the code snippet multiple times (in a loop) to provide a statistically reliable measurement of execution time. It reports the best average time taken, minimizing the impact of random fluctuations and system load. It returns the average time taken per execution and can help identify performance bottlenecks in your code.

```
[x**2 for x in range(10)]
```

```
[0, 1, 4, 9, 16, 25, 36, 49, 64, 81]
```

TABLE 8.1 Comparison of Python Lists versus NumPy ndarrays

Feature	Python List	NumPy ndarray
Performance	Slow for numerical operations due to Python's dynamic typing and lack of optimization	Optimized for speed, especially with large datasets and numerical computations
Homogeneity	Supports mixed data types (e.g., integers, strings, objects)	Requires uniform data types for efficient memory usage and computation
Indexing/Slicing	Basic single-element access and simple slicing	Advanced multidimensional slicing and Boolean indexing
Structure	1D collection (nested lists mimic multidimensionality)	Native support for N-dimensions (e.g., 2D matrices, 3D tensors)
Operations	Limited to basic operations (append, remove, etc.)	Element-wise math operations $(+, -, *, /)$ and linear algebra functions
Memory Usage	Higher memory overhead for storing type information	Compact storage due to fixed data types (e.g., int32, float64)
Broadcasting	Not supported (requires manual iteration)	Automatic alignment of arrays with different shapes
Functionality	Minimal built-in math functions	Rich library of mathematical/statistical functions
Data Handling	Better for general-purpose, heterogeneous data	Optimized for numerical/scientific homogeneous data

```
import numpy as np

np.arange(10) ** 2
```

```
array([ 0,  1,  4,  9, 16, 25, 36, 49, 64, 81])
```

```
SIZE = 10
```

```
%timeit -n 1000 [x**2 for x in range(SIZE)]
%timeit -n 1000 np.arange(SIZE) ** 2
```

```
4.38 µs ± 1.66 µs per loop (mean ± std. dev. of 7 runs, 1000 loops each)
1.56 µs ± 490 ns per loop (mean ± std. dev. of 7 runs, 1000 loops each)
```

```
SIZE = 100
```

```
%timeit -n 1000 [x**2 for x in range(SIZE)]
%timeit -n 1000 np.arange(SIZE) ** 2
```

```
28.8 µs ± 1.32 µs per loop (mean ± std. dev. of 7 runs, 1000 loops each)
1.55 µs ± 324 ns per loop (mean ± std. dev. of 7 runs, 1000 loops each)
```

```
SIZE = 1000
```

```
%timeit -n 1000 [x**2 for x in range(SIZE)]
%timeit -n 1000 np.arange(SIZE) ** 2
```

```
308 µs ± 8.04 µs per loop (mean ± std. dev. of 7 runs, 1000 loops each)
2.72 µs ± 343 ns per loop (mean ± std. dev. of 7 runs, 1000 loops each)
```

8.3.2 Explanation

NumPy's `ndarray` can achieve efficiency compared to Python lists due to several key factors:

1. Data Types: `ndarray` requires that all elements be of the same data type. This allows NumPy to optimize memory storage and processing speed since it knows exactly how much space each element occupies and how to handle it efficiently. On the other hand, `list` can contain elements of varying types. This flexibility comes at the cost of performance, as each element requires additional overhead to manage and can lead to inefficiencies in computation.
2. Memory Allocation: `ndarray` stores data in a contiguous block of memory. This improves cache performance and allows for efficient vectorized operations, where multiple elements are processed simultaneously. On the other hand, `list` stores data in separate objects and may be scattered in memory, leading to slower access times and less efficient processing.
3. Vectorization: `ndarray` supports vectorized operations, where operations are applied to entire arrays (or subarrays) at once, leveraging low-level optimizations and efficient computation in C or Fortran. On the other hand, Python lists have operations usually performed in Python loops, which are slower due to the interpreted nature of Python and lack of hardware acceleration.
4. Broadcasting: NumPy uses broadcasting to perform operations on arrays of different shapes in a memory-efficient manner, without creating intermediate copies of arrays. However, Python lists lack built-in support for broadcasting, making similar operations cumbersome and less efficient to implement manually.
5. Pre-compiled Functions: Many of NumPy's functions are implemented in C or Fortran, which are much faster than equivalent Python code due to lower-level optimizations. But, operations in Python lists are performed using pure Python code, which is generally slower than compiled code.

In summary, NumPy arrays are designed to maximize computational efficiency and memory usage for numerical tasks, whereas Python lists are more general purpose and flexible but less optimized for numerical computations.

TABLE 8.2 Why NumPy ndarrays Outperform Python Lists

Feature	Python List	NumPy ndarray
Data Types	Mixed types (e.g., numbers, text, objects). Like a messy toolbox.	Same type (e.g., all integers). Like a neatly sorted toolbox.
Memory Storage	Data scattered in memory. Like books in different rooms, which is slow to collect.	Data stored in one connected block. Like books on a single shelf, which is easy to grab.
Math Operations	Requires slow Python loops. Like counting apples one by one.	Does math on entire arrays at once. Like weighing all apples in a basket together.
Handling Shapes	No built-in rules for mismatched sizes. You adjust manually.	Automatically adjusts sizes (broadcasting). Like resizing gloves to fit all hands.
Behind the Code	Runs in Python (like a translator converting instructions slowly).	Runs in pre-compiled C/Fortran (like a native speaker giving direct commands).

Here is a summary for the reasons why NumPy's `ndarray` outperform Python's `list` in Table 8.2.

8.3.3 Practice

Task: Change the variable `SIZE` in previous demonstration, and test the performance when `SIZE` is 10000 and 100000.

```
# Your code is here
```

8.4 LESSON: NDARRAY CREATION

8.4.1 Demonstration

The `np.array()` constructor in NumPy is used to create a new `ndarray` from existing data. `np.array()` takes a sequence-like input (such as a list or tuple) and converts it into a NumPy array. For instance, the following code creates a one-dimensional array `arr` with the elements `[1, 2, 3, 4]`:

```
arr = np.array([1, 2, 3, 4])
arr
```

```
array([1, 2, 3, 4])
```

You can create multidimensional arrays by passing nested sequences. For instance, the following code creates a two-dimensional array `matrix` with shape `(2, 3)`:

```
matrix = np.array([[1, 2, 3], [4, 5, 6]])
matrix
```

```
array([[1, 2, 3],
       [4, 5, 6]])
```

You can specify the data type of the array elements using the `dtype` parameter. For instance, the following code creates an array of type `float` with elements `[1.0, 2.0, 3.0]`:

```
arr_float = np.array([1, 2, 3], dtype=float)
arr_float
```

```
array([1., 2., 3.])
```

The `np.arange()` function in NumPy is used to create arrays with regularly spaced values over a specified range. It is often used for creating sequences of numbers for iteration or mathematical operations.

The basic syntax is `np.arange([start, ]stop, [step, ]dtype=None)`, where:

- `start` (optional): The starting value of the sequence (inclusive). Defaults to 0 if not specified.
- `stop`: The end value of the sequence (exclusive).
- `step` (optional): The spacing between values. Defaults to 1 if not specified.
- `dtype` (optional): The desired data type of the array. If not specified, it is inferred from the input values.

`np.arange()` is a convenient function for generating arrays with a specified range and step size, useful for creating sequences and ranges in numerical computations.

Basic usage with default start and step:

```
arr = np.arange(5) # Output: array([0, 1, 2, 3, 4])
arr
```

```
array([0, 1, 2, 3, 4])
```

Specifying start, stop, and step:

```
arr = np.arange(2, 10, 2) # Output: array([2, 4, 6, 8])
arr
```

```
array([2, 4, 6, 8])
```

Creating an array with floating-point numbers:

```
arr = np.arange(0.5, 3.0, 0.5) # Output: array([0.5, 1. , 1.5, 2. , 2.5])
arr
```

```
array([0.5, 1. , 1.5, 2. , 2.5])
```

reshape() is a convenient way to organize the ndarray to any shape:

```
arr=np.arange(12).reshape(3, 4)
arr
```

```
array([[ 0,  1,  2,  3],
       [ 4,  5,  6,  7],
       [ 8,  9, 10, 11]])
```

```
arr = arr.reshape(2, 6)
arr
```

```
array([[ 0,  1,  2,  3,  4,  5],
       [ 6,  7,  8,  9, 10, 11]])
```

```
arr = arr.reshape(3, 2, 2)
arr
```

```
array([[[ 0,  1],
        [ 2,  3]],

       [[ 4,  5],
        [ 6,  7]],

       [[ 8,  9],
        [10, 11]]])
```

8.4.2   Retrieve ndarray Metadata

NumPy provides several useful attributes and functions to retrieve information about an ndarray. Here's a brief overview of the most commonly used ones:

- type(): Returns the type of the NumPy array object itself.
- size: Returns the total number of elements in the array.
- ndim: Returns the number of dimensions (axes) of the array.
- shape: Returns a tuple representing the dimensions of the array. Each element in the tuple represents the size of the array along a particular axis.
- dtype: Returns the data type of the array elements.

These attributes and functions provide essential details about the structure, type, and properties of a NumPy array, helping to understand and manipulate data effectively.

```
# Define a function for checking
def ndarr_info(arr):
  print(arr)
  print(f'''Object type: {type(arr)},
  Array size: {np.size(arr)},
  Array dimensions: {arr.ndim},
  Array shape: {arr.shape},
  Array data type: {arr.dtype}''')
```

```
arr = np.array([1,2,3,4,5])
ndarr_info(arr)
```

```
[1 2 3 4 5]
```

```
Object type: <class 'numpy.ndarray'>,
  Array size: 5,
  Array dimensions: 1,
  Array shape: (5,),
  Array data type: int64
```

```
arr = np.arange(0.1, 0.5, 0.1)
ndarr_info(arr)
```

```
[0.1 0.2 0.3 0.4]
Object type: <class 'numpy.ndarray'>,
  Array size: 4,
  Array dimensions: 1,
  Array shape: (4,),
  Array data type: float64
```

```
arr = np.array([[[1],[2]],[[3],[4]],[[5],[6]]])
ndarr_info(arr)
```

```
[[[1]
  [2]]

 [[3]
  [4]]

 [[5]
  [6]]]
Object type: <class 'numpy.ndarray'>,
  Array size: 6,
  Array dimensions: 3,
  Array shape: (3, 2, 1),
  Array data type: int64
```

8.4.3 Practice

The following tasks require you to create several **ndarray** objects. You can use the function **ndarr_info()** to check the **ndarray** object.

Task: Create a one-dimensional NumPy array containing the integers from 1 to 5.

```
arr = np.array([1, 2, 3, 4, 5])
ndarr_info(arr)
```

```
[1 2 3 4 5]
Object type: <class 'numpy.ndarray'>,
  Array size: 5,
  Array dimensions: 1,
  Array shape: (5,),
  Array data type: int64
```

Task: Create a two-dimensional NumPy array with the following data:

```
[[1, 2, 3],
 [4, 5, 6]]
```

```
arr = np.array([[1, 2, 3], [4, 5, 6]])
ndarr_info(arr)
```

```
[[1 2 3]
 [4 5 6]]
Object type: <class 'numpy.ndarray'>,
  Array size: 6,
  Array dimensions: 2,
  Array shape: (2, 3),
  Array data type: int64
```

Task: Create a 1D array of integers from 10 to 14, but with a data type of `float`.

```
arr = np.array([10, 11, 12, 13, 14], dtype=float)
ndarr_info(arr)
```

```
[10. 11. 12. 13. 14.]
Object type: <class 'numpy.ndarray'>,
  Array size: 5,
  Array dimensions: 1,
  Array shape: (5,),
  Array data type: float64
```

Task: Create a three-dimensional NumPy array with shape (2, 2, 2) filled with values ranging from 1 to 8.

```
arr = np.array([[[1, 2], [3, 4]], [[5, 6], [7, 8]]])
ndarr_info(arr)
```

```
[[[1 2]
  [3 4]]

 [[5 6]
  [7 8]]]
Object type: <class 'numpy.ndarray'>,
  Array size: 8,
  Array dimensions: 3,
  Array shape: (2, 2, 2),
  Array data type: int64
```

Task: Use `np.arange()` to create a 1D array of values from 5 to 15 (exclusive) with a step of 2.

```
arr = np.arange(5, 15, 2)
ndarr_info(arr)
```

```
[ 5  7  9 11 13]
Object type: <class 'numpy.ndarray'>,
  Array size: 5,
  Array dimensions: 1,
  Array shape: (5,),
  Array data type: int64
```

Task: Use `np.arange()` to create an array of floating-point numbers from 0.5 to 2.0 with a step of 0.5.

```
arr = np.arange(0.5, 2.0, 0.5)
ndarr_info(arr)
```

```
[0.5 1.  1.5]
Object type: <class 'numpy.ndarray'>,
  Array size: 3,
  Array dimensions: 1,
  Array shape: (3,),
  Array data type: float64
```

Task: Convert the following nested list into a NumPy array:

```
[[10, 20],
 [30, 40],
 [50, 60]]
```

```
arr = np.array([[10, 20], [30, 40], [50, 60]])
ndarr_info(arr)
```

```
[[10 20]
 [30 40]
 [50 60]]
Object type: <class 'numpy.ndarray'>,
  Array size: 6,
  Array dimensions: 2,
  Array shape: (3, 2),
  Array data type: int64
```

Task: Use np.array() to create a 1D array with elements [3.5, 2.5, 1.5] and explicitly set the data type to int.

```
arr = np.array([3.5, 2.5, 1.5], dtype=int)
ndarr_info(arr)
```

```
[3 2 1]
Object type: <class 'numpy.ndarray'>,
  Array size: 3,
  Array dimensions: 1,
  Array shape: (3,),
  Array data type: int64
```

Task: Create a 1D array with 10 even numbers from 2, 4, to 20 using np.arange(), and then reshape it into a 2x5 array.

```
arr = np.arange(2, 21, 2).reshape(2, 5)
print(arr)
```

```
[[ 2  4  6  8 10]
 [12 14 16 18 20]]
```

8.5   LESSON: ACCESS 1D NDARRAY

8.5.1   Demonstration

Accessing elements in a one-dimensional NumPy array is straightforward and similar to accessing elements in a Python list. In sum:

- Single Index: `arr[index]` returns the element at the specified position.
- Negative Index: `arr[-index]` accesses elements from the end of the array.
- Slicing: `arr[start:stop:step]` retrieves a subarray with optional start, stop, and step parameters.

Accessing Single Elements: Retrieve a single element from the array using its index by using the index in square brackets `[]`.

```
arr = np.array([10, 20, 30, 40, 50])
print(arr[2])    # Output: 30
```

30

Negative Indexing: Access elements from the end of the array using negative indices by using negative indices to count from the end of the array.

```
arr = np.array([10, 20, 30, 40, 50])
print(arr[-1])    # Output: 50 (last element)
```

50

Slicing: Retrieve a subarray or slice of the original array by using the colon `:` to specify the start, stop, and step.

```
arr = np.array([10, 20, 30, 40, 50])
print('arr:', arr)
print('arr[:3]:', arr[:3]) # Output: [10 20 30]
print('arr[3:]:', arr[3:]) # Output: [40 50]
print('arr[1:3]:', arr[1:3]) # Output: [20 30]
print('arr[1:-1]:', arr[1:-1]) # Output: [20 30 40]
```

```
arr: [10 20 30 40 50]
arr[:3]: [10 20 30]
arr[3:]: [40 50]
arr[1:3]: [20 30]
arr[1:-1]: [20 30 40]
```

Accessing with Step: Retrieve elements with a specific step size by using the step parameter in slicing to skip elements.

```
arr = np.array([10, 20, 30, 40, 50])
print(arr[::2])    # Output: [10 30 50]
print(arr[::-1])   # Output: [50 40 30 20 10]
print(arr[1::2])   # Output: [20 40]
print(arr[:-1:2])  # Output: [10 30]
```

```
[10 30 50]
[50 40 30 20 10]
[20 40]
[10 30]
```

8.5.2 Practice

Task: Let `arr` be a NumPy array with values in the list `[1, 2, 3, 4, 5]`.

```
arr = np.array([1, 2, 3, 4, 5])
arr
```

```
array([1, 2, 3, 4, 5])
```

Task: Show the first element of `arr`.

```
arr[0]
```

```
1
```

Task: Show the last element of `arr`.

```
arr[-1]
```

```
5
```

Task: Show the first three elements of `arr`.

```
arr[:3]
```

```
array([1, 2, 3])
```

Task: Show the last three elements of `arr`.

```
arr[2:]
```

```
array([3, 4, 5])
```

Task: Show the elements of `arr` whose index is odd (1, 3, 5, ...).

```
arr[1::2]
```

```
array([2, 4])
```

Task: Show the elements of `arr` except the last one.

```
arr[:-1]
```

```
array([1, 2, 3, 4])
```

Task: Show the elements of `arr` in the reversed order.

```
arr[::-1]
```

```
array([5, 4, 3, 2, 1])
```

8.6 LESSON: ACCESS 2D NDARRAY

8.6.1 Demonstration

Here we have a 2D `ndarray` with shape (3, 3) and values from 1 to 9:

```
mda = np.array([
        [1, 2, 3],
        [4, 5, 6],
        [7, 8, 9]
    ])
```

We can retrieve a row by using the index of the row directly.

```
row2 = mda[1]
row2, type(row2), row2.ndim
```

(array([4, 5, 6]), numpy.ndarray, 1)

Retrieving a cell within a row could require two steps: we first retrieve that row, then retrieve the cell from that row.

```
row3 = mda[2]
row3cell2 = row3[1]
row3cell2
```

8

We can save the effort by combining the two steps together: we first specify the index of the row, then add the index of the cell, separating the two indices by a comma, within the brackets.

```
row3cell2 = mda[2,1]
row3cell2
```

8

We can retrieve all rows by slicing. Similar to 1D `ndarray`, we need to specify the `start:end:step` within the brackets.

```
all_rows = mda[0:len(mda)]
all_rows
```

```
array([[1, 2, 3],
       [4, 5, 6],
       [7, 8, 9]])
```

```
all_rows = mda[:]
all_rows
```

```
array([[1, 2, 3],
       [4, 5, 6],
       [7, 8, 9]])
```

Retrieving a column is different than retrieving a row. We should first slicing all rows, then specify the index of the cell of all rows, which is the column we want.

```
col2 = mda[:,1]
col2
```

array([2, 5, 8])

Column slicing is also different but similar to row slicing.

```
cols2and3 = mda[:,1:]
cols2and3
```

```
array([[2, 3],
       [5, 6],
       [8, 9]])
```

```
cols2and3 = mda[:,-2:]
cols2and3
```

```
array([[2, 3],
       [5, 6],
       [8, 9]])
```

8.6.2 Practice

Task: Let X be a ndarray with shape as (3, 4), and filled from 0 to 11.

```
X = np.arange(12).reshape(3, 4)
X
```

```
array([[ 0,  1,  2,  3],
       [ 4,  5,  6,  7],
       [ 8,  9, 10, 11]])
```

Task: Show the first row of X.

```
X[0]
```

```
array([0, 1, 2, 3])
```

Task: Show the first column of X.

```
X[:,0]
```

```
array([0, 4, 8])
```

Task: Show the first element of the first row of X.

```
X[0,0]
```

```
0
```

Task: Show the last row of X.

```
X[-1]
```

```
array([ 8,  9, 10, 11])
```

Task: Show the last column of X.

```
X[:,-1]
```

```
array([ 3,  7, 11])
```

Task: Show the last element of the last row of X.

```
X[-1,-1]
```

```
11
```

Task: Show all the rows except the last row of X.

```
X[:-1]
```

```
array([[0, 1, 2, 3],
       [4, 5, 6, 7]])
```

Task: Show all the columns except the last column of X.

```
X[:,:-1]
```

```
array([[ 0,  1,  2],
       [ 4,  5,  6],
       [ 8,  9, 10]])
```

Task: Show the first two elements of the first two rows of X.

```
X[:2,:2]
```

```
array([[0, 1],
       [4, 5]])
```

8.7   LESSON: NDARRAY MANIPULATION

8.7.1   Demonstration

We can modify the value of a cell in a `ndarray` by assignments.

```
arr = np.array([1, 2, 3, 4])
print(arr)
arr[0] = 9
print(arr)
```

```
[1 2 3 4]
[9 2 3 4]
```

```
arr = np.array([1, 2, 3, 4]).reshape(2, 2)
print(arr)
arr[0, 0] = 9
print(arr)
```

```
[[1 2]
 [3 4]]
[[9 2]
 [3 4]]
```

We can modify the value of some cells in a `ndarray` by assignments too.

```
mda = np.array([
        [1, 2, 3],
        [4, 5, 6],
        [7, 8, 9]
    ])
print(mda)
print('-' * 20)

# Make all elements of the first row as 2
mda[0, :] = 2
print(mda)
```

```
[[1 2 3]
 [4 5 6]
 [7 8 9]]
--------------------
[[2 2 2]
 [4 5 6]
 [7 8 9]]
```

```
mda = np.array([
        [1, 2, 3],
        [4, 5, 6],
        [7, 8, 9]
    ])
print(mda)
print('-' * 20)

# Add 2 to all elements of the first row
mda[0, :] += 2
print(mda)
```

```
[[1 2 3]
 [4 5 6]
 [7 8 9]]
--------------------
[[3 4 5]
 [4 5 6]
 [7 8 9]]
```

```
mda = np.array([
        [1, 2, 3],
        [4, 5, 6],
        [7, 8, 9]
    ])
print(mda)
print('-' * 20)

# Add 2 to first 2 elements of the first 2 row
mda[:2, :2] += 2
print(mda)
```

```
[[1 2 3]
 [4 5 6]
 [7 8 9]]
--------------------
[[3 4 3]
 [6 7 6]
 [7 8 9]]
```

```
mda = np.array([
        [1, 2, 3],
        [4, 5, 6],
        [7, 8, 9]
    ])
v = [10, 20, 30]

# Add a row vector to one row
```

```
mda[0] += v
print(mda)
```

```
[[11 22 33]
 [ 4  5  6]
 [ 7  8  9]]
```

```
mda = np.array([
        [1, 2, 3],
        [4, 5, 6],
        [7, 8, 9]
    ])
v = [10, 20, 30]

# Add a row vector to one column
mda[:,0] += v
print(mda)
```

```
[[11  2  3]
 [24  5  6]
 [37  8  9]]
```

```
mda = np.array([
        [1, 2, 3],
        [4, 5, 6],
        [7, 8, 9]
    ])
v = [10, 20, 30]

# Add a row vector to all rows
mda[:] += v
print(mda)
```

```
[[11 22 33]
 [14 25 36]
 [17 28 39]]
```

Summary, here are the approaches we can use to manipulate a `ndarray`:

- Single Elements: `arr[index] = new_value`
- Multiple Elements: `arr[start:stop] = new_values`
- Rows/Columns in 2D Arrays: `arr[row_index] = new_values` or `arr[:, column_index] = new_values`
- Adding a Vector to a Matrix: `matrix + vector` (uses broadcasting)

These techniques provide a flexible approach to modify and update `ndarray` data efficiently.

8.7.2 Practice

Task: Create a `ndarray` arr with value [0, 2, 4, 6, 8].

```
arr = np.array([0, 2, 4, 6, 8])
arr
```

```
array([0, 2, 4, 6, 8])
```

Task: Change the third element of the `arr` to 100.

```
print(arr) # Output: [0 2 4 6 8]
arr[2] = 100
print(arr)   # Output: [  0   2 100   6 8]
```

```
[0 2 4 6 8]
[  0   2 100   6   8]
```

Task: Set elements from index 2 to 4 of `arr` to [10, 20, 30].

```
print(arr) # Output: [0 2 100 6 8]
arr[2:] = [10, 20, 30]
print(arr)   # Output: [ 0   2 10 20 30]
```

```
[  0   2 100   6   8]
[ 0   2 10 20 30]
```

Task: Create a 2D `ndarray` `arr` with values from 1 to 9 and shape (3, 3).

```
arr = np.array([[1, 2, 3], [4, 5, 6], [7, 8, 9]])
print(arr)
```

```
[[1 2 3]
 [4 5 6]
 [7 8 9]]
```

Task: Change the second row of `arr` to `[100, 200, 300]`.

```
print(arr)
arr[1] = [100, 200, 300]
print(arr)
```

```
[[1 2 3]
 [4 5 6]
 [7 8 9]]
[[  1   2   3]
 [100 200 300]
 [  7   8   9]]
```

Task: Set the last column of `arr` to `[50, 60, 70]`.

```
print(arr)
arr[:, 2] = [50, 60, 70]
print(arr)
```

```
[[  1   2   3]
 [100 200 300]
 [  7   8   9]]
[[  1   2  50]
 [100 200  60]
 [  7   8  70]]
```

Task: Add the following vector `[10, 20, 30]` to each row `arr`.

```
print(arr)
vector = np.array([10, 20, 30])
arr +=vector
print(arr)
```

```
[[  1   2  50]
 [100 200  60]
 [  7   8  70]]
[[ 11  22  80]
 [110 220  90]
 [ 17  28 100]]
```

Task: Subtract 5 from every element in `arr`.

```
print(arr)
arr -= 5
print(arr)
```

```
[[ 11  22  80]
 [110 220  90]
 [ 17  28 100]]
[[  6  17  75]
 [105 215  85]
 [ 12  23  95]]
```

Task: Multiply every element in `arr` by 3.

```
print(arr)
arr *= 3
print(arr)
```

```
[[  6  17  75]
 [105 215  85]
 [ 12  23  95]]
[[ 18  51 225]
 [315 645 255]
 [ 36  69 285]]
```

8.8 LESSON: OPERATIONS IN NDARRAY

8.8.1 Demonstration

NumPy `ndarray` supports vectorized operations for efficient computation on arrays. This feature enables element-wise operations, meaning operations are performed independently on each element of the array. Element-wise operations in NumPy are performed using optimized C and Fortran libraries, which are much faster than Python loops or list comprehensions. Vectorized operations simplify code by removing the need for explicit loops and making mathematical operations more readable. NumPy operations are designed to handle large datasets efficiently, leveraging low-level optimizations that improve performance for numerical computations.

Addition (+): Adds corresponding elements of two arrays or adds a scalar to every element of an array.

```
arr1 = np.array([1, 2, 3])
arr2 = np.array([4, 5, 6])
result = arr1 + arr2 # Output: array([5, 7, 9])
result
```

```
array([5, 7, 9])
```

Subtraction (−): Subtracts corresponding elements of one array from another or subtracts a scalar from every element of an array.

```
arr1 = np.array([10, 20, 30])
arr2 = np.array([1, 2, 3])
result = arr1 - arr2 # Output: array([ 9, 18, 27])
result
```

```
array([ 9, 18, 27])
```

Multiplication (∗): Multiplies corresponding elements of two arrays or multiplies each element of an array by a scalar.

```
arr1 = np.array([1, 2, 3])
arr2 = np.array([4, 5, 6])
result = arr1 * arr2 # Output: array([ 4, 10, 18])
result
```

```
array([ 4, 10, 18])
```

Division (/): Divides corresponding elements of one array by another or divides each element of an array by a scalar.

```
arr1 = np.array([10, 20, 30])
arr2 = np.array([1, 2, 3])
result = arr1 / arr2 # Output: array([10., 10., 10.])
result
```

```
array([10., 10., 10.])
```

In summary, operations on lists are not inherently element-wise. For example, adding two lists concatenates them rather than performing element-wise addition. To perform element-wise operations, you need to use loops or list comprehensions:

```
list1 = [1, 2, 3]
list2 = [4, 5, 6]
result = list1 + list2
result
```

```
[1, 2, 3, 4, 5, 6]
```

```
list1 = [1, 2, 3]
list2 = [4, 5, 6]
result = [x + y for x, y in zip(list1, list2)] # Output: [5, 7, 9]
result
```

```
[5, 7, 9]
```

On the other hand, NumPy `ndarray` supports direct element-wise operations. This means operations like addition, subtraction, multiplication, and division are applied

to each element of the array automatically and efficiently. This vectorized approach
is much faster than using loops due to internal optimizations and compiled code.

```
arr1 = np.array([1, 2, 3])
arr2 = np.array([4, 5, 6])
result = arr1 + arr2 # Output: array([5, 7, 9])
result
```

```
array([5, 7, 9])
```

8.8.2 Practice

Task: Create ndarray arr1 from a list [1, 2, 3] and arr2 from a list [6, 5, 4].

```
arr1 = np.array([1, 2, 3])
arr2 = np.array([6, 5, 4])
arr1, arr2
```

```
(array([1, 2, 3]), array([6, 5, 4]))
```

Task: Add arr1 and arr2 and save the result to arr3.

```
arr3 = arr1 + arr2
arr1, arr2, arr3
```

```
(array([1, 2, 3]), array([6, 5, 4]), array([7, 7, 7]))
```

Task: Subtract arr2 from arr1 and save it to arr3.

```
arr3 = arr1 - arr2
arr1, arr2, arr3
```

```
(array([1, 2, 3]), array([6, 5, 4]), array([-5, -3, -1]))
```

Task: Subtract arr2 from arr1 and save it to arr3.

```
arr3 = arr2 - arr1
arr1, arr2, arr3
```

```
(array([1, 2, 3]), array([6, 5, 4]), array([5, 3, 1]))
```

Task: Multiply arr1 with arr2 and save it to arr3.

```
arr3 = arr1 * arr2
arr1, arr2, arr3
```

```
(array([1, 2, 3]), array([6, 5, 4]), array([ 6, 10, 12]))
```

Task: Divide arr1 from arr2 and save it to arr3.

```
arr3 = arr2 / arr1
arr1, arr2, arr3
```

```
(array([1, 2, 3]),
 array([6, 5, 4]),
 array([6.        , 2.5       , 1.33333333]))
```

Task: Divide `arr2` from `arr1` and save it to `arr3`.

```
arr3 = arr1 / arr2
arr1, arr2, arr3
```

```
(array([1, 2, 3]),
 array([6, 5, 4]),
 array([0.16666667, 0.4       , 0.75      ]))
```

Task: Raise each element of the `arr1` to the power of 3 and save it to `arr3`.

```
arr3 = arr1 **3
arr1, arr3
```

```
(array([1, 2, 3]), array([ 1,  8, 27]))
```

Task: Raise each element of the `arr2` to the power of 2 and save it to `arr3`.

```
arr3 = arr2 **2
arr2, arr3
```

```
(array([6, 5, 4]), array([36, 25, 16]))
```

Task: Compute the modulus of each element in `arr1` with 3 and save it to `arr3`.

```
arr3 = arr1 % 3
arr1, arr3
```

```
(array([1, 2, 3]), array([1, 2, 0]))
```

Task: Compare each element in `arr2` with 5 and save the result of `>5` to `arr3`.

```
arr3 = arr2 > 5
arr2, arr3
```

```
(array([6, 5, 4]), array([ True, False, False]))
```

Task: Check each element in `arr1` for even numbers and save the result to `arr3`.

```
arr3 = arr1 % 2 == 0
arr1, arr3
```

```
(array([1, 2, 3]), array([False,  True, False]))
```

8.9   INTERACT WITH GENAI

Here are some questions and prompts you can interact with generative AI tools, including ChatGPT.

- Define ndarray and its differences from Python lists.
- Explain ndarray's central role in NumPy.
- Describe ndarray's efficient data storage.
- Highlight key ndarray features: shape, dtype, and strides.
- Explain NumPy's performance advantages over Python loops.
- Create an ndarray from a Python list.

- Reshape ndarray into 2D or 3D arrays.
- Demonstrate ndarray slicing and indexing.
- Generate ndarrays with zeros, ones, or random values.
- Perform element-wise operations on ndarrays.
- Analyze ndarray shape's impact on data structure.
- Explore ndarray's element type constraints.
- Compare ndarray and nested list multidimensional handling.
- Explain NumPy's vectorization optimization.
- Distinguish shallow and deep ndarray copies.
- Demonstrate creating ndarrays with `np.view()`.
- Perform matrix operations with ndarrays.
- Conduct statistical analysis using ndarrays.
- Simplify machine learning data preparation.
- Identify and prevent ndarray reshaping errors.
- Handle ndarray dimension mismatches.
- Understand dtype's impact on calculations.

8.10 EXPLORE MORE OF NDARRAY

At the end, here is the official documentation of `ndarray`: https://numpy.org/doc/stable/reference/generated/numpy.ndarray.html

## CHAPTER 9

NumPy

W E JUST LEARNED the `ndarray` data structure, which is the core data structure of the NumPy package. While `ndarray` allows efficient handling of large datasets and complex calculations, NumPy goes even further by offering a wide range of features that make it essential for data manipulation. NumPy is crucial in fields like data science, machine learning, and engineering because it simplifies and speeds up calculations, allowing users to focus on problem-solving rather than coding performance.

In this chapter, we are going to explore the universal functions for fast element-wise operations, statistical methods for data understanding and analysis, tools for linear algebra to solve equations or manipulate matrices, and random number generation for simulations and modeling. We will also learn a practical features, masking, which lets you filter or modify data based on conditions, perfect for tasks like cleaning datasets or handling missing values. We will learn together how NumPy turns complex numerical tasks into simple, efficient operations.

Are you excited? Let's get started!

9.1 UNIVERSAL FUNCTIONS

9.1.1 Demonstration

Universal functions, commonly known as ufuncs, are a core feature of NumPy that allow for efficient, element-wise operations on arrays. These functions are designed to operate on each element of the array independently and are implemented in C for high performance. Universal functions support broadcasting, which enables operations between arrays of different shapes. Universal functions apply the function to each element of the array, making them highly efficient for array computations. Universal functions support broadcasting, allowing operations on arrays of different shapes without explicit loops. Implemented in C, universal functions are optimized for speed, making array operations faster compared to Python loops. At last,

DOI: 10.1201/9781003624868-9

universal functions can handle arrays of different shapes and dimensions, provided they adhere to broadcasting rules.

Addition (`np.add()`): Adds corresponding elements of two arrays or adds a scalar to every element of an array.

```python
import numpy as np

arr1 = np.array([1, 2, 3])
arr2 = np.array([4, 5, 6])
result = np.add(arr1, arr2)
print(result)   # Output: [5 7 9]
```

[5 7 9]

Subtraction (`np.subtract()`): Subtracts corresponding elements of one array from another or subtracts a scalar from every element.

```python
arr1 = np.array([10, 20, 30])
arr2 = np.array([1, 2, 3])
result = np.subtract(arr1, arr2)
print(result)   # Output: [ 9 18 27]
```

[9 18 27]

Multiplication (`np.multiply()`): Multiplies corresponding elements of two arrays or multiplies each element by a scalar.

```python
arr1 = np.array([2, 4, 6])
arr2 = np.array([1, 3, 5])
result = np.multiply(arr1, arr2)
print(result)   # Output: [ 2 12 30]
```

[2 12 30]

Division (`np.divide()`): Divides corresponding elements of one array by another or divides each element by a scalar.

```python
arr1 = np.array([100, 200, 300])
arr2 = np.array([10, 20, 30])
result = np.divide(arr1, arr2)
print(result)   # Output: [10. 10. 10.]
```

[10. 10. 10.]

Sine (`np.sin()`): Computes the sine of each element in the array.

```python
arr = np.array([0, np.pi/2, np.pi])
result = np.sin(arr)
print(result)   # Output: [0. 1. 0.]
```

[0.0000000e+00 1.0000000e+00 1.2246468e-16]

Cosine (`np.cos()`): Computes the cosine of each element in the array.

```python
arr = np.array([0, np.pi/2, np.pi])
result = np.cos(arr)
print(result)   # Output: [1. 0. -1.]
```

```
[ 1.000000e+00  6.123234e-17 -1.000000e+00]
```

Tangent (np.tan()): Computes the tangent of each element in the array.

```python
arr = np.array([0, np.pi/4, np.pi/2])
result = np.tan(arr)
print(result)   # Output: [0.        1.        1.63312394e+16]
```

```
[0.00000000e+00 1.00000000e+00 1.63312394e+16]
```

Natural Logarithm (np.log()): Computes the natural logarithm (base e) of each element.

```python
arr = np.array([1, np.e, np.e**2])
result = np.log(arr)
print(result)   # Output: [0. 1. 2.]
```

```
[0. 1. 2.]
```

Exponential (np.exp()): Computes the exponential (e^x) of each element.

```python
arr = np.array([0, 1, 2])
result = np.exp(arr)
print(result)   # Output: [1.         2.71828183 7.3890561 ]
```

```
[1.         2.71828183 7.3890561 ]
```

Square Root (np.sqrt()): Computes the square root of each element.

```python
arr = np.array([1, 4, 9])
result = np.sqrt(arr)
print(result)   # Output: [1. 2. 3.]
```

```
[1. 2. 3.]
```

Power (np.power()): Raises each element to the specified power.

```python
arr = np.array([2, 3, 4])
result = np.power(arr, 3)
print(result)   # Output: [ 8 27 64]
```

```
[ 8 27 64]
```

Broadcasting allows ufuncs to operate on arrays of different shapes. It automatically expands the smaller array to match the shape of the larger one.

```python
arr = np.array([[1, 2, 3], [4, 5, 6]])
scalar = 10
result = arr + scalar
print(result)
# Output:
# [[11 12 13]
#  [14 15 16]]
```

```
[[11 12 13]
 [14 15 16]]
```

9.1.2 Practice

Task: Create two NumPy arrays, a with elements [1, 2, 3, 4, 5] and b with elements [10, 20, 30, 40, 50]. Compute the element-wise product of these arrays.

```python
a = np.array([1, 2, 3, 4, 5])
b = np.array([10, 20, 30, 40, 50])
product = np.multiply(a, b)
print(product)
```

```
[ 10  40  90 160 250]
```

Task: Create a 2x3 NumPy array A with elements [[1, 2, 3], [4, 5, 6]]. Add a one-dimensional array b with elements [10, 20, 30] to each row of A using broadcasting.

```python
A = np.array([[1, 2, 3], [4, 5, 6]])
b = np.array([10, 20, 30])
result = A + b
print(result)
```

```
[[11 22 33]
 [14 25 36]]
```

Task: Create a NumPy array x with elements [-1, 0, 1, 2, 3]. Apply the np.exp (exponential) function to each element of the array.

```python
x = np.array([-1, 0, 1, 2, 3])
exp_result = np.exp(x)
print(exp_result)
```

```
[ 0.36787944  1.          2.71828183  7.3890561  20.08553692]
```

Task: Create a NumPy array angles with elements $[0, \pi/2, \pi, 3\pi/2, 2\pi]$. Compute the sine of each element in the array using the np.sin function. Hint: You can use np.pi for π.

```python
angles = np.array([0, np.pi/2, np.pi, 3*np.pi/2, 2*np.pi])
sine_values = np.sin(angles)
print(sine_values)
```

```
[ 0.0000000e+00  1.0000000e+00  1.2246468e-16 -1.0000000e+00
 -2.4492936e-16]
```

9.2 STATISTICAL METHODS

9.2.1 Demonstration

NumPy provides a comprehensive suite of statistical functions to analyze and interpret data. These functions allow you to compute essential statistical measures efficiently and handle large datasets with ease. Below is a detailed introduction to some of the most commonly used statistical methods in NumPy.

```
# Create a dummy ndarray
arr = np.array([1, 2, 2, 3, 3, 3]).reshape(3, 2)
arr
```

```
array([[1, 2],
       [2, 3],
       [3, 3]])
```

Mean (np.mean()): Computes the average of all elements in the array or along a specified axis.

```
mean = np.mean(arr)
mean
```

```
2.3333333333333335
```

```
mean = np.mean(arr[0])
mean
```

```
1.5
```

Median (np.median()): Computes the median value of the array elements or along a specified axis. The median is the middle value when the data is sorted.

```
median = np.median(arr)
median
```

```
2.5
```

```
median = np.median(arr[0])
median
```

```
1.5
```

```
median = np.median(arr[:,0])
median
```

```
2.0
```

```
median = np.median(arr, axis = 1)
median
```

```
array([1.5, 2.5, 3. ])
```

```
median = np.median(arr, axis = 0)
median
```

```
array([2., 3.])
```

Standard Deviation (np.std()): Computes the standard deviation of the array elements, which measures the amount of variation or dispersion from the mean.

```
std_dev = np.std(arr)
print(std_dev)
```

```
0.7453559924999298
```

Variance (`np.var()`): Computes the variance of the array elements, which measures the spread of the numbers in the dataset.

```
variance = np.var(arr)
print(variance)
```

0.5555555555555555

Percentiles (`np.percentile()`): Computes the nth percentile of the array elements. The percentile is a value below which a given percentage of observations fall.

```
percentile_25 = np.percentile(arr, 25)
percentile_75 = np.percentile(arr, 75)
print(f'25th percentile: {percentile_25}')   # Output: 25th percentile: 2.0
print(f'75th percentile: {percentile_75}')   # Output: 75th percentile: 3.0
```

```
25th percentile: 2.0
75th percentile: 3.0
```

9.2.2 Practice

Task: Create a NumPy array with the elements [0, 1, 2, 3, 4, 5, 6, 7, 8, 9, 10] and compute the mean of the array.

```
arr = np.arange(11)
mean = np.mean(arr)
print(mean)
```

5.0

Task: Generate an array of 20 random integers between 1 and 100. Calculate the median of the array.

```
arr = np.random.randint(1, 101, 20)
median = np.median(arr)
print(median)
```

56.5

Task: Construct a NumPy array with the elements [4, 8, 15, 16, 23, 42]. Compute the standard deviation of the array.

```
arr = np.array([4, 8, 15, 16, 23, 42])
std_dev = np.std(arr)
print(std_dev)
```

12.315302134607444

Task: Create an array of 15 random floats between 0 and 1. Compute the variance of the array.

```
arr = np.random.rand(15)
variance = np.var(arr)
print(variance)
```

0.07049010237451717

Task: Generate an array of 30 random integers between 50 and 150. Calculate the 25th percentile of the array.

```
arr = np.random.randint(50, 151, 30)
percentile_25 = np.percentile(arr, 25)
print(percentile_25)
```

80.5

Task: Create a NumPy array with elements [12, 15, 14, 10, 8, 9, 10, 11, 9, 12]. Find the range of the array (max value - min value).

```
arr = np.array([12, 15, 14, 10, 8, 9, 10, 11, 9, 12])
range_value = np.max(arr) - np.min(arr)
print(range_value)
```

7

9.3   LINEAR ALGEBRA

9.3.1   Demonstration

Linear algebra is a fundamental aspect of NumPy, and it provides powerful tools for numerical computations involving vectors, matrices, and their operations. Let's dive into the key components and functions of linear algebra in NumPy with detailed explanations and examples.

In NumPy, matrices are represented using the `ndarray` object, which can have 1 or more dimensions.

```
A = np.array([[1, 2], [3, 4]])
print('Matrix A:')
print(A)

# Creating a vector (1D array)
v = np.array([1, 2, 3])
print('Vector v:')
print(v)
```

```
Matrix A:
[[1 2]
 [3 4]]
Vector v:
[1 2 3]
```

Matrix Addition and Subtraction:

```
# Create a Matrix B
B = np.array([[5, 6], [7, 8]])
print('Matrix B:')
print(B)

# Matrix addition
C = A + B
```

```
print('Matrix C (A + B):')
print(C)
```

```
Matrix B:
[[5 6]
 [7 8]]
Matrix C (A + B):
[[ 6  8]
 [10 12]]
```

Multiplication (Element-wise and Dot Product):

```
# Element-wise multiplication
D = A * B
print('Matrix D (Element-wise A * B):')
print(D)

# Dot product (matrix multiplication)
E = np.dot(A, B)
print('Matrix E (Dot product A.dot(B)):')
print(E)
```

```
Matrix D (Element-wise A * B):
[[ 5 12]
 [21 32]]
Matrix E (Dot product A.dot(B)):
[[19 22]
 [43 50]]
```

Matrix Inverse and Transpose:

```
# Computing the inverse of a matrix
A_inv = np.linalg.inv(A)
print('Inverse of Matrix A:')
print(A_inv)

# Computing the transpose of a matrix
A_transpose = A.T
print('Transpose of Matrix A:')
print(A_transpose)
```

```
Inverse of Matrix A:
[[-2.   1. ]
 [ 1.5 -0.5]]
Transpose of Matrix A:
[[1 3]
 [2 4]]
```

Eigenvalues and eigenvectors are fundamental in many numerical computations, such as principal component analysis (PCA) and solving differential equations.

```
# Computing eigenvalues and eigenvectors
eigenvalues, eigenvectors = np.linalg.eig(A)
print('Eigenvalues of Matrix A:')
print(eigenvalues)
```

```
print('Eigenvectors of Matrix A:')
print(eigenvectors)
```

```
Eigenvalues of Matrix A:
[-0.37228132  5.37228132]
Eigenvectors of Matrix A:
[[-0.82456484 -0.41597356]
 [ 0.56576746 -0.90937671]]
```

These examples cover the foundational aspects of linear algebra in NumPy and demonstrate its utility in solving practical problems. Each operation and function plays a crucial role in various computational tasks, making NumPy a powerful tool for numerical computing and data analysis.

9.3.2 Practice

Given three matrices below, complete following tasks:

```
# Run this cell for the practice

A = np.arange(6).reshape(2, 3)
B = np.arange(6, 12).reshape(2, 3)
C = np.arange(6, 12).reshape(3, 2)

A, B, C
```

```
(array([[0, 1, 2],
       [3, 4, 5]]),
 array([[ 6,  7,  8],
       [ 9, 10, 11]]),
 array([[ 6,  7],
       [ 8,  9],
       [10, 11]]))
```

Task: Compute the sum of A and B.

```
result = A + B
result
```

```
array([[ 6,  8, 10],
       [12, 14, 16]])
```

Task: Subtract B from A.

```
result = A - B
result
```

```
array([[-6, -6, -6],
       [-6, -6, -6]])
```

Task: Subtract A from B.

```
result = B - A
result
```

```
array([[6, 6, 6],
       [6, 6, 6]])
```

Task: Element-wise multiplication of A and B.

```
result = A * B
result
```

```
array([[ 0,  7, 16],
       [27, 40, 55]])
```

Task: Compute the Dot product (matrix multiplication) of A and C.

```
result = A.dot(C)
result
```

```
array([[ 28,  31],
       [100, 112]])
```

Task: Compute the dot product of A' s transpose and B.

```
result = A.transpose().dot(B)
result
```

```
array([[27, 30, 33],
       [42, 47, 52],
       [57, 64, 71]])
```

Task: Compute the dot product of A and B's transpose.

```
result = A.dot(B.transpose())
result
```

```
array([[ 23,  32],
       [ 86, 122]])
```

9.4   RANDOM GENERATION

9.4.1   Demonstration

Random number generation is a crucial aspect of data analysis, simulations, and machine learning. NumPy provides a powerful set of tools for generating random numbers and performing random sampling. The `numpy.random` module includes various functions to generate random numbers from different distributions, shuffle arrays, and set random seeds for reproducibility.

`numpy.random.seed()` initializes the random number generator to a known state, ensuring that random numbers generated are the same across runs. This is common in classrooms and demonstrations. In practice, we do not set the seed because we want to pursue the randomness.

```
np.random.seed(42)    # Set the random seed
random_numbers1 = np.random.rand(3)
np.random.seed(42)    # Reset the random seed
random_numbers2 = np.random.rand(3)

print(random_numbers1)   # Output: [0.37454012 0.95071431 0.73199394]
print(random_numbers2)   # Output: [0.37454012 0.95071431 0.73199394]
```

```
[0.37454012 0.95071431 0.73199394]
[0.37454012 0.95071431 0.73199394]
```

Generates random numbers between a specified range, typically between 0 and 1.

```
random_array = np.random.rand(2, 3)
print(random_array)
# Output might be:
# [[0.37454012 0.95071431 0.73199394]
#  [0.59865848 0.15601864 0.15599452]
```

```
[[0.37454012 0.95071431 0.73199394]
 [0.59865848 0.15601864 0.15599452]]
```

```
random_array = np.random.uniform(2, 3, size = (2, 3))
print(random_array)
# Output might be:
# [[2.15601864 2.15599452 2.05808361]
#  [2.86617615 2.60111501 2.70807258]]
```

```
[[2.15601864 2.15599452 2.05808361]
 [2.86617615 2.60111501 2.70807258]]
```

Generates random numbers following a normal (Gaussian) distribution with a specified mean and standard deviation.

```
normal_array = np.random.randn(2, 3)
print(normal_array)
# Output might be:
# [[ 0.49671415 -0.1382643   0.64768854]
#  [ 1.52302986 -0.23415337 -0.23413696]]
```

```
[[ 0.49671415 -0.1382643   0.64768854]
 [ 1.52302986 -0.23415337 -0.23413696]]
```

Generates random integers between specified low and high values.

```
random_integers = np.random.randint(1, 10, size=(2, 3))
print(random_integers)
# Output might be:
# [[7 4 8]
#  [5 7 3]]
```

```
[[7 4 8]
 [5 7 3]]
```

9.4.2 Practice

Task: Generate an array of five random floats between 0 and 1 using NumPy's uniform distribution function.

```
# Generate 5 random floats between 0 and 1
random_floats = np.random.uniform(0, 1, 5)
print(random_floats)
# Output: Array of 5 random floats between 0 and 1
```

```
[0.61838601 0.38246199 0.98323089 0.46676289 0.85994041]
```

Task: Generate an array of seven random integers between 10 and 50 (inclusive) using NumPy's uniform distribution function.

```python
# Generate 7 random integers between 10 and 50 (inclusive)
random_integers = np.random.randint(10, 51, 7)
print(random_integers)
# Output: Array of 7 random integers between 10 and 50
```

```
[16 30 18 48 27 13 34]
```

Task: Generate an array of four random floats from a normal distribution with a mean of 0 and standard deviation of 1.

```python
# Generate 4 random floats from a normal distribution
random_floats = np.random.randn(4)
print(random_floats)
```

```
[-0.11564828 -0.3011037  -1.47852199 -0.71984421]
```

Task: Generate an array of six random integers from a normal distribution with a mean of 50 and standard deviation of 10. Round the values to the nearest integer.

```python
# Generate 6 random floats from a normal distribution
random_floats = np.random.normal(50, 10, 6)

# Round to nearest integer
random_integers = np.round(random_floats).astype(int)
print(random_integers)
```

```
[45 61 53 32 53 46]
```

Task: Generate an array of four random floats between 5 and 15 using NumPy's uniform distribution function.

```python
# Generate 4 random floats between 5 and 15
random_floats = np.random.uniform(5, 15, 4)
print(random_floats)
# Output: Array of 4 random floats between 5 and 15
```

```
[ 9.31945019  7.9122914  11.11852895  6.39493861]
```

Task: Generate an array of four random floats from a normal distribution with a mean of 10 and standard deviation of 2.

```python
# Generate 4 random floats from a normal distribution
random_floats = np.random.normal(10, 2, 4)
print(random_floats)
```

```
[ 8.18395185  7.1753926  12.93129754  9.5484474 ]
```

Task: Generate a 3-by-3 matrix of random integers between 100 and 200 (inclusive) using NumPy's uniform distribution function.

```
random_matrix = np.random.randint(100, 201, size=(3, 3))
print(random_matrix)
```

```
[[150 154 163]
 [102 200 150]
 [106 120 172]]
```

Task: Generate a 2-by-4 matrix of random floats from a normal distribution with a mean of 5 and standard deviation of 3.

```
# Generate a 2 by 4 matrix of random floats from a normal distribution
random_matrix = np.random.normal(5, 3, size=(2, 4))
print(random_matrix)
```

```
[[ 3.19808393  4.12491875  3.19488016 10.55683455]
 [ 4.95950833  1.82686721  7.46763474  1.33746905]]
```

9.5 MASKING

9.5.1 Demonstration

Masking in NumPy is a powerful feature that allows you to perform operations on specific subsets of an array based on conditions. It enables you to filter and manipulate data efficiently without the need for explicit loops. This is particularly useful for handling and analyzing large datasets where you need to apply conditions to select or modify elements.

Conditional masking involves applying conditions to create a mask directly from the array elements. This allows you to filter or modify elements based on specific criteria.

```
mask = (array condition)
```

```
# Create an array
arr = np.array([1, 2, 3, 4, 5, 6])

# Create a mask for even numbers
even_mask = arr % 2 == 0

print(even_mask)
# Output: [False  True False  True False  True]

# Use the mask to select even numbers
even_numbers = arr[even_mask]
print(even_numbers)
# Output: [2 4 6]
```

```
[False  True False  True False  True]
[2 4 6]
```

Advanced masking involves combining multiple masks or using masks with other NumPy functions for complex data operations.

```
# Create an array
arr = np.array([10, 20, 30, 40, 50])

# Create masks for different conditions
mask1 = arr > 20
mask2 = arr < 50

# Combine masks using logical operations
combined_mask = mask1 & mask2

print(combined_mask)
# Output: [False False  True  True  False]

# Use the combined mask to filter values
filtered_values = arr[combined_mask]
print(filtered_values)
# Output: [30 40]
```

```
[False False   True   True False]
[30 40]
```

Handle NaN (Not a Number) values in arrays by creating masks to identify or replace NaNs.

```
numpy.isnan(array)
```

```
# Create an array with NaN values
arr = np.array([1, 2, np.nan, 4, np.nan])

# Create a mask for NaN values
nan_mask = np.isnan(arr)

print(nan_mask)
# Output: [False False  True False  True]
```

```
[False False   True False   True]
```

9.5.2   Practice

Task: Create a NumPy array with values ranging from −5 to 5. Create a mask to select only the positive values from this array.

```
# Create the array
arr = np.arange(-5, 6)

# Create the mask for positive values
mask = arr > 0

# Select positive values
positive_values = arr[mask]
print(positive_values)  # Output: [1 2 3 4 5]
```

```
[1 2 3 4 5]
```

Task: Create a NumPy array with random integers from −10 to 10. Replace all negative values with zero using masking.

```python
# Create the array with random integers
arr = np.random.randint(-10, 11, size=10)

# Create the mask for negative values
mask = arr < 0

# Replace negative values with zero
arr[mask] = 0
print(arr)
```

```
[ 0 10  0  1  1  6  0  5  4  4]
```

Task: Create a NumPy array with values from 1 to 20. Create a mask to select values between 7 and 15 (inclusive).

```python
# Create the array
arr = np.arange(1, 21)

# Create the mask for values between 7 and 15
mask = (arr >= 7) & (arr <= 15)

# Select values within the range
values_in_range = arr[mask]
print(values_in_range)   # Output: [ 7  8  9 10 11 12 13 14 15]
```

```
[ 7  8  9 10 11 12 13 14 15]
```

Task: Create a 3-by-3 NumPy array with values from 1 to 9. Create a mask to select values greater than 5.

```python
# Create a 3 by 3 array
arr = np.arange(1, 10).reshape(3, 3)

# Create the mask for values greater than 5
mask = arr > 5

# Select values greater than 5
values_gt_5 = arr[mask]
print(values_gt_5)   # Output: [6 7 8 9]
```

```
[6 7 8 9]
```

Task: Create a NumPy array with the following values: [1, 2, 3, 4, 5]. Replace all occurrences of the number 3 with 0.

```python
# Create the array
arr = np.array([1, 2, 3, 4, 5])

# Create the mask for the value 3
mask = arr == 3

# Replace 3 with 0
```

```
arr[mask] = 0
print(arr)   # Output: [1 2 0 4 5]
```

[1 2 0 4 5]

Task: Create a 4-by-4 NumPy array with values from 1 to 16. Create a mask to select elements where the value is even.

```
# Create a 4 by 4 array
arr = np.arange(1, 17).reshape(4, 4)

# Create the mask for even values
mask = arr % 2 == 0

# Select even values
even_values = arr[mask]
print(even_values)   # Output: [ 2  4  6  8 10 12 14 16]
```

[2 4 6 8 10 12 14 16]

Task: Create a NumPy array with values from 1 to 20. Create a mask to select values that are greater than 10 and also even.

```
# Create the array
arr = np.arange(1, 21)

# Create the mask for values greater than 10 and even
mask = (arr > 10) & (arr % 2 == 0)

# Select values that meet both conditions
filtered_values = arr[mask]
print(filtered_values)   # Output: [12 14 16 18 20]
```

[12 14 16 18 20]

Task: Create a 1D NumPy array with values from 1 to 10. Use a mask to increment all values greater than 5 by 10.

```
# Create the array
arr = np.arange(1, 11)

# Create the mask for values greater than 5
mask = arr > 5

# Increment values greater than 5 by 10
arr[mask] += 10
print(arr)   # Output: [ 1  2  3  4  5 15 16 17 18 19]
```

[1 2 3 4 5 16 17 18 19 20]

9.6 INTERACT WITH GENAI

Here are some questions and prompts you can interact with generative AI tools, including ChatGPT.

- Describe NumPy's performance enhancement in numerical computations.
- Highlight key NumPy features: ndarrays, broadcasting, universal functions.
- Explain NumPy's foundational role in data science and machine learning.
- Generate sequences using `arange()` and `linspace()`.
- Demonstrate element-wise array operations.
- Calculate statistical measures with NumPy functions.
- Explain the role of dtype in NumPy arrays.
- Explore multidimensional array handling.
- Discuss broadcasting's utility.
- Describe NumPy's random number generation.
- Define universal functions (ufuncs) and their computational optimization.
- Explain NumPy's broadcasting mechanism.
- Discuss vectorization for large-scale computations.
- Analyze masked arrays for handling missing data.
- Solve linear algebra problems.
- Perform numerical integration and differentiation.
- Simplify data cleaning and transformation.
- Address shape mismatch errors.
- Debug NumPy performance issues.
- Investigate unexpected NumPy operation results.

9.7 EXPLORE MORE NUMPY

The absolute basics: https://numpy.org/doc/stable/user/absolute_beginners.html

Official documentation: https://numpy.org/doc/stable/user/index.html

## CHAPTER 10

Series

IN PYTHON, set and dict are mapping structures that store data in unique, efficient ways. set is an unordered collection of unique items, while dict maps keys to values. These structures make it easy to search, update, or retrieve data using their key or value. Building on these concepts, the data structure Series in the pandas package offers a similar structure but with more functionality. Like a dictionary, a Series maps labels to values, but it also includes the ability to access data by position (like a list or array). This indexing system, both label index and position index, makes the Series both flexible and powerful. Series is designed for handling structured data. It supports numerical operations, works seamlessly with missing values, and integrates well with pandas DataFrames for advanced data manipulation. For example, a Series can represent a single column in a dataset or a time series with labeled entries. Series is popular because it bridges simplicity and efficiency, making it an essential tool for data analysis. In this chapter, we'll explore how the label-index and position-index work, and how to use Series for filtering, calculations, and organizing data efficiently.

Are you ready? Let's get started!

10.1 WHAT IS A SERIES

10.1.1 Explanation

A Series in pandas is a one-dimensional array-like object that can hold various data types such as integers, floats, strings, and Python objects. It is similar to a column in a spreadsheet or a database table.

```
import numpy as np
import pandas as pd
```

DOI: 10.1201/9781003624868-10

10.2   CREATE A SERIES

10.2.1   Demonstration

You can create a `Series` using `pd.Series()` function in pandas.

```python
# Create a series from a ndarray
data = pd.Series(np.arange(5))
print(data)
```

```
0    0
1    1
2    2
3    3
4    4
dtype: int64
```

```python
# Create a series from a list
data = pd.Series([0, 2, 4, 5, 6])
print(data)
```

```
0    0
1    2
2    4
3    5
4    6
dtype: int64
```

```python
# Create a series from a tuple
data = pd.Series((0, 2, 4, 5, 6))
print(data)
```

```
0    0
1    2
2    4
3    5
4    6
dtype: int64
```

```python
# Create a series from a range
data = pd.Series(range(5))
print(data)
```

```
0    0
1    1
2    2
3    3
4    4
dtype: int64
```

Indexing is a critical aspect of `Series` in pandas. It helps in identifying and accessing elements efficiently. Each element in a `Series` has an identifier called an index. When you create a `Series` without specifying an index, pandas automatically assigns an integer index starting from 0.

You can explicitly define an index when creating a `Series`. This index can be anything like strings, dates, or even a mix of different types.

```
# Creating a Series with custom index
data = pd.Series([1, 2, 3, 4, 5],
                 index=['a', 'b', 'c', 'd', 'e'])
print(data)
```

```
a    1
b    2
c    3
d    4
e    5
dtype: int64
```

```
# Creating a Series with custom index
num = [2, 3, 5, 7, 13]
data = pd.Series(num, index=num)
data
```

```
2     2
3     3
5     5
7     7
13    13
dtype: int64
```

You can modify the index of an existing `Series` using the `rename()` method or by directly setting the `index` attribute.

```
data = data.rename({2: 'a', 3: 'b'})
data
```

```
a     2
b     3
5     5
7     7
13    13
dtype: int64
```

```
data.index = ['x', 'y', 'z', 'w', 'v']
print(data)
```

```
x     2
y     3
z     5
w     7
v     13
dtype: int64
```

`Series` now allows duplicate indices.

```
data = pd.Series([1, 2, 3, 4, 5],
                 index = ['a', 'a', 'b', 'b', 'b'])
data
```

```
a    1
```

```
a    2
b    3
b    4
b    5
dtype: int64
```

10.2.2 Practice

Task: Create a `Series` from the list `[1.0, 2, 3, 4, 5]`.

```
data = pd.Series([1.0, 2, 3, 4, 5])
print(data)
```

```
0    1.0
1    2.0
2    3.0
3    4.0
4    5.0
dtype: float64
```

Task: Create a `Series` from the a `ndarray` with values from 0 to 10.

```
data = pd.Series(np.arange(10))
print(data)
```

```
0    0
1    1
2    2
3    3
4    4
5    5
6    6
7    7
8    8
9    9
dtype: int64
```

Task: Create a `Series` from a `tuple` `('a', 'c', 'd', 'b', 'g')`.

```
data = pd.Series(('a', 'c', 'd', 'b', 'g'))
print(data)
```

```
0    a
1    c
2    d
3    b
4    g
dtype: object
```

Task: Create a `Series` from a `list` `[10, 20, 30, 40, 50]` with indices `['a', 'b', 'c', 'd', 'e']`.

```
data = [10, 20, 30, 40, 50]
index = ['a', 'b', 'c', 'd', 'e']
```

```
s = pd.Series(data, index=index)
print(s)
```

```
a    10
b    20
c    30
d    40
e    50
dtype: int64
```

Task: Modify the index of the `Series` created above to `['w', 'x', 'y', 'z', 'u']`.

```
s.index = ['w', 'x', 'y', 'z', 'u']
print(s)
```

```
w    10
x    20
y    30
z    40
u    50
dtype: int64
```

10.3   ACCESSING A SERIES

10.3.1   Demonstration

Accessing elements in a `Series` is straightforward and can be done using several methods. Here, we'll explore various techniques to access elements by position, index label, slicing, and Boolean indexing.

You can use integer positions (similar to accessing elements in a `list` or NumPy array) to access elements in a `Series`. This is done using the `iloc` attribute.

```
data = [10, 20, 30, 40, 50]
s = pd.Series(data)

# Accessing the first element (position 0)
print(s.iloc[0])    # Output: 10

# Accessing the last element (position -1)
print(s.iloc[-1])   # Output: 50

# Accessing a range of elements
print(s.iloc[1:4])   # Output:
                     # 1    20
                     # 2    30
                     # 3    40
                     # dtype: int64
```

```
10
50
1    20
2    30
3    40
dtype: int64
```

You can use index labels to access elements. This is done using the `loc` attribute or directly using the square bracket notation if the `Series` has an explicit index.

```python
# Creating a Series with a custom index
data = [10, 20, 30, 40, 50]
index = ['a', 'b', 'c', 'd', 'e']
s = pd.Series(data, index=index)

# Accessing elements using index labels
print(s['a'])  # Output: 10
print(s.loc['c'])  # Output: 30

# Accessing a range of elements using index labels
print(s['b':'d'])  # Output:
                   # b    20
                   # c    30
                   # d    40
                   # dtype: int64
```

```
10
30
b    20
c    30
d    40
dtype: int64
```

You can access multiple elements by passing a `list` of positions or index labels.

```python
# Accessing multiple elements by position
print(s.iloc[[0, 2, 4]])  # Output:
                          # a    10
                          # c    30
                          # e    50
                          # dtype: int64

# Accessing multiple elements by index labels
print(s.loc[['a', 'c', 'e']])  # Output:
                               # a    10
                               # c    30
                               # e    50
                               # dtype: int64
```

```
a    10
c    30
e    50
dtype: int64
a    10
c    30
e    50
dtype: int64
```

Boolean indexing allows you to filter elements based on a condition.

```python
# Boolean indexing to filter elements greater than 25
filtered = s[s > 25]
print(filtered)  # Output:
```

```
                # c      30
                # d      40
                # e      50
                # dtype: int64
```

```
c    30
d    40
e    50
dtype: int64
```

If a `Series` has duplicate indices, accessing elements by index label returns all matching elements.

```
# Creating a Series with duplicate indices
data = [10, 20, 30, 40, 50]
index = ['a', 'a', 'b', 'b', 'c']
s = pd.Series(data, index=index)

# Accessing elements with duplicate indices
print(s['a'])   # Output:
                # a    10
                # a    20
                # dtype: int64

# Accessing a subset with duplicate indices
print(s.loc['b'])   # Output:
                    # b    30
                    # b    40
                    # dtype: int64
```

```
a    10
a    20
dtype: int64
b    30
b    40
dtype: int64
```

The `.at` and `.iat` methods provide faster access for individual elements by label and position, respectively.

```
# Accessing elements using .at (label-based)
print(s.at['c'])   # Output: 50

# Accessing elements using .iat (position-based)
print(s.iat[2])   # Output: 30
```

```
50
30
```

10.3.2 Practice

```
# Given the Series below for the following tasks
data = ['Atlanta', 'Boston', 'Chicago', 'Dallas', 'El Paso']
index = ['a', 'b', 'c', 'd', 'e']
s = pd.Series(data, index=index)
```

Task: Access the first element of the Series s.

```
# Accessing the first element
print(s.iloc[0])   # Output: Atlanta
```

Atlanta

Task: Access the last element of the Series s.

```
# Accessing the last element
print(s.iloc[-1])   # Output: El Paso
```

El Paso

Task: Access the element with index 'b' from the Series s.

```
# Accessing element with index 'b'
print(s['b'])   # Output: Boston
```

Boston

Task: Get a slice of the Series s from position 1 to 3.

```
# Slicing the Series by position
print(s.iloc[1:4])   # Output:
                     # b      Boston
                     # c      Chicago
                     # d      Dallas
                     # dtype: object
```

```
b     Boston
c     Chicago
d     Dallas
dtype: object
```

Task: Get a slice of the Series s from index 'b' to 'd'.

```
# Slicing the Series by index label
print(s['b':'d'])   # Output:
                    # b      Boston
                    # c      Chicago
                    # d      Dallas
                    # dtype: object
```

```
b     Boston
c     Chicago
d     Dallas
dtype: object
```

Task: Access the elements at positions 0, 2, and 4 from the Series s.

```
# Accessing multiple elements by position
print(s.iloc[[0, 2, 4]])   # Output:
                           # a      Atlanta
                           # c      Chicago
                           # e      El Paso
                           # dtype: object
```

```
a    Atlanta
c    Chicago
e    El Paso
dtype: object
```

Task: Access the elements with indices `'a'`, `'c'`, and `'e'` from the `Series` s.

```python
# Accessing multiple elements by index label
print(s.loc[['a', 'c', 'e']])   # Output:
                                 # a      Atlanta
                                 # c      Chicago
                                 # e      El Paso
                                 # dtype: object
```

```
a    Atlanta
c    Chicago
e    El Paso
dtype: object
```

Task: Filter the elements with alphabetical order `>='C'` from the `Series` s.

```python
# Boolean indexing to filter elements
filtered = s[s > 'C']
print(filtered)   # Output:
                  # c      Chicago
                  # d      Dallas
                  # e      El Paso
                  # dtype: object
```

```
c    Chicago
d    Dallas
e    El Paso
dtype: object
```

Task: Access the element with index `'c'` and the element at position 2 from the `Series` s.

```python
# Accessing element using .at
print(s.at['c'])   # Output: Chicago

# Accessing element using .iat
print(s.iat[2])   # Output: Chicago
```

```
Chicago
Chicago
```

Task: Access all elements with index `'a'` from the `Series` created with data `[5, 10, 15, 20, 25]` and index `['a', 'a', 'b', 'b', 'c']`.

```python
# Series creation
data = ['Atlanta', 'Austin', 'Boston', 'Boulder', 'Chicago']
index = ['a', 'a', 'b', 'b', 'c']
s = pd.Series(data, index=index)

# Accessing elements with duplicate indices
print(s['a'])   # Output:
```

```
# a    Atlanta
# a    Austin
# dtype: object
```

```
a    Atlanta
a    Austin
dtype: object
```

10.4 MATH OPERATIONS

10.4.1 Demonstration

Pandas `Series` supports a wide range of mathematical operations, making it a powerful tool for data manipulation and analysis. These operations can be applied element-wise, and pandas aligns Series by their index labels, allowing for easy data handling.

You can perform basic arithmetic operations such as addition, subtraction, multiplication, and division on `Series`.

```
s1 = pd.Series([1, 2, 3, 4, 5])
s2 = pd.Series([10, 20, 30, 40, 50])

# Addition
print(s1 + s2)  # Output:
                # 0    11
                # 1    22
                # 2    33
                # 3    44
                # 4    55
                # dtype: int64

# Subtraction
print(s1 - s2)  # Output:
                # 0    -9
                # 1    -18
                # 2    -27
                # 3    -36
                # 4    -45
                # dtype: int64

# Multiplication
print(s1 * s2)  # Output:
                # 0    10
                # 1    40
                # 2    90
                # 3    160
                # 4    250
                # dtype: int64

# Division
print(s1 / s2)  # Output:
                # 0    0.1
                # 1    0.1
                # 2    0.1
```

```
# 3    0.1
# 4    0.1
# dtype: float64
```

```
0    11
1    22
2    33
3    44
4    55
dtype: int64
0    -9
1    -18
2    -27
3    -36
4    -45
dtype: int64
0     10
1     40
2     90
3    160
4    250
dtype: int64
0    0.1
1    0.1
2    0.1
3    0.1
4    0.1
dtype: float64
```

Pandas `Series` works seamlessly with NumPy functions, allowing for complex mathematical operations.

```
# Applying NumPy functions
print(np.sqrt(s1))   # Output:
                     # 0    1.000000
                     # 1    1.414214
                     # 2    1.732051
                     # 3    2.000000
                     # 4    2.236068
                     # dtype: float64

print(np.exp(s1))    # Output:
                     # 0      2.718282
                     # 1      7.389056
                     # 2     20.085537
                     # 3     54.598150
                     # 4    148.413159
                     # dtype: float64
```

```
0    1.000000
1    1.414214
2    1.732051
3    2.000000
4    2.236068
dtype: float64
0      2.718282
```

```
1       7.389056
2      20.085537
3      54.598150
4     148.413159
dtype: float64
```

Pandas provides various aggregation functions to compute summary statistics.

```python
# Sum
print(s1.sum())    # Output: 15

# Mean
print(s1.mean())   # Output: 3.0

# Standard Deviation
print(s1.std())    # Output: 1.5811388300841898

# Minimum
print(s1.min())    # Output: 1

# Maximum
print(s1.max())    # Output: 5
```

```
15
3.0
1.5811388300841898
1
5
```

Pandas aligns `Series` by their index labels during operations, and you can handle missing data using methods like `fillna()`.

```python
s3 = pd.Series([1, 2, 3], index=['a', 'b', 'c'])
s4 = pd.Series([4, 5, 6], index=['b', 'c', 'd'])

# Addition with alignment
print(s3 + s4)    # Output:
                  # a    NaN
                  # b    6.0
                  # c    8.0
                  # d    NaN
                  # dtype: float64

# Filling missing values
print((s3 + s4).fillna(0))    # Output:
                              # a    0.0
                              # b    6.0
                              # c    8.0
                              # d    0.0
                              # dtype: float64
```

```
a    NaN
b    6.0
c    8.0
d    NaN
dtype: float64
```

```
a    0.0
b    6.0
c    8.0
d    0.0
dtype: float64
```

You can apply custom functions to `Series` using the `apply()` method.

```
# Custom function to square each element
def square(x):
    return x * x

print(s1.apply(square))    # Output:
                           # 0    1
                           # 1    4
                           # 2    9
                           # 3    16
                           # 4    25
                           # dtype: int64
```

```
0     1
1     4
2     9
3    16
4    25
dtype: int64
```

10.4.2 Practice

```
# Given two Series below, complete following tasks
s1 = pd.Series([1, 2, 3, 4, 5], index = ['a', 'b', 'c', 'd', 'e'])
s2 = pd.Series([10, 20, 30, 40, 50], index = ['e', 'd', 'c', 'b', 'a'])
```

Task: Add s1 and s2 and save it to `result`.

```
result = s1 + s2
result
```

```
a    51
b    42
c    33
d    24
e    15
dtype: int64
```

Task: Subtract s2 from s1 and save it to `result`.

```
result = s1 - s2
result
```

```
a    -49
b    -38
c    -27
d    -16
e     -5
dtype: int64
```

Task: Multiply s1 and s2 and save it to `result`.

```
result = s1 * s2
result
```

```
a    50
b    80
c    90
d    80
e    50
dtype: int64
```

Task: Divide s1 by s2 and save it to `result`.

```
result = s1 / s2
result
```

```
a    0.02
b    0.05
c    0.10
d    0.20
e    0.50
dtype: float64
```

Task: Apply the NumPy `sqrt` function to s1.

```
result = np.sqrt(s1)
result
```

```
a    1.000000
b    1.414214
c    1.732051
d    2.000000
e    2.236068
dtype: float64
```

Task: Calculate the sum of s1.

```
# Calculating the sum of the Series
result = s1.sum()
result
```

```
15
```

Task: Calculating the mean of s1.

```
# Calculating the mean of the Series
result = s1.mean()
result
```

```
3.0
```

Task: Calculate the standard deviation of s1.

```
# Calculating the std of the Series
result = s1.std()
result
```

```
1.5811388300841898
```

Task: Create a `Series` s3 with values [1, 2, None, 4, 5] and fill missing values with 0.

```python
# Creating a Series with missing data
s3 = pd.Series([1, 2, None, 4, 5])

# Filling missing values with 0
result = s3.fillna(0)
result
```

```
0    1.0
1    2.0
2    0.0
3    4.0
4    5.0
dtype: float64
```

Task: Create two `Series`, s4 with values [1, 2, 3] and index ['a', 'b', 'c'], and s5 with values [4, 5, 6] and index ['b', 'c', 'd'], and add them together.

```python
# Creating Series with different indices
s4 = pd.Series([1, 2, 3], index=['a', 'b', 'c'])
s5 = pd.Series([4, 5, 6], index=['b', 'c', 'd'])

# Adding Series with different indices
result = s4 + s5
result
```

```
a    NaN
b    6.0
c    8.0
d    NaN
dtype: float64
```

Task: Adding above s4 and s5 and fill missing value as 0.

```python
# Adding Series with different indices
result = (s4 + s5).fillna(0)
result
```

```
a    0.0
b    6.0
c    8.0
d    0.0
dtype: float64
```

10.5 INTERACT WITH GENAI

Here are some questions and prompts you can interact with generative AI tools, including ChatGPT.

- What is a Pandas `Series`, and how is it different from a Python `list` or NumPy array?
- What are the main components of a `Series`, such as index and values?
- How does a `Series` handle missing data?

- Why is the index in a `Series` more powerful than a regular `list`?
- Create a `Series` from a Python `list` and a NumPy array.
- Access elements in a `Series` using position and label-based indexing.
- Perform element-wise arithmetic on a `Series`.
- Create a `Series` with custom indices and access elements by index.
- What is the role of the index in a Pandas `Series`?
- How is a `Series` different from a Python dictionary?
- Can a `Series` have non-unique indices? What are the effects?
- How do you align two `Series` with different indices in operations?
- What is the dtype of a `Series`, and how does it affect operations?
- Why is a `Series` more efficient than a Python `list` for large datasets?
- How can you convert a `Series` to other structures like lists or dictionaries?
- How can you use a `Series` for time series data?
- How can you calculate the frequency distribution using a `Series`?
- How can you use a `Series` to store labeled data, like product prices or student grades?
- How can you handle missing data in a `Series` with `fillna()` or `dropna()`?
- What happens when you access a `Series` with a non-existent label?
- How do you reset or change the index of a `Series`?
- What are common performance issues when using a `Series`, and how can you avoid them?

10.6   EXPLORE MORE OF SERIES

At the end, here is the official documentation of pandas `Series`: https://pandas.pydata.org/pandas-docs/stable/reference/api/pandas.Series.html

## CHAPTER 11

DataFrame

$\mathbf{D}$ ATAFRAME is a powerful data structure in the pandas library for Python. DataFrame is a two-dimensional labeled data structure that is widely used for data manipulation and analysis tasks. It is similar to a spreadsheet or a SQL table, where data is organized into rows and columns. In this chapter, we will explore the fundamentals of DataFrame, including its creation, accessing individual elements and subsets of data, manipulation techniques, and statistical analysis.

Are you ready? Let's get started!

11.1 WHAT IS A DATAFRAME

11.1.1 Explanation

A DataFrame in pandas is a two-dimensional labeled data structure, resembling a table or spreadsheet, where data is organized into rows and columns. Each column represents a different variable or feature, while each row corresponds to a specific observation or data point. The columns and rows are labeled, allowing for easy identification and manipulation of data elements. One of the primary advantages of using DataFrames is their flexibility in handling heterogeneous data types within a single structure. This versatility enables users to store and analyze various types of data, including numerical, categorical, and textual data, all within the same DataFrame object.

Additionally, DataFrames offer powerful functionalities for data manipulation and analysis. Users can perform a wide range of operations, such as filtering, sorting, grouping, merging, and aggregating data, with ease. This makes DataFrames ideal for tasks such as data cleaning, preprocessing, exploration, and transformation, which are essential steps in the data analysis workflow. Furthermore, pandas provides extensive support for data input and output operations, allowing users to seamlessly import data from different sources, such as CSV files, Excel spreadsheets, SQL databases, and more, and export processed data for further analysis or visualization.

DOI: 10.1201/9781003624868-11

The versatility and usability of `DataFrame` make it a popular tool in various applications across different domains. Data scientists, analysts, researchers, and professionals in fields such as finance, marketing, healthcare, and academia leverage `DataFrame` for tasks such as data wrangling, exploratory data analysis, statistical modeling, machine learning, and reporting. Whether its analyzing sales trends, forecasting stock prices, predicting customer behavior, or conducting scientific research, `DataFrame` provides a flexible and efficient framework for managing and analyzing data, making it a must-have of modern data analysis workflows.

11.1.2 Test Your Understanding

1. What is a `DataFrame` in pandas?
   a) A one-dimensional labeled data structure
   b) A two-dimensional labeled data structure
   c) A multidimensional labeled data structure
   d) A non-labeled data structure
   > Correct answer: b) A two-dimensional labeled data structure. Because a `DataFrame` in pandas is a two-dimensional labeled data structure where data is organized into rows and columns, resembling a table or spreadsheet.
2. Which of the following operations can be performed on a `DataFrame`?
   a) Data cleaning and preprocessing
   b) Exploratory data analysis
   c) Statistical modeling and machine learning
   d) All of the above
   > Correct answer: All of the above. `DataFrame` in pandas offers extensive functionalities for various data analysis tasks, including data cleaning, preprocessing, exploratory data analysis, statistical modeling, machine learning, and more. `DataFrame` is a versatile tool that supports a wide range of operations across different domains and applications.

11.2 CREATE A DATAFRAME

11.2.1 Demonstration

In pandas, there are several ways to create a `DataFrame`, allowing users to efficiently organize and analyze data from different sources. One common method is to create a `DataFrame` from a dictionary, where each key value pair represents a column name and the corresponding data. This approach provides flexibility in constructing DataFrames from structured data stored in dictionaries, making it suitable for various data manipulation tasks. Note: since the `DataFrame` is built-in in pandas package, don't forget to import pandas package before playing with dataframe.

```
import pandas as pd

# Create a DataFrame from a dictionary
data = {'Name': ['Alice', 'Bob', 'Charlie'],
        'Age': [25, 30, 35],
        'City': ['New York', 'Los Angeles', 'Chicago']}
df_dict = pd.DataFrame(data)
print("DataFrame created from dictionary:")
print(df_dict)
```

```
DataFrame created from dictionary:
      Name  Age          City
0    Alice   25      New York
1      Bob   30   Los Angeles
2  Charlie   35       Chicago
```

In this DataFrame:

1. The Name column represents the names of individuals.
2. The Age column represents the ages of the individuals.
3. The City column represents the cities where the individuals reside.

For example, Alice is 25 years old and lives in New York, Bob is 30 years old and lives in Los Angeles, and Charlie is 35 years old and lives in Chicago.

Another method for creating a DataFrame is by using NumPy arrays. NumPy is a powerful library for numerical computing in Python, and pandas seamlessly integrates with NumPy to create DataFrames from arrays. This approach is particularly useful for working with numerical data, as NumPy arrays provide efficient storage and operations for numerical computations.

```
import numpy as np

# Create a DataFrame from a NumPy array
temperature_data = np.array([[25, 30, 20], [28, 32, 22], [23, 29, 19]])
df_temperature = pd.DataFrame(temperature_data,
                              columns=['Monday', 'Tuesday', 'Wednesday'],
                              index=['New York', 'Los Angeles', 'Chicago'])
print("DataFrame created from NumPy array:")
print(df_temperature)
```

```
DataFrame created from NumPy array:
             Monday  Tuesday  Wednesday
New York         25       30         20
Los Angeles      28       32         22
Chicago          23       29         19
```

In this DataFrame:

1. Each row represents the temperature recorded on a specific day (Monday, Tuesday, Wednesday).
2. Each column represents the temperature recorded in a different city (New York, Los Angeles, Chicago).

For example, the temperature in New York on Monday is 25 degrees Celsius, the temperature in Los Angeles on Tuesday is 32 degrees Celsius, and so on.

Additionally, DataFrames can be constructed from pandas Series objects, which are one-dimensional labeled arrays. By combining multiple Series objects, users can create a DataFrame with labeled rows and columns, providing a convenient way to organize and analyze data in pandas.

```python
# Create a DataFrame from pandas Series objects
sales_q1 = pd.Series([1000, 1500, 1200], name='Q1',
                    index=['Product A', 'Product B', 'Product C'])
sales_q2 = pd.Series([1100, 1600, 1300], name='Q2',
                    index=['Product A', 'Product B', 'Product C'])
sales_q3 = pd.Series([1200, 1700, 1400], name='Q3',
                    index=['Product A', 'Product B', 'Product C'])
df_sales = pd.concat([sales_q1, sales_q2, sales_q3], axis=1)
print("DataFrame created from pandas Series:")
print(df_sales)
```

```
DataFrame created from pandas Series:
            Q1     Q2     Q3
Product A   1000   1100   1200
Product B   1500   1600   1700
Product C   1200   1300   1400
```

In this DataFrame:

1. Each row represents the sales revenue for a specific quarter (Q1, Q2, Q3).
2. Each column represents the sales revenue generated by a different product (Product A, Product B, Product C).

For example, the sales revenue for Product A in Q1 is 1000, in Q2 is 1100, and in Q3 is 1200.

11.2.2   Practice

Task: Create a DataFrame from a dictionary where keys represent countries and values represent their respective populations. Countries and their populations are as follows:

- India 1,428,627,663
- China 1,425,671,352
- United States 339,996,563
- Indonesia 277,534,122
- Pakistan 240,485,658
- Nigeria 223,804,632
- Brazil 216,422,446
- Bangladesh 172,954,319
- Russia 144,444,359
- Mexico 128,455,567

```
# Your code is here

import pandas as pd

# Create a dictionary with countries and their populations
population_data = {
    'Country': ['India', 'China', 'United States', 'Indonesia', 'Pakistan',
                'Nigeria', 'Brazil', 'Bangladesh', 'Russia', 'Mexico'],
    'Population': [1428627663, 1425671352, 339996563, 277534122, 240485658,
                   223804632, 216422446, 172954319, 144444359, 128455567]
}

# Create a DataFrame from the dictionary
df_population = pd.DataFrame(population_data)

# Display the DataFrame
print(df_population)
```

```
         Country  Population
0          India  1428627663
1          China  1425671352
2  United States   339996563
3      Indonesia   277534122
4       Pakistan   240485658
5        Nigeria   223804632
6         Brazil   216422446
7     Bangladesh   172954319
8         Russia   144444359
9         Mexico   128455567
```

Task: Generate a `DataFrame` from a NumPy array containing random values, with column names `'X'`, `'Y'`, and `'Z'`.

```
# Your code is here

import pandas as pd
import numpy as np

# Generate a NumPy array with random values
random_data = np.random.randn(5, 3)

# Create a DataFrame with column names 'X', 'Y', and 'Z'
df_random = pd.DataFrame(random_data, columns=['X', 'Y', 'Z'])

# Display the DataFrame
print(df_random)
```

```
          X         Y         Z
0  1.359543 -0.769306 -0.395408
1 -0.054183  2.314917  0.564761
2 -0.935918  0.473582  1.504356
3 -1.179814 -1.795447  0.513292
4 -0.844447 -1.384335  0.809767
```

Task: Construct a `DataFrame` from pandas `Series` objects representing the average temperatures in different cities for three week days. The cities, weekdays, and temperatures are as follows:

- New York City: Monday(18), Tuesday(22), Wednesday(12)
- Denver: Monday(8), Tuesday(2), Wednesday(-1)
- Seattle: Monday(12), Tuesday(13), Wednesday(10)

```python
# Your code is here

# Create pandas Series objects for each city and weekday
ny_temperatures = pd.Series([18, 22, 12],
                        index=['Monday', 'Tuesday', 'Wednesday'],
                        name='New York City')
denver_temperatures = pd.Series([8, 2, -1],
                            index=['Monday', 'Tuesday', 'Wednesday'],
                            name='Denver')
seattle_temperatures = pd.Series([12, 13, 10],
                            index=['Monday', 'Tuesday', 'Wednesday'],
                            name='Seattle')

# Concatenate the Series objects to create a DataFrame
df_temperatures = pd.concat([ny_temperatures,
                        denver_temperatures,
                        seattle_temperatures], axis=1)

# Display the DataFrame
print(df_temperatures)
```

```
           New York City  Denver  Seattle
Monday                18       8       12
Tuesday               22       2       13
Wednesday             12      -1       10
```

11.3   ACCESS ELEMENTS IN A DATAFRAME USING LABELS

11.3.1   Demonstration

To access elements in a DataFrame, we have various methods available, including accessing one row, multiple rows, one column, multiple columns, a sub-dataframe (selected rows and columns), and individual cells. We can use both labels and indices to perform these operations.

To access elements using labels, we use the .loc[] indexer. We can specify row and column labels or indices to retrieve specific elements or subsets of data from the DataFrame.

```python
# Create a sample DataFrame
data = {'A': [1, 2, 3],
        'B': [4, 5, 6],
        'C': [7, 8, 9]}
df = pd.DataFrame(data, index=['X', 'Y', 'Z'])
```

```
# Display the DataFrame
print(df)
```

```
   A  B  C
X  1  4  7
Y  2  5  8
Z  3  6  9
```

```
# Accessing one row using labels
print('Accessing one row using labels:')
print(df.loc['Y'])
```

```
Accessing one row using labels:
A    2
B    5
C    8
Name: Y, dtype: int64
```

```
# Accessing multiple rows using labels
print('Accessing multiple rows using labels:')
print(df.loc[['X', 'Z']])
```

```
Accessing multiple rows using labels:
   A  B  C
X  1  4  7
Z  3  6  9
```

```
# Accessing one column using labels
print('Accessing one column using labels:')
print(df['B'])
```

```
Accessing one column using labels:
X    4
Y    5
Z    6
Name: B, dtype: int64
```

```
# Accessing multiple columns using labels
print('Accessing multiple columns using labels:')
print(df[['A', 'C']])
```

```
Accessing multiple columns using labels:
   A  C
X  1  7
Y  2  8
Z  3  9
```

```
# Accessing a sub-dataframe (some rows and columns) using labels
print('Accessing a sub-dataframe using labels:')
print(df.loc[['Y', 'Z'], ['B', 'C']])
```

```
Accessing a sub-dataframe using labels:
   B  C
Y  5  8
Z  6  9
```

```
# Accessing one cell using labels
print('Accessing one cell using labels:')
print(df.loc['Y', 'B'])
```

```
Accessing one cell using labels:
5
```

```
# Accessing one cell using labels
print('Accessing one cell using labels:')
print(df.at['Y', 'B'])
```

```
Accessing one cell using labels:
5
```

11.3.2   Practice

```
# Let's use the dataframe we created previously

# Create pandas Series objects for each city and weekday
df = pd.DataFrame({'New York City':[18, 22, 12],
                   'Denver':[8, 2, -1],
                   'Seattle': [12, 13, 10]},
                  index = ['Monday', 'Tuesday', 'Wednesday'])
# Display the DataFrame
print(df)
```

```
           New York City  Denver  Seattle
Monday                18       8       12
Tuesday               22       2       13
Wednesday             12      -1       10
```

Task: Access the temperature for New York City on Tuesday.

```
print(df.at['Tuesday', 'New York City'])
```

```
22
```

Task: Access the temperatures for Denver on Monday and Wednesday.

```
print(df.loc[['Monday', 'Wednesday'], 'Denver'])
```

```
Monday        8
Wednesday    -1
Name: Denver, dtype: int64
```

Task: Access the temperature for Seattle on Wednesday.

```
print(df.loc['Wednesday', 'Seattle'])
```

```
10
```

Task: Access the temperatures for all cities on Monday.

```
print(df.loc['Monday'])
```

```
New York City    18
Denver            8
Seattle          12
```

```
Name: Monday, dtype: int64
```

Task: Access the temperatures for New York City.

```
print(df['New York City'])
```

```
Monday       18
Tuesday      22
Wednesday    12
Name: New York City, dtype: int64
```

Task: Access the temperatures except for New York City.

```
print(df[['Denver', 'Seattle']])
```

```
           Denver  Seattle
Monday          8       12
Tuesday         2       13
Wednesday      -1       10
```

11.4 ACCESS ELEMENTS IN A DATAFRAME USING INDICES

11.4.1 Demonstration

To access elements using indices, we use the `.iloc[]` indexer. With these indexers, we can specify row and column labels or indices to retrieve specific elements or subsets of data from the DataFrame.

```
# Create a sample DataFrame
data = {'A': [1, 2, 3],
        'B': [4, 5, 6],
        'C': [7, 8, 9]}
df = pd.DataFrame(data, index=['X', 'Y', 'Z'])

# Accessing one row using indices
print('Accessing one row using indices:')
print(df.iloc[1])
```

```
Accessing one row using indices:
A    2
B    5
C    8
Name: Y, dtype: int64
```

```
# Accessing multiple rows using indices
print('Accessing multiple rows using indices:')
print(df.iloc[[0, 2]])
```

```
Accessing multiple rows using indices:
   A  B  C
X  1  4  7
Z  3  6  9
```

```
# Accessing one column using indices
print('Accessing one column using indices:')
print(df.iloc[:, 1])
```

```
Accessing one column using indices:
X    4
Y    5
Z    6
Name: B, dtype: int64
```

```
# Accessing multiple columns using indices
print('Accessing multiple columns using indices:')
print(df.iloc[:, [0, 2]])
```

```
Accessing multiple columns using indices:
   A  C
X  1  7
Y  2  8
Z  3  9
```

```
# Accessing a sub-dataframe (some rows and columns) using indices
print('Accessing a sub-dataframe using indices:')
print(df.iloc[[0, 2], [1, 2]])
```

```
Accessing a sub-dataframe using indices:
   B  C
X  4  7
Z  6  9
```

```
# Accessing one cell using indices
print('Accessing one cell using indices:')
print(df.iloc[1, 1])
```

```
Accessing one cell using indices:
5
```

```
# Accessing one cell using indices
print('Accessing one cell using indices:')
print(df.iat[1, 1])
```

```
Accessing one cell using indices:
5
```

11.4.2   Practice

```
# Let's use the dataframe we created previously

# Create pandas Series objects for each city and weekday
df = pd.DataFrame({'New York City':[18, 22, 12],
                   'Denver':[8, 2, -1],
                   'Seattle': [12, 13, 10]},
                  index = ['Monday', 'Tuesday', 'Wednesday'])
# Display the DataFrame
print(df)
```

```
          New York City  Denver  Seattle
Monday               18       8       12
```

Tuesday	22	2	13
Wednesday	12	-1	10

Task: Access the temperature for Denver on Monday using index.

```
print(df.iloc[0, 1])
```

8

Task: Access the temperatures for New York City and Seattle on Tuesday using index.

```
print(df.iloc[1, [0, 2]])
```

```
New York City    22
Seattle          13
Name: Tuesday, dtype: int64
```

Task: Access the temperature for Seattle on Wednesday using index.

```
print(df.iloc[2, 2])
```

10

Task: Access the temperatures for all cities on Monday and Wednesday using index.

```
print(df.iloc[[0, 2]])
```

	New York City	Denver	Seattle
Monday	18	8	12
Wednesday	12	-1	10

11.4.3 Test Your Understanding

Task: Compare accessing elements in a `DataFrame` by labels and by indices. What are the pros and cons of them?

Answer: Accessing elements in a `DataFrame` can be done either by labels (using `.loc[]` indexer) or by indices (using `.iloc[]` indexer).

Accessing by Labels: Using labels allows for more intuitive access to specific rows and columns based on their names. Labels can be non-numeric and can represent meaningful identifiers, making the code more readable. However, accessing elements by labels may be slower compared to using indices, especially with large DataFrames. Also, typos or incorrect labels may lead to KeyError, making it slightly more error-prone.

Accessing by Indices: Accessing elements by indices tends to be faster than using labels, especially with large DataFrames, as it involves integer-based indexing. Using indices provides a clear indication of the position of elements within the DataFrame. However, indices are numeric and may not provide meaningful context, making the code less intuitive. Indices are sequential and fixed, so changes in the `DataFrame` structure (e.g., reordering rows/columns) can affect the code's reliability.

In summary, accessing elements by labels offers intuitiveness and flexibility, while accessing by indices provides better performance and explicitness. The choice between the two methods depends on factors such as the size of the DataFrame, the readability of the code, and the specific requirements of the task at hand.

11.5   MANIPULATE ROWS IN A DATAFRAME

11.5.1   Demonstration

Adding, removing, changing labels, and modifying values of rows in a `DataFrame` are common operations in data manipulation.

To add a new row, you can use the `.loc[]` indexer and specify the new index label along with the data for the row. This allows for flexibility in adding rows with custom index labels and corresponding values.

For removing rows, you can utilize the `.drop()` method and specify the index labels of the rows to be removed. This method provides a straightforward way to eliminate unwanted rows from the DataFrame.

To change the label of a row, the `.rename()` method can be employed, allowing for the renaming of index labels while keeping the data intact. This method is useful for updating row labels to better reflect the data or to maintain consistency.

Finally, to modify values of specific cells within rows, you can directly access the `DataFrame` using index labels and column names, and then assign new values to the desired cells.

```python
# Create a sample DataFrame
data = {'A': [1, 2, 3],
        'B': [4, 5, 6]}
df = pd.DataFrame(data, index=['X', 'Y', 'Z'])
print('Original dataframe:')
print(df)
```

```
Original dataframe:
   A  B
X  1  4
Y  2  5
Z  3  6
```

```python
# Adding a new row
df.loc['W'] = [7, 8]
print('After adding a new row:')
print(df)
```

```
After adding a new row:
   A  B
X  1  4
Y  2  5
Z  3  6
W  7  8
```

```
# Removing a row
df = df.drop('Y')
print('After removing a row:')
print(df)
```

```
After removing a row:
   A  B
X  1  4
Z  3  6
W  7  8
```

```
# Removing a row in place
df.drop('X', inplace = True)
print('After removing a row:')
print(df)
```

```
After removing a row:
   A  B
Z  3  6
W  7  8
```

```
# Changing label of a row
df = df.rename(index={'Z': 'Z_new'})
print('After changing the label of a row:')
print(df)
```

```
After changing the label of a row:
       A  B
Z_new  3  6
W      7  8
```

```
# Changing value of a cell
df.at['X', 'A'] = 10
print('After changing the value of a cell:')
print(df)
```

```
After changing the value of a cell:
          A    B
Z_new   3.0  6.0
W       7.0  8.0
X      10.0  NaN
```

11.5.2 Practice

```
# Let's use the dataframe we created previously

# Create pandas Series objects for each city and weekday
df = pd.DataFrame({'New York City':[18, 22, 12],
                   'Denver':[8, 2, -1],
                   'Seattle': [12, 13, 10]},
                index = ['Monday', 'Tuesday', 'Wednesday'])
# Display the DataFrame
print(df)
```

```
         New York City  Denver  Seattle
Monday              18       8       12
Tuesday             22       2       13
```

```
Wednesday              12      -1      10
```

Task: Add a new row for Thursday with temperatures [20, 15, 18] for New York City, Denver, and Seattle, respectively.

```python
df.loc['Thursday'] = [20, 15, 18]
print(df)
```

```
            New York City  Denver  Seattle
Monday                 18       8       12
Tuesday                22       2       13
Wednesday              12      -1       10
Thursday               20      15       18
```

Task: Remove the row for Tuesday from the `DataFrame`.

```python
df = df.drop('Tuesday')
print(df)
```

```
            New York City  Denver  Seattle
Monday                 18       8       12
Wednesday              12      -1       10
Thursday               20      15       18
```

Task: Change the index label of the row for Wednesday to Wed for all cities.

```python
df = df.rename(index={'Wednesday': 'Wed'})
print(df)
```

```
            New York City  Denver  Seattle
Monday                 18       8       12
Wed                    12      -1       10
Thursday               20      15       18
```

Task: Modify the temperature for New York City on Monday to 25.

```python
df.at['Monday', 'New York City'] = 25
print(df)
```

```
            New York City  Denver  Seattle
Monday                 25       8       12
Wed                    12      -1       10
Thursday               20      15       18
```

Task: Modify the temperature for Seattle on Wed to 15.

```python
df.at['Wed', 'Seattle'] = 15
print(df)
```

```
            New York City  Denver  Seattle
Monday                 25       8       12
Wed                    12      -1       15
Thursday               20      15       18
```

11.6   MANIPULATE COLUMNS IN A DATAFRAME

11.6.1   Demonstration

Adding, removing, changing labels, and modifying values of rows in a `DataFrame` are common operations in data manipulation.

Adding, removing, changing labels, and modifying values of columns in a `DataFrame` are essential operations in data manipulation.

To add a new column, you can directly assign a `Series` or `list` to a new column label, or use the `.insert()` method to insert a column at a specific position.

For removing columns, you can utilize the `.drop()` method and specify the column labels to be removed along with the axis parameter set to 1.

To change the label of a column, you can directly assign a new label to the column using the `.rename()` method, specifying the current column label and the new label.

Finally, to modify values of specific cells within columns, you can directly access the `DataFrame` using column names and index labels, then assign new values to the desired cells.

```python
# Create a sample DataFrame
data = {'A': [1, 2, 3],
        'B': [4, 5, 6],
        'C': [7, 8, 9]}
df = pd.DataFrame(data, index=['X', 'Y', 'Z'])
print('Original dataframe:')
print(df)
```

```
Original dataframe:
   A  B  C
X  1  4  7
Y  2  5  8
Z  3  6  9
```

```python
# Adding a new column
df['D'] = [0, 0, 0]
print('After adding a new column:')
print(df)
```

```
After adding a new column:
   A  B  C  D
X  1  4  7  0
Y  2  5  8  0
Z  3  6  9  0
```

```python
# Removing a column
df = df.drop(columns=['B'])
print('After removing column B:')
print(df)
```

```
After removing column B:
   A  C  D
```

```
X   1   7   0
Y   2   8   0
Z   3   9   0
```

```
# Removing a column
df = df.drop('D', axis = 1)
print('After removing column D:')
print(df)
```

```
After removing column D:
   A  C
X  1  7
Y  2  8
Z  3  9
```

```
# Changing label of a column
df = df.rename(columns={'A': 'New_A'})
print('After renaming column A to New_A:')
print(df)
```

```
After renaming column A to New_A:
   New_A  C
X      1  7
Y      2  8
Z      3  9
```

```
# Changing value of a cell
df.at['Z', 'New_A'] = 10
print('After changing value of a cell')
print(df)
```

```
After changing value of a cell
   New_A  C
X      1  7
Y      2  8
Z     10  9
```

11.6.2 Practice

```
# Let's use the dataframe we created previously

# Create pandas Series objects for each city and weekday
df = pd.DataFrame({'New York City':[18, 22, 12],
                   'Denver':[8, 2, -1],
                   'Seattle': [12, 13, 10]},
                  index = ['Monday', 'Tuesday', 'Wednesday'])
# Display the DataFrame
print(df)
```

```
           New York City  Denver  Seattle
Monday                18       8       12
Tuesday               22       2       13
Wednesday             12      -1       10
```

Task: Add a new column Chicago with temperatures [20, 18, 15].

```
df['Chicago'] = [20, 18, 15]
print(df)
```

```
          New York City  Denver  Seattle  Chicago
Monday               18       8       12       20
Tuesday              22       2       13       18
Wednesday            12      -1       10       15
```

Task: Remove the column for Denver.

```
df = df.drop(columns=['Denver'])
print(df)
```

```
          New York City  Seattle  Chicago
Monday               18       12       20
Tuesday              22       13       18
Wednesday            12       10       15
```

Task: Change the label of the column for New York City to NYC.

```
df = df.rename(columns={'New York City': 'NYC'})
print(df)
```

```
          NYC  Seattle  Chicago
Monday     18       12       20
Tuesday    22       13       18
Wednesday  12       10       15
```

Task: Modify the temperature for Tuesday in Seattle to 14.

```
df.at['Tuesday', 'Seattle'] = 14
print(df)
```

```
          NYC  Seattle  Chicago
Monday     18       12       20
Tuesday    22       14       18
Wednesday  12       10       15
```

Task: Modify the temperature for Monday in Chicago to 22.

```
df.at['Monday', 'Chicago'] = 22
print(df)
```

```
          NYC  Seattle  Chicago
Monday     18       12       22
Tuesday    22       14       18
Wednesday  12       10       15
```

11.7 MERGING DATAFRAMES

11.7.1 Demonstration

Merging DataFrames by columns involves combining them based on common keys present in their columns. This operation is similar to joining tables in a database based on a common column.

Different Joining Methods:

1. Inner Join: This method returns only the rows where the keys are present in both DataFrames.
2. Outer Join: This method returns all rows from both DataFrames and fills in missing values with NaN where keys are not present in both DataFrames.
3. Left Join: This method returns all rows from the left DataFrame and fills in missing values with NaN where keys are not present in the right DataFrame.
4. Right Join: This method returns all rows from the right DataFrame and fills in missing values with NaN where keys are not present in the left DataFrame.

```python
# Sample DataFrames
df1 = pd.DataFrame({'Key': ['A', 'B', 'C'], 'Value1': [1, 2, 3]})
print('df1')
print(df1)
df2 = pd.DataFrame({'Key': ['B', 'C', 'D'], 'Value2': [4, 5, 6]})
print('\ndf2')
print(df2)
```

```
df1
  Key  Value1
0   A       1
1   B       2
2   C       3

df2
  Key  Value2
0   B       4
1   C       5
2   D       6
```

```python
# Inner Join
inner_merged = pd.merge(df1, df2, on='Key', how='inner')
print('Inner Join:')
print(inner_merged)
```

```
Inner Join:
  Key  Value1  Value2
0   B       2       4
1   C       3       5
```

```python
# Outer Join
outer_merged = pd.merge(df1, df2, on='Key', how='outer')
print('Outer Join:')
print(outer_merged)
```

```
Outer Join:
  Key  Value1  Value2
0   A     1.0     NaN
1   B     2.0     4.0
2   C     3.0     5.0
3   D     NaN     6.0
```

```
# Left Join
left_merged = pd.merge(df1, df2, on='Key', how='left')
print('Left Join Based on df1:')
print(left_merged)
```

```
Left Join Based on df1:
  Key  Value1  Value2
0   A       1     NaN
1   B       2     4.0
2   C       3     5.0
```

```
# Right Join
right_merged = pd.merge(df1, df2, on='Key', how='right')
print('Right Join Based on df2:')
print(right_merged)
```

```
Right Join Based on df2:
  Key  Value1  Value2
0   B     2.0       4
1   C     3.0       5
2   D     NaN       6
```

11.7.2 Practice

```
# Create pandas Series objects for some cities and weekdays
df1 = pd.DataFrame({'Weekday': ['Monday', 'Tuesday', 'Wednesday'],
                    'New York City':[18, 22, 12],
                    'Denver':[8, 2, -1],
                    'Seattle': [12, 13, 10]})
# Display the DataFrame
print(df1)
```

```
# Create pandas Series objects for some cities and weekdays
df2 = pd.DataFrame({'Weekday': ['Tuesday', 'Wednesday', 'Thursday'],
                    'Jersey City':[12, 5, 5],
                    'Boston': [13, 10, 5],
                    'Chicago': [18, 15,5]})
# Display the DataFrame
print(df2)
```

```
     Weekday  New York City  Denver  Seattle
0     Monday             18       8       12
1    Tuesday             22       2       13
2  Wednesday             12      -1       10
     Weekday  Jersey City  Boston  Chicago
0    Tuesday           12      13       18
1  Wednesday            5      10       15
2   Thursday            5       5        5
```

Task: Perform an inner joining on `Weekday` to merge `df1` and `df2`.

```
# Inner Join
inner_merged = pd.merge(df1, df2, on = 'Weekday', how='inner')
print('\nInner Join:')
print(inner_merged)
```

```
Inner Join:
      Weekday  New York City  Denver  Seattle  Jersey City  Boston  Chicago
0     Tuesday             22       2       13           12      13       18
1   Wednesday             12      -1       10            5      10       15
```

Task: Perform an outer joining on `Weekday` to merge `df1` and `df2`.

```
# Outer Join
outer_merged = pd.merge(df1, df2, on = 'Weekday', how='outer')
print('\nOuter Join:')
print(outer_merged)
```

```
Outer Join:
      Weekday  New York City  Denver  Seattle  Jersey City  Boston  Chicago
0      Monday           18.0     8.0     12.0          NaN     NaN      NaN
1     Tuesday           22.0     2.0     13.0         12.0    13.0     18.0
2   Wednesday           12.0    -1.0     10.0          5.0    10.0     15.0
3    Thursday            NaN     NaN      NaN          5.0     5.0      5.0
```

Task: Perform a left joining on `Weekday` to merge `df1` and `df2`.

```
# Left Join
left_merged = pd.merge(df1, df2, on = 'Weekday', how='left')
print('\nLeft Join Based on df1:')
print(left_merged)
```

```
Left Join Based on df1:
      Weekday  New York City  Denver  Seattle  Jersey City  Boston  Chicago
0      Monday             18       8       12          NaN     NaN      NaN
1     Tuesday             22       2       13         12.0    13.0     18.0
2   Wednesday             12      -1       10          5.0    10.0     15.0
```

Task: Perform a right joining on `Weekday` to merge `df1` and `df2`.

```
# Right Join
right_merged = pd.merge(df1, df2, on = 'Weekday', how='right')
print('\nRight Join Based on df2:')
print(right_merged)
```

```
Right Join Based on df2:
      Weekday  New York City  Denver  Seattle  Jersey City  Boston  Chicago
0     Tuesday           22.0     2.0     13.0           12      13       18
1   Wednesday           12.0    -1.0     10.0            5      10       15
2    Thursday            NaN     NaN      NaN            5       5        5
```

11.8   CONCATENATING DATAFRAMES

11.8.1   Demonstration

Concatenation in pandas is a method of combining DataFrames along a particular axis, either rows or columns. It allows you to stack DataFrames together to create a new DataFrame.

Different Ways of Stacking:

1. Vertical Stacking (Along Rows): This involves stacking DataFrames on top of each other along the row axis. It is achieved using the `concat()` function with `axis=0`.

2. Horizontal Stacking (Along Columns): This involves stacking DataFrames next to each other along the column axis. It is achieved using the `concat()` function with `axis=1`.

```python
# Sample DataFrames
df1 = pd.DataFrame({'A': [1, 2, 3], 'B': [4, 5, 6]})
df2 = pd.DataFrame({'A': [7, 8, 9], 'B': [1, 2, 4]})
print(df1)
print(df2)
```

```
   A  B
0  1  4
1  2  5
2  3  6
   A  B
0  7  1
1  8  2
2  9  4
```

```python
# Vertical Stacking (Along Rows)
vertical_stacked = pd.concat([df1, df2], axis=0)
print('Vertical Stacking:')
print(vertical_stacked)
```

```
Vertical Stacking:
   A  B
0  1  4
1  2  5
2  3  6
0  7  1
1  8  2
2  9  4
```

```python
# Horizontal Stacking (Along Columns)
horizontal_stacked = pd.concat([df1, df2], axis=1)
print('Horizontal Stacking:')
print(horizontal_stacked)
```

```
Horizontal Stacking:
   A  B  A  B
0  1  4  7  1
1  2  5  8  2
2  3  6  9  4
```

11.8.2   Practice

```
# Create pandas Series objects for some cities and weekdays
df1 = pd.DataFrame({'Weekday': ['Monday', 'Tuesday', 'Wednesday'],
                    'New York City':[18, 22, 12],
                    'Denver':[8, 2, -1]})
# Display the DataFrame
print(df1)

# Create pandas Series objects for some cities and weekdays
df2 = pd.DataFrame({'Weekday': ['Tuesday', 'Wednesday', 'Thursday'],
                    'Jersey City':[12, 5, 5],
                    'Boston': [13, 10, 5]})
# Display the DataFrame
print(df2)
```

```
     Weekday  New York City  Denver
0      Monday             18       8
1     Tuesday             22       2
2   Wednesday             12      -1
     Weekday  Jersey City  Boston
0     Tuesday           12      13
1   Wednesday            5      10
2    Thursday            5       5
```

Task: Stacking df1 and df2 vertically.

```
# Vertical Stacking (Along Rows)
vertical_stacked = pd.concat([df1, df2], axis=0)
print('Vertical Stacking:')
print(vertical_stacked)
```

```
Vertical Stacking:
     Weekday  New York City  Denver  Jersey City  Boston
0      Monday           18.0     8.0          NaN     NaN
1     Tuesday           22.0     2.0          NaN     NaN
2   Wednesday           12.0    -1.0          NaN     NaN
0     Tuesday            NaN     NaN         12.0    13.0
1   Wednesday            NaN     NaN          5.0    10.0
2    Thursday            NaN     NaN          5.0     5.0
```

Task: Stacking df1 and df2 horizontally.

```
# Horizontal Stacking (Along Columns)
horizontal_stacked = pd.concat([df1, df2], axis=1)
print('\nHorizontal Stacking:')
print(horizontal_stacked)
```

```
Horizontal Stacking:
     Weekday  New York City  Denver    Weekday  Jersey City  Boston
0      Monday             18       8    Tuesday           12      13
1     Tuesday             22       2  Wednesday            5      10
2   Wednesday             12      -1   Thursday            5       5
```

11.8.3 Practice More

Task: Do these concatenation make sense? Can you modify the df1 and df2, so they can be stacked vertically for a meaningful result?

```python
# Create pandas Series objects for some cities and weekdays
df1 = pd.DataFrame({'Weekday': ['Monday', 'Tuesday', 'Wednesday'],
                    'New York City':[18, 22, 12],
                    'Denver':[8, 2, -1]})
# Display the DataFrame
print(df1)

# Create pandas Series objects for some cities and weekdays
df2 = pd.DataFrame({'Weekday': ['Thursday', 'Friday', 'Saturday'],
                    'New York City':[8, 2, 12],
                    'Denver':[3, 2, 10]})
# Display the DataFrame
print(df2)

# Vertical Stacking (Along Rows)
vertical_stacked = pd.concat([df1, df2], axis=0)
print('\nMeaningful Vertical Stacking:')
print(vertical_stacked)
```

```
     Weekday  New York City  Denver
0     Monday             18       8
1    Tuesday             22       2
2  Wednesday             12      -1
     Weekday  New York City  Denver
0   Thursday              8       3
1     Friday              2       2
2   Saturday             12      10

Meaningful Vertical Stacking:
     Weekday  New York City  Denver
0     Monday             18       8
1    Tuesday             22       2
2  Wednesday             12      -1
0   Thursday              8       3
1     Friday              2       2
2   Saturday             12      10
```

Task: Can you modify the df1 and df2, so they can be stacked horizontally for a meaningful result?

```python
# Create pandas Series objects for some cities and weekdays
df1 = pd.DataFrame({'Weekday': ['Monday', 'Tuesday', 'Wednesday'],
                    'New York City':[18, 22, 12],
                    'Denver':[8, 2, -1]})
# Display the DataFrame
print(df1)

# Create pandas Series objects for some cities and weekdays
df2 = pd.DataFrame({'Boston':[8, 2, 12],
                    'Jersey City':[3, 2, 10]})
```

```
# Display the DataFrame
print(df2)

# Horizontal Stacking (Along Columns)
horizontal_stacked = pd.concat([df1, df2], axis=1)
print('\nMeaningful Horizontal Stacking:')
print(horizontal_stacked)
```

```
     Weekday  New York City  Denver
0     Monday             18       8
1    Tuesday             22       2
2  Wednesday             12      -1
     Boston  Jersey City
0         8            3
1         2            2
2        12           10


Meaningful Horizontal Stacking:
     Weekday  New York City  Denver  Boston  Jersey City
0     Monday             18       8       8            3
1    Tuesday             22       2       2            2
2  Wednesday             12      -1      12           10
```

11.8.4   Test Your Understanding

What are the differences between merging and concatenation methods to combine multiple DataFrames in pandas?

Answer: Merging and concatenation are both techniques used to combine multiple DataFrames in pandas, but they have different purposes and behaviors.

Merging is used to combine DataFrames based on one or more keys present in their columns. It is similar to the SQL join operation and is typically used when you want to combine datasets with related information. Concatenation is used to combine DataFrames along a particular axis (usually rows or columns). It is useful for stacking DataFrames together, either vertically or horizontally.

When merging DataFrames, pandas aligns the rows based on common keys in their columns. It can perform different types of joins such as inner, outer, left, or right join, depending on how you specify the how parameter. Concatenating DataFrames simply stacks them together along the specified axis. It does not perform any alignment based on keys, and it does not check for duplicates or perform any kind of data alignment.

The result of merging DataFrames is a new `DataFrame` with rows that match the specified conditions based on the keys used for merging. The result of concatenating DataFrames is a new `DataFrame` with the combined rows or columns from the original DataFrames, depending on the axis of concatenation.

In summary, merging is used to combine DataFrames based on common keys, while concatenation is used to stack DataFrames together along a particular axis without considering keys or performing any kind of alignment based on values.

11.9   INTERACT WITH GENAI

Here are some questions and prompts you can interact with generative AI tools, including ChatGPT.

- What is a `DataFrame` in Pandas, and how is it different from a `Series`?
- Why is the `DataFrame` widely used for data analysis?
- How does a `DataFrame` handle different data types across columns?
- Create a `DataFrame` from a dictionary of lists or a NumPy array.
- Access rows and columns in a `DataFrame` using labels or positions.
- Add a new column to a `DataFrame` using existing data.
- Filter rows in a `DataFrame` based on a condition in a column.
- Use the `groupby()` method to aggregate data in a `DataFrame`.
- What is the difference between a `DataFrame` and a `Series` in Pandas?
- Can a `DataFrame` have duplicate row indices or column labels? What are the implications?
- How does slicing work for columns and rows in a `DataFrame`?
- How do you merge or join DataFrames using `merge()` or `concat()`?
- What is the difference between `loc[]` and `iloc[]` for accessing `DataFrame` elements?
- Calculate statistics for each group in a dataset, like mean sales per region.
- Reshape a `DataFrame` using pivot tables or `melt()`.
- What happens if you access a column or row that doesn't exist in a `DataFrame`?
- How do you effectively handle missing or NaN values in a `DataFrame`?
- How can you debug alignment issues when working with multiple `DataFrame`?
- What are common mistakes when manipulating `DataFrame` indices or using group operations?

11.10   EXPLORE MORE OF DATAFRAME

At the end, here are the official documentations of `DataFrame`:

- User guide: https://pandas.pydata.org/docs/reference/frame.html
- More on pandas: https://pandas.pydata.org/docs/reference/index.html

## CHAPTER 12

Pandas

P ANDAS IS A PYTHON package designed for fast, flexible, and expressive data
structures, making it easy and intuitive to work with relational or labeled data.
It aims to be a fundamental tool for practical data analysis in Python, with the
broader goal of being the most powerful and flexible open-source data analysis tool
available in any language. Pandas is already making significant strides toward this
goal. Are you ready? Let's go!

12.1   WHAT IS PANDAS

12.1.1   Import of Pandas

```
# import packages

import numpy as np
import pandas as pd
```

12.1.2   Key Features of Pandas

Pandas is ideal for various types of data:

- Tabular Data: Similar to SQL tables or Excel spreadsheets with heterogeneously
  typed columns.
- Time Series Data: Both ordered and unordered time series data.
- Matrix Data: Homogeneous or heterogeneous matrix data with row and column
  labels.
- Observational/Statistical Data: Any form of data, whether labeled or unlabeled.

The primary data structures in pandas are:

- Series: One-dimensional data.
- DataFrame: Two-dimensional data, similar to R's data.frame but more powerful.

DOI: 10.1201/9781003624868-12

Pandas is built on NumPy and integrates well within the scientific computing environment, alongside many other third-party libraries.

12.1.3 Exploration

Task: Search and find how pandas is named.

Solution by Wikipedia: The name is derived from the term "panel data," an econometrics term for data sets that include observations over multiple time periods for the same individuals, as well as a play on the phrase "Python data analysis."

12.2 USEFUL FUNCTIONALITIES

12.2.1 Demonstration

There are many useful `DataFrame` functions can greatly aid in data exploration and analysis. Among these, `info()` provides a concise summary of the `DataFrame`, including the data types of each column and the number of non-null values. This function is particularly useful for understanding the structure of the `DataFrame` and identifying any missing values.

Additionally, `head()` and `tail()` are handy for quickly inspecting the first and last few rows of the `DataFrame`, respectively. This allows users to get a glimpse of the data and understand its format without needing to display the entire `DataFrame`, which can be especially helpful for large datasets.

```python
# Creating a dummy dataset
data = {
    'A': [1, 2, 3, 4, 5, 7, 9],
    'B': ['a', 'b', 'c', 'd', 'e', 'f', 'g'],
    'C': [10.5, 20.5, 30.5, 40.5, 50.5, 51, 51.5]
}
df = pd.DataFrame(data)
print('The DataFrame')
print(df)
```

```
The DataFrame
   A  B     C
0  1  a  10.5
1  2  b  20.5
2  3  c  30.5
3  4  d  40.5
4  5  e  50.5
5  7  f  51.0
6  9  g  51.5
```

```python
# Displaying summary information about the DataFrame
print('The structure of the DataFrame')
print(df.info())
```

```
The structure of the DataFrame
<class 'pandas.core.frame.DataFrame'>
```

```
RangeIndex: 7 entries, 0 to 6
Data columns (total 3 columns):
 #   Column  Non-Null Count  Dtype
---  ------  --------------  -----
 0   A       7 non-null      int64
 1   B       7 non-null      object
 2   C       7 non-null      float64
dtypes: float64(1), int64(1), object(1)
memory usage: 296.0+ bytes
None
```

```
# Displaying the first five rows of the DataFrame
print('The first 5 of the DataFrame')
print(df.head())
```

```
The first 5 of the DataFrame
   A  B     C
0  1  a  10.5
1  2  b  20.5
2  3  c  30.5
3  4  d  40.5
4  5  e  50.5
```

```
# Displaying the first three rows of the DataFrame
print('The first 3 of the DataFrame')
print(df.head(3))
```

```
The first 3 of the DataFrame
   A  B     C
0  1  a  10.5
1  2  b  20.5
2  3  c  30.5
```

```
# Displaying the last five rows of the DataFrame
print('The last 5 of the DataFrame')
print(df.tail())
```

```
The last 5 of the DataFrame
   A  B     C
2  3  c  30.5
3  4  d  40.5
4  5  e  50.5
5  7  f  51.0
6  9  g  51.5
```

```
# Displaying the last three rows of the DataFrame
print('The last 3 of the DataFrame')
print(df.tail(3))
```

```
The last 3 of the DataFrame
   A  B     C
4  5  e  50.5
5  7  f  51.0
6  9  g  51.5
```

12.2.2 Practice

```
# Create a dummy dataset
data = {
    'Name': ['Alice', 'Bob', 'Charlie',
            'David', 'Emma', 'Harry', 'Ron'],
    'Age': [25, 30, 35, 40, 45, 42, 23],
    'City': ['New York', 'Los Angeles', 'Chicago',
            'Houston', 'Phoenix', 'London', 'Boston']
}

df = pd.DataFrame(data)
print(df)
```

```
      Name  Age         City
0    Alice   25     New York
1      Bob   30  Los Angeles
2  Charlie   35      Chicago
3    David   40      Houston
4     Emma   45      Phoenix
5    Harry   42       London
6      Ron   23       Boston
```

Task: Display the information about the `df`.

```
print(df.info())
```

```
<class 'pandas.core.frame.DataFrame'>
RangeIndex: 7 entries, 0 to 6
Data columns (total 3 columns):
 #   Column  Non-Null Count  Dtype
---  ------  --------------  -----
 0   Name    7 non-null      object
 1   Age     7 non-null      int64
 2   City    7 non-null      object
dtypes: int64(1), object(2)
memory usage: 296.0+ bytes
None
```

Task: Display the first five rows of the `df`.

```
print(df.head())
```

```
      Name  Age         City
0    Alice   25     New York
1      Bob   30  Los Angeles
2  Charlie   35      Chicago
3    David   40      Houston
4     Emma   45      Phoenix
```

Task: Display the first two rows of the `df`.

```
print(df.head(2))
```

```
    Name  Age         City
0  Alice   25     New York
1    Bob   30  Los Angeles
```

Task: Display the last five rows of the df.

```
print(df.tail())
```

```
      Name  Age     City
2  Charlie   35  Chicago
3    David   40  Houston
4     Emma   45  Phoenix
5    Harry   42   London
6      Ron   23   Boston
```

Task: Display the last four rows of the df.

```
print(df.tail(4))
```

```
    Name  Age     City
3  David   40  Houston
4   Emma   45  Phoenix
5  Harry   42   London
6    Ron   23   Boston
```

12.3   DESCRIPTIVE STATISTICS FOR NUMERICAL COLUMNS

12.3.1   Demonstration

Let's discuss descriptive statistics for numerical columns, focusing on central tendency, variance, position, and the `describe()` method.

Central Tendency:

1. Mean: Represents the average value of the data, calculated by summing all values and dividing by the number of observations.

2. Median: The middle value of the data when sorted in ascending order, indicating the central value that separates the higher and lower halves of the dataset.

```python
# Sample DataFrame representing monthly sales for different products
sales_data = {
    'Product A': [55000, 62000, 48000, 51000, 59000],
    'Product B': [4800, 5100, 5900, 5500, 6200],
    'Product C': [12000, 55000, 151000, 5000, 480]
}

# Create DataFrame
sales_df = pd.DataFrame(sales_data,
                        index=['Jan', 'Feb', 'Mar', 'Apr', 'May'])

# Central Tendency
mean_sales = sales_df.mean()
median_sales = sales_df.median()

# Output
print('Central Tendency:')
print('Mean Sales:')
```

```
print(mean_sales)
print('\nMedian Sales:')
print(median_sales)
```

```
Central Tendency:
Mean Sales:
Product A    55000.0
Product B     5500.0
Product C    44696.0
dtype: float64

Median Sales:
Product A    55000.0
Product B     5500.0
Product C    12000.0
dtype: float64
```

Variance:

1. Minimum and Maximum: The smallest and largest values in the data, respectively, providing insights into the range of values present.

2. Range: The difference between the maximum and minimum values, indicating the spread or dispersion of the data.

3. Standard Deviation: Measures the dispersion of the data points around the mean, providing insights into the variability of the dataset.

4. Variance: The average of the squared differences from the mean, offering another measure of data dispersion.

```
# Variance
min_sales = sales_df.min()
max_sales = sales_df.max()
range_sales = max_sales - min_sales
std_dev_sales = sales_df.std()
variance_sales = sales_df.var()

# Output
print('Variance:')
print('Minimum Sales:')
print(min_sales)
print('\nMaximum Sales:')
print(max_sales)
print('\nRange of Sales:')
print(range_sales)
print('\nStandard Deviation of Sales:')
print(std_dev_sales)
print('\nVariance of Sales:')
print(variance_sales)
```

```
Variance:
Minimum Sales:
Product A    48000
Product B     4800
Product C      480
```

```
dtype: int64

Maximum Sales:
Product A      62000
Product B       6200
Product C     151000
dtype: int64

Range of Sales:
Product A      14000
Product B       1400
Product C     150520
dtype: int64

Standard Deviation of Sales:
Product A      5700.877125
Product B       570.087713
Product C     63258.533654
dtype: float64

Variance of Sales:
Product A     3.250000e+07
Product B     3.250000e+05
Product C     4.001642e+09
dtype: float64
```

Position:

1. Percentiles: Values below which a certain percentage of data points fall, providing insights into the distribution of the dataset.

2. Quartiles: Values that divide the dataset into four equal parts, each containing 25% of the data, indicating the spread of the dataset.

The describe() Method:

1. describe(): A method that generates descriptive statistics summarizing the central tendency, dispersion, and shape of the dataset, including count, mean, standard deviation, minimum, maximum, and percentiles.

```python
# Position
percentiles_sales = sales_df.quantile([0.01, 0.1, 0.4, 0.99])
quartiles_sales = sales_df.quantile([0.25, 0.5, 0.75])

# Output
print('Position:')
print('Percentiles of Sales: 1%, 10%, 40%, 99%')
print(percentiles_sales)
print('Quartiles of Sales: Q1, Q2, Q3')
print(quartiles_sales)

# Describe Method
description_sales = sales_df.describe()
```

```
print('\nDescribe Method for Sales DataFrame:')
print(description_sales)
```

```
Position:
Percentiles of Sales: 1%, 10%, 40%, 99%
      Product A   Product B   Product C
0.01     48120.0     4812.0        660.8
0.10     49200.0     4920.0       2288.0
0.40     53400.0     5340.0       9200.0
0.99     61880.0     6188.0     147160.0
Quartiles of Sales: Q1, Q2, Q3
      Product A   Product B   Product C
0.25     51000.0     5100.0       5000.0
0.50     55000.0     5500.0      12000.0
0.75     59000.0     5900.0      55000.0
```

```
Describe Method for Sales DataFrame:
           Product A      Product B       Product C
count       5.000000       5.000000        5.000000
mean    55000.000000    5500.000000    44696.000000
std      5700.877125     570.087713    63258.533654
min     48000.000000    4800.000000      480.000000
25%     51000.000000    5100.000000     5000.000000
50%     55000.000000    5500.000000    12000.000000
75%     59000.000000    5900.000000    55000.000000
max     62000.000000    6200.000000   151000.000000
```

12.3.2 Practice

```
# Creating a dummy dataset
data = {
    'ID': [1, 2, 3, 4, 5],
    'Age': [25, 30, 35, 40, 45],
    'Height (cm)': [170, 175, 180, 185, 190],
    'Weight (kg)': [65, 70, 75, 80, 85]
}
df = pd.DataFrame(data)
print(df)
```

```
   ID  Age  Height (cm)  Weight (kg)
0   1   25          170           65
1   2   30          175           70
2   3   35          180           75
3   4   40          185           80
4   5   45          190           85
```

Task: Calculate the mean age.

```
mean_age = df['Age'].mean()
print('Mean Age:', mean_age)
```

```
Mean Age: 35.0
```

Task: Calculate the median height.

```
median_height = df['Height (cm)'].median()
print('Median Height:', median_height)
```

Median Height: 180.0

Task: Calculate the standard deviation of weight.

```
std_weight = df['Weight (kg)'].std()
print('Standard Deviation of Weight:', std_weight)
```

Standard Deviation of Weight: 7.905694150420948

Task: Find the maximum age.

```
max_age = df['Age'].max()
print('Maximum Age:', max_age)
```

Maximum Age: 45

Task: Calculate the range of heights.

```
height_range = df['Height (cm)'].max() - df['Height (cm)'].min()
print('Height Range:', height_range)
```

Height Range: 20

Task: Get a summary of stats using `describe()`.

```
df.describe()
```

12.4   DESCRIPTIVE STATISTICS FOR CATEGORICAL COLUMNS

12.4.1   Demonstration

Descriptive statistics for `DataFrame` categorical columns provide insights into the distribution of categorical values within the dataset. Three commonly used methods for analyzing categorical data are `value_counts()`, `unique()`, and `nunique()`. Here's a brief explanation of each method:

`value_counts()`: This method returns a `Series` containing counts of unique values in the categorical column. It helps identify the frequency of each unique value in the column, providing insights into the distribution of categorical data.

`unique()`: The `unique()` method returns an array of unique values present in the categorical column. It is useful for quickly identifying the distinct categories within the column.

`nunique()`: This method returns the number of unique values in the categorical column. It provides a count of the distinct categories present, allowing for easy determination of the cardinality of the categorical variable.

```
# Sample DataFrame representing student grades by subject
grades_data = {
    'StudentID': [1, 2, 3, 4, 5, 6],
```

```
    'Subject': ['Math', 'Science', 'Math',
                'English', 'Science', 'English'],
    'Grade': ['A', 'B', 'B', 'C', 'A', 'B']
}

# Create DataFrame
grades_df = pd.DataFrame(grades_data)
```

```
# Count each unique value
print('Value Counts:')
print(grades_df['Subject'].value_counts())
print(grades_df['Grade'].value_counts())
```

```
Value Counts:
Math       2
Science    2
English    2
Name: Subject, dtype: int64
B    3
A    2
C    1
Name: Grade, dtype: int64
```

```
# Display unique values
print('Unique Values:')
print('Subject:', grades_df['Subject'].unique())
print('Grade:', grades_df['Grade'].unique())
```

```
Unique Values:
Subject: ['Math' 'Science' 'English']
Grade: ['A' 'B' 'C']
```

```
# Count the number of unique values
print('Number of Unique Values:')
print('Subject:', grades_df['Subject'].nunique())
print('Grade:', grades_df['Grade'].nunique())
```

```
Number of Unique Values:
Subject: 3
Grade: 3
```

12.4.2 Practice

```
# Creating a dummy dataset
data = {
    'ID': [1, 2, 3, 4, 5],
    'Gender': ['Male', 'Female', 'Male', 'Female', 'Male'],
    'Education': ['College', 'College', 'College',
                  'Graduate', 'Graduate'],
    'Marital Status': ['Single', 'Married', 'Married',
                       'Single', 'Divorced']
}
df = pd.DataFrame(data)
print(df)
```

```
   ID  Gender Education Marital Status
```

```
0   1    Male    College        Single
1   2  Female    College       Married
2   3    Male    College       Married
3   4  Female  Graduate        Single
4   5    Male  Graduate       Divorced
```

Task: Count the number of each gender.

```
gender_counts = df['Gender'].value_counts()
print('Gender Counts:')
print(gender_counts)
```

```
Gender Counts:
Male      3
Female    2
Name: Gender, dtype: int64
```

Task: Get the unique education levels.

```
unique_education = df['Education'].unique()
print('Unique Education Levels:')
print(unique_education)
```

```
Unique Education Levels:
['College' 'Graduate']
```

Task: Count the frequency of each marital status.

```
marital_counts = df['Marital Status'].value_counts()
print('Marital Status Counts:')
print(marital_counts)
```

```
Marital Status Counts:
Single      2
Married     2
Divorced    1
Name: Marital Status, dtype: int64
```

12.5 LESSON: GROUPBY() AND AGGREGATION

12.5.1 Demonstration

Aggregation methods, such as `groupby()` in pandas, are essential for summarizing and analyzing data based on specific criteria. Here's an introduction to some common aggregation methods:

GroupBy: The `groupby()` method splits the `DataFrame` into groups based on specified criteria. It allows you to perform operations on these groups independently or aggregate data within each group.

Aggregation Functions: Pandas provides various aggregation functions, such as `sum`, `mean`, `median`, `count`, `min`, and `max`. These functions compute summary statistics for each group in the DataFrame.

Custom Aggregation: You can define custom aggregation functions to perform specialized calculations within each group. This allows for flexibility in summarizing data based on unique requirements.

```
# Let's reate a dummy DataFrame
data = {
    'Group': ['A', 'A', 'B', 'B', 'B', 'C', 'C', 'C', 'C'],
    'Value1': [10, 20, 30, 40, 50, 60, 70, 80, 90],
    'Value2': [1, 2, 3, 4, 5, 6, 7, 8, 9]
}

df = pd.DataFrame(data)

print('Dummy DataFrame:')
print(df)
```

```
Dummy DataFrame:
  Group  Value1  Value2
0     A      10       1
1     A      20       2
2     B      30       3
3     B      40       4
4     B      50       5
5     C      60       6
6     C      70       7
7     C      80       8
8     C      90       9
```

```
# Group by 'Group' column
grouped = df.groupby('Group')

# Calculate the mean of each group
print('Mean:')
print(grouped.mean())
```

```
Mean:
       Value1  Value2
Group
A        15.0     1.5
B        40.0     4.0
C        75.0     7.5
```

```
# Calculate the sum of each group
print('Sum:')
print(grouped.sum())
```

```
Sum:
       Value1  Value2
Group
A          30       3
B         120      12
C         300      30
```

```
# Calculate the minimum value of each group
print('Minimum:')
print(grouped.min())
```

```
Minimum:
      Value1  Value2
Group
A         10       1
B         30       3
C         60       6
```

```
# Calculate the maximum value of each group
print('Maximum:')
print(grouped.max())
```

```
Maximum:
      Value1  Value2
Group
A         20       2
B         50       5
C         90       9
```

```
# Count the number of rows in each group
print('Count:')
print(grouped.size())
```

```
Count:
Group
A    2
B    3
C    4
dtype: int64
```

```
# Calculate the median of each group
print('Median:')
print(grouped.median())
```

```
Median:
      Value1  Value2
Group
A       15.0     1.5
B       40.0     4.0
C       75.0     7.5
```

12.5.2   Practice

```
# Create a dummy dataset
data = {
    'City': ['New York', 'Los Angeles', 'Chicago',
             'New York', 'Los Angeles', 'Chicago'],
    'Temperature': [70, 75, 68, 72, 77, 70],
    'Humidity': [50, 55, 60, 52, 57, 62],
    'Wind_Speed': [5, 7, 3, 6, 8, 4]
}

df = pd.DataFrame(data)
print(df)
```

```
        City  Temperature  Humidity  Wind_Speed
0   New York           70        50           5
```

```
1  Los Angeles        75        55        7
2      Chicago        68        60        3
3     New York        72        52        6
4  Los Angeles        77        57        8
5      Chicago        70        62        4
```

Task: Group by City and find the average temperature.

```
avg_temp = df.groupby('City')['Temperature'].mean()
print('Average Temperature by City:\n', avg_temp)
```

```
Average Temperature by City:
 City
Chicago         69.0
Los Angeles     76.0
New York        71.0
Name: Temperature, dtype: float64
```

Task: Group by City and find the maximum humidity.

```
max_humidity = df.groupby('City')['Humidity'].max()
print('Maximum Humidity by City:\n', max_humidity)
```

```
Maximum Humidity by City:
 City
Chicago         62
Los Angeles     57
New York        52
Name: Humidity, dtype: int64
```

Task: Group by City and find the minimum wind speed.

```
min_wind_speed = df.groupby('City')['Wind_Speed'].min()
print('Minimum Wind Speed by City:\n', min_wind_speed)
```

```
Minimum Wind Speed by City:
 City
Chicago         3
Los Angeles     7
New York        5
Name: Wind_Speed, dtype: int64
```

12.6   HANDLING MISSING DATA

12.6.1   Demonstration

You can detect missing values using `isna()` or `isnull()`, which are equivalent.

```
import pandas as pd
import numpy as np

data = {
    'A': [1, 2, np.nan, 4],
    'B': [np.nan, 2, 3, 4],
    'C': [1, np.nan, np.nan, 4]
```

```
}
df = pd.DataFrame(data)

# Detecting missing values
print(df.isna())   # or df.isnull()

# Counting missing values in each column
print(df.isna().sum())
```

```
        A      B      C
0  False   True  False
1  False  False   True
2   True  False   True
3  False  False  False
A    1
B    1
C    2
dtype: int64
```

You can fill missing values using the `fillna()` method.

```
# Filling missing values with a specific value
df_filled = df.fillna(0)
print(df_filled)

# Filling missing values with the mean of the column
df_filled_mean = df.fillna(df.mean())
print(df_filled_mean)
```

```
     A    B    C
0  1.0  0.0  1.0
1  2.0  2.0  0.0
2  0.0  3.0  0.0
3  4.0  4.0  4.0
          A    B    C
0  1.000000  3.0  1.0
1  2.000000  2.0  2.5
2  2.333333  3.0  2.5
3  4.000000  4.0  4.0
```

You can drop rows or columns with missing values using the `dropna()` method.

```
# Dropping rows with any missing values
df_dropped_rows = df.dropna()
print(df_dropped_rows)

# Dropping columns with any missing values
df_dropped_columns = df.dropna(axis=1)
print(df_dropped_columns)

# Dropping rows only if all values are missing
df_dropped_all = df.dropna(how='all')
print(df_dropped_all)
```

```
     A    B    C
3  4.0  4.0  4.0
Empty DataFrame
```

```
Columns: []
Index: [0, 1, 2, 3]
     A    B    C
0  1.0  NaN  1.0
1  2.0  2.0  NaN
2  NaN  3.0  NaN
3  4.0  4.0  4.0
```

12.6.2 Practice

Given a `DataFrame` with missing values as below, complete the following tasks.

```
# Run this cell for this practice

data = {
    'Atlanta': [47, 48, np.nan, 52],
    'Boston': [np.nan, 32, 31, 37],
    'Chicago': [43, np.nan, np.nan, 45],
    'Dallas': [56, 53, 58, 65]
}

df = pd.DataFrame(data)
print(df)
```

```
   Atlanta  Boston  Chicago  Dallas
0     47.0     NaN     43.0      56
1     48.0    32.0      NaN      53
2      NaN    31.0      NaN      58
3     52.0    37.0     45.0      65
```

Task: Given the `DataFrame` df with some missing values, fill all the missing values with zero.

```
# Fill missing values with zero
df_filled_zero = df.fillna(0)
print(df_filled_zero)
```

```
   Atlanta  Boston  Chicago  Dallas
0     47.0     0.0     43.0      56
1     48.0    32.0      0.0      53
2      0.0    31.0      0.0      58
3     52.0    37.0     45.0      65
```

Task: Given the `DataFrame` df with some missing values, fill all the missing values with the mean of their respective columns.

```
# Fill missing values with mean of each column
df_filled_mean = df.fillna(df.mean())
print(df_filled_mean)
```

```
   Atlanta     Boston  Chicago  Dallas
0     47.0  33.333333     43.0      56
1     48.0  32.000000     44.0      53
2     49.0  31.000000     44.0      58
3     52.0  37.000000     45.0      65
```

Task: Given the `DataFrame` df with some missing values, fill all the missing values with the median of their respective columns.

```
# Fill missing values with median of each column
df_filled_median = df.fillna(df.median())
print(df_filled_median)
```

	Atlanta	Boston	Chicago	Dallas
0	47.0	32.0	43.0	56
1	48.0	32.0	44.0	53
2	48.0	31.0	44.0	58
3	52.0	37.0	45.0	65

Task: Given the `DataFrame` df with some missing values, drop all rows that contain any missing values.

```
# Drop rows with any missing values
df_dropped_rows = df.dropna()
print(df_dropped_rows)
```

	Atlanta	Boston	Chicago	Dallas
3	52.0	37.0	45.0	65

Task: Given the `DataFrame` df with some missing values, drop all columns that contain any missing values.

```
# Drop columns with any missing values
df_dropped_columns = df.dropna(axis=1)
print(df_dropped_columns)
```

	Dallas
0	56
1	53
2	58
3	65

12.7 HANDLING DUPLICATE VALUES

In data preprocessing, managing duplicate values is a crucial step to ensure data quality. pandas provides several methods to detect, filter, and drop duplicate values.

12.7.1 Demonstration

You can detect duplicate rows in a `DataFrame` using the `duplicated()` method. This method returns a Boolean series, indicating whether each row is a duplicate or not.

```
data = {
    'A': [1, 2, 2, 2, 4],
    'B': [1, 2, 2, 2, 4],
    'C': [1, 2, 2, 3, 4]
}
df = pd.DataFrame(data)
print(df)
```

```
# Detecting duplicates
duplicates = df.duplicated()
print(duplicates)
```

```
   A  B  C
0  1  1  1
1  2  2  2
2  2  2  2
3  2  2  3
4  4  4  4
0    False
1    False
2     True
3    False
4    False
dtype: bool
```

By default, `duplicated()` considers all columns. You can specify a subset of columns to check for duplicates using the **subset** parameter.

```
# Detecting duplicates based on column 'A'
duplicates_A = df.duplicated(subset='A')
print(duplicates_A)
```

```
0    False
1    False
2     True
3     True
4    False
dtype: bool
```

```
# Detecting duplicates based on column 'C'
duplicates_C = df.duplicated(subset='C')
print(duplicates_C)
```

```
0    False
1    False
2     True
3    False
4    False
dtype: bool
```

To filter out duplicate rows, you can use the `duplicated()` method in combination with Boolean indexing. The ~ sign is the **not** operator that flips the Boolean value.

```
# Filtering out duplicate rows
unique_rows = df[~df.duplicated()]
print(unique_rows)
```

```
   A  B  C
0  1  1  1
1  2  2  2
3  2  2  3
4  4  4  4
```

```
# Filtering out duplicate rows based on Column 'A'
unique_rows_A = df[~df.duplicated(subset='A')]
print(unique_rows_A)
```

```
   A  B  C
0  1  1  1
1  2  2  2
4  4  4  4
```

The `drop_duplicates()` method removes duplicate rows from a DataFrame. By default, it keeps the first occurrence of each duplicate row and drops the rest.

```
# Dropping duplicate rows
df_unique = df.drop_duplicates()
print(df_unique)
```

```
   A  B  C
0  1  1  1
1  2  2  2
3  2  2  3
4  4  4  4
```

You can also specify which columns to consider when identifying duplicates using the subset parameter.

```
# Dropping duplicates based on column 'A'
df_unique_A = df.drop_duplicates(subset='A')
print(df_unique_A)
```

```
   A  B  C
0  1  1  1
1  2  2  2
4  4  4  4
```

To keep the last occurrence of each duplicate row instead of the first, use the `keep` parameter with the value `'last'`.

```
# Dropping duplicates and keeping the last occurrence
df_unique_last = df.drop_duplicates(keep='last')
print(df_unique_last)
```

```
   A  B  C
0  1  1  1
2  2  2  2
3  2  2  3
4  4  4  4
```

Additionally, you can drop duplicates in place without creating a new `DataFrame` by setting the `inplace` parameter to `True`.

```
# Dropping duplicates in place
df.drop_duplicates(inplace=True)
print(df)
```

```
   A  B  C
0  1  1  1
1  2  2  2
```

```
3  2  2  3
4  4  4  4
```

12.7.2 Practice

Given a DataFrame with duplicate values as below, complete the following tasks.

```
# Run this cell for this practice

data = {
    'Mon': [47, 48, 48, 52, 52],
    'Tue': [32, 32, 31, 37, 37],
    'Wed': [43, 42, 42, 45, 45],
    'Thu': [56, 53, 58, 65, 65],
    'Fri': [56, 53, 58, 65, 65]
}
index = ['Atlanta', 'Boston', 'Chicago', 'Dallas', 'dallas']
df = pd.DataFrame(data, index=index)
print(df)
```

```
         Mon  Tue  Wed  Thu  Fri
Atlanta   47   32   43   56   56
Boston    48   32   42   53   53
Chicago   48   31   42   58   58
Dallas    52   37   45   65   65
dallas    52   37   45   65   65
```

Task: Given the DataFrame df, detect which rows are duplicates.

```
# Detecting duplicate rows
duplicates = df.duplicated()
print(duplicates)
```

```
Atlanta    False
Boston     False
Chicago    False
Dallas     False
dallas      True
dtype: bool
```

Task: Given the DataFrame df, drop all duplicate rows and keep only the first occurrence.

```
# Dropping duplicate rows
df_unique = df.drop_duplicates()
print(df_unique)
```

```
         Mon  Tue  Wed  Thu  Fri
Atlanta   47   32   43   56   56
Boston    48   32   42   53   53
Chicago   48   31   42   58   58
Dallas    52   37   45   65   65
```

Task: Given the DataFrame df, drop all duplicate rows and keep only the last occurrence.

```
# Dropping duplicate rows
df_unique = df.drop_duplicates(keep='last')
print(df_unique)
```

```
          Mon  Tue  Wed  Thu  Fri
Atlanta    47   32   43   56   56
Boston     48   32   42   53   53
Chicago    48   31   42   58   58
dallas     52   37   45   65   65
```

Task: Given the `DataFrame` df, drop duplicate rows based on column Mon.

```
# Dropping duplicate rows based on column 'Mon'
df_unique_Mon = df.drop_duplicates(subset='Mon')
print(df_unique_Mon)
```

```
          Mon  Tue  Wed  Thu  Fri
Atlanta    47   32   43   56   56
Boston     48   32   42   53   53
Dallas     52   37   45   65   65
```

Task: Given the `DataFrame` df, drop duplicate rows based on column Fri.

```
# Dropping duplicate rows based on column 'Fri'
df_unique_Fri = df.drop_duplicates(subset='Fri')
print(df_unique_Fri)
```

```
          Mon  Tue  Wed  Thu  Fri
Atlanta    47   32   43   56   56
Boston     48   32   42   53   53
Chicago    48   31   42   58   58
Dallas     52   37   45   65   65
```

12.8 INTERACT WITH GENAI

Here are some questions and prompts you can interact with generative AI tools, including ChatGPT.

- What is Pandas, and why is it a popular library for data analysis in Python?
- How does Pandas simplify working with structured data?
- What are the main use cases for Pandas in data manipulation and analysis?
- Why is Pandas considered essential for data science workflows?
- Filter rows in a `DataFrame` based on a condition.
- Create a small `DataFrame` and sort it by a specific column.
- What is the significance of the index in Pandas?
- Can Pandas handle time series data effectively? If so, how?
- What are some scenarios where using Pandas might not be the best choice?
- How does Pandas integrate with other libraries like NumPy and Matplotlib?
- How do you optimize performance when working with DataFrames in Pandas?
- Discuss how Pandas handles categorical data and its benefits.
- Use Pandas for exploratory data analysis on a real-world dataset.
- Merge or join multiple DataFrames using Pandas methods.

- Clean a messy dataset using Pandas, such as removing duplicates and handling missing values.
- Use Pandas for financial data analysis, like calculating moving averages.
- Prepare data for machine learning models with Pandas.
- How do you debug issues with incorrectly parsed data types in a Pandas DataFrame?
- Why might a Pandas operation give unexpected results?

12.9   EXPLORE MORE OF PANDAS

At the end, here are the official documentations of pandas:

- 10 minutes to pandas: https://pandas.pydata.org/pandas-docs/stable/user_guide/10min.html
- Cookbook: https://pandas.pydata.org/pandas-docs/stable/user_guide/cookbook.html#cookbook
- User guide: https://pandas.pydata.org/pandas-docs/stable/user_guide/index.html

III

Data Visualization

S ECTION III: DATA VISUALIZATION focuses on the powerful tools available in Python for creating insightful data visualizations. You'll explore three essential packages: Matplotlib, Seaborn, and Plotly, each offering unique capabilities for visualizing data. The section covers a variety of plot types, including scatter, line, area, bar, histogram, and pie charts, with an emphasis on how to effectively use color, size, and shape to distinguish different data points. Additionally, you'll learn how to create interactive visualizations using Plotly, enabling more dynamic exploration of data. By mastering these tools, you'll be able to present data in a way that is both informative and visually appealing.

By the end of this section, you will be able to:

- Create a wide range of static plots using Matplotlib to visualize data effectively.

- Utilize Seaborn for more advanced and professional visualizations.

- Understand and apply the use of color, size, and shape to enhance data differentiation in plots.

- Develop interactive data visualizations using Plotly to allow for more engaging data exploration.

- Choose the appropriate visualization techniques and tools to best represent different types of data.

## CHAPTER 13

Matplotlib (Basic)

D ATA VISUALIZATION IS ESSENTIAL for effectively delivering information, making complex data easier to understand. Matplotlib, a widely used Python library, offers a simple and intuitive way to create visualizations. You will learn the basics of Matplotlib, from creating a simple plot to customize it to meet your specific needs. You'll learn how to plot data points, adjust labels and titles, and modify visual elements to enhance clarity. By the end, you'll have a solid foundation for using Matplotlib to present data more effectively. Are you ready? Let's get started!

13.1 INTRODUCTION

13.1.1 Explanation

Matplotlib is a powerful and widely used plotting library in Python, designed for creating static, animated, and interactive visualizations. It serves as a fundamental tool for data scientists and analysts, enabling them to convert complex datasets into comprehensible graphs and charts. The importance of Matplotlib lies in its versatility and ease of use; it can produce a wide range of plots, including line charts, bar charts, histograms, scatter plots, and more, with just a few lines of code. This makes it essential for exploratory data analysis and presenting findings effectively. Among its pros, Matplotlib offers extensive customization options, fine control over plot aesthetics, and integration with other libraries like NumPy and pandas. However, it has some cons, such as a steeper learning curve for beginners due to its vast array of functions and sometimes cumbersome syntax for complex visualizations. Despite these drawbacks, Matplotlib remains a cornerstone in the Python data visualization ecosystem, appreciated for its robustness and comprehensive capabilities.

To utilize the Matplotlib package in Python, users need to import the `pyplot` module. The conventional way to do this is by using the alias `plt` for simplicity and convenience. This is done by including the following line at the beginning of your script: `import matplotlib.pyplot as plt`. This practice is widely adopted in the data

DOI: 10.1201/9781003624868-13

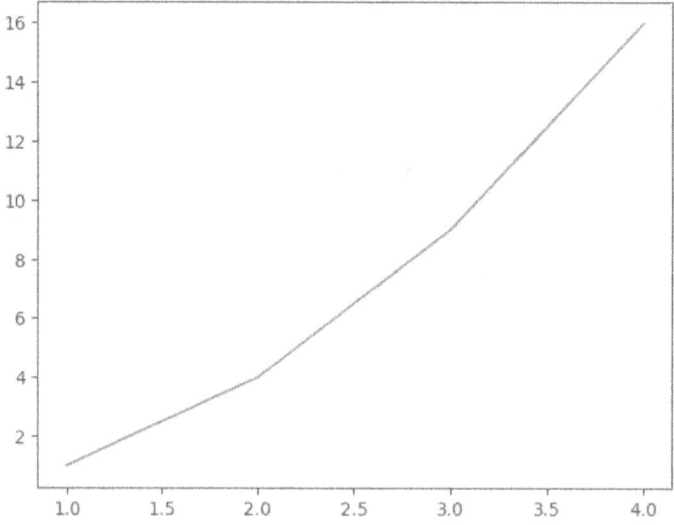

Figure 13.1   A basic line plot showing a single line representing data.

science community, ensuring that your code is consistent with common conventions and easily understood by others.

```
import matplotlib.pyplot as plt
```

13.2   A SIMPLE PLOT

13.2.1   Demonstration

Let's start with creating a simple line plot (Figure 13.1) to get familiar with Matplotlib.

Syntax: `plt.plot(x, y)`

- x: The data for the x-axis.
- y: The data for the y-axis.

```
# Sample data
x = [1, 2, 3, 4]
y = [1, 4, 9, 16]

# Plotting the data
plt.plot(x, y)

# Display the plot
plt.show()
```

13.2.2   Practice

We use the following dummy datasets for the practices:

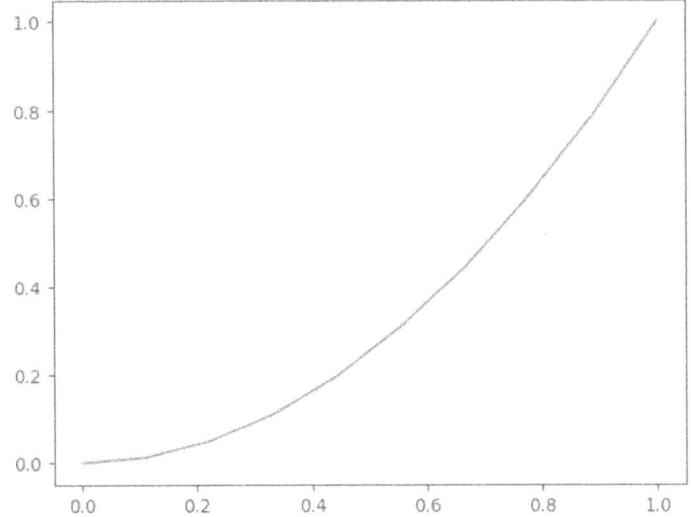

Figure 13.2 A line plot comparing two variables d1 and d2.

```
# Run this cell for all the practices
import numpy as np

d1 = np.linspace(0, 1, 10)
d2 = d1 ** 2
d3 = d1 ** 0.5
```

Task: Make a simple plot for d1 vs d2 (Figure 13.2).

```
plt.plot(d1, d2)
```

Task: Make a plot for d1 vs d3 (Figure 13.3).

```
plt.plot(d1, d3)
```

13.3 TITLES AND LABELS

The plots we created previously are good, but too simple. They are missing key information, such as what are the labels of the x-axes and y-axes, and what is the title, etc. Let's add some flavors.

13.3.1 Demonstration

Adding titles and labels helps in understanding what the plot represents and the axes values. It makes the plot more informative and easier to read (Figure 13.4).

Syntax:

- `plt.title('Title')`: Adds a title to the plot.
- `plt.xlabel('Label')`: Adds a label to the x-axis.
- `plt.ylabel('Label')`: Adds a label to the y-axis.

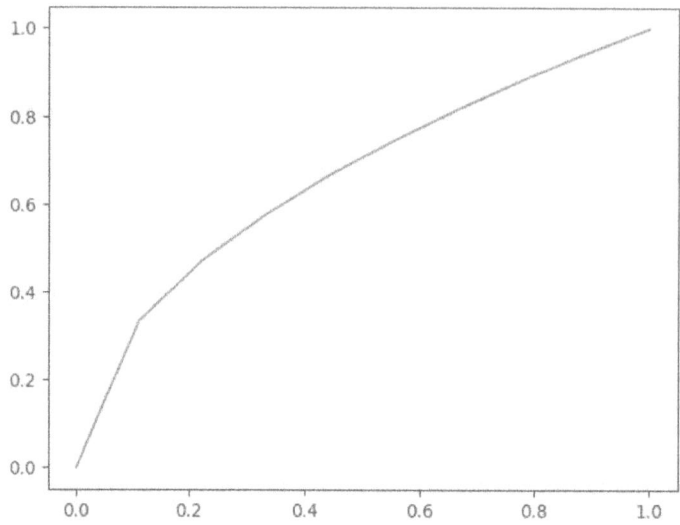

Figure 13.3 A line plot comparing two variables d1 and d3.

```
# Sample data
x = [1, 2, 3, 4]
y = [1, 4, 9, 16]

# Plotting the data
plt.plot(x, y)

# Adding title and labels
plt.title('Simple Line Plot')
plt.xlabel('X-axis')
plt.ylabel('Y-axis')

# Display the plot
plt.show()
```

13.3.2 Practice

Task: Plot d1 vs d2, make title as `'Square'`, x-label as `'x'`, y-label as `'x square'` (Figure 13.5).

```
# Plotting d1 vs d2
plt.plot(d1, d2)

# Adding title to the plot
plt.title('Square')

# Adding label to the x-axis
plt.xlabel('x')

# Adding label to the y-axis
plt.ylabel('x square')
```

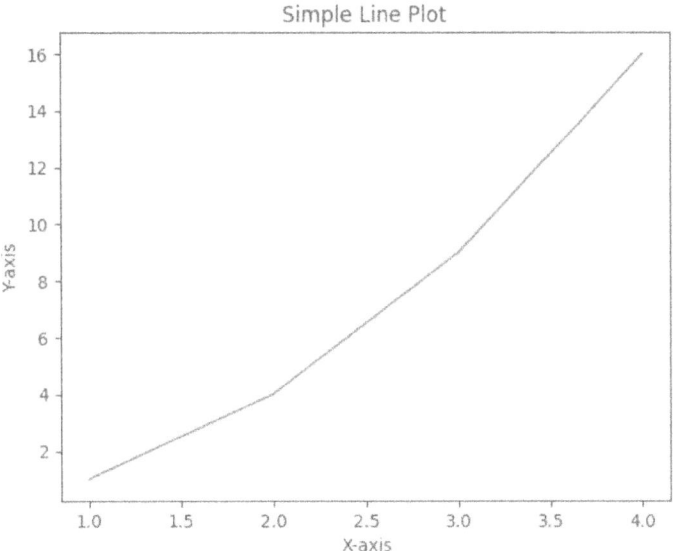

Figure 13.4 A line plot with a title describing the data and labels on the x and y axes.

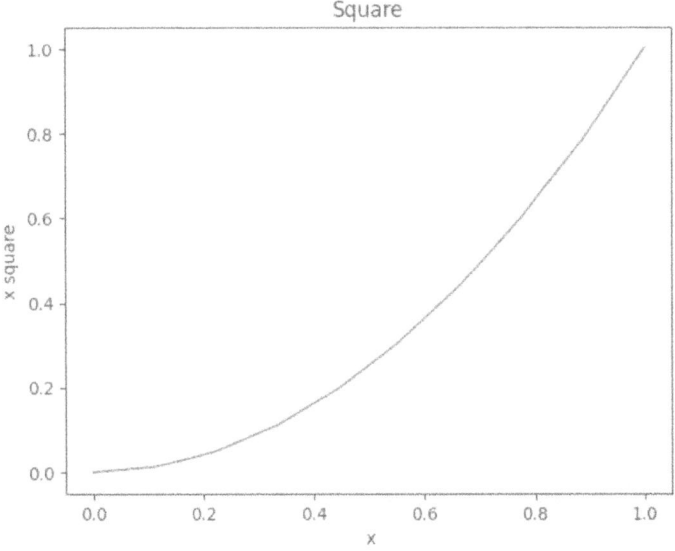

Figure 13.5 A line plot comparing d1 and d2, with a title and labels for clarity.

```
# Displaying the plot
plt.show()
```

Task: Plot d1 vs d3, make title as `'Square Root'`, x-label as `'x'`, y-label as `'x sqrt'` (Figure 13.6).

```
# Plotting d1 vs d3
plt.plot(d1, d3)
```

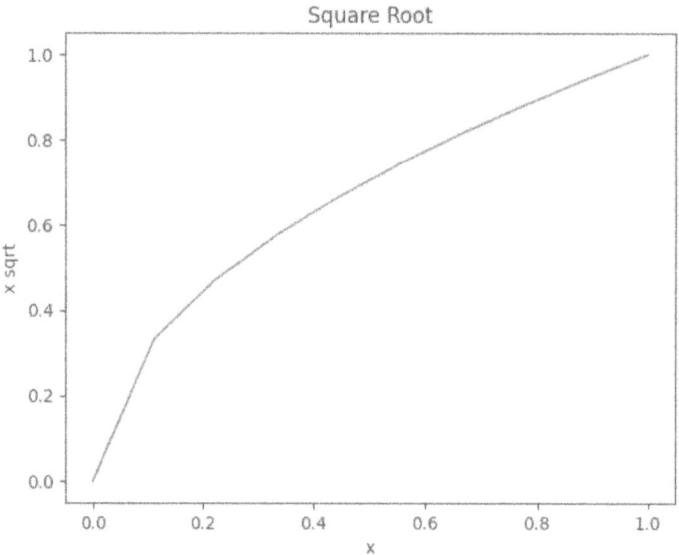

Figure 13.6 A line plot comparing d1 and d3, with a title and axis labels.

```python
# Adding title to the plot
plt.title('Square Root')

# Adding label to the x-axis
plt.xlabel('x')

# Adding label to the y-axis
plt.ylabel('x sqrt')

# Displaying the plot
plt.show()
```

13.4 LEGEND

13.4.1 Demonstration

Legends help in identifying different data series in a plot, especially when multiple lines or datasets are plotted together (Figure 13.7).

Syntax:

- `plt.plot(x, y, label='Label')`: Adds a label to the plot.
- `plt.legend()`: Displays the legend on the plot.

```python
# Sample data
x = [1, 2, 3, 4]
y1 = [1, 4, 9, 16]
y2 = [1, 2, 3, 4]

# Plotting the data
plt.plot(x, y1, label='Square')
```

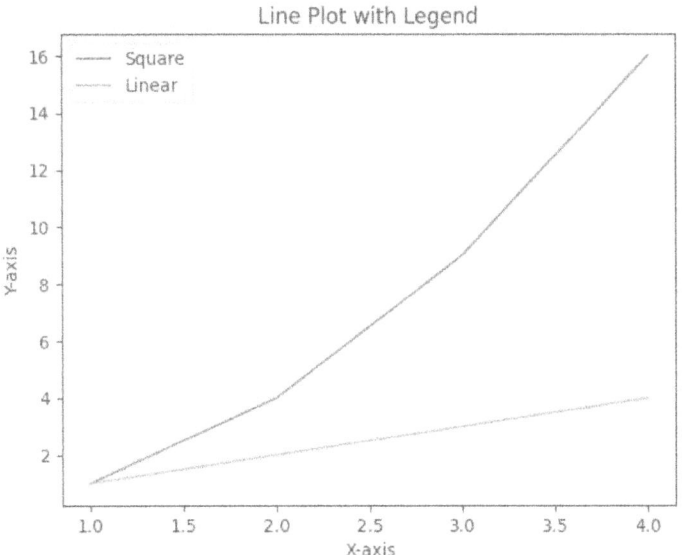

Figure 13.7 A line plot with a legend to distinguish between data series.

```
plt.plot(x, y2, label='Linear')

# Adding title, labels, and legend
plt.title('Line Plot with Legend')
plt.xlabel('X-axis')
plt.ylabel('Y-axis')
plt.legend()

# Display the plot
plt.show()
```

13.4.2 Practice

Task: Plot d1 vs d2, plot label as `'Square'`. Plot d1 vs d3, plot label as `'Square Root'`. Make x-label as `'x'`. Make the title as `'Square vs SQRT'`. Create the legend (Figure 13.8).

```
plt.plot(d1, d2, label = 'Square')
plt.plot(d1, d3, label = 'Square Root')
plt.xlabel('x')
plt.title('Square VS SQRT')
plt.legend()
plt.show()
```

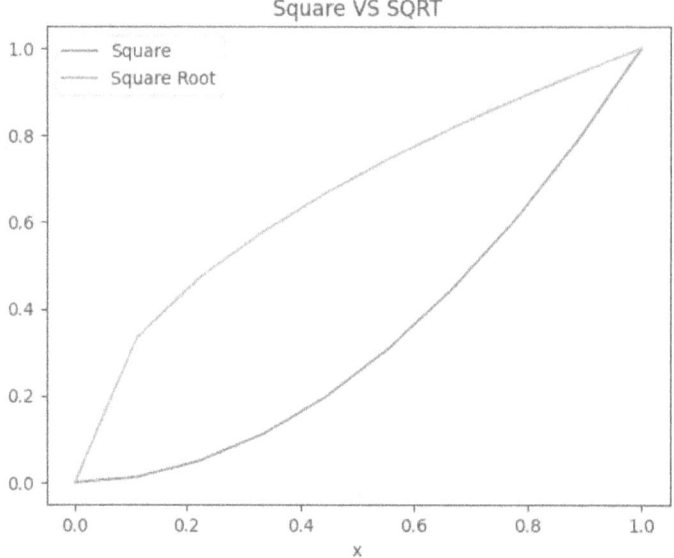

Figure 13.8   A line plot of d1 and d2, including a legend to identify each line.

13.5   CUSTOMIZATION

13.5.1   Demonstration

Customizing plots involves changing colors, line styles, and markers to make plots visually appealing and easier to distinguish (Figure 13.9).

Syntax:

- plt.plot(x, y, color='color', linestyle='style', marker='marker', label='Label'): Customizes the line plot.

```python
# Sample data
x = [1, 2, 3, 4]
y1 = [1, 4, 9, 16]
y2 = [1, 2, 3, 4]

# Plotting the data with customizations
plt.plot(x, y1, color='g', linestyle='--', marker='o', label='Square')
plt.plot(x, y2, color='b', linestyle='-', marker='x', label='Linear')

# Adding title, labels, legend, and grid
plt.title('Customized Line Plot')
plt.xlabel('X-axis')
plt.ylabel('Y-axis')
plt.legend()
plt.grid(True)

# Display the plot
plt.show()
```

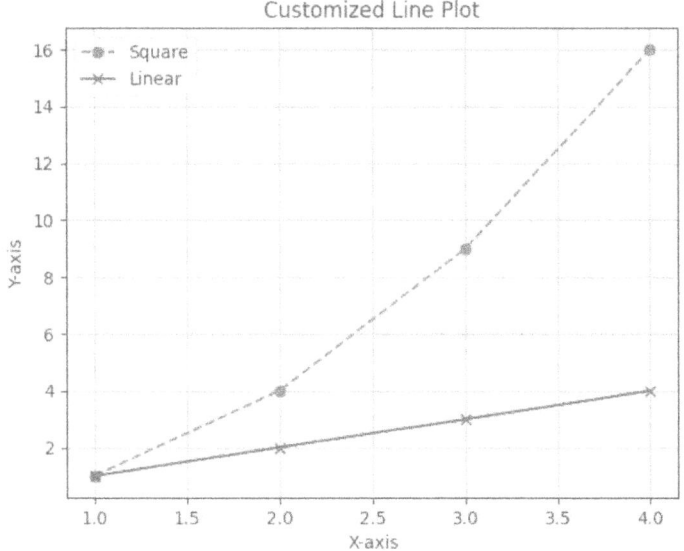

Figure 13.9 A plot displaying two customized lines with different styles.

There are plenty of ways to customize your plot with Matplotlib. We summarized some common settings for color, linestyle, marker, and marker size in Table 13.1.

13.5.2 Practice

Task: Create a data visualization (Figure 13.10) that:

- Plot d1 vs d2, with color as `'r'`, linestyle as `':'`, marker as `'d'`, plot label as `'Square'`.
- Plot d1 vs d3, with color as `'b'`, linestyle as `'-'`, marker as `'h'`, plot label as `'Square Root'`.
- Make x-label as `'x'`.
- Make title as `'Square VS SQRT'`.
- Create the grid.
- Create the legend.

```
plt.plot(d1, d2, color='r', linestyle=':', marker='d', label = 'Square')
plt.plot(d1, d3, color='b', linestyle='-', marker='h', label = 'SQRT')
plt.xlabel('x')
plt.title('Square VS SQRT')
plt.grid()
plt.legend()
plt.show()
```

TABLE 13.1 Matplotlib Plot Customization

Category	Code	Explanation
Color	`color='r'`	Red
Color	`color='g'`	Green
Color	`color='b'`	Blue
Color	`color='k'`	Black
Color	`color='y'`	Yellow
Color	`color='m'`	Magenta
Color	`color='c'`	Cyan
Color	`color='#1f77b4'`	Hex code for custom colors
Linestyle	`linestyle='-'`	Solid line
Linestyle	`linestyle='--'`	Dashed line
Linestyle	`linestyle='-.'`	Dash-dot line
Linestyle	`linestyle=':'`	Dotted line
Marker	`marker='o'`	Circle marker
Marker	`marker='s'`	Square marker
Marker	`marker='x'`	X marker
Marker	`marker='*'`	Star marker
Marker	`marker='d'`	Diamond marker
Marker	`marker='v'`	Triangle down marker
Marker	`marker='p'`	Pentagon marker
Marker	`marker='h'`	Hexagon marker
Marker Size	`markersize=5`	Small markers
Marker Size	`markersize=10`	Medium markers
Marker Size	`markersize=15`	Large markers

13.6 ANNOTATION

13.6.1 Demonstration

Annotations are useful for highlighting specific data points or adding extra information to the plot (Figure 13.11).

Syntax:

- `plt.annotate('Text', xy=(x, y), xytext=(x_text, y_text), arrowprops=dict())`: Adds an annotation with an arrow pointing to the specified data point.

```
# Sample data
x = [1, 2, 3, 4, 5, 6]
y = [1, 4, 9, 16, 15, 12]

# Plotting the data
plt.plot(x, y)
```

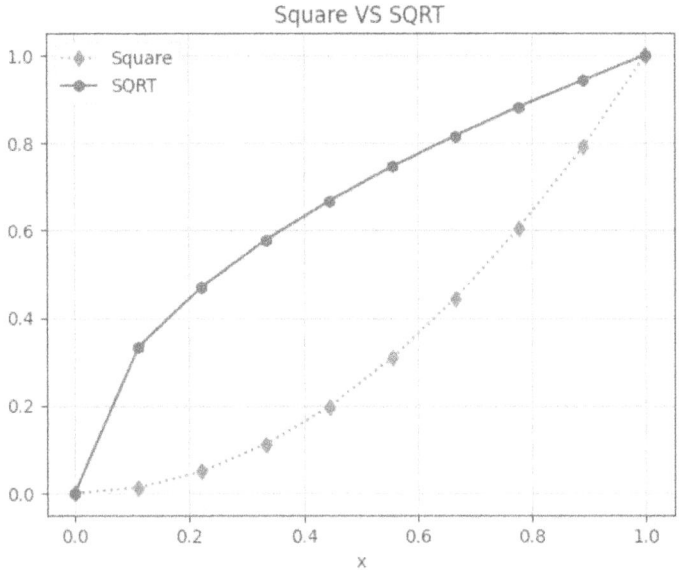

Figure 13.10 A plot showing two customized lines for variables d1, d2, and d3.

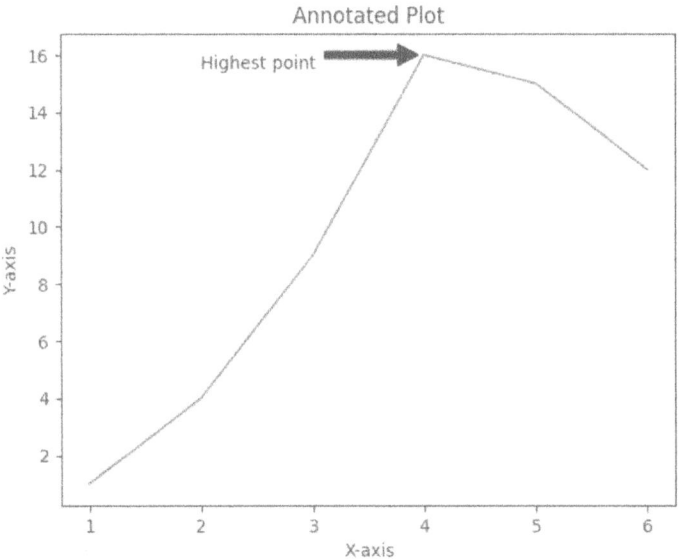

Figure 13.11 A line plot with an annotation highlighting a specific point on the line.

```
# Adding title, labels, and annotation
plt.title('Annotated Plot')
plt.xlabel('X-axis')
plt.ylabel('Y-axis')
plt.annotate('Highest point', xy=(4, 16), xytext=(2, 15.5),
             arrowprops=dict(facecolor='black', shrink=0.05))

# Display the plot
plt.show()
```

13.7 SUBPLOTS

13.7.1 Demonstration

Creating subplots allows you to display multiple plots in a single figure, which is useful for comparing different datasets or visualizations (Figure 13.12).

Syntax: `fig, axs = plt.subplots(nrows, ncols)`

- nrows: Number of rows of subplots.
- ncols: Number of columns of subplots.

```python
# Sample data
x = np.linspace(0, 1, 10)
y1 = x*2
y2 = x**2
y3 = x**3
y4 = np.sqrt(x)


# Creating subplots
fig, axs = plt.subplots(2, 2)

# Plotting the data
axs[0,0].plot(x, y1, color='g', linestyle='--', marker='o')
axs[0,0].set_title('Square')

axs[0,1].plot(x, y2, color='b', linestyle='-', marker='x')
axs[0,1].set_title('Linear')

axs[1,0].plot(x, y3, color='r', linestyle='-', marker='D')
axs[1,0].set_title('Cube')

axs[1,1].plot(x, y4, color='y', linestyle='-', marker='d')
axs[1,1].set_title('Sqrt')

# Display the plots
plt.tight_layout(pad=0.4, w_pad=0.5, h_pad=1.0)
plt.show()
```

There is an alternative way of creating subplots using `plt.subplot(nrows, ncols, index)` (Figure 13.13).

Syntax: `plt.subplot(nrows, ncols, index)`

- nrows: Number of rows of subplots.
- ncols: Number of columns of subplots.
- index: The position of the subplot you are currently working on.

Using `plt.subplot(nrows, ncols, index)` provides a flexible way to manage multiple plots in a single figure. You specify the total number of rows and columns of subplots, and the index indicates the position of the current subplot. This method is useful for creating more complex grid layouts of plots.

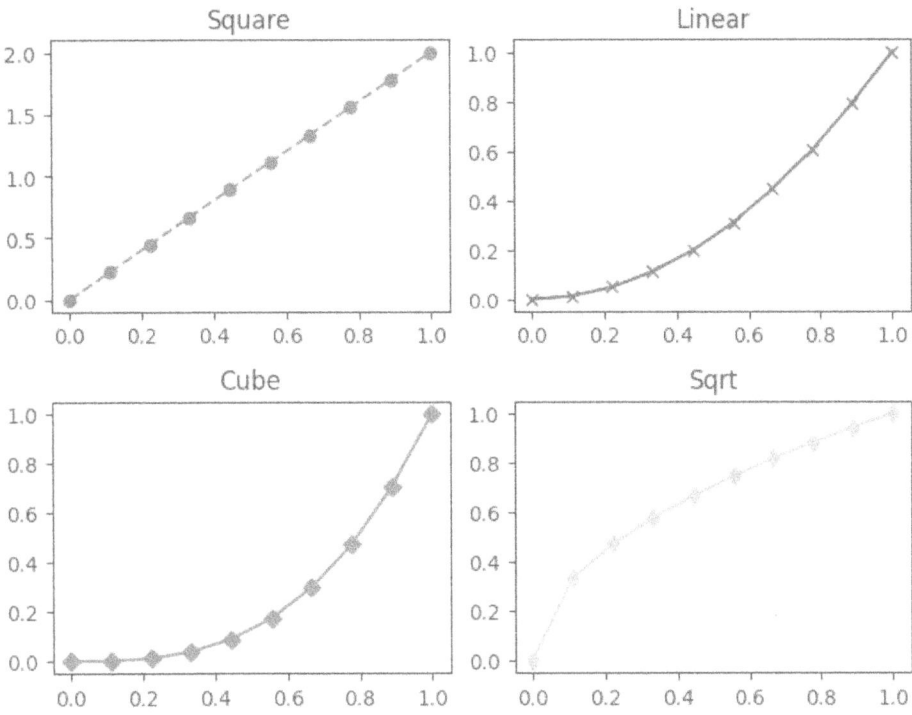

Figure 13.12 A plot with four subplots, each with its own title.

```
plt.subplot(2, 2, 1)
plt.plot(x, y1, color='g', linestyle=':', marker='o', label = 'Linear')
plt.legend()
plt.subplot(2, 2, 2)
plt.plot(x, y2, color='b', linestyle=':', marker='x', label = 'Square')
plt.legend()
plt.subplot(2, 2, 3)
plt.plot(x, y3, color='r', linestyle=':', marker='D', label = 'Cube')
plt.legend()
plt.subplot(2, 2, 4)
plt.plot(x, y4, color='y', linestyle=':', marker='d', label = 'Sqrt')
plt.legend()
plt.show()
```

13.8 INTERACT WITH GENAI

Here are some questions and prompts you can interact with generative AI tools, including ChatGPT.

- Why is Matplotlib widely used for data visualization in Python?
- What is the purpose of labels, titles, legends, and grids?
- How do subplots help organize multiple visualizations in a single figure?
- What is the purpose of a legend in a plot, and how do you add one in Matplotlib?
- What are some ways to control the placement and styling of legends?

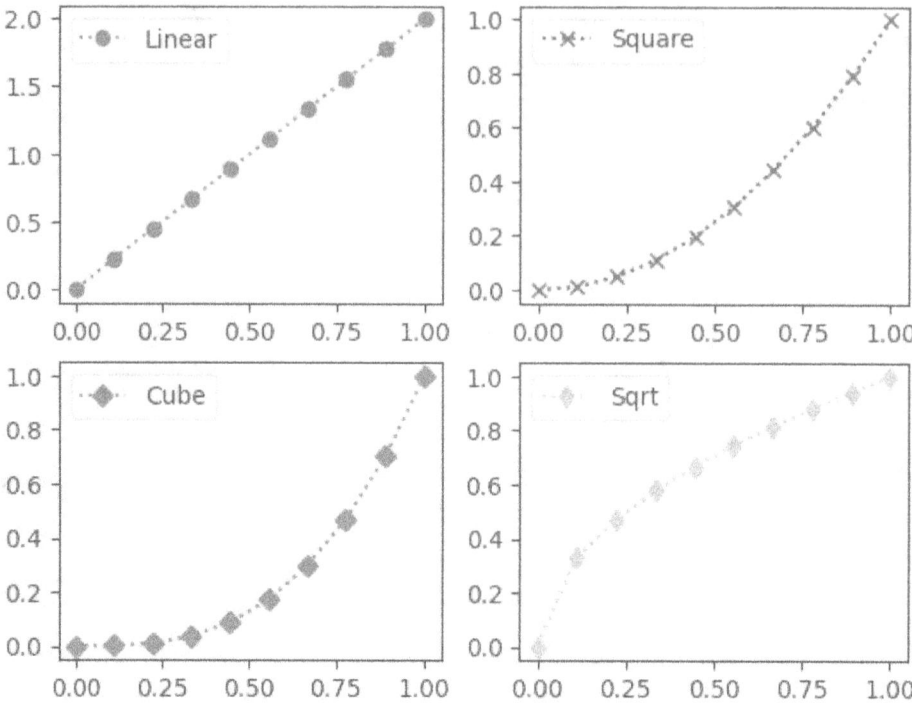

Figure 13.13 A plot with four subplots, each with its own legend.

- How to use line styles and markers together to make a plot more informative?
- What is a common mistake when adding annotations, and how can it be avoided?

## CHAPTER 14

Matplotlib (Advanced)

BUILDING ON THE BASIC understanding of Matplotlib, we will learn a variety of advanced plots to better visualize different types of data. We'll explore bar charts, histograms, scatter plots, pie charts, box plots, heatmaps, etc., learning how to customize each one to highlight key insights. Additionally, we'll discuss how to choose the right plot for different datasets, helping you present information clearly and effectively. By the end of this chapter, you'll be equipped with the skills to create diverse visualizations and make data-driven decisions with confidence. Are you ready? Let's get started!

14.1 INTRODUCTION

Matplotlib is a comprehensive library for creating static, animated, and interactive visualizations in Python. It is particularly adept at producing plots that look like those from MATLAB. This tutorial introduces different types of plots available in Matplotlib, using various dummy datasets, and explains their purposes.

```python
import matplotlib.pyplot as plt
import numpy as np
```

14.2 LINE PLOT

14.2.1 Demonstration

A line plot is useful for displaying data trends over intervals. It shows information as a series of data points connected by straight line segments.

Syntax: `plt.plot(x, y, options)`

The following line plot (Figure 14.1) shows the temperature variation over five days. Adding a title and labels helps understand what the axes represent.

DOI: 10.1201/9781003624868-14

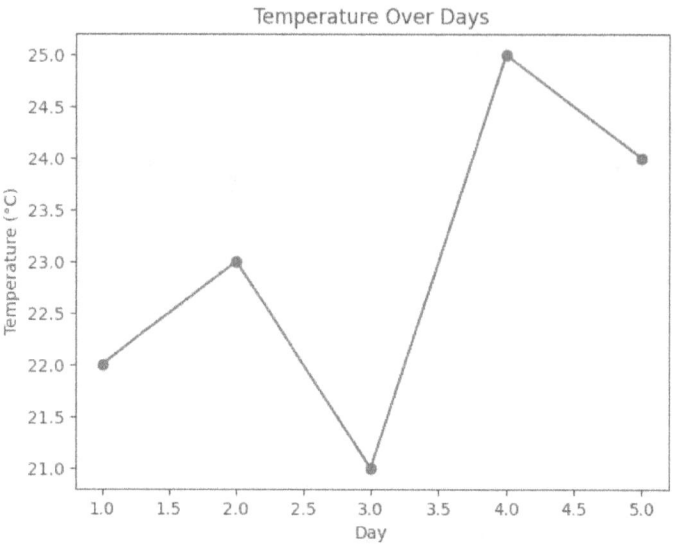

Figure 14.1   A line plot illustrating temperature changes over several days.

```python
# Dummy data
days = [1, 2, 3, 4, 5]
temperatures = [22, 23, 21, 25, 24]

# Creating the line plot
plt.plot(days, temperatures, marker='o', linestyle='-', color='b')

# Adding title and labels
plt.title('Temperature Over Days')
plt.xlabel('Day')
plt.ylabel('Temperature (°C)')

# Show plot
plt.show()
```

14.2.2   Practice

Task: Create a simple line plot (Figure 14.2) with x values [1, 2, 3, 4, 5] and y values [1, 9, 4, 6, 15].

```python
x = [1, 2, 3, 4, 5]
y = [1, 9, 4, 6, 15]

plt.plot(x, y)
plt.title('Simple Line Plot')
plt.xlabel('X values')
plt.ylabel('Y values')
plt.show()
```

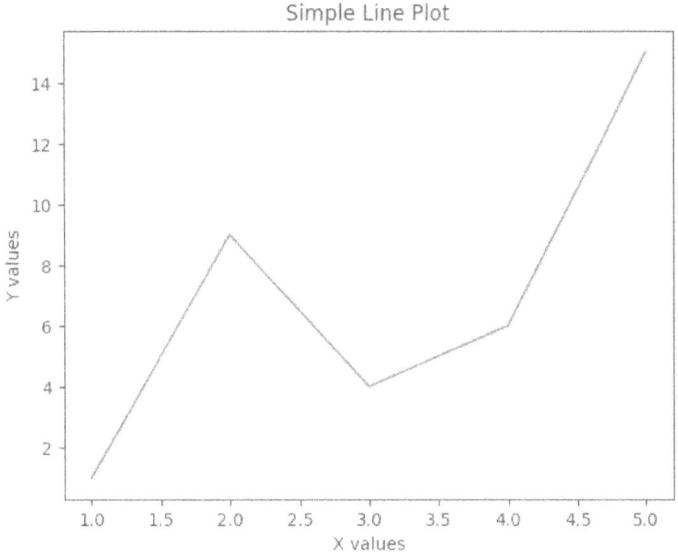

Figure 14.2 A simple line plot displaying data trends.

14.3 BAR PLOT

14.3.1 Demonstration

Bar plots are useful for comparing quantities across different categories.

Syntax: `plt.bar(x, height, options)`

The following bar plot (Figure 14.3) compares values across four categories. Different colors enhance visual distinction between bars.

```python
# Dummy data
categories = ['A', 'B', 'C', 'D']
values = [5, 7, 3, 8]

# Creating the bar plot
plt.bar(categories, values, color=['r', 'g', 'b', 'c'])

# Adding title and labels
plt.title('Category Values')
plt.xlabel('Category')
plt.ylabel('Values')

# Show plot
plt.show()
```

14.3.2 Practice

Task: Create a bar plot (Figure 14.4) with categories ['A', 'B', 'C', 'D'] and values [4, 7, 1, 8].

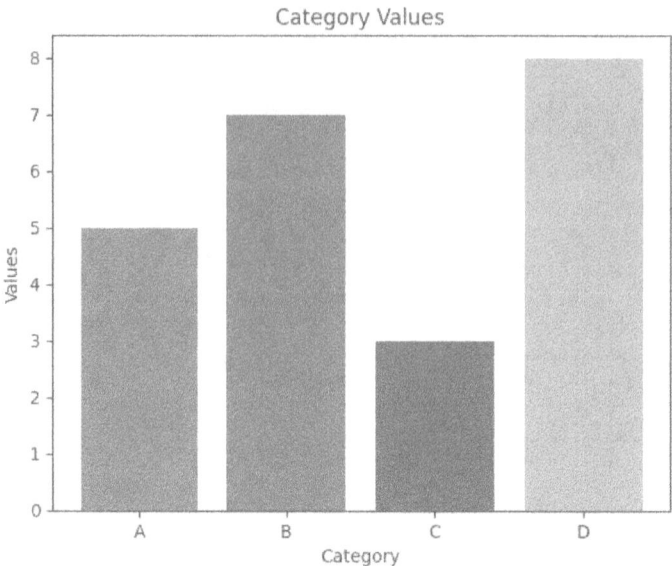

Figure 14.3 A bar plot representing categorical values with bars of varying heights.

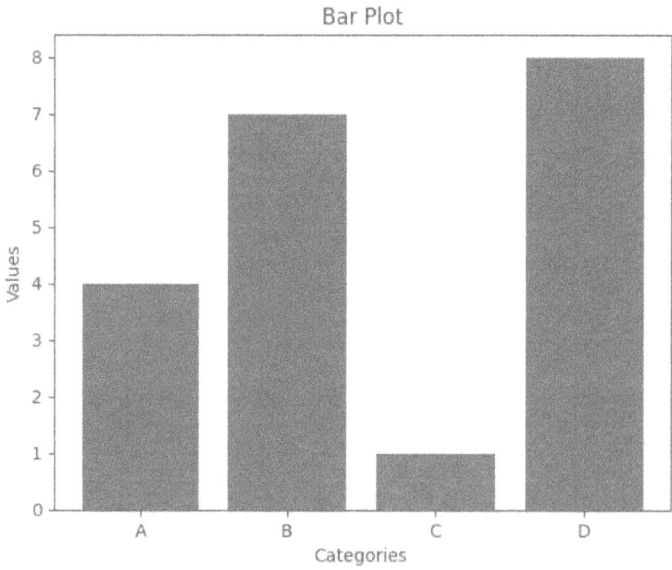

Figure 14.4 A basic bar plot showing comparisons between categories.

```python
categories = ['A', 'B', 'C', 'D']
values = [4, 7, 1, 8]

plt.bar(categories, values, color='blue')
plt.title('Bar Plot')
plt.xlabel('Categories')
plt.ylabel('Values')
plt.show()
```

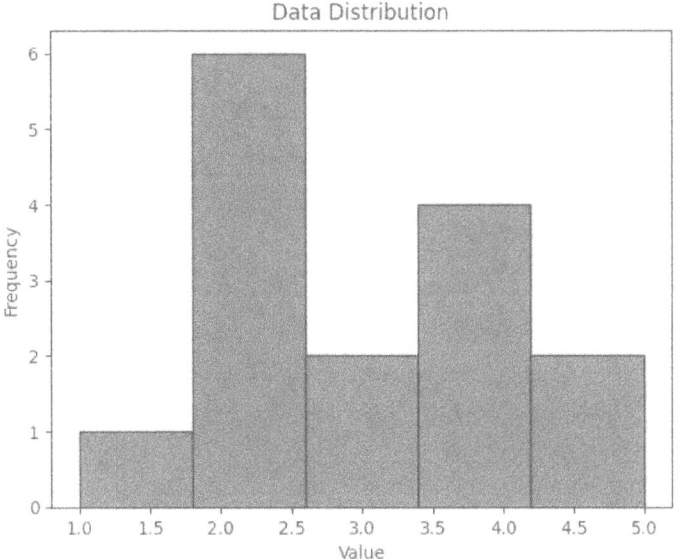

Figure 14.5 A histogram plot displaying the distribution of data.

14.4 HISTOGRAM

14.4.1 Demonstration

Histograms are used to represent the distribution of a dataset by dividing it into bins and counting the number of observations in each bin.

Syntax: plt.hist(x, bins, options)

The following histogram (Figure 14.5) shows the distribution of data values. Bins help to understand the frequency of each range of values.

```python
# Dummy data
data = [1, 3, 2, 4, 3, 2, 4, 4, 2, 4, 2, 2, 5, 2, 5]

# Creating the histogram
plt.hist(data, bins=5, edgecolor='black')

# Adding title and labels
plt.title('Data Distribution')
plt.xlabel('Value')
plt.ylabel('Frequency')

# Show plot
plt.show()
```

14.4.2 Practice

Task: Create a histogram (Figure 14.6) with the 100 random integers within [0, 100] and 5 bins.

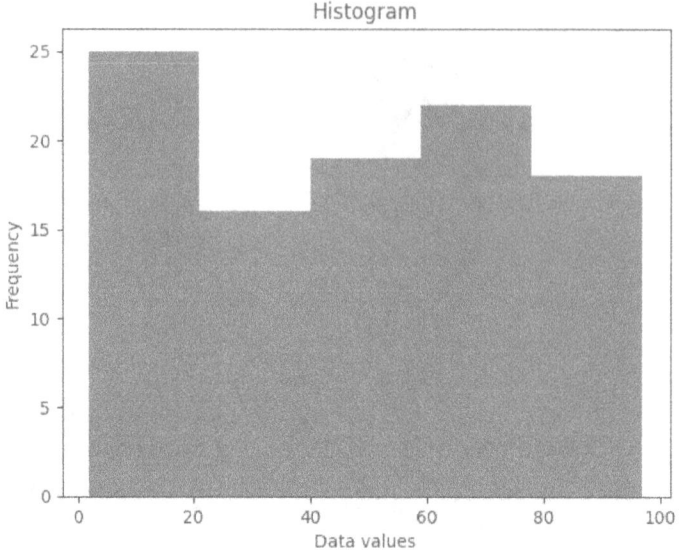

Figure 14.6 A histogram showing the distribution of random integers.

```
data = np.random.randint(0, 100, 100)

plt.hist(data, bins=5)
plt.title('Histogram')
plt.xlabel('Data values')
plt.ylabel('Frequency')
plt.show()
```

14.5 SCATTER PLOT

14.5.1 Demonstration

Scatter plots are useful for showing the relationship between two variables.

Syntax: plt.scatter(x, y, options)

The following scatter plot (Figure 14.7) shows the relationship between the x and y variables. Each point represents a pair of values.

```
# Dummy data
x = [5, 7, 8, 7, 2, 17, 2, 9, 4, 11]
y = [99, 86, 87, 88, 100, 86, 103, 87, 94, 78]

# Creating the scatter plot
plt.scatter(x, y, color='g')

# Adding title and labels
plt.title('Scatter Plot of X vs Y')
plt.xlabel('X')
plt.ylabel('Y')
```

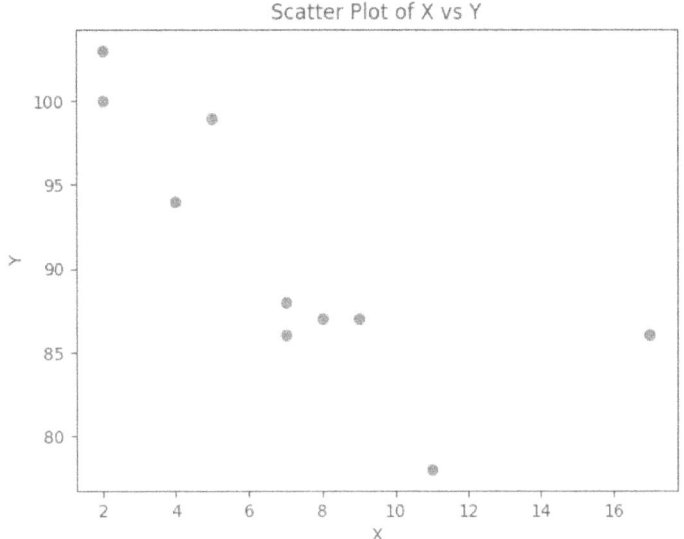

Figure 14.7 A basic scatter plot showing data points.

```
# Show plot
plt.show()
```

14.5.2 Practice

Task: Create a scatter plot (Figure 14.8) with x values [1, 2, 3, 4, 5] and y values [2, 3, 5, 7, 11].

```
x = [1, 2, 3, 4, 5]
y = [2, 3, 5, 7, 11]

plt.scatter(x, y, color='red')
plt.title('Scatter Plot')
plt.xlabel('X values')
plt.ylabel('Y values')
plt.show()
```

14.6 PIE CHART

14.6.1 Demonstration

Pie charts are useful for showing the proportion of different categories.

Syntax: plt.pie(data, options)

The following pie chart (Figure 14.9) shows the proportion of different fruits in a dataset. The autopct parameter displays the percentage of each category.

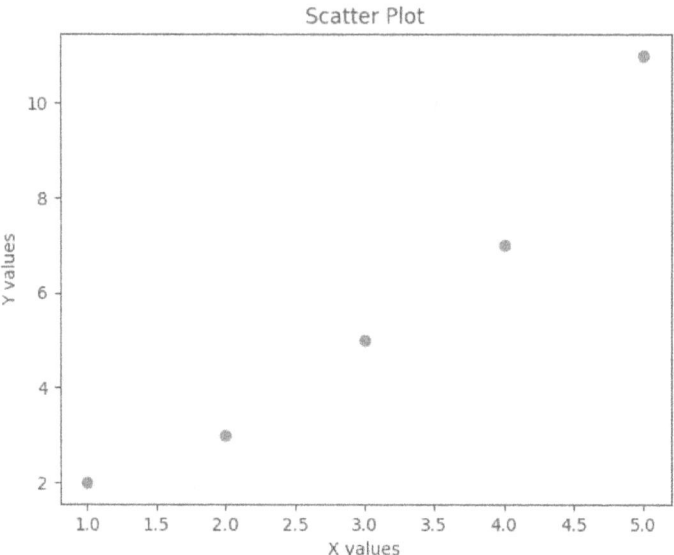

Figure 14.8 A scatter plot displaying the relationship between variables x and y.

```
# Dummy data
labels = ['Apple', 'Banana', 'Cherry', 'Date']
sizes = [15, 30, 45, 10]

# Creating the pie chart
plt.pie(sizes, labels=labels, colors=['r', 'y', 'c', 'm'])

# Adding title
plt.title('Fruit Proportions')

# Show plot
plt.show()
```

14.6.2 Practice

Task: Create a pie chart (Figure 14.10) with labels ['Apple', 'Samsung', 'Google', 'Others'] for the smart-phone industry and their market shares [30, 28, 22, 20].

```
labels = ['Apple', 'Samsung', 'Google', 'Others']
sizes = [30, 28, 22, 20]

plt.pie(sizes, labels=labels)
plt.title('Pie Chart')
plt.show()
```

Fruit Proportions

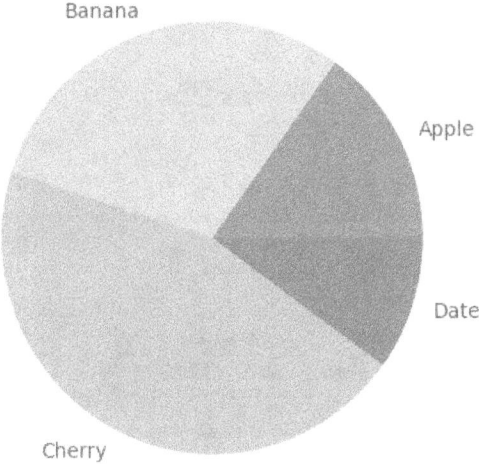

Figure 14.9 A pie plot illustrating fruit proportions with slices representing each fruit.

Pie Chart

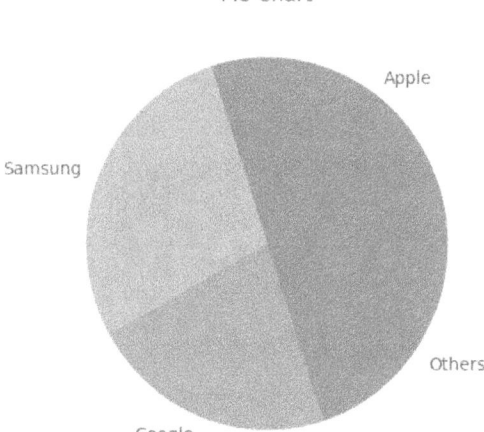

Figure 14.10 A pie plot showing the market share of different smartphone companies.

14.7 BOX PLOT

14.7.1 Demonstration

Box plots are useful for visualizing the distribution of a dataset through its quartiles.

Syntax: `plt.boxplot(data, options)`

The following box plot (Figure 14.11) visualizes the spread and skewness of the dataset. It highlights the median, quartiles, and potential outliers.

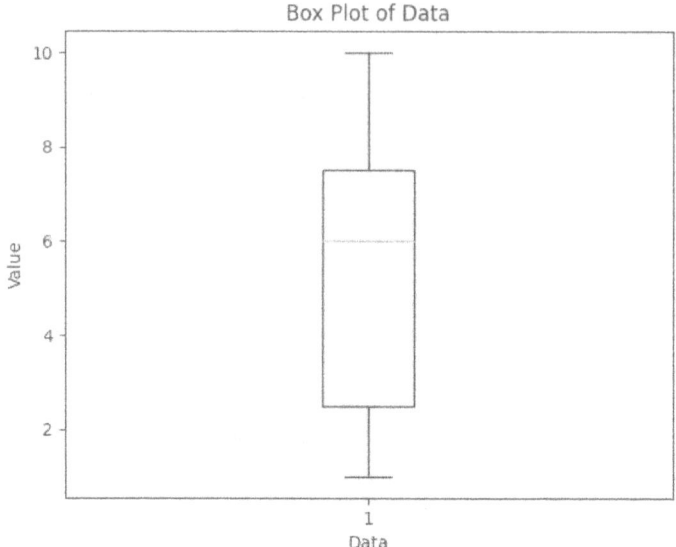

Figure 14.11 A basic box plot displaying the distribution of data.

```python
# Dummy data
data = [1, 2, 2, 3, 4, 6, 6, 7, 8, 9, 10]

# Creating the box plot
plt.boxplot(data)

# Adding title and labels
plt.title('Box Plot of Data')
plt.xlabel('Data')
plt.ylabel('Value')

# Show plot
plt.show()
```

14.7.2 Practice

Task: Create a box plot (Figure 14.12) for the 100 random floats within [0, 1]

```python
data = np.random.rand(100)

plt.boxplot(data)
plt.title('Box Plot')
plt.ylabel('Values')
plt.show()
```

14.8 HEATMAP

14.8.1 Demonstration

Heatmaps are useful for visualizing matrix-like data.

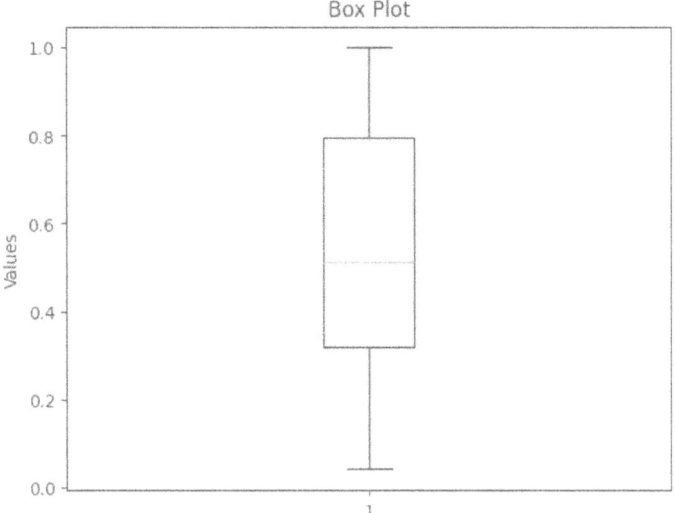

Figure 14.12 A basic box plot for random integers.

Syntax: `plt.imshow(data, options)`

The following heatmap (Figure 14.13) represents random data values in a matrix format. Different colors represent different data ranges.

```python
import numpy as np

# Dummy data
matrix = np.random.rand(10,10)

# Creating the heatmap
plt.imshow(matrix, cmap='viridis')

# Adding title
plt.title('Heatmap of Random Data')

# Show plot
plt.show()
```

14.8.2 Practice

Task: Create a heatmap (Figure 14.14) for a 4x4 matrix with random values.

```python
data = np.random.rand(4, 4)

plt.imshow(data)
plt.title('Heatmap')
plt.colorbar()
plt.show()
```

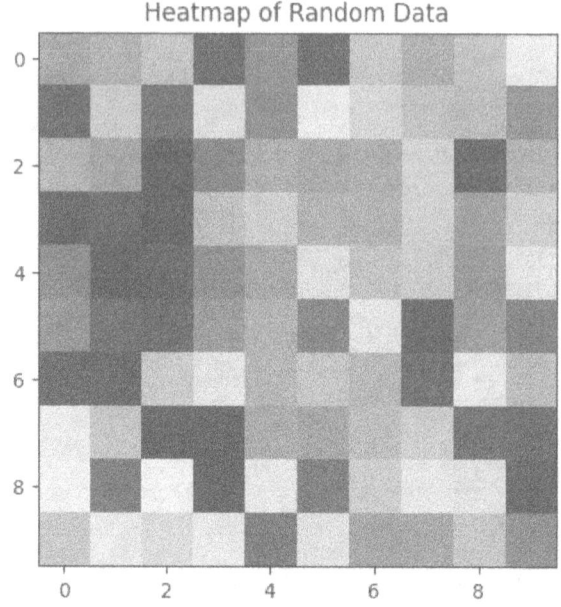

Figure 14.13 A heatmap visualizing random data with color intensity.

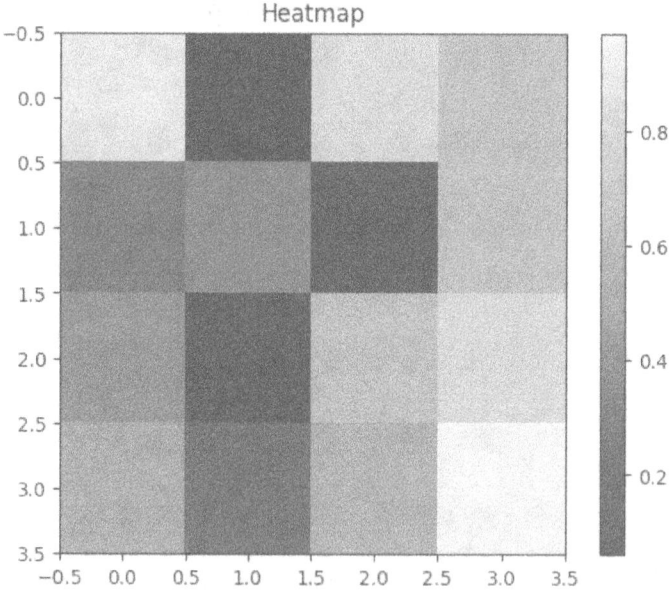

Figure 14.14 A heatmap displaying random data using a color gradient.

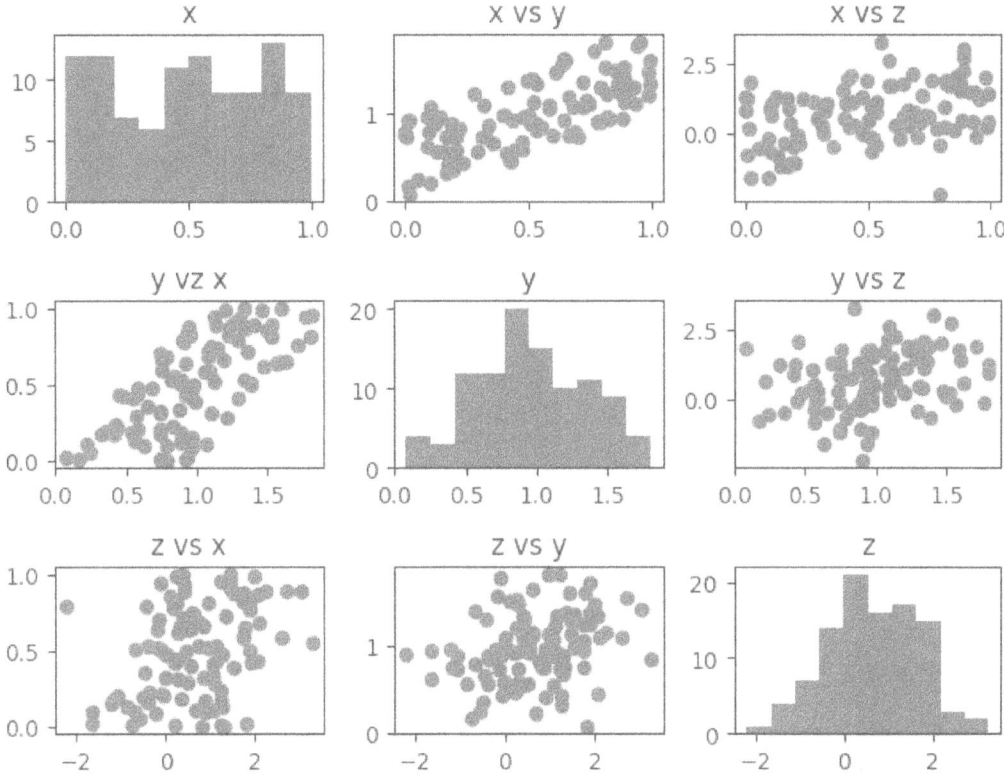

Figure 14.15 A plot with nine subplots arranged in a grid.

14.9 SUBPLOTS AGAIN

14.9.1 Demonstration

We have learned subplots that enable us to put multiple plots together. Let's revisit it and organize various type of plots together to make it a dashboard (Figure 14.15).

```python
# Make two dummy datasets
x = sorted(np.random.rand(100))
y = x + np.random.rand(100)
z = x + np.random.randn(100)

# Creating subplots
fig, axs = plt.subplots(3, 3)
axs[0,0].hist(x, bins=10)
axs[0,0].set_title('x')

axs[0,1].scatter(x, y)
axs[0,1].set_title('x vs y')

axs[0,2].scatter(x, z)
axs[0,2].set_title('x vs z')
```

```
axs[1,0].scatter(y, x)
axs[1,0].set_title('y vz x')

axs[1,1].hist(y, bins=10)
axs[1,1].set_title('y')

axs[1,2].scatter(y, z)
axs[1,2].set_title('y vs z')

axs[2,0].scatter(z, x)
axs[2,0].set_title('z vs x')

axs[2,1].scatter(z, y)
axs[2,1].set_title('z vs y')

axs[2,2].hist(z, bins=10)
axs[2,2].set_title('z')

# Display the plots
plt.tight_layout(pad=0.4, w_pad=0.5, h_pad=1.0)
plt.show()
```

14.9.2 Practice

Task: Create multiple line plots (Figure 14.16) in a single figure with x values [1, 2, 3, 4, 5] and two sets of y values [2, 3, 5, 4, -1] and [4, 2, 8, 9, 5].

```
x = [1, 2, 3, 4, 5]
y1 = [2, 3, 5, 4, -1]
y2 = [4, 2, 8, 9, 5]

plt.plot(x, y1, label='y1')
plt.plot(x, y2, label='y2')
plt.title('Multiple Line Plots')
plt.xlabel('X values')
plt.ylabel('Y values')
plt.legend()categories = ['A', 'B', 'C', 'D']
plt.show()
```

Task: Create multiple line plots (Figure 14.17) in a single figure with x values [1, 2, 3, 4, 5] and two sets of y values [2, 3, 5, 4, -1], label as year2020, and [4, 2, 8, 9, 5], label as year2024, with the category as ['Agent1', 'Agent2', 'Agent3', 'Agent4', 'Agent5']. Create a 2 by 2 multiplots that has:

1. A line plot of x values as x, y1 and y2 values as y in the same plot.
2. A scatter plot of y1 and y2.
3. A bar plot of y1 and category.
4. A bar plot of y2 and category.

```
x = [1, 2, 3, 4, 5]
y1 = [2, 3, 5, 4, -1]
y2 = [4, 2, 8, 9, 5]
category = ['Agent1', 'Agent2', 'Agent3', 'Agent4', 'Agent5']
```

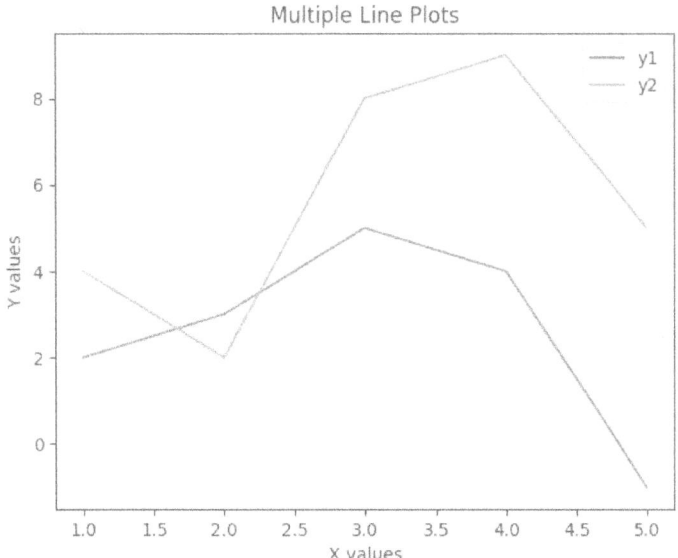

Figure 14.16 A plot displaying multiple lines, each representing a different relationship.

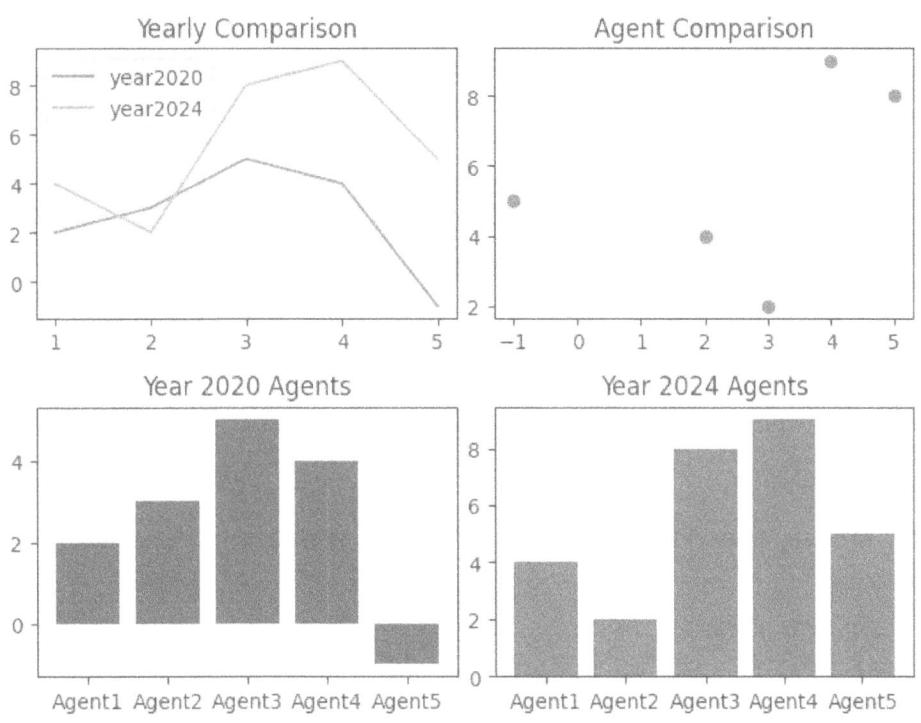

Figure 14.17 A plot divided into four subplots for comparing data.

```
fig, axs = plt.subplots(2, 2)

axs[0, 0].plot(x, y1, label='year2020')
```

TABLE 14.1 Matplotlib Plot Types

Plot Type	Basic Syntax	Scenario
Line Plot	`plt.plot(x, y)`	Shows trends or changes over time. Ideal for continuous data. Example: Tracking daily temperature changes over a month.
Bar Plot	`plt.bar(x, y)`	Compares categories or groups. Suitable for categorical data. Example: Comparing sales across different product categories.
Horizontal Bar	`plt.barh(x, y)`	Compares categories horizontally, useful for long labels. Example: Visualizing the population of countries with long names.
Histogram	`plt.hist(data)`	Displays the distribution of a dataset. Ideal for frequency analysis. Example: Analyzing the distribution of students' test scores.
Scatter Plot	`plt.scatter(x, y)`	Shows relationships between two variables. Example: Examining the relationship between hours studied and exam scores.
Pie Chart	`plt.pie(data)`	Represents proportions of a whole. Best for percentage distribution. Example: Showing the market share of smartphone brands.
Box Plot	`plt.boxplot(data)`	Displays data distribution, highlighting median and outliers. Example: Comparing monthly salaries across departments.
Heatmap	`plt.imshow(data)`	Visualizes matrix-like data, often for correlation or intensity maps. Example: Representing the correlation between multiple economic indicators.

```python
axs[0, 0].plot(x, y2, label='year2024')
axs[0, 0].set_title('Yearly Comparison')
axs[0, 0].legend()

axs[0, 1].scatter(y1, y2)
axs[0, 1].set_title('Agent Comparison')

axs[1, 0].bar(category, y1, color='blue')
axs[1, 0].set_title('Year 2020 Agents')

axs[1, 1].bar(category, y2, color='Green')
axs[1, 1].set_title('Year 2024 Agents')

plt.tight_layout(pad=0.4, w_pad=0.5, h_pad=1.0)
plt.show()
```

We summarize the different types of plots in Table 14.1.

14.10   INTERACT WITH GENAI

Here are some questions and prompts you can interact with generative AI tools, including ChatGPT.

- What are the different types of plots available in Matplotlib, and when should each be used?
- Provide an example of a histogram to show the distribution of test scores.
- What is the difference between a bar plot and a histogram?
- How do you customize the size and color of points in a scatter plot?
- Can you add labels to each slice of a pie chart? If so, how?
- What does a box plot reveal about a dataset's median and variability?
- How do you determine the number of bins to use in a histogram?
- How can you create grouped bar plots to compare data across multiple categories?
- Discuss how to use subplots to display multiple types of plots (e.g., scatter and line) in a single figure.
- How can you use a stacked bar plot to visualize cumulative data?
- How to customize the angles, colors, and explode properties of a pie chart?
- Why might a box plot not display outliers, and how can you enable them?

14.11   EXPLORE MORE OF MATPLOTLIB

At the end, here are the official documentations of Matplotlib:

- Quick guide: https://matplotlib.org/stable/users/explain/quick_start.html
- Plot types: https://matplotlib.org/stable/plot_types/index
- User guide: https://matplotlib.org/stable/users/index

## CHAPTER 15

Seaborn

W E will continue our journey in data visualization by exploring Seaborn, a powerful library built on top of Matplotlib that simplifies the process of creating beautiful and informative plots. We'll learn how to generate different types of visualizations, including relational, distribution, and categorical plots, making it easier to uncover patterns in data. Additionally, we'll learn how to create advanced plots with colors, styles, facet grids, and `LMplot`, and discover how to create multiple plots for richer data insights. Are you ready? Let's get started!

15.1 INTRODUCTION

15.1.1 Explanation

Seaborn is a Python data visualization library based on Matplotlib. It provides a high-level interface for drawing attractive and informative statistical graphics. It is particularly well-suited for visualizing data from pandas DataFrames and arrays of data, making it a valuable tool for data analysis and exploration.

There are many reasons of the popularity of Seaborn. Its high-level interface makes it easy to create complex visualizations with just a few lines of code. It comes with a variety of built-in themes and color palettes to make your plots look more aesthetically pleasing. Seaborn works seamlessly with pandas DataFrames, making it easy to visualize data stored in these structures. Many functions of Seaborn automatically estimate and plot linear regression models, KDE plots, etc.

While Seaborn is powerful and easy to use, it is built on top of Matplotlib, which offers more flexibility and control over plot customization. Although Seaborn simplifies many aspects of data visualization, understanding all its features and parameters can take some time. For very large datasets, Seaborn may be slower than Matplotlib due to its higher-level interface and additional functionality.

In summary, seaborn is an excellent tool for creating attractive and informative statistical visualizations with minimal effort. Its integration with Pandas and Matplotlib

DOI: 10.1201/9781003624868-15

makes it a powerful addition to any data scientist's toolkit. As we proceed with this tutorial, we'll explore more features and capabilities of Seaborn, including various plot types, customization options, and advanced functionalities.

15.1.2 Major categories

Seaborn categorizes plots into three main general types:

1. Relational Plots: Used to understand the relationship between two or more variables.
2. Distribution Plots: Used to visualize the distribution of a dataset.
3. Categorical Plots: Used to visualize the relationship between categorical data and other variables.

15.1.3 Get started

Similar to Matplotlib, we need to import Seaborn package to use it. In convention, we use `import seaborn as sns` to give an alias `sns` for Seaborn. In this demonstration, we will use the built-in dataset, `tips` in Seaborn.

```
# Load packages
import seaborn as sns
import matplotlib.pyplot as plt
import pandas as pd

# Load the tips dataset for this tutorial
tips = sns.load_dataset('tips')
```

```
tips.info()
```

```
<class 'pandas.core.frame.DataFrame'>
RangeIndex: 244 entries, 0 to 243
Data columns (total 7 columns):
 #   Column      Non-Null Count  Dtype
---  ------      --------------  -----
 0   total_bill  244 non-null    float64
 1   tip         244 non-null    float64
 2   sex         244 non-null    category
 3   smoker      244 non-null    category
 4   day         244 non-null    category
 5   time        244 non-null    category
 6   size        244 non-null    int64
dtypes: category(4), float64(2), int64(1)
memory usage: 7.4 KB
```

15.2 RELATIONAL PLOTS

15.2.1 Demonstration

Statistical analysis involves exploring how variables in a dataset interact and how these interactions are influenced by other variables. Visualization plays a crucial role

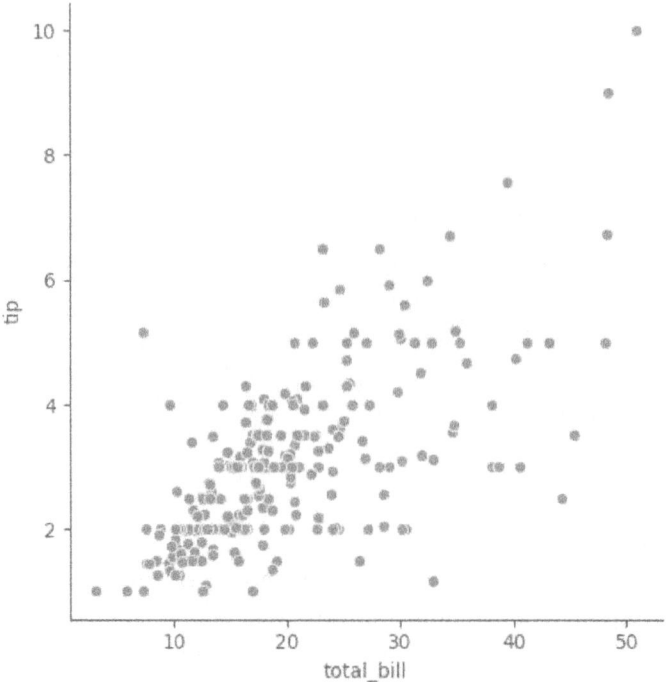

Figure 15.1   A scatter plot showing the correlation between total bill and tip amounts.

in this process because it allows the human eye to detect trends and patterns that signify relationships.

The function `relplot()` operates at the figure level and is used to visualize statistical relationships through two main types of plots: scatter plots and line plots.

Scatter Plot (`kind='scatter'`): A scatter plot is the default plot type for `relplot()`. It shows the relationship between two numerical variables (Figure 15.1).

```
# Create a scatter plot
sns.relplot(data=tips, x='total_bill', y='tip', kind='scatter')

# Show the plot
plt.show()
```

Line Plot (`kind='line'`): A line plot is used to show the relationship between two numerical variables, with data points connected by lines. It is useful for visualizing trends over time or ordered categories.

If there are multiple measurements for the same value of the x variable, the default behavior in seaborn is to aggregate the multiple measurements at each x value by plotting the mean and the 95% confidence interval around the mean (Figure 15.2).

```
# Create a line plot
sns.relplot(data=tips, x='size', y='total_bill', kind='line')
```

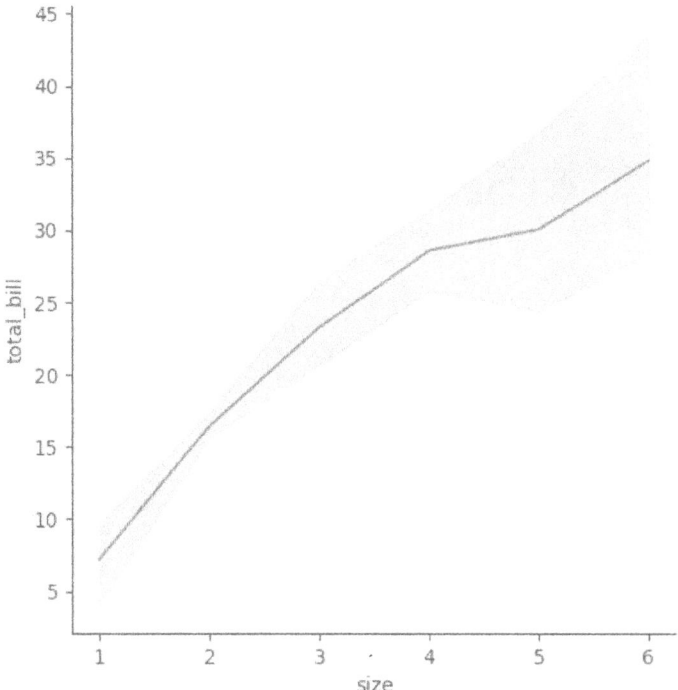

Figure 15.2 A line plot displaying the relationship between total bill and party size.

```
# Show the plot
plt.show()
```

15.2.2 Practice

Task: Create a scatter relational plot (Figure 15.3) for `'time'` and `'total_bill'`.

```
# Create a scatter plot
sns.relplot(data=tips, x='time', y='total_bill')

# Show the plot
plt.show()
```

Task: Create a line relational plot (Figure 15.4) for `'time'` and `'total_bill'`.

```
# Create a line plot
sns.relplot(data=tips, x='time', y='total_bill', kind='line')

# Show the plot
plt.show()
```

Task: Create a scatter relational plot (Figure 15.5) for `'day'` and `'total_bill'`.

```
# Create a scatter plot
sns.relplot(data=tips, x='day', y='total_bill')
```

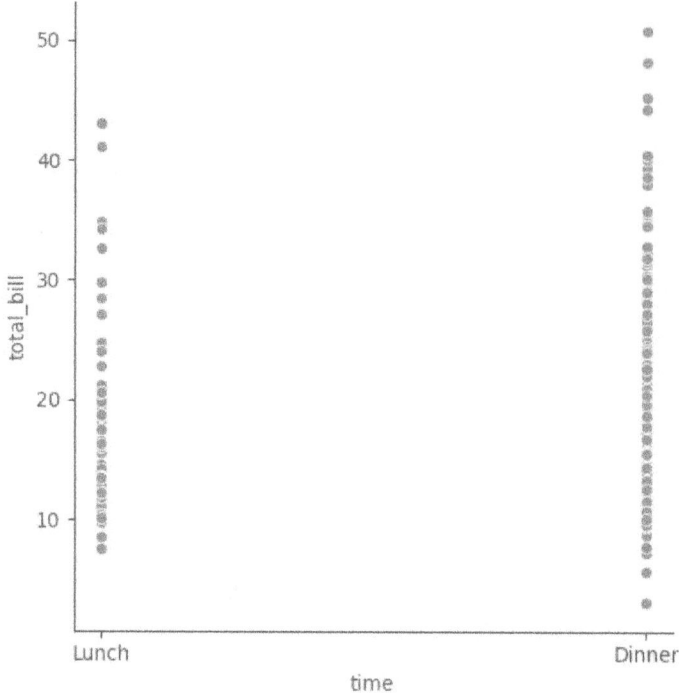

Figure 15.3   A scatter plot showing the relationship between total bill amount and time of day.

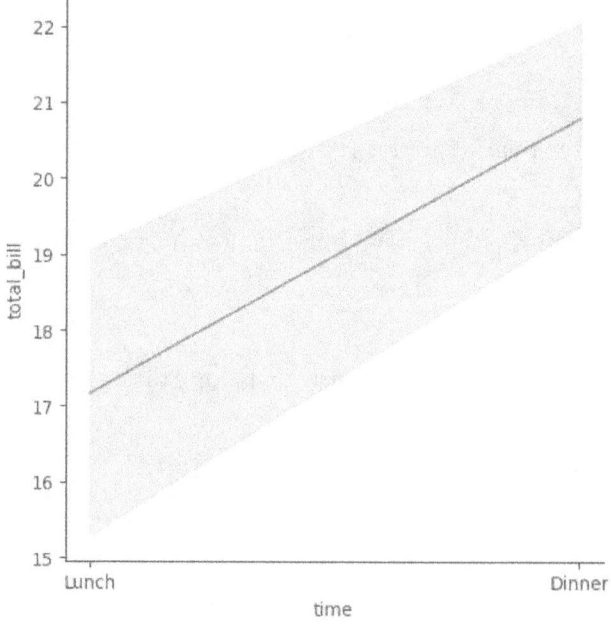

Figure 15.4   A line plot showing how total bill amount varies with the time of day.

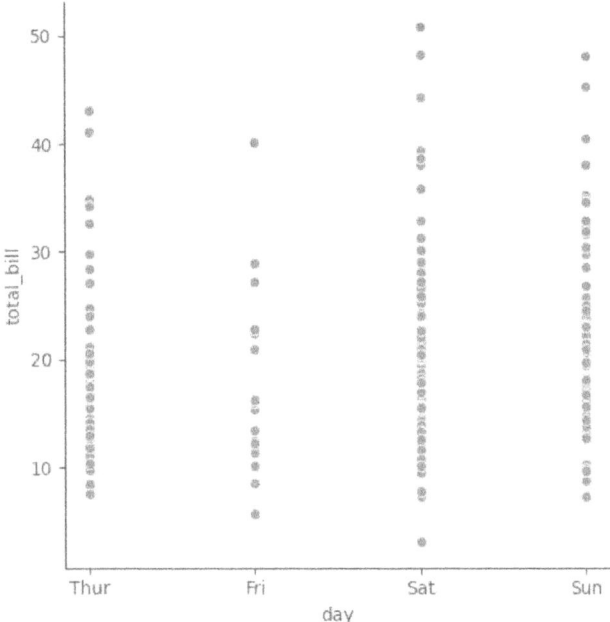

Figure 15.5 A scatter plot showing the relationship between total bill and day of the week.

```
# Show the plot
plt.show()
```

Task: Create a line relational plot (Figure 15.6) for `'day'` and `'total_bill'`.

```
# Create a line plot
sns.relplot(data=tips, x='day', y='total_bill', kind='line')

# Show the plot
plt.show()
```

15.3 DISTRIBUTION PLOTS

15.3.1 Demonstration

The `displot()` function in Seaborn is for visualizing the distribution of a dataset.

Histogram (`kind='hist'`): A histogram displays the distribution of a dataset by dividing the data into bins and counting the number of observations in each bin. The following histogram (Figure 15.7) shows the distribution of the total bill amounts in the 'tips' dataset.

```
# Create a histogram
sns.displot(tips, x='total_bill', kind='hist')
```

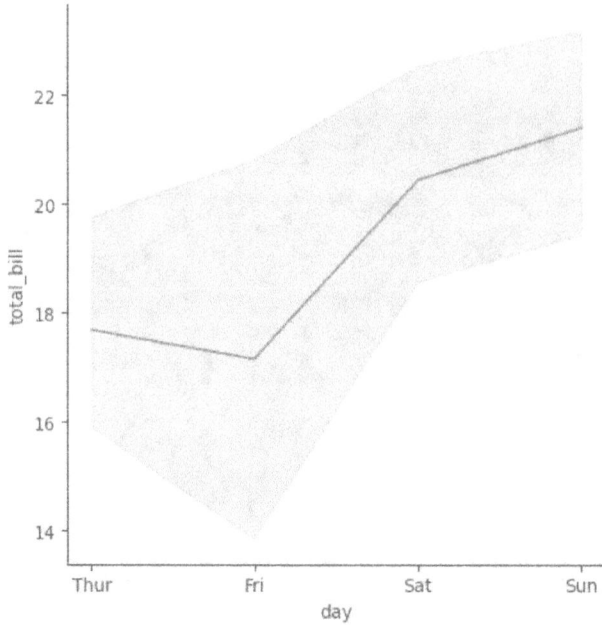

Figure 15.6   A line plot showing total bill amounts across different days of the week.

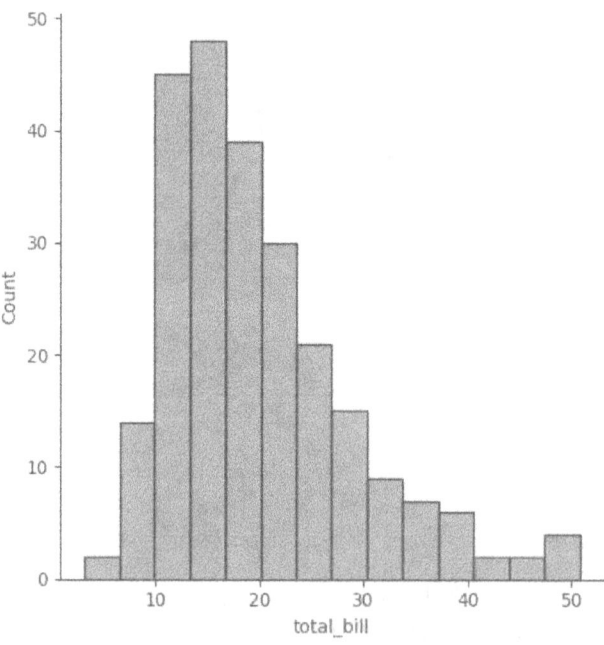

Figure 15.7   A basic histogram plot showing the distribution of total bill amounts.

```
# Show the plot
plt.show()
```

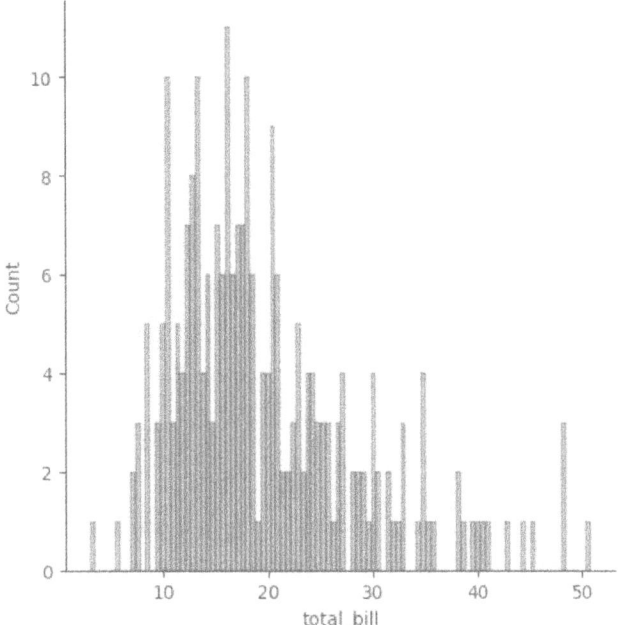

Figure 15.8 A histogram plot of total bill amounts with more bins for finer detail.

We can change the number of bins by using the keywords `bins` to modify the granularity of the distribution (Figure 15.8).

```
# Create a histogram with 100 bins
sns.displot(tips, x='total_bill', kind='hist', bins = 100)

# Show the plot
plt.show()
```

Kernel Density Estimate Plot (`kind='kde'`): A kernel density estimate (KDE) plot is a smoothed version of the histogram, which estimates the probability density function of the data. The following KDE plot (Figure 15.9) shows the smoothed distribution of the total bill amounts in the 'tips' dataset.

```
# Create a KDE plot
sns.displot(tips, x='total_bill', kind='kde')

# Show the plot
plt.show()
```

Empirical Cumulative Distribution Function Plot (`kind='ecdf'`): An ECDF plot shows the proportion of observations less than or equal to a particular value, providing a cumulative view of the data distribution. The following ECDF plot (Figure 15.10) displays the cumulative distribution of the total bill amounts in the 'tips' dataset.

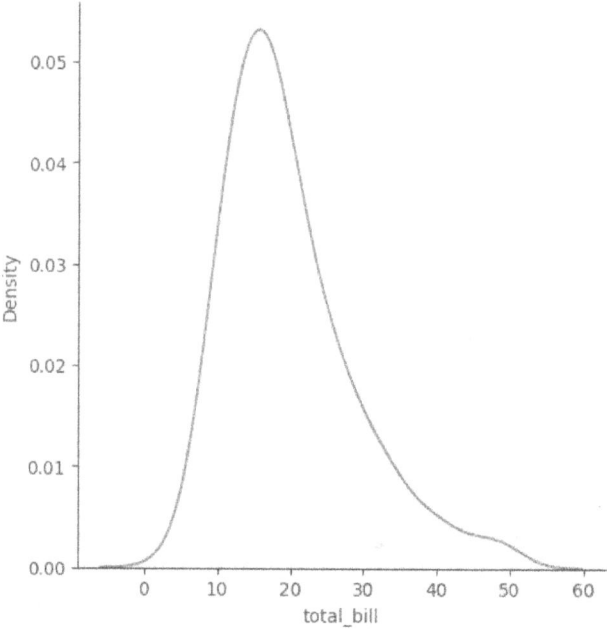

Figure 15.9 A KDE plot showing the probability density of total bill amounts.

```
# Create an ECDF plot
sns.displot(tips, x='total_bill', kind='ecdf')

# Show the plot
plt.show()
```

15.3.2 Practice

Here are some coding problems to help you practice using the `displot()` function in Seaborn with the 'tips' dataset. These problems will use different attributes of the dataset to create various types of distribution plots.

Task: Create a histogram (Figure 15.11) to visualize the distribution of tip amounts in the 'tips' dataset.

```
# Create a histogram of tip amounts
sns.displot(tips, x='tip', kind='hist')

# Show the plot
plt.show()
```

Task: Create a KDE plot (Figure 15.12) to visualize the distribution of tip amounts.

```
# Create a KDE plot of tips
sns.displot(tips, x='tip', kind='kde')

# Show the plot
plt.show()
```

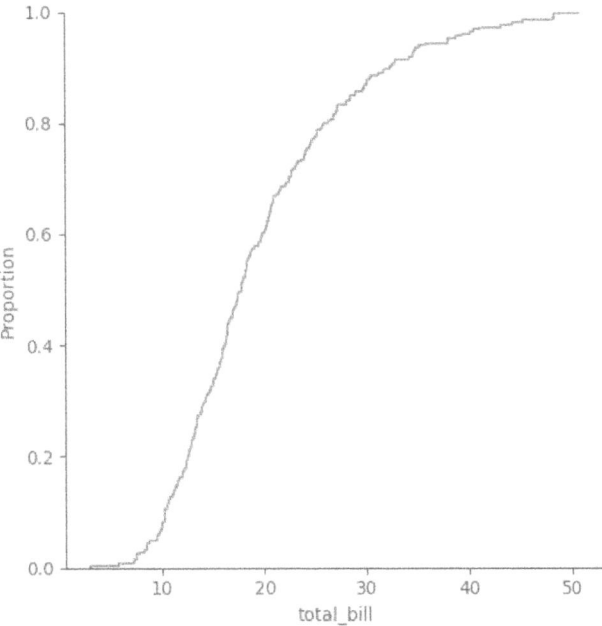

Figure 15.10 An empirical cumulative distribution function (ECDF) plot for total bill amounts.

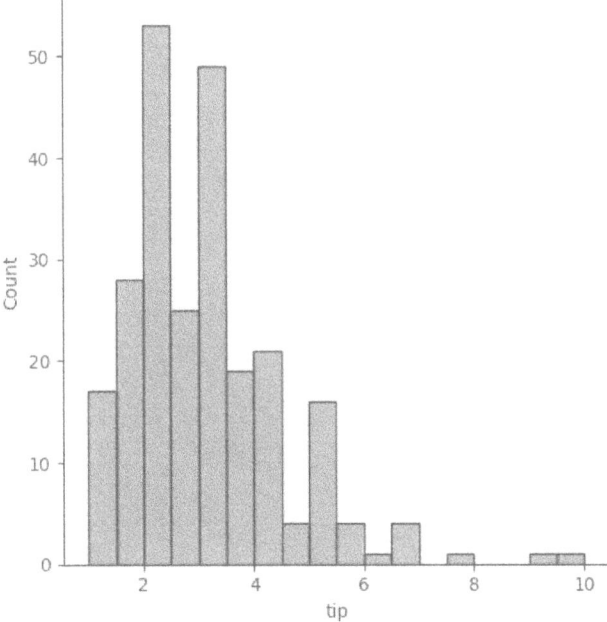

Figure 15.11 A histogram plot showing the distribution of tip amounts.

Task: Create an ECDF plot (Figure 15.13) to visualize tip amounts.

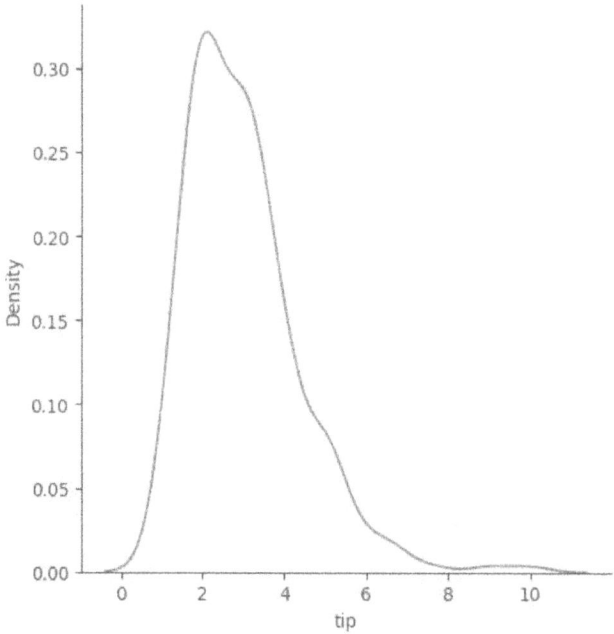

Figure 15.12 A kernel density estimation (KDE) plot for tip amounts.

```
# Create an ECDF plot of tip percentages
sns.displot(tips, x='tip', kind='ecdf')

# Show the plot
plt.show()
```

Task: Create a histogram (Figure 15.14) to visualize the distribution of the size of dining parties.

```
# Create a histogram of the size of dining parties
sns.displot(tips, x='size', kind='hist')

# Show the plot
plt.show()
```

Task: Create a KDE plot (Figure 15.15) to visualize the distribution of size.

```
# Create a KDE plot of size
sns.displot(tips, x='size', kind='kde')

# Show the plot
plt.show()
```

Task: Create a ECDF plot (Figure 15.16) to visualize the distribution of size.

```
# Create a ECDF plot of size
sns.displot(tips, x='size', kind='ecdf')
```

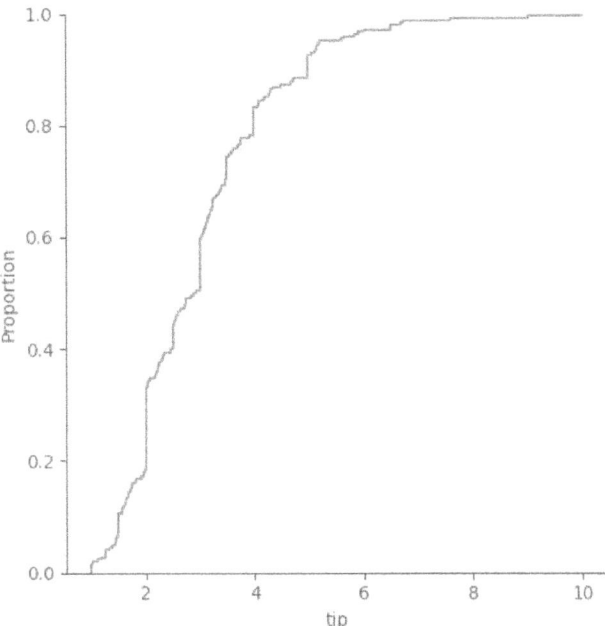

Figure 15.13 An empirical cumulative distribution function (ECDF) plot for tip amounts.

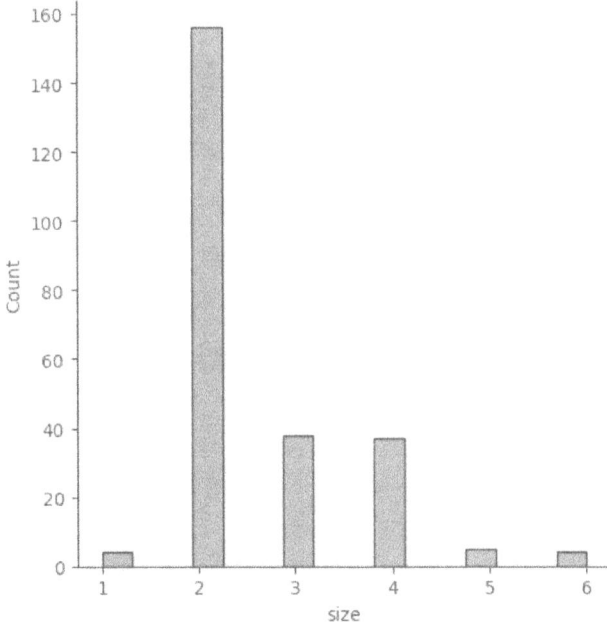

Figure 15.14 A histogram plot showing the distribution of party size.

```
# Show the plot
plt.show()
```

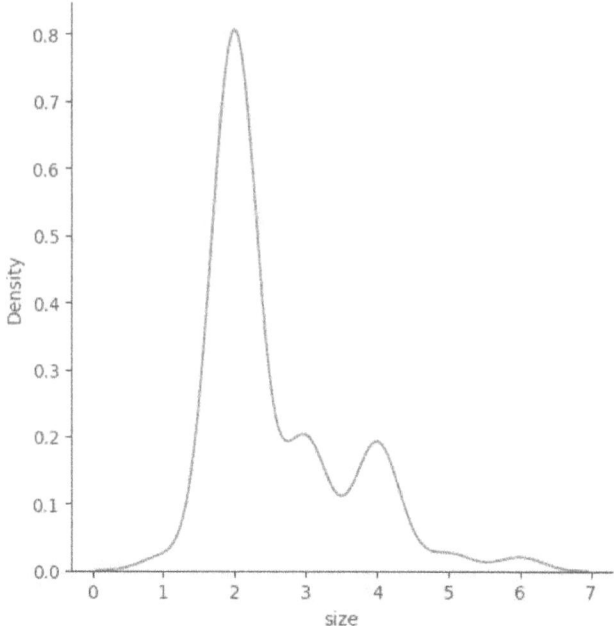

Figure 15.15 A kernel density estimation (KDE) plot for tip amounts.

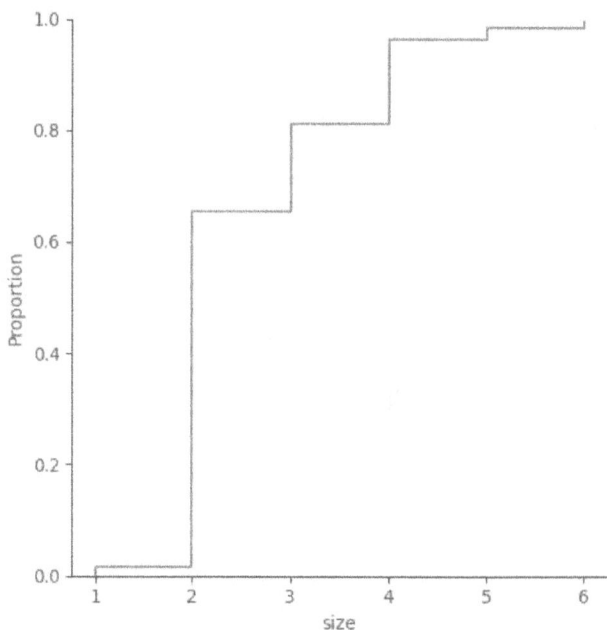

Figure 15.16 An empirical cumulative distribution function (ECDF) plot for tip amounts.

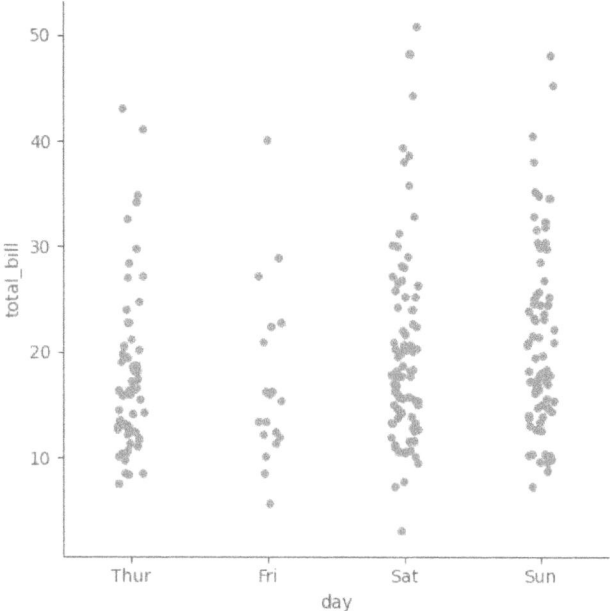

Figure 15.17 A strip plot showing the distribution of total bill amounts across different days.

15.4 CATEGORICAL PLOTS

15.4.1 Demonstration

The `catplot()` function in Seaborn visualizes the relationship between categorical data and other variables. By using the `kind` parameter, you can create strip plots, swarm plots, box plots, violin plots, bar plots, and point plots to explore the relationship between categorical variables and other data in your dataset. The 'tips' dataset provides an excellent starting point for practicing these techniques.

Strip Plot (`kind='strip'`): A strip plot shows individual data points along an axis, which can be useful for visualizing the distribution of data points within categories. The following strip plot (Figure 15.17) displays the distribution of total bill amounts for each day of the week.

```
# Create a strip plot
sns.catplot(data=tips, x='day', y='total_bill', kind='strip')

# Show the plot
plt.show()
```

Swarm Plot (`kind='swarm'`): A swarm plot is similar to a strip plot but adjusts the positions of the data points to prevent them from overlapping, providing a clearer view of the distribution. The following swarm plot (Figure 15.18) shows the distribution of total bill amounts for each day of the week without overlapping points.

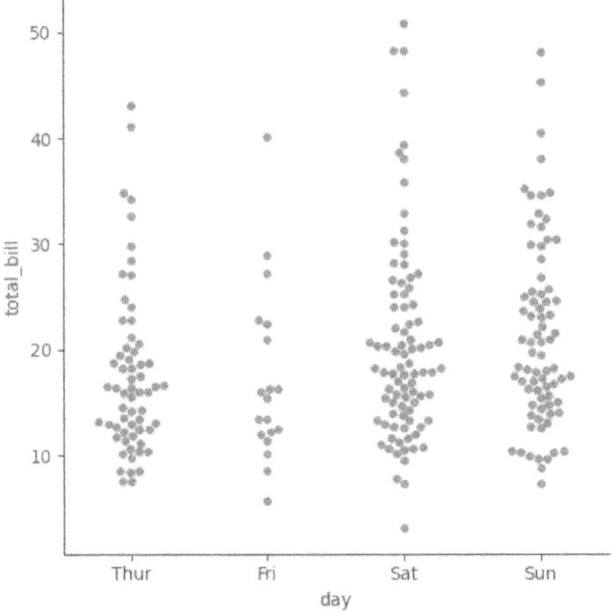

Figure 15.18 A swarm plot showing the distribution of total bill amounts across different days, avoiding overlap.

```
# Create a swarm plot
sns.catplot(data=tips, x='day', y='total_bill', kind='swarm')

# Show the plot
plt.show()
```

Box Plot (`kind='box'`): A box plot shows the distribution of data based on a five-number summary: minimum, first quartile (Q1), median, third quartile (Q3), and maximum. It also highlights outliers. The following box plot (Figure 15.19) visualizes the distribution of total bill amounts for each day of the week.

```
# Create a box plot
sns.catplot(data=tips, x='day', y='total_bill', kind='box')

# Show the plot
plt.show()
```

Violin Plot (`kind='violin'`): A violin plot combines aspects of a box plot and a KDE plot, showing the distribution of the data across different categories. The following violin plot (Figure 15.20) displays the distribution of total bill amounts for each day of the week, including the density of the data.

```
# Create a violin plot
sns.catplot(data=tips, x='day', y='total_bill', kind='violin')

# Show the plot
plt.show()
```

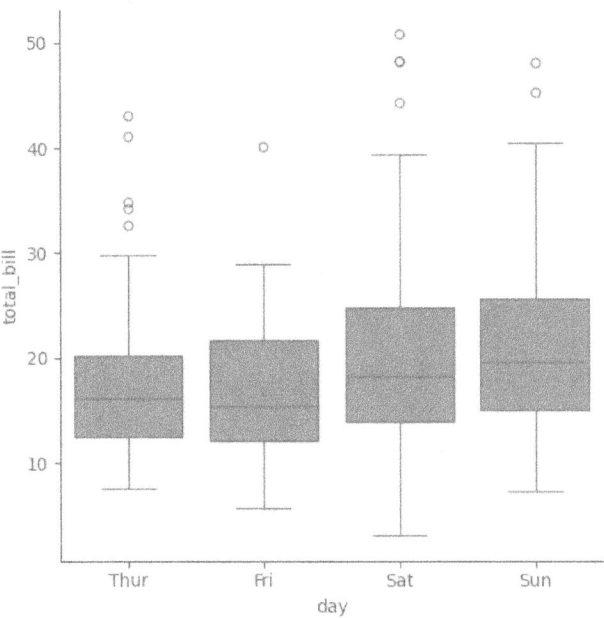

Figure 15.19 A box plot showing the distribution of total bill amounts for each day.

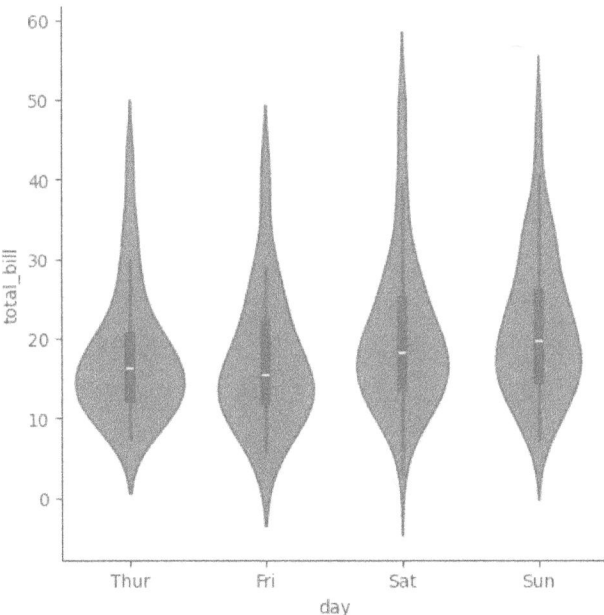

Figure 15.20 A violin plot combining box plot and KDE to show the distribution of total bill amounts per day.

Bar Plot (`kind='bar'`): A bar plot shows the central tendency of the data for each category along with error bars to indicate variability. The following bar plot (Figure

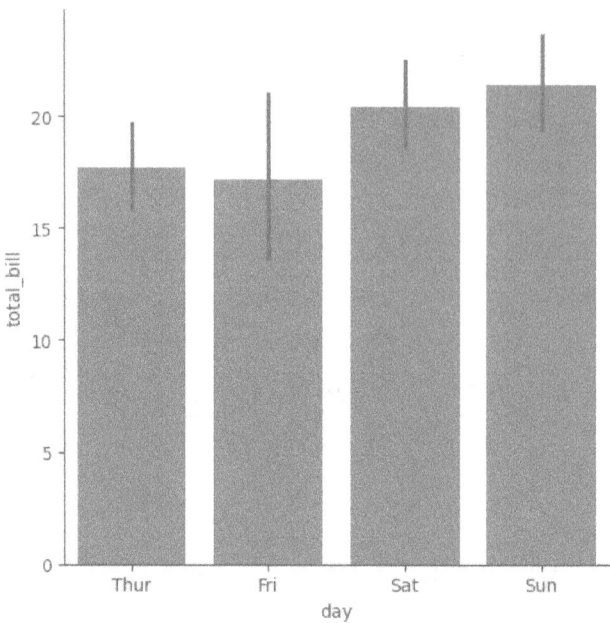

Figure 15.21 A bar plot comparing total bill amounts across different days.

15.21) displays the average total bill amounts for each day of the week, with error bars indicating the standard error.

```
# Create a bar plot
sns.catplot(data=tips, x='day', y='total_bill', kind='bar')

# Show the plot
plt.show()
```

Point Plot (`kind='point'`): A point plot is similar to a bar plot but uses points and lines to show the central tendency and variability of the data for each category. The following point plot (Figure 15.22) visualizes the average total bill amounts for each day of the week, with lines indicating the standard error.

```
# Create a point plot
sns.catplot(data=tips, x='day', y='total_bill', kind='point')

# Show the plot
plt.show()
```

15.4.2 Practice

Here are some coding problems to help you practice using the `catplot()` function in Seaborn with the 'tips' dataset. These problems focus on different attributes and use the `kind` parameter to create various types of categorical plots.

Task: Create a strip plot (Figure 15.23) showing the distribution of the 'tip' column for different times of day ('time').

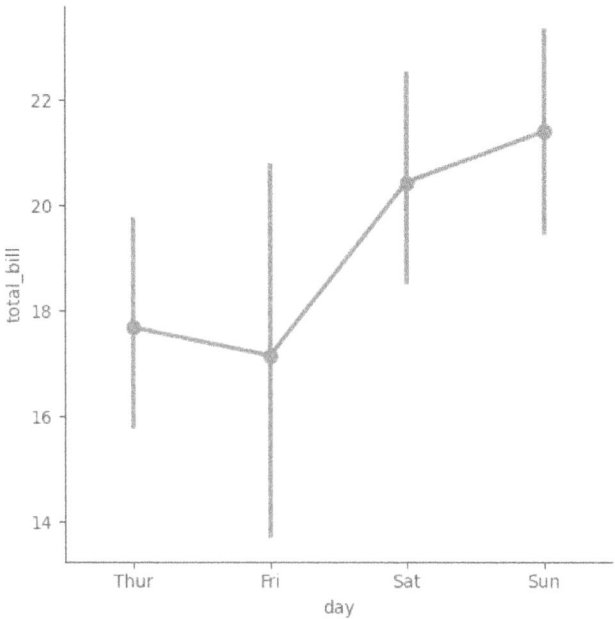

Figure 15.22 A point plot illustrating the average total bill amount for each day.

```
# Create a strip plot of tips by time of day
sns.catplot(data=tips, x='time', y='tip', kind='strip')

# Show the plot
plt.show()
```

Task: Create a swarm plot (Figure 15.24) showing the distribution of the 'total_bill' column for different sexes ('sex').

```
# Create a swarm plot of total bill by sex
sns.catplot(data=tips, x='sex', y='total_bill', kind='swarm')

# Show the plot
plt.show()
```

Task: Calculate the tip percentage for each entry in the dataset and create a box plot (Figure 15.25) to visualize the distribution of tip percentages for different days of the week ('day').

```
# Calculate tip percentage
tips['tip_percentage'] = tips['tip'] / tips['total_bill'] * 100

# Create a box plot of tip percentages by day
sns.catplot(data=tips, x='day', y='tip_percentage', kind='box')

# Show the plot
plt.show()
```

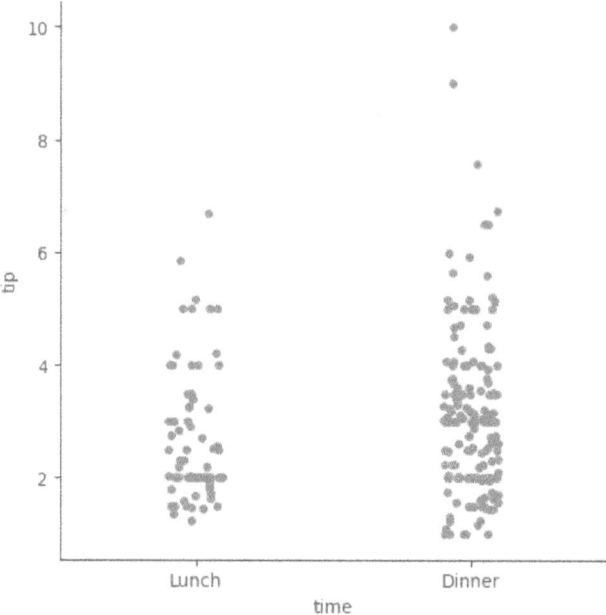

Figure 15.23 A strip plot showing the distribution of tip amounts over time.

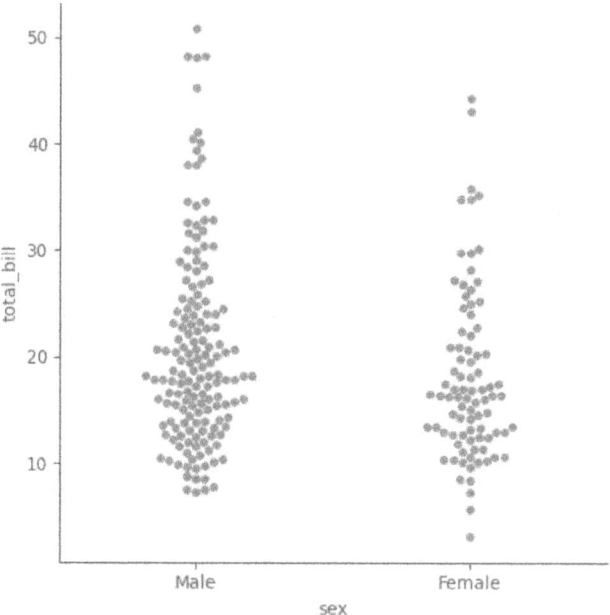

Figure 15.24 A strip plot showing the distribution of total bill amounts by gender.

Task: Create a violin plot (Figure 15.26) to visualize the distribution of the 'total_bill' column for smokers and non-smokers ('smoker').

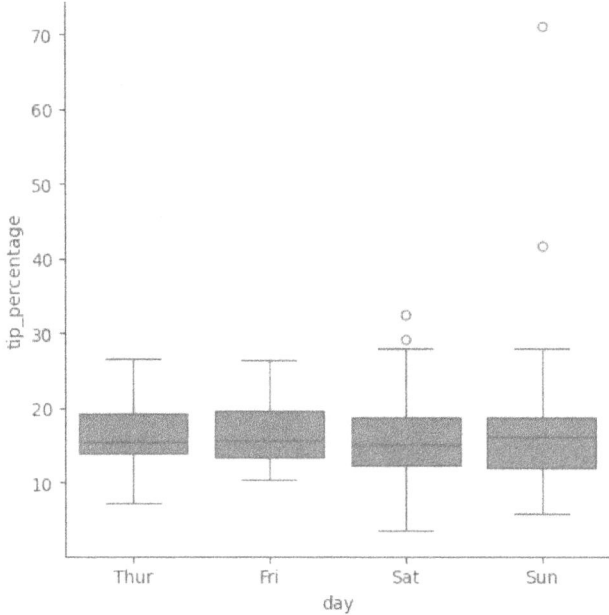

Figure 15.25   A box plot comparing tip percentages across different days.

```python
# Create a violin plot of total bill by smoker status
sns.catplot(data=tips, x='smoker', y='total_bill', kind='violin')

# Show the plot
plt.show()
```

Task: Create a bar plot (Figure 15.27) to visualize the average 'tip' amounts for different sexes ('sex'), with error bars indicating the standard error.

```python
# Create a bar plot of average tips by sex
sns.catplot(data=tips, x='sex', y='tip', kind='bar')

# Show the plot
plt.show()
```

Task: Create a point plot (Figure 15.28) to visualize the average 'tip' amounts for different days of the week ('day'), with lines indicating the standard error.

```python
# Create a point plot of average tip by day
sns.catplot(data=tips, x='day', y='tip', kind='point')

# Show the plot
plt.show()
```

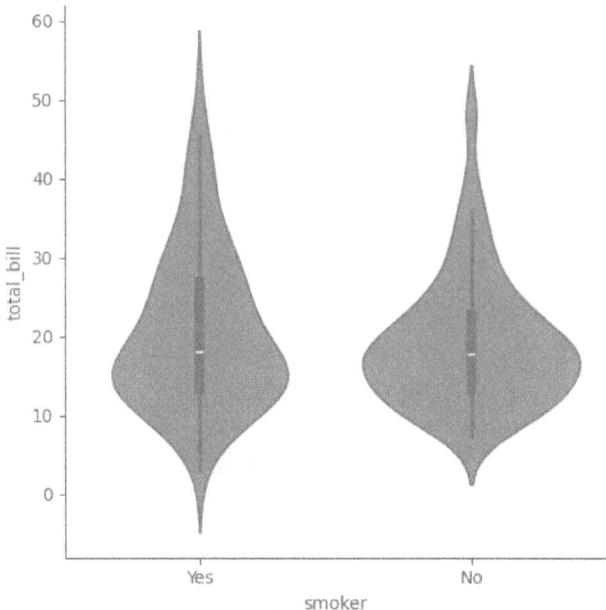

Figure 15.26 A violin plot showing the distribution of total bill amounts for smokers and non-smokers.

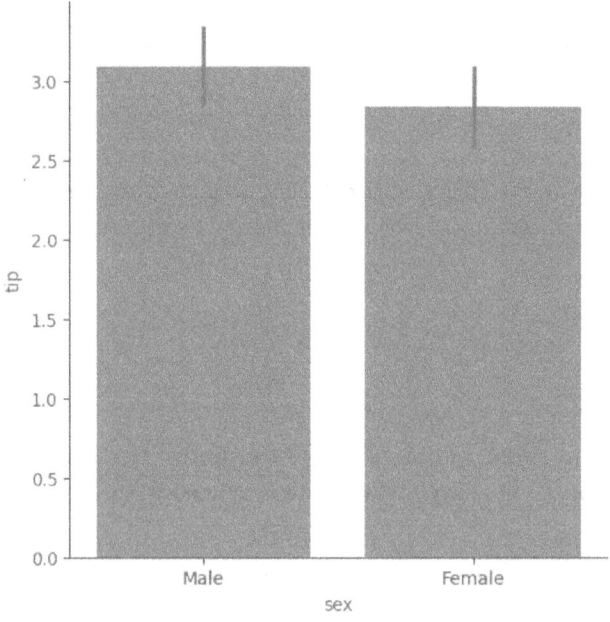

Figure 15.27 A bar plot comparing tip amounts between genders.

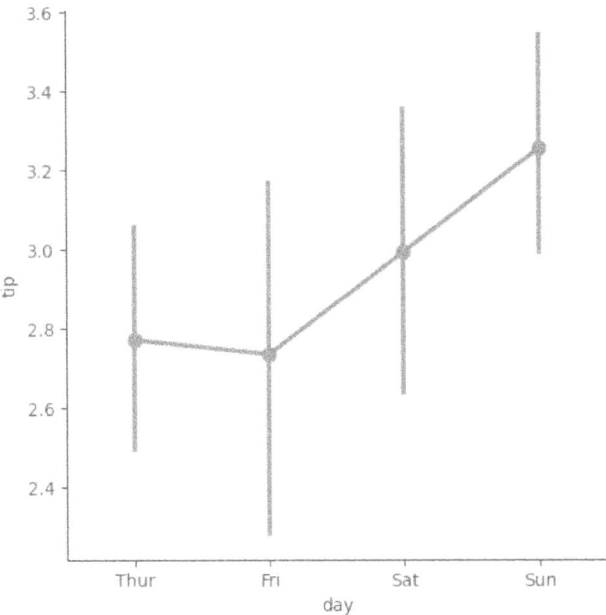

Figure 15.28 A point plot showing the average tip amount for each day.

15.5 ADDING COLORS

15.5.1 Demonstration

The hue parameter in Seaborn enhances visualizations by adding a categorical dimension through color differentiation. With hue, you can create more informative and visually appealing visualizations that help uncover deeper insights from your data. This lesson will demonstrate how to use the hue parameter with various types of plots in relplot(), displot(), and catplot() functions using the 'tips' dataset. The examples provided demonstrate how to use hue with various kinds of plots to enhance your data analysis.

Using hue with relplot(): The relplot() function can create scatter plots and line plots. In the following scatter plot (Figure 15.29), data points are colored based on the customer's gender, allowing comparison of the relationship between total bill and tip amounts for males and females.

```
# Create a scatter plot with hue
sns.relplot(data=tips, x='total_bill', y='tip', hue='sex', kind='scatter')

# Show the plot
plt.show()
```

In the following line plot (Figure 15.30), the lines are colored based on the customer's gender, showing the trend of total bill amounts with party size for males and females.

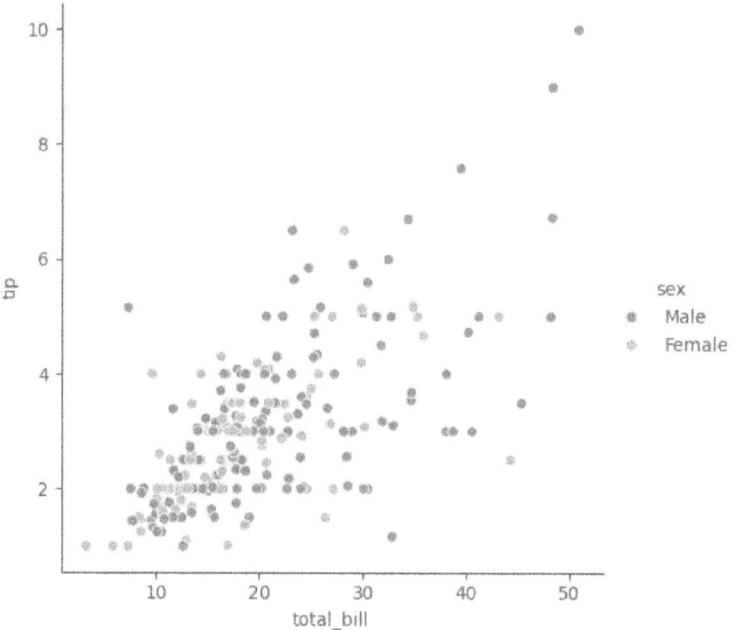

Figure 15.29 A scatter plot of total bill and tip, with color indicating sex.

```python
# Create a line plot with hue
sns.relplot(data=tips, x='size', y='total_bill', hue='sex', kind='line')

# Show the plot
plt.show()
```

Using `hue` with `displot()`: The `displot()` function can create histograms, KDE plots, and ECDF plots. In the following histogram (Figure 15.31), bars are colored based on the customer's gender, providing a comparison of tip amount distributions between males and females.

```python
# Create a histogram with hue
sns.displot(data=tips, x='tip', hue='sex', kind='hist')

# Show the plot
plt.show()
```

To avoid the overlapping of bars, you can use the `multiple` parameter to make a stacked histogram (Figure 15.32).

```python
# Create a histogram with hue and stacking
sns.displot(data=tips, x='tip', hue='sex', kind='hist', multiple='stack')

# Show the plot
plt.show()
```

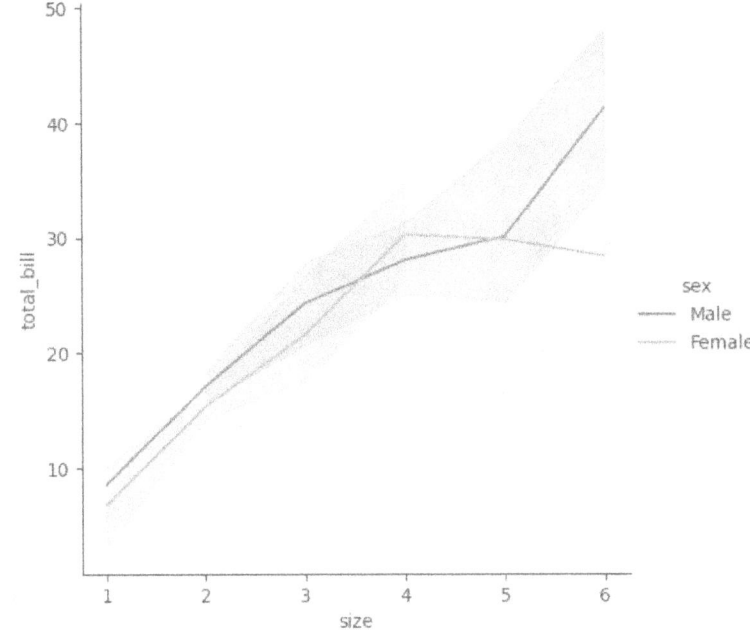

Figure 15.30 A line plot of total bill and size, with color indicating sex.

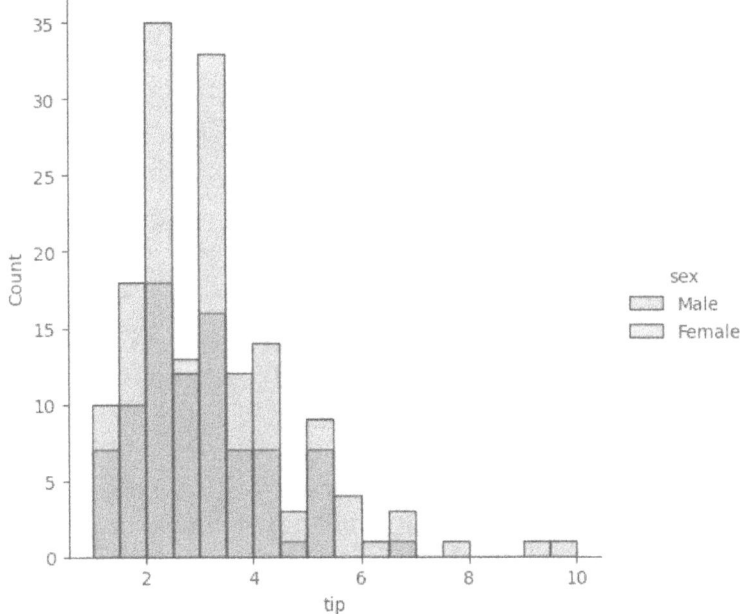

Figure 15.31 A histogram plot of tip amounts, with color differentiating categories.

In the following KDE plot (Figure 15.33), the distributions of tip amounts are colored based on whether the customer is a smoker, allowing for comparison of tip distributions between smokers and non-smokers.

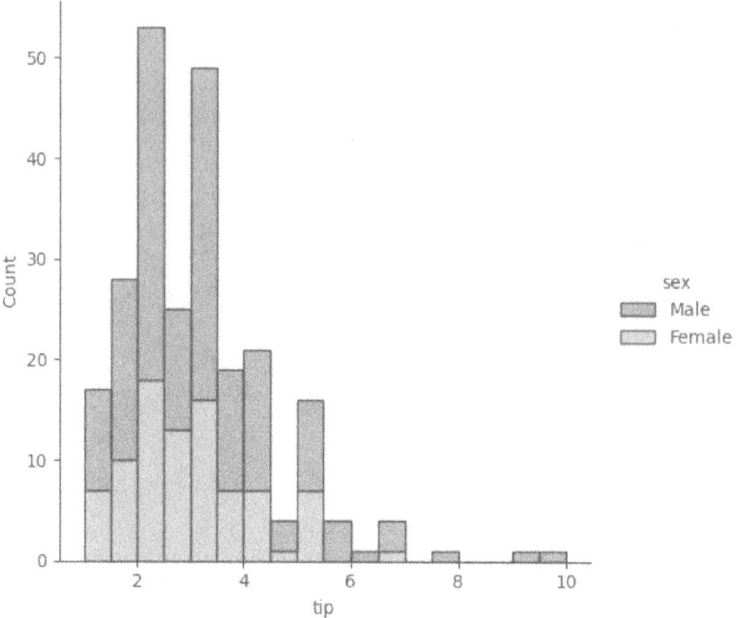

Figure 15.32 A stacked histogram plot of tip amounts, grouped by a categorical variable.

```
# Create a KDE plot with hue
sns.displot(data=tips, x='tip', hue='smoker', kind='kde')

# Show the plot
plt.show()
```

To avoid the overlapping of bars, you can use the `multiple` parameter to make a stacked KDE plot (Figure 15.34).

```
# Create a KDE plot with hue and stacking
sns.displot(data=tips, x='tip', hue='smoker', kind='kde', multiple='stack')

# Show the plot
plt.show()
```

In the following ECDF plot (Figure 15.35), lines are colored based on the day of the week, providing a cumulative view of total bill distributions across different days.

```
# Create an ECDF plot with hue
sns.displot(data=tips, x='total_bill', hue='day', kind='ecdf')

# Show the plot
plt.show()
```

The `catplot()` function can create strip plots, swarm plots, box plots, violin plots, bar plots, and point plots. In the following strip plot (Figure 15.36), data points are

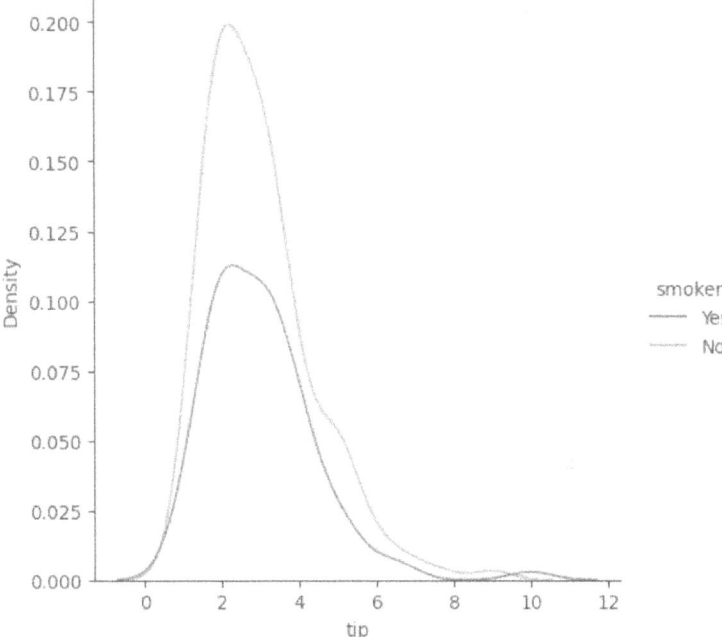

Figure 15.33 A kernel density estimation (KDE) plot of tip amounts, with color for categories.

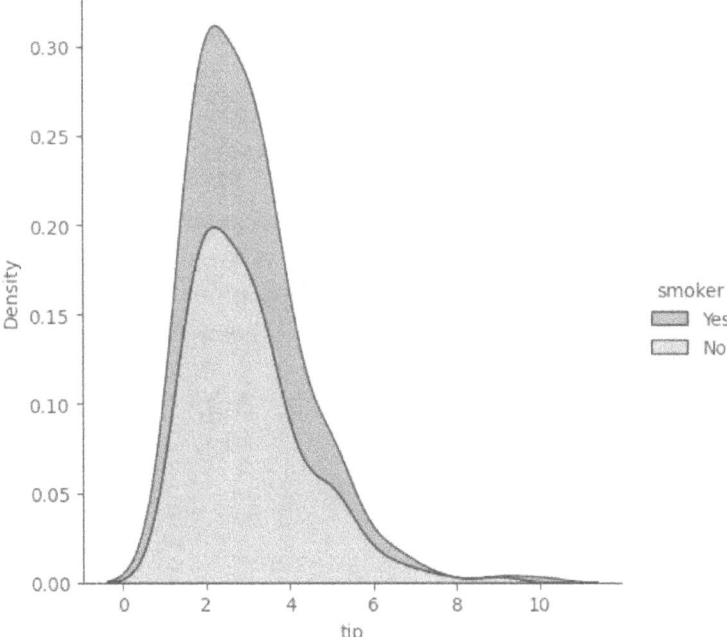

Figure 15.34 A stacked KDE plot of tip amounts, grouped by a categorical variable.

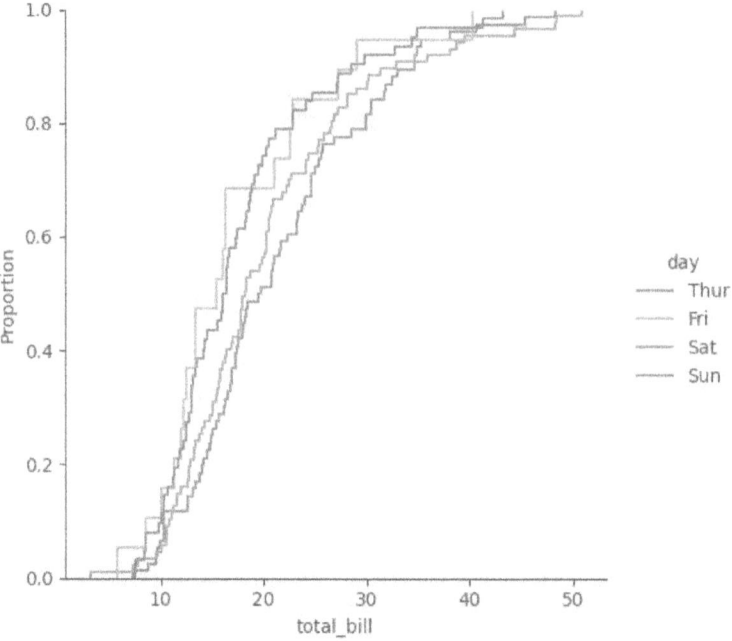

Figure 15.35 An empirical cumulative distribution function (ECDF) plot for total bill with color for categories.

colored based on whether the customer is a smoker, showing the distribution of total bill amounts across different days.

```
# Create a strip plot with hue
sns.catplot(data=tips, x='day', y='total_bill', hue='smoker', kind='strip')

# Show the plot
plt.show()
```

In the following swarm plot (Figure 15.37), data points are colored based on the customer's gender, visualizing the distribution of tips across different days.

```
# Create a swarm plot with hue
sns.catplot(data=tips, x='day', y='tip', hue='sex', kind='swarm')

# Show the plot
plt.show()
```

In the following box plot (Figure 15.38), boxes are colored based on the customer's gender, comparing the distribution of total bill amounts for lunch and dinner between males and females.

```
# Create a box plot with hue
sns.catplot(data=tips, x='time', y='total_bill', hue='sex', kind='box')
```

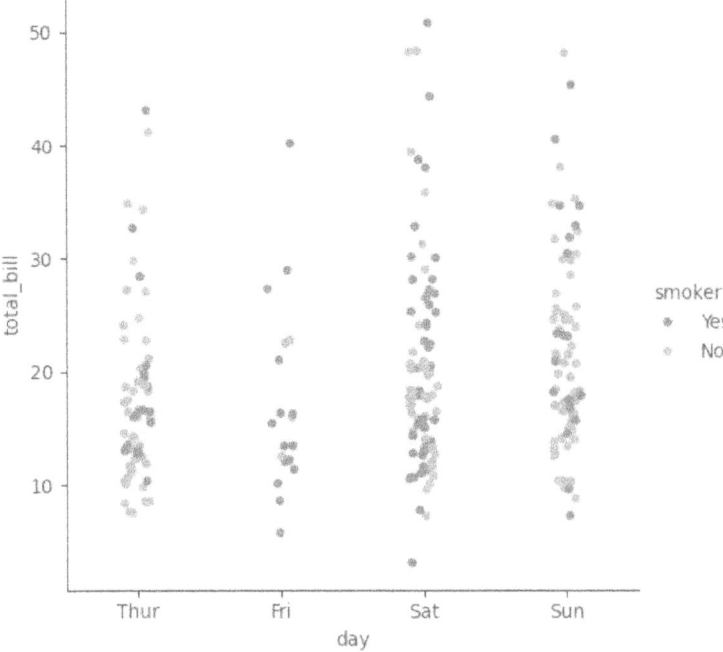

Figure 15.36 A strip plot of total bill over day, with color differentiating categories.

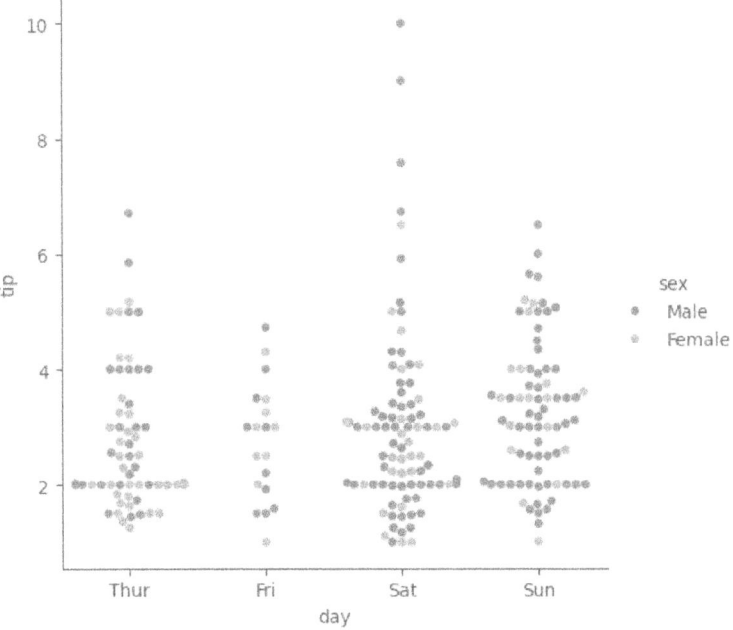

Figure 15.37 A strip plot of tip over day, with color differentiating categories.

```
# Show the plot
plt.show()
```

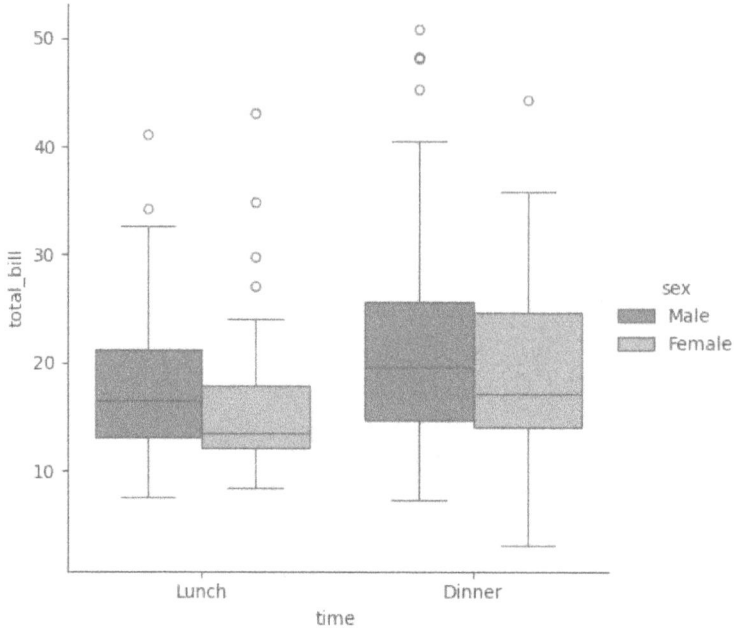

Figure 15.38 A box plot of total bill over time, with color differentiating categories.

In the following violin plot (Figure 15.39), distributions are colored based on the customer's gender, showing the density of tips for lunch and dinner between males and females.

```
# Create a violin plot with hue
sns.catplot(data=tips, x='time', y='tip', hue='sex', kind='violin')

# Show the plot
plt.show()
```

A standard violin plot is symmetric. If you'd like keep half of the violin to save space, you can utilize the **split** parameter to create a compact violin plot (Figure 15.40).

```
# Create a violin plot with hue and make the split as True
sns.catplot(data=tips, x='time', y='tip',
            hue='sex', kind='violin', split=True)

# Show the plot
plt.show()
```

In the following bar plot (Figure 15.41), bars are colored based on the customer's gender, comparing the average total bill amounts across different days between males and females.

```
# Create a bar plot with hue
sns.catplot(data=tips, x='day', y='total_bill', hue='sex', kind='bar')
```

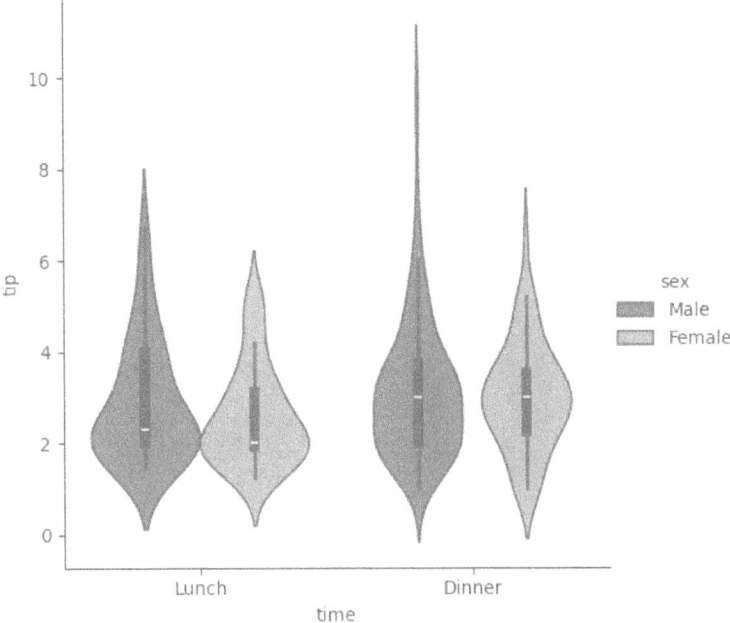

Figure 15.39 A violin plot of tip over time, with color differentiating categories.

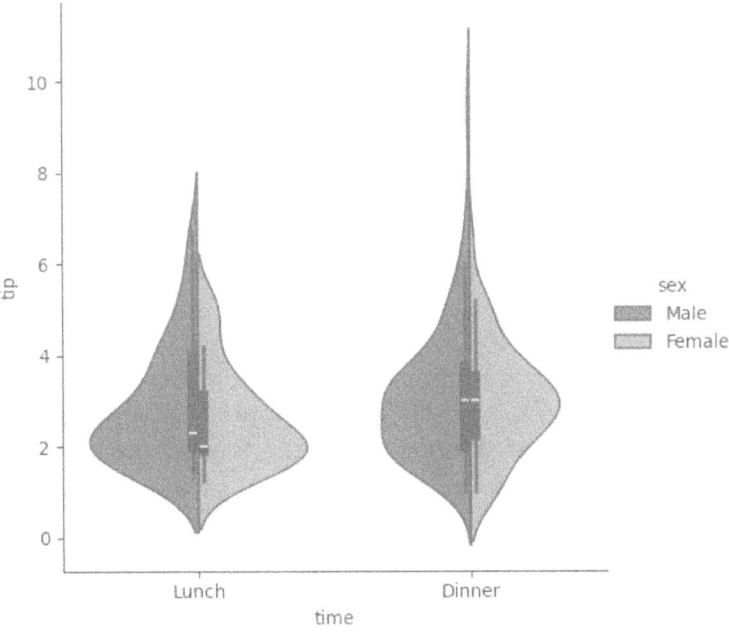

Figure 15.40 A compact violin plot of tip over time, with color differentiating categories.

```
# Show the plot
plt.show()
```

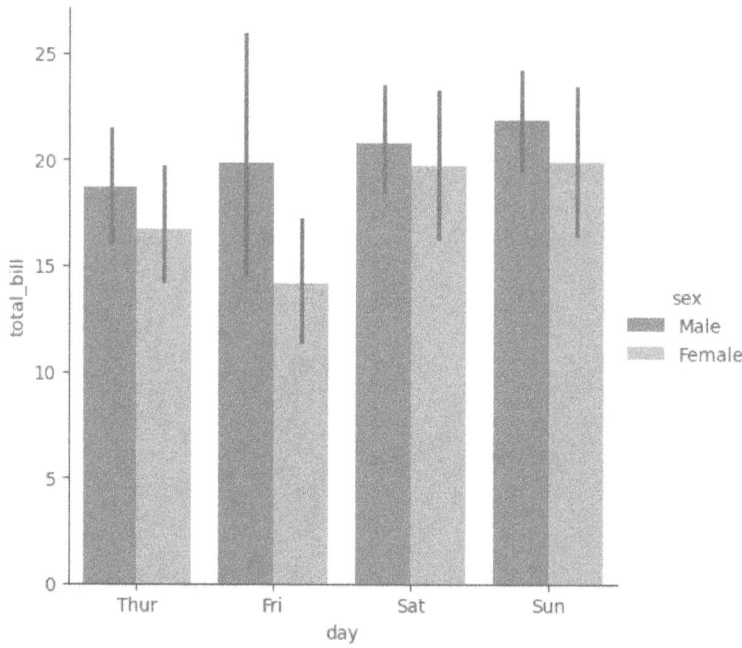

Figure 15.41 A bar plot of total bill over day, with color differentiating categories.

In the following point plot (Figure 15.42), points and lines are colored based on whether the customer is a smoker, visualizing the average tip amounts across different days for smokers and non-smokers.

```python
# Create a point plot with hue
sns.catplot(data=tips, x='day', y='tip', hue='smoker', kind='point')

# Show the plot
plt.show()
```

15.5.2 Practice

Here are some practice problems to help you understand and apply the **hue** parameter in Seaborn. we'll use different attributes from the 'tips' dataset that were not used in the previous demonstrations.

Task: Create a scatter plot (Figure 15.43) to visualize the relationship between 'total_bill' and 'tip', with points colored based on the 'day' attribute.

```python
# Create a scatter plot with hue based on day
sns.relplot(data=tips, x='total_bill', y='tip', hue='day', kind='scatter')

# Show the plot
plt.show()
```

Task: Create a KDE plot (Figure 15.44) to visualize the distribution of 'total_bill', with lines colored based on the 'time' attribute.

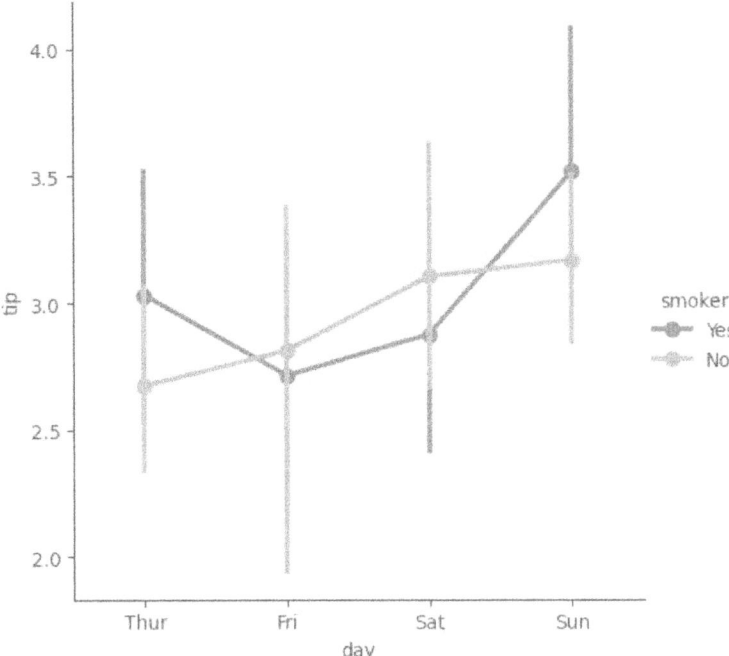

Figure 15.42 A point plot of tip over day, with color differentiating categories.

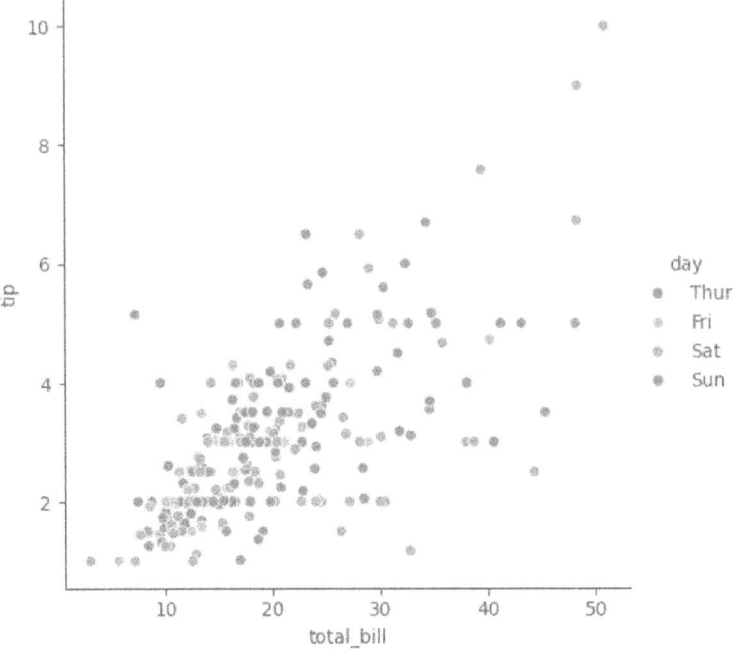

Figure 15.43 A scatter plot of tip and total bill, with color differentiating categories.

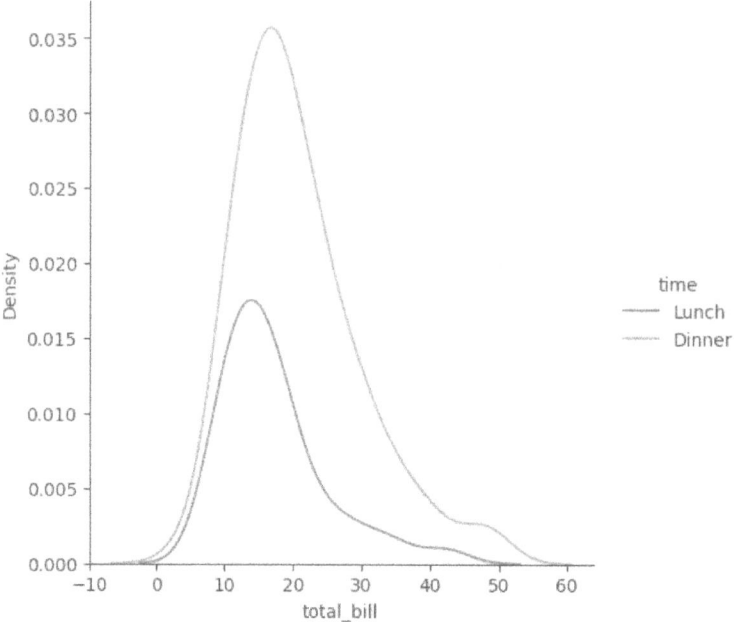

Figure 15.44 A KDE plot of total bill, with color differentiating categories.

```
# Create a KDE plot with hue based on time
sns.displot(data=tips, x='total_bill', hue='time', kind='kde')

# Show the plot
plt.show()
```

Task: Create an ECDF plot (Figure 15.45) to visualize the cumulative distribution of 'tip', with lines colored based on the 'sex' attribute.

```
# Create an ECDF plot with hue based on sex
sns.displot(data=tips, x='tip', hue='sex', kind='ecdf')

# Show the plot
plt.show()
```

Task: Create a violin plot (Figure 15.46) to visualize the distribution of 'total_bill', with sections colored based on the 'smoker' attribute.

```
# Create a violin plot with hue based on smoker status
sns.catplot(data=tips, x='day', y='total_bill',
            hue='smoker', kind='violin')

# Show the plot
plt.show()
```

Task: Create a bar plot (Figure 15.47) to visualize the average 'tip' amounts for each day, with bars colored based on the 'time' attribute.

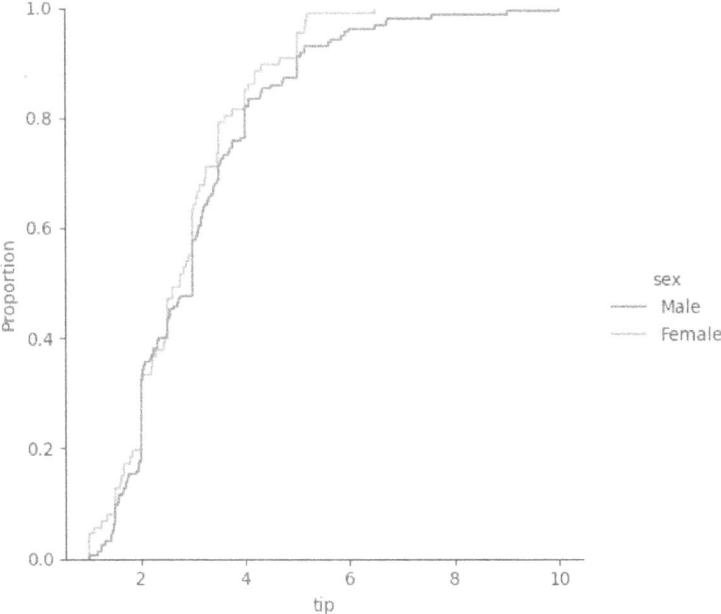

Figure 15.45 An ECDF plot of tip, with color differentiating categories.

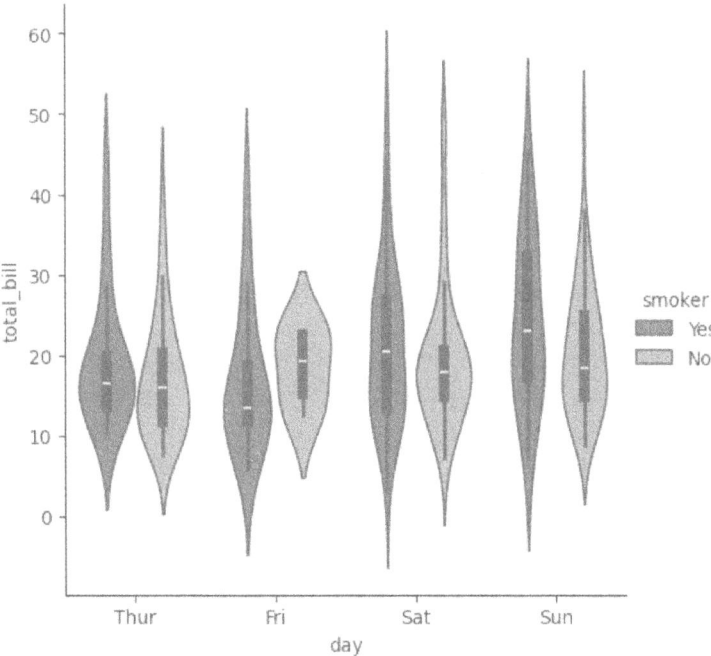

Figure 15.46 A violin plot of total bill over day, with color differentiating categories.

```
# Create a bar plot with hue based on time
sns.catplot(data=tips, x='day', y='tip', hue='time', kind='bar')
```

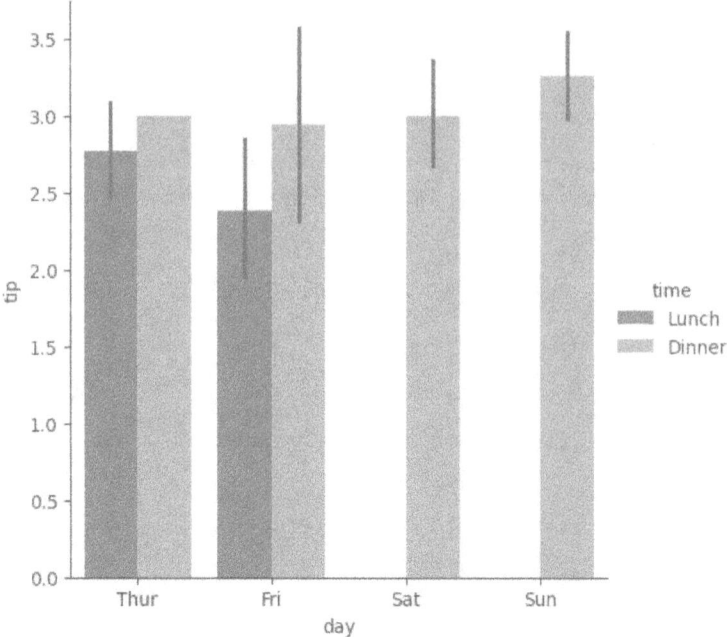

Figure 15.47 A bar plot of tip over day, with color differentiating categories.

```
# Show the plot
plt.show()
```

Task: Create a point plot (Figure 15.48) to visualize the average 'total_bill' amounts for each party size, with points colored based on the 'smoker' attribute.

```
# Create a point plot with hue based on smoker status
sns.catplot(data=tips, x='size', y='total_bill',
            hue='smoker', kind='point')

# Show the plot
plt.show()
```

15.6   MORE STYLES

15.6.1   Demonstration

In Seaborn, the `style` and `size` parameters add more dimensions to your visualizations by differentiating data points with varying marker styles and sizes. This can help make your plots more informative and easier to interpret.

In the following scatter plot (Figure 15.49):

- `hue='smoker'`: Colors the data points based on whether the customer is a smoker.
- `style='sex'`: Differentiates the data points with different marker styles based on the customer's gender.

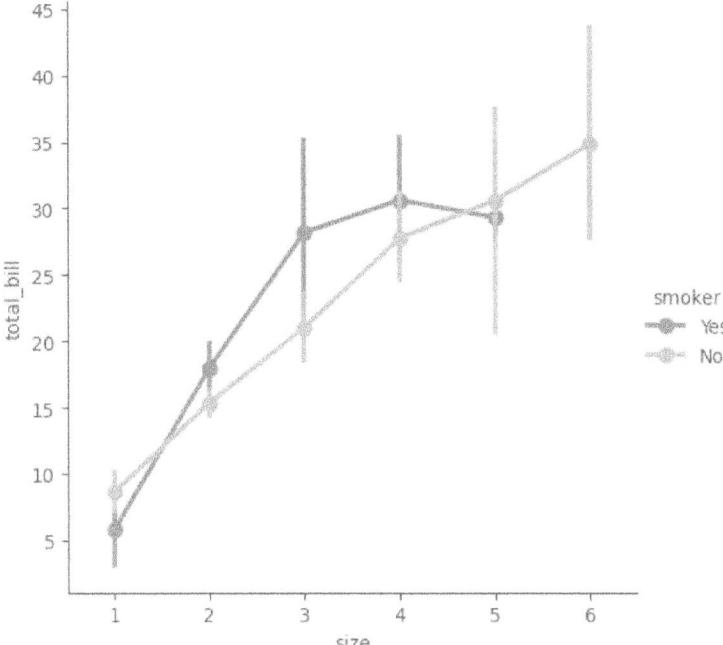

Figure 15.48 A point plot of total bill over size, with color differentiating categories.

- `size='size'`: Varies the size of the data points based on the party size.

```
# Create a scatter plot with style and size
sns.relplot(data=tips, x='total_bill', y='tip',
           hue='smoker', style='sex', size='size', kind='scatter')

# Show the plot
plt.show()
```

In the following line plot (Figure 15.50):

- `hue='sex'`: Colors the lines based on the customer's gender.
- `style='smoker'`: Differentiates the lines with different styles based on whether the customer is a smoker.
- `markers=True`: Adds markers to the lines.
- `dashes=False`: Uses solid lines for all categories.

```
# Create a line plot with style
sns.relplot(data=tips, x='size', y='total_bill',
           hue='sex', style='smoker', kind='line')

# Show the plot
plt.show()
```

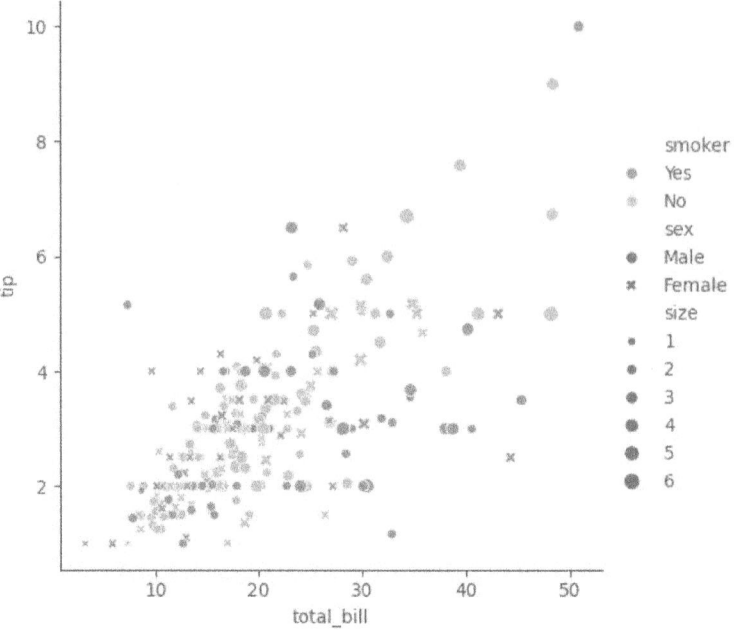

Figure 15.49 A scatter plot of total bill and tip, with both style and size variations.

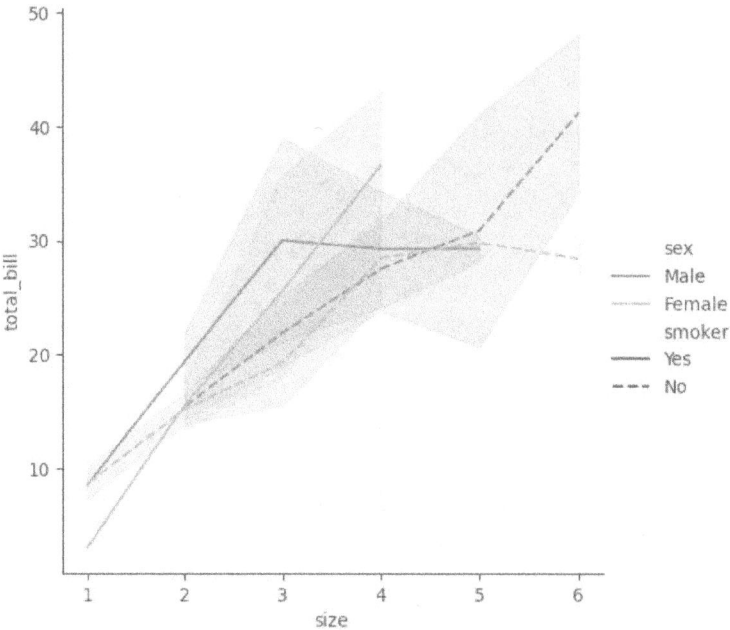

Figure 15.50 A line plot of total bill and size, with different line styles.

15.6.2   Practice

Here are some practice problems to help you understand and apply the `style` and `size` parameters in Seaborn using the 'tips' dataset.

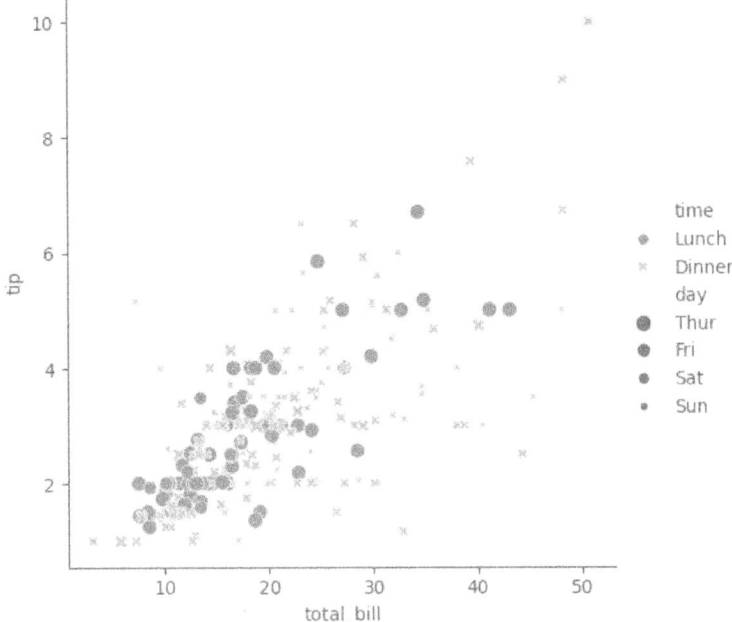

Figure 15.51 A scatter plot of total bill and tip, with both style and size variations.

Task: Create a scatter plot (Figure 15.51) to visualize the relationship between `total_bill` and `tip`, using different marker styles based on the `time` of day and varying the marker sizes based on the `day` of the week.

```
# Create a scatter plot with style and size
sns.relplot(data=tips, x='total_bill', y='tip',
            hue='time', style='time',
            size='day', kind='scatter')

# Show the plot
plt.show()
```

Task: Create a line plot (Figure 15.52) to visualize the relationship between `size` of the party and `total_bill`, using different line styles based on the `smoker` status.

```
# Create a line plot with style
sns.relplot(data=tips, x='size', y='total_bill',
            hue='smoker', style='smoker',
            kind='line', markers=True, dashes=True)

# Show the plot
plt.show()
```

Task: Create a scatter plot (Figure 15.53) to visualize the relationship between `tip` and `size` of the party, using different marker styles based on `sex` and varying the marker sizes based on `total_bill`.

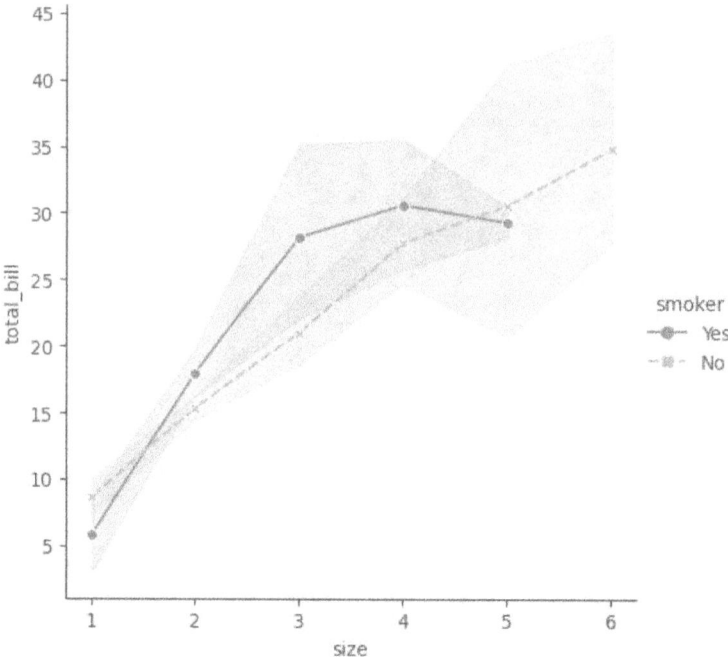

Figure 15.52 A line plot of total bill and size, with different line styles.

```
# Create a scatter plot with style and size
sns.relplot(data=tips, x='tip', y='size',
            hue='sex', style='sex',
            size='total_bill', kind='scatter')

# Show the plot
plt.show()
```

15.7 FACET GRIDS

15.7.1 Demonstration

Facet grids are a powerful feature in Seaborn that allow you to create multiple subplots based on the values of one or more categorical variables. This helps in visualizing complex datasets by breaking down the data into smaller, more manageable plots, making it easier to identify patterns and relationships within subsets of the data.

In Seaborn, facet grids can be created using the `FacetGrid` class or higher-level functions like `relplot()`, `catplot()`, and `displot()`.

The `relplot()` function can create scatter and line plots with facet grids. we'll demonstrate a scatter plot with facets based on `smoker` and `time`.

In the following scatter plot (Figure 15.54):

- `col='smoker'`: Creates separate columns for smokers and non-smokers.

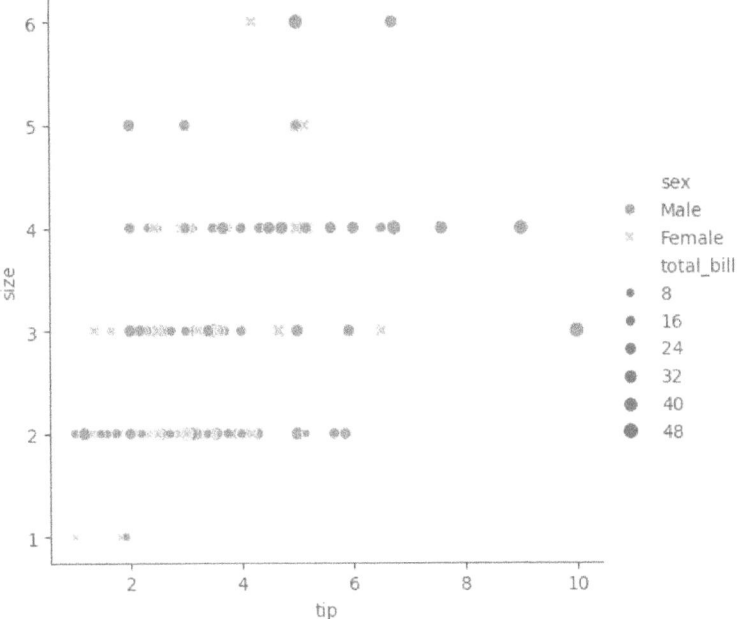

Figure 15.53 A scatter plot of size and tip, with style and size variations.

- row='time': Creates separate rows for lunch and dinner.
- hue='sex': Colors the data points based on the customer's gender.

```
# Create a scatter plot with facets based on smoker and time
sns.relplot(data=tips, x='total_bill', y='tip',
            col='smoker', row='time',
            hue='sex', kind='scatter')

# Show the plot
plt.show()
```

The displot() function can create histograms, KDE plots, and ECDF plots with facet grids. we'll demonstrate a histogram with facets based on smoker.

In the following histogram (Figure 15.55):

- col='smoker': Creates separate columns for smokers and non-smokers.
- kde=True: Adds a KDE plot on top of the histograms.

```
# Create a histogram with facets based on day
sns.displot(data=tips, x='total_bill', col='smoker', kde=True)

# Show the plot
plt.show()
```

The catplot() function can create various types of categorical plots with facet grids. we'll demonstrate a box plot with facets based on time. In the following box plot (Figure 15.56):

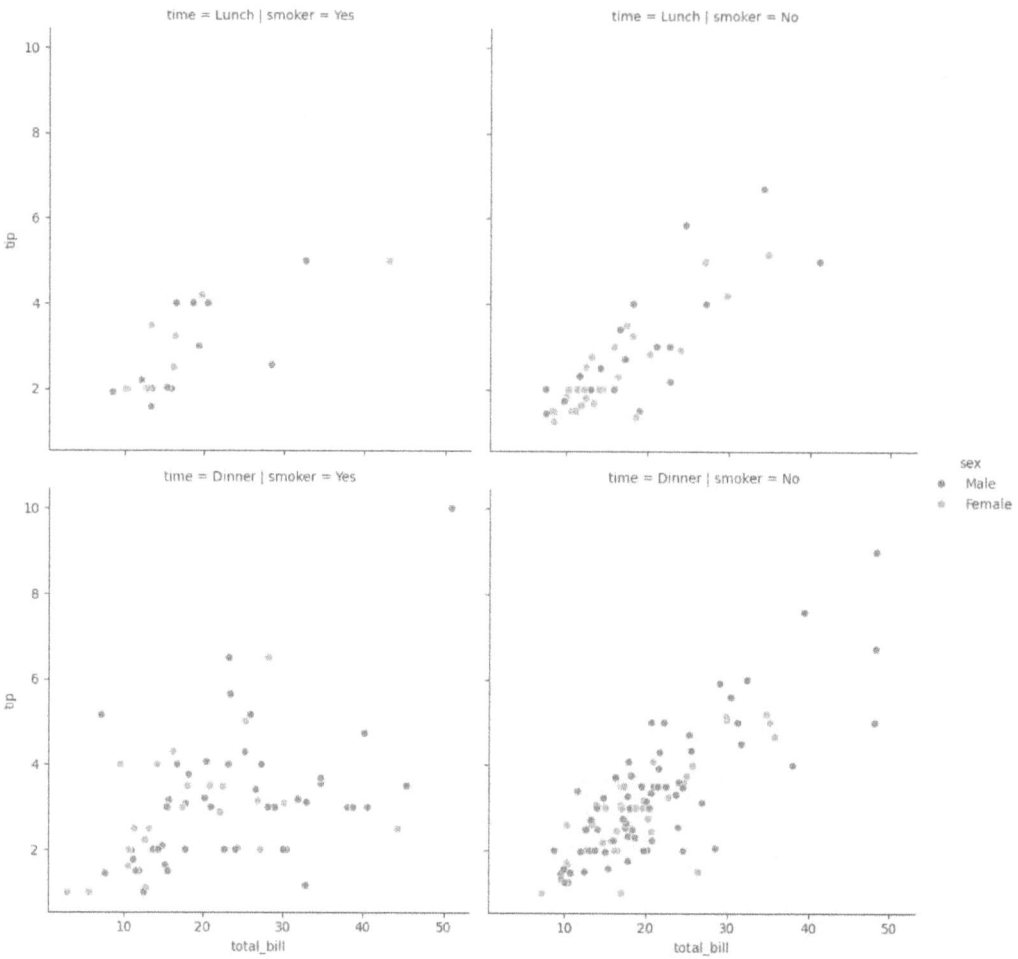

Figure 15.54 A scatter plot with data points grouped by smoker status and time.

- `col='time'`: Creates separate columns for lunch and dinner.
- `x='day'`: Shows the distribution of `total_bill` for each day of the week.
- `kind='box'`: Specifies the type of plot as a box plot.

```python
# Create a box plot with facets based on time
sns.catplot(data=tips, x='day', y='total_bill', col='time', kind='box')

# Show the plot
plt.show()
```

15.7.2 Practice

Here are some practice problems to help you understand and apply facet grids in Seaborn using the 'tips' dataset. These problems use different attributes that were not used in the demonstrations.

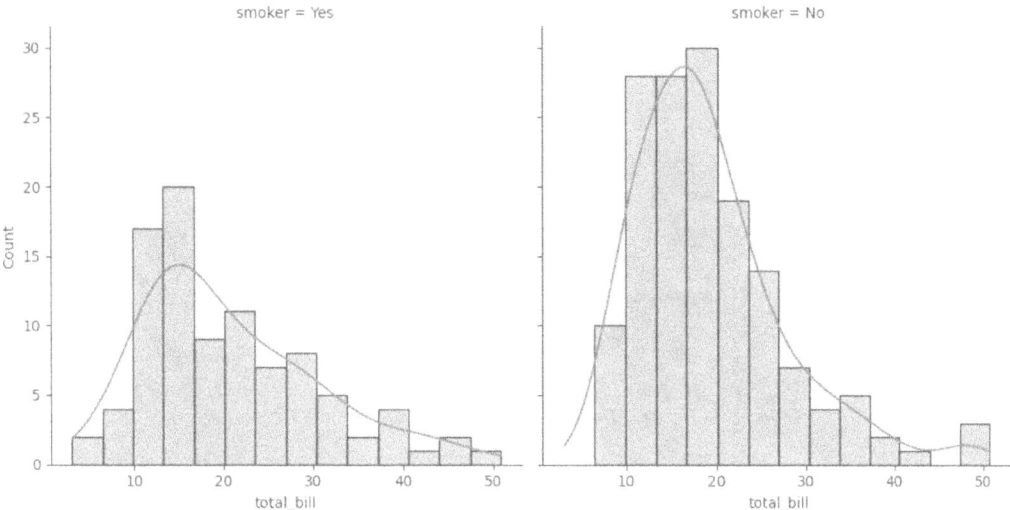

Figure 15.55 A histogram with data distribution separated by day.

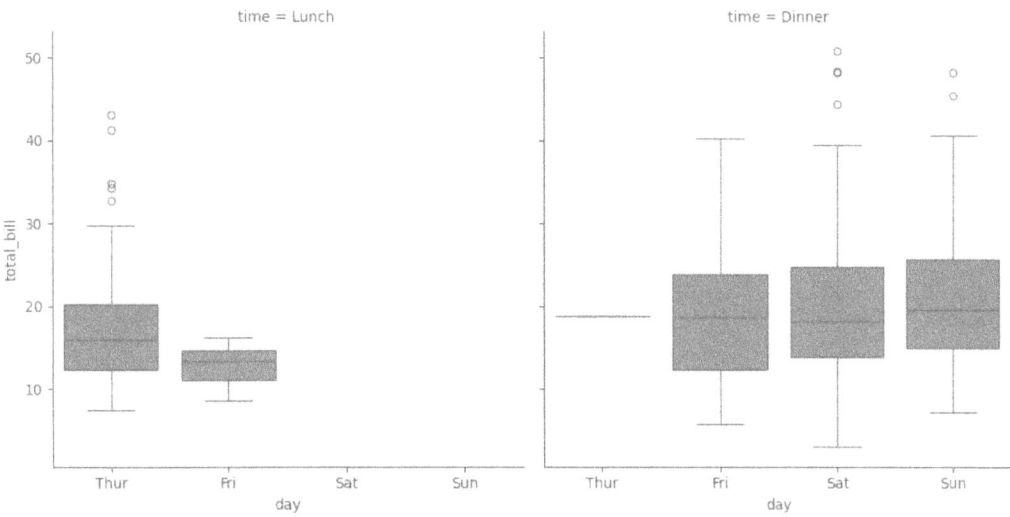

Figure 15.56 A box plot showing data distribution grouped by time.

Task: Create a scatter plot (Figure 15.57) to visualize the relationship between `total_bill` and `tip`, using separate facets for each `day` of the week and differentiating the data points by `time`.

```python
# Create a scatter plot with facets based on day and time
sns.relplot(data=tips, x='total_bill', y='tip',
            col='day', hue='time', kind='scatter')

# Show the plot
plt.show()
```

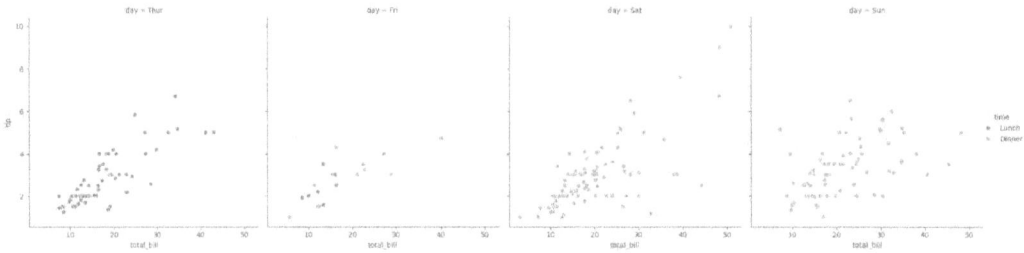

Figure 15.57 A scatter plot with data points arranged in facets based on day and time.

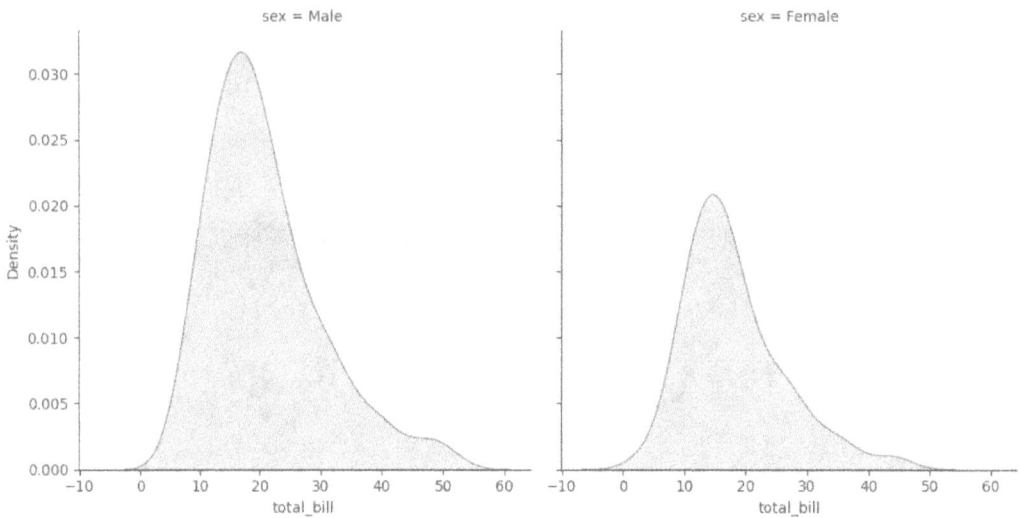

Figure 15.58 A kernel density estimation (KDE) plot with data separated by gender.

Task: Create a KDE plot (Figure 15.58) to visualize the distribution of `total_bill`, using separate facets for each `sex` and adding the KDE plot for each subset.

```
# Create a KDE plot with facets based on sex
sns.displot(data=tips, x='total_bill', col='sex', kind='kde', fill=True)

# Show the plot
plt.show()
```

Task: Create a bar plot (Figure 15.59) to visualize the average `total_bill` for each day, using separate facets for `time` and differentiating the bars by `smoker` status.

```
# Create a bar plot with facets based on time and smoker status
sns.catplot(data=tips, x='day', y='total_bill',
            col='time', hue='smoker', kind='bar')

# Show the plot
plt.show()
```

Task: Create a violin plot (Figure 15.60) to visualize the distribution of `tip` for each day, using separate facets for `smoker` status and `sex`.

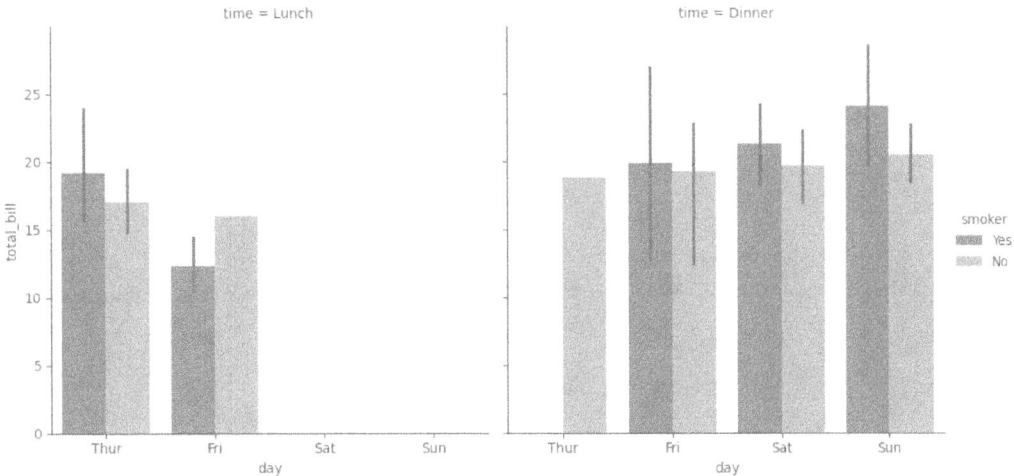

Figure 15.59 A bar plot with data categorized by time and smoker status.

```
# Create a violin plot with facets based on smoker status and sex
sns.catplot(data=tips, x='day', y='tip',
            col='smoker', row='sex', kind='violin')

# Show the plot
plt.show()
```

Task: Create a histogram (Figure 15.61) to visualize the distribution of `tip`, using separate facets for `time` and differentiating the bars by `day`.

```
# Create a histogram with facets based on time and day
sns.displot(data=tips, x='tip', col='time', hue='day', multiple='stack')

# Show the plot
plt.show()
```

15.8 LESSON: LMPLOT

15.8.1 Demonstration

`lmplot` is a powerful function in Seaborn designed for visualizing linear relationships between variables. It combines the capabilities of a scatter plot and a regression line plot, providing a simple and intuitive way to explore and understand relationships in your data. The `lmplot` function is particularly useful for performing linear regression analysis and visualizing the results.

Key Features of `lmplot`:

- **Scatter Plot with Regression Line**: Displays data points and fits a linear regression model, plotting the regression line.
- **Faceted Plots**: Easily create multiple plots based on subsets of the data.

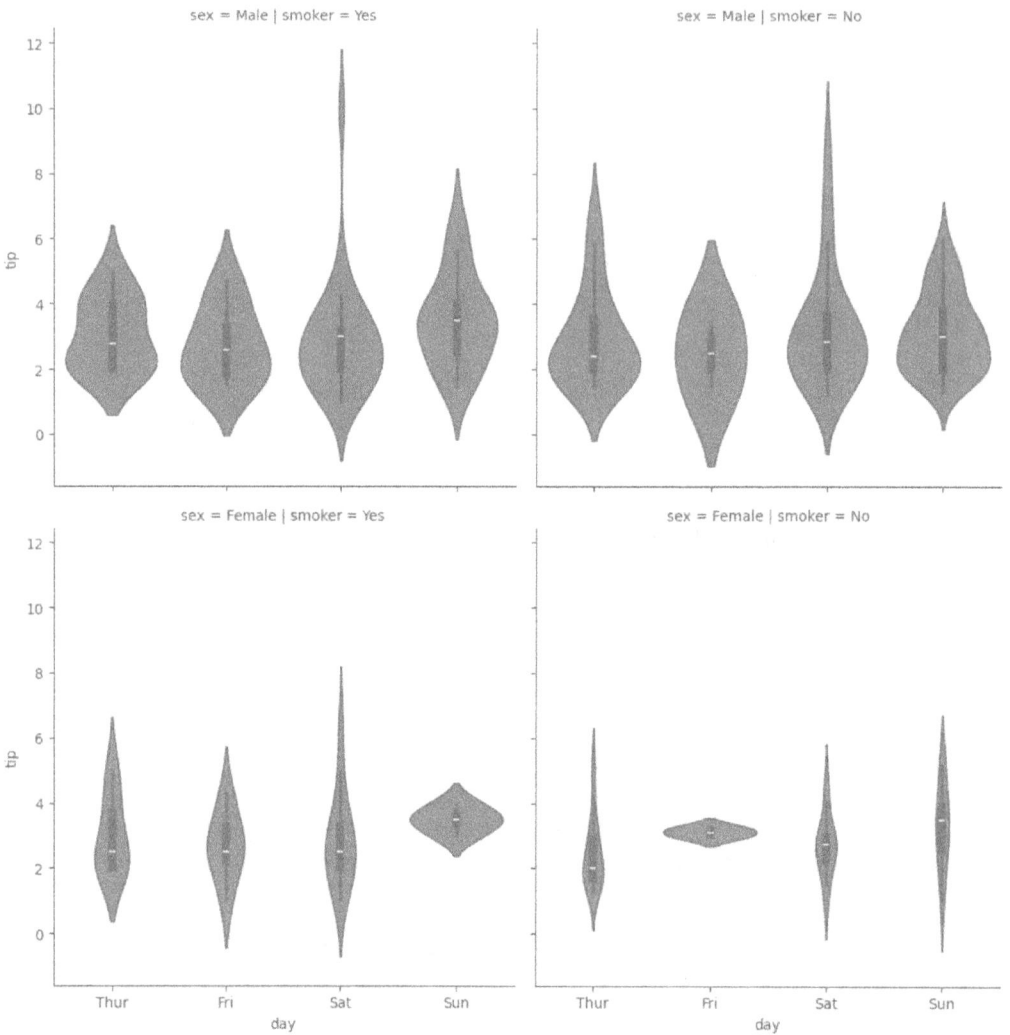

Figure 15.60 A violin plot with data distribution grouped by smoker status and gender.

- **Statistical Information**: Provides insights into the linear relationships and helps in understanding correlations.

The basic syntax of `lmplot` is:

```
sns.lmplot(data=dataset, x='x_variable', y='y_variable',
  hue='hue_variable', col='col_variable', row='row_variable')
```

- `data`: The dataset containing the variables to plot.
- `x`: Name of the variable for the x-axis.
- `y`: Name of the variable for the y-axis.
- `hue`: (Optional) Categorical variable that determines the color of the points and lines.

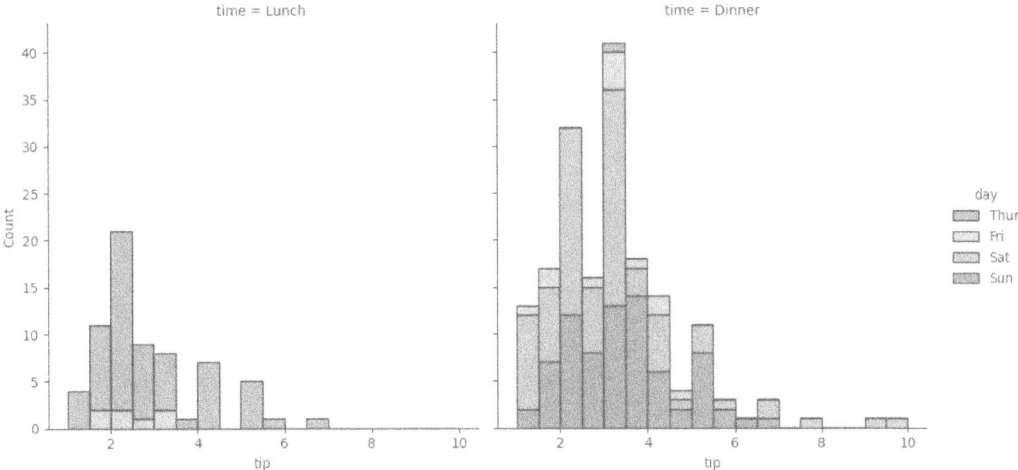

Figure 15.61   A histogram with data distribution grouped by time and day.

- col: (Optional) Categorical variable that creates separate plots for each category.
- row: (Optional) Categorical variable that creates separate plots for each category in rows.

Let's create a basic lmplot (Figure 15.62) to visualize the relationship between total_bill and tip.

```
# Create a basic lmplot
sns.lmplot(data=tips, x='total_bill', y='tip')

# Show the plot
plt.show()
```

We can use the hue parameter to differentiate data points by a categorical variable, such as sex (Figure 15.63).

```
# Create an lmplot with hue based on sex
sns.lmplot(data=tips, x='total_bill', y='tip', hue='sex')

# Show the plot
plt.show()
```

We can also use the col to create separate plots for each category of the smoker (Figure 15.64).

```
# Create an lmplot with facets based on smoker status
sns.lmplot(data=tips, x='total_bill', y='tip', col='smoker')

# Show the plot
plt.show()
```

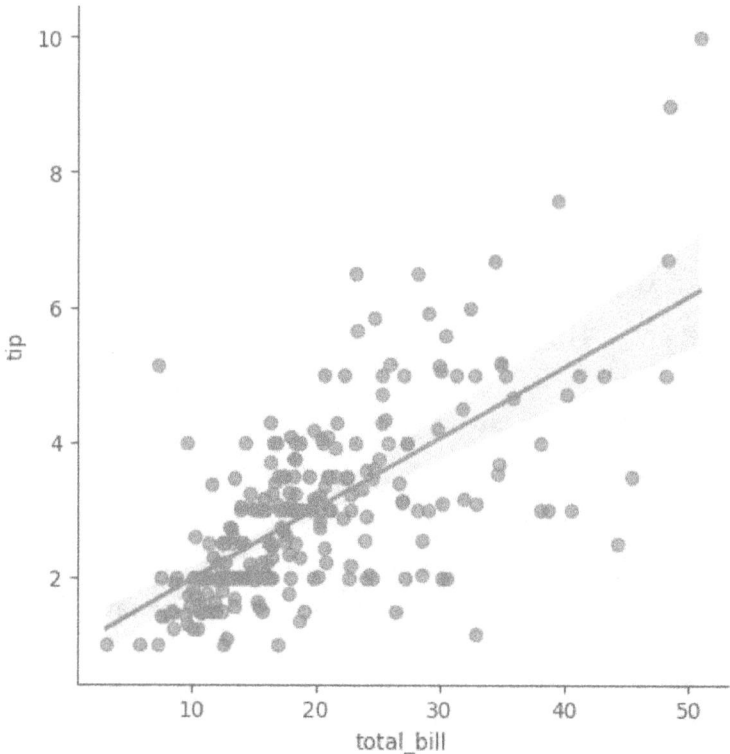

Figure 15.62 A basic linear model plot.

We can use both `col` and `row` to create a grid of plots for `smoker` and `time` (Figure 15.65).

```python
# Create an lmplot with multiple facets based on smoker status and time
sns.lmplot(data=tips, x='total_bill', y='tip',
           col='smoker', row='time')

# Show the plot
plt.show()
```

15.8.2 Practice

The `lmplot` function in Seaborn is used to create linear regression plots. It allows you to visualize the linear relationship between two variables, along with confidence intervals and various customizations. Here are some practice problems to help you understand and apply `lmplot` using the 'tips' dataset with different attributes.

Task: Create a linear regression plot (Figure 15.66) to visualize the relationship between `size` and `tip`.

```python
# Create a simple linear regression plot
sns.lmplot(data=tips, x='size', y='tip')
```

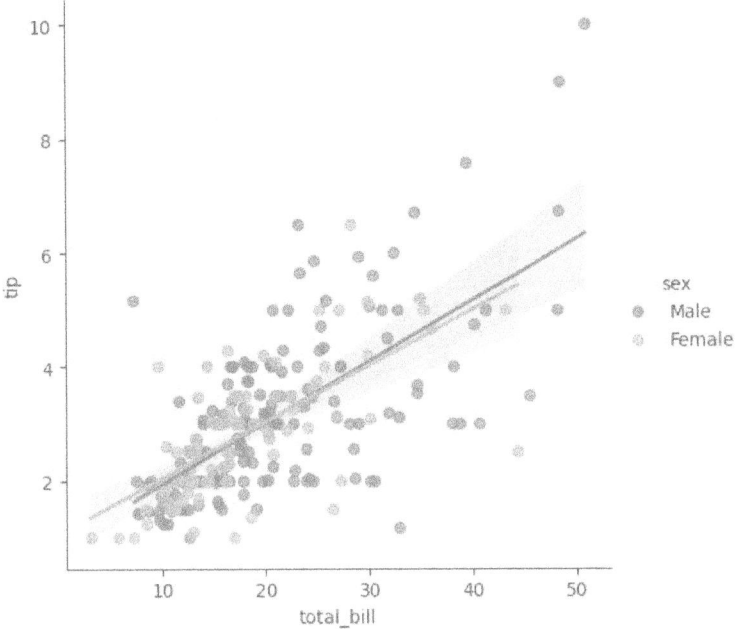

Figure 15.63 A linear model plot with color differentiating categories by gender.

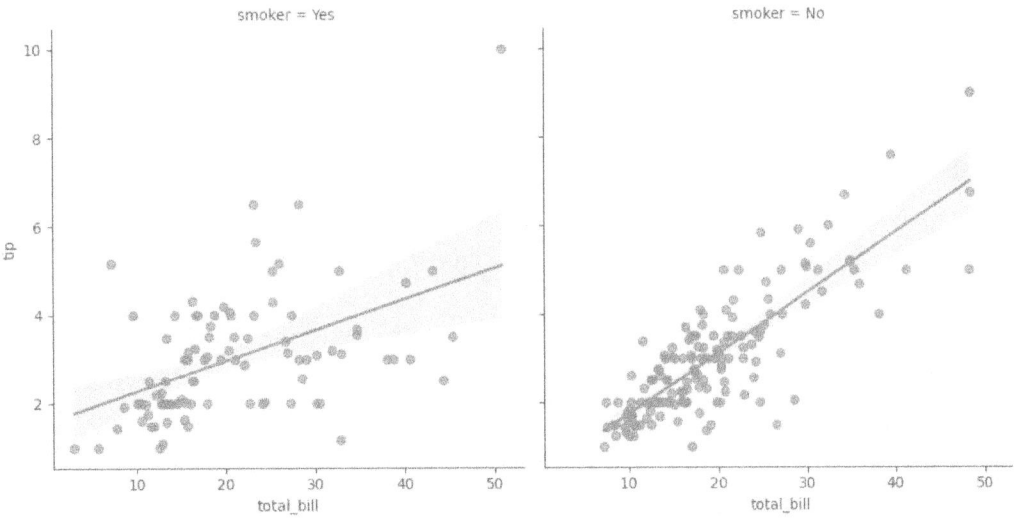

Figure 15.64 A linear model plot with data separated by smoker status.

```
# Show the plot
plt.show()
```

Task: Create a linear regression plot (Figure 15.67) to visualize the relationship between `size` and `tip`, differentiating the data points by `sex`.

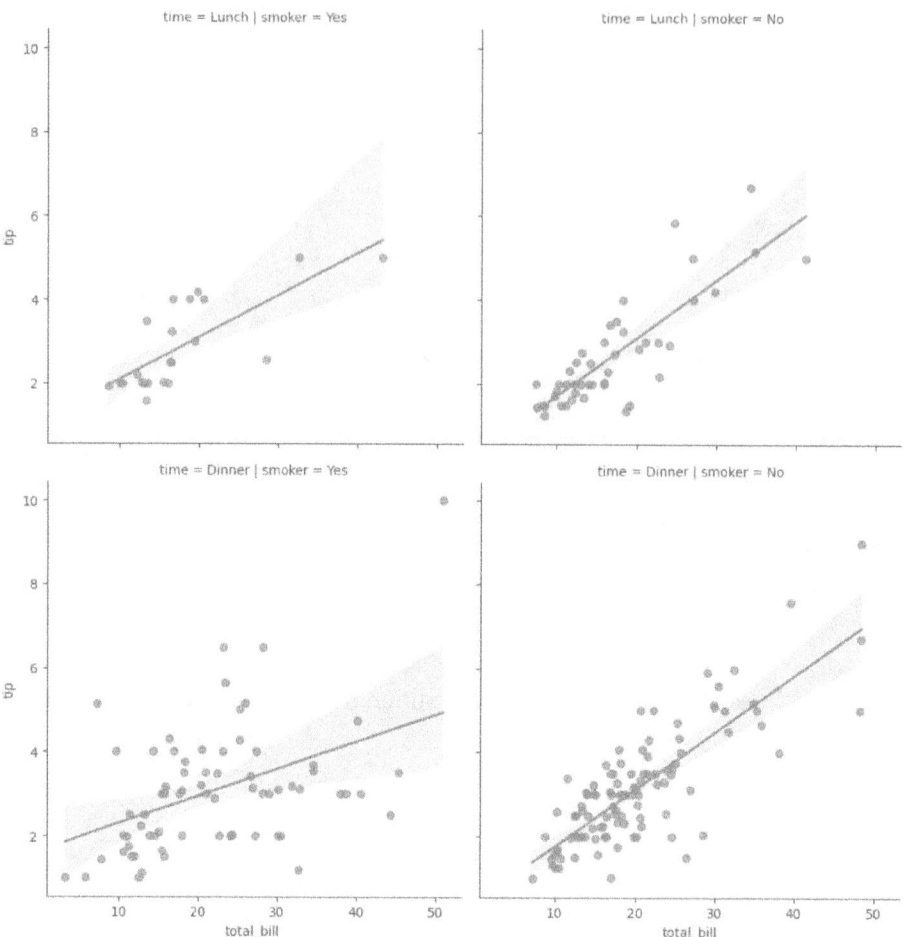

Figure 15.65 A linear model plot with data faceted by smoker status and time.

```
# Create a linear regression plot with hue based on sex
sns.lmplot(data=tips, x='size', y='tip', hue='sex')

# Show the plot
plt.show()
```

Task: Create a linear regression plot (Figure 15.68) to visualize the relationship between `size` and `tip`, using separate facets for each `time` of day.

```
# Create a linear regression plot with facets based on time
sns.lmplot(data=tips, x='size', y='tip', col='time')

# Show the plot
plt.show()
```

Task: Create a linear regression plot (Figure 15.69) to visualize the relationship between `size` and `tip`, using separate facets for each `day` of the week and differentiating the data points by `smoker` status.

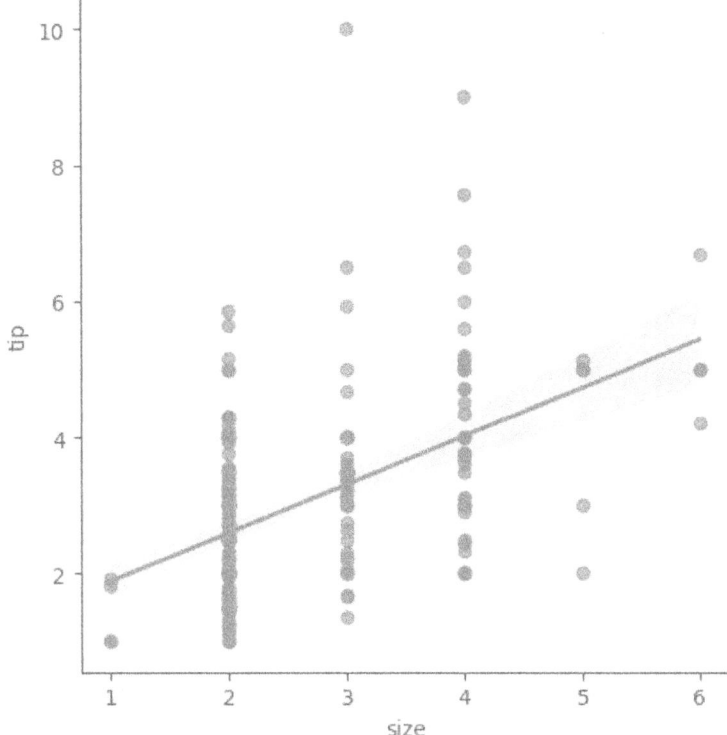

Figure 15.66 A simple linear model plot.

```
# Create a linear regression plot with multiple facets
sns.lmplot(data=tips, x='size', y='tip', col='day', hue='smoker')

# Show the plot
plt.show()
```

Task: Create a linear regression plot (Figure 15.70) to visualize the relationship between **size** and **tip**, fitting a second-order polynomial regression.

```
# Create a linear regression plot with polynomial order 2
sns.lmplot(data=tips, x='size', y='tip', order=2)

# Show the plot
plt.show()
```

15.9 MULTIPLE PLOTS

15.9.1 Demonstration

Multiplots in Seaborn are powerful tools for visualizing relationships between multiple variables in a dataset. They help in identifying patterns, correlations, and distributions in a comprehensive manner. In this section, we will introduce two key multiplot functions: `pairplot` and `jointplot`.

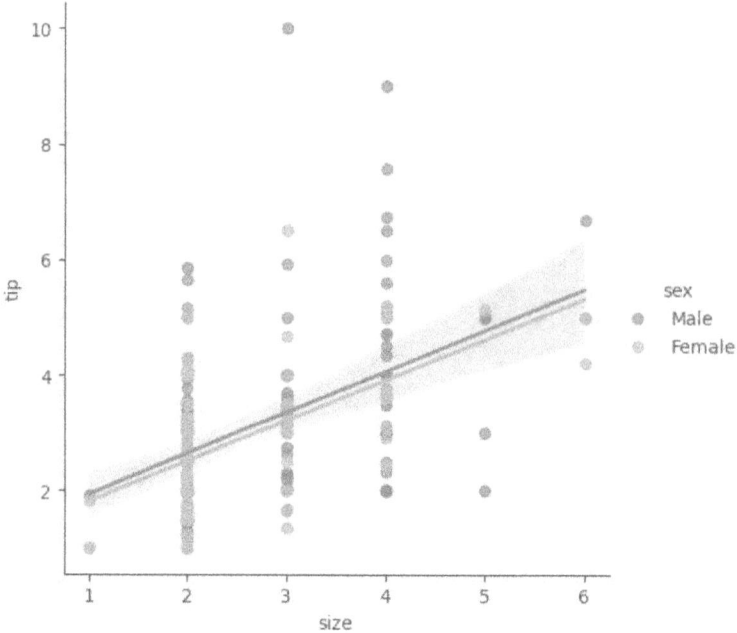

Figure 15.67 A linear model plot with color differentiating categories by gender.

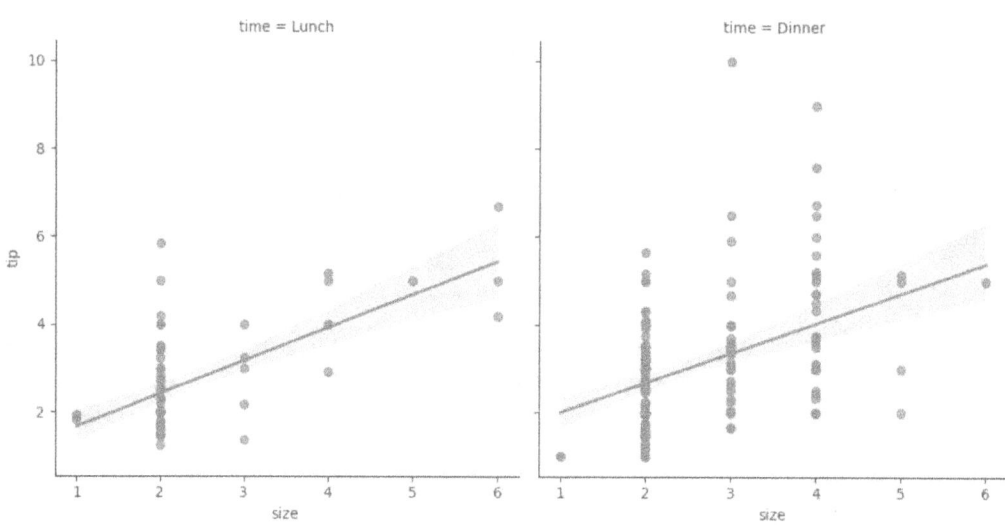

Figure 15.68 A linear model plot with data faceted by time.

The `pairplot` function creates a grid of plots, where each variable in the dataset is plotted against each other. It helps in visualizing the pairwise relationships and the distribution of each variable (Figure 15.71).

```
# Create a pairplot with hue based on the 'sex' attribute
sns.pairplot(tips, hue='sex')
```

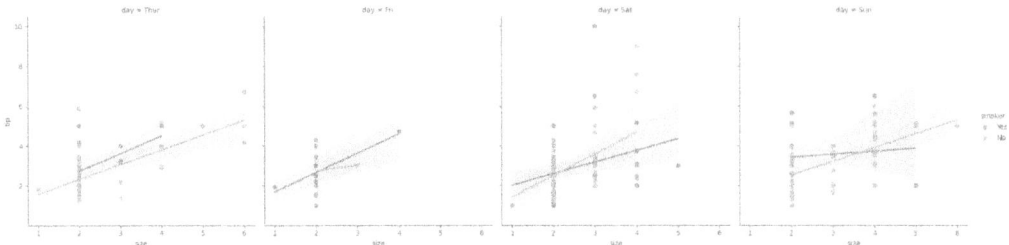

Figure 15.69 A linear model plot with multiple facets for different categories.

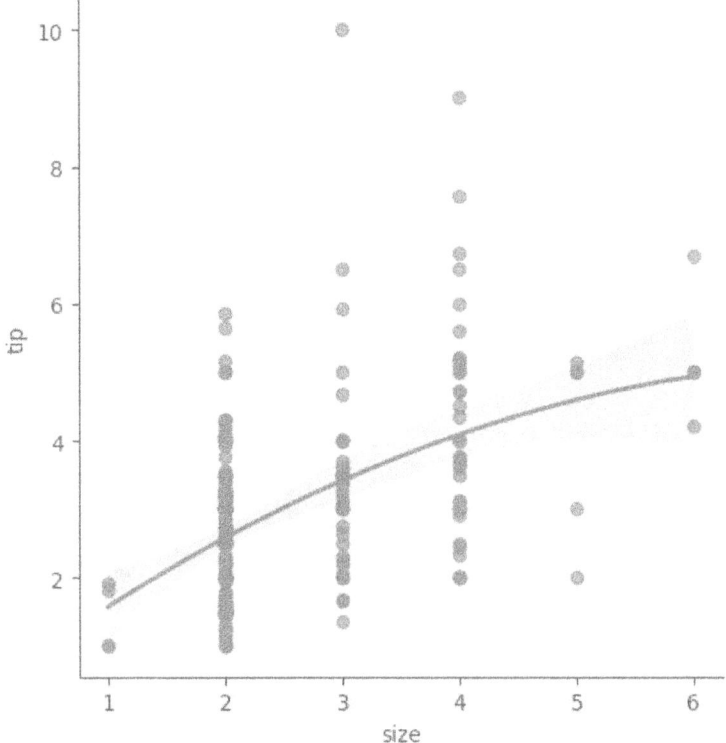

Figure 15.70 A linear model plot with a polynomial curve of order 2.

```
# Show the plot
plt.show()
```

The jointplot function creates a bivariate plot with marginal histograms or density plots. It helps in visualizing the relationship between two variables, along with their individual distributions (Figure 15.72).

```
# Create a jointplot for the relationship between 'total_bill' and 'tip'
sns.jointplot(x='total_bill', y='tip', data=tips, kind='scatter')

# Show the plot
plt.show()
```

We can do color differentiation using the `hue` in `pairplot` (Figure 15.73):

```python
# Create a pairplot with regression lines and hue based on 'sex'
sns.pairplot(tips, hue='sex', kind='reg')

# Show the plot
plt.show()
```

We can create a KDE `jointplot` using `kind='kde'` (Figure 15.74):

```python
# Show the relationship between 'total_bill' and 'tip' with KDE
sns.jointplot(x='total_bill', y='tip', data=tips, kind='kde')

# Show the plot
plt.show()
```

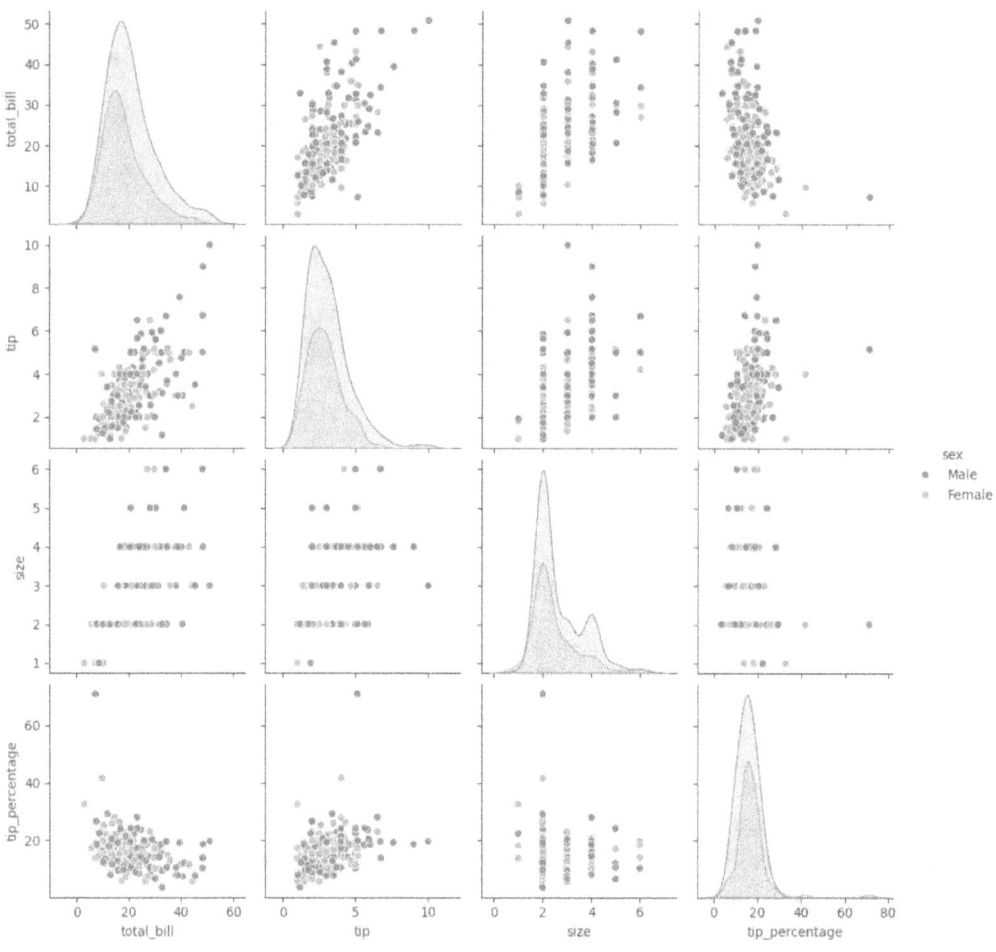

Figure 15.71 A pair plot showing relationships between multiple variables, with color for gender.

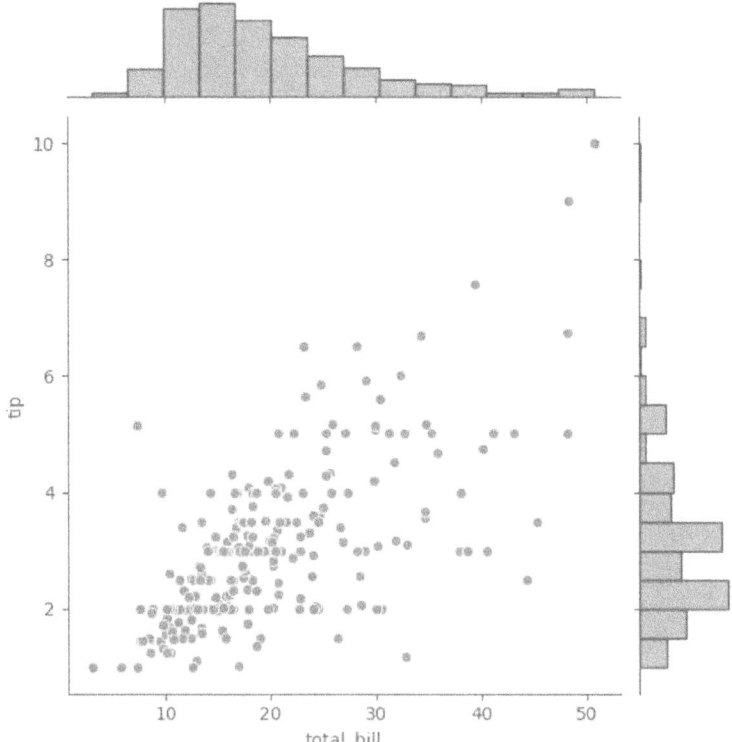

Figure 15.72 A joint plot showing the relationship between total bill and tip.

While we can create various plots using the `kind` parameter in the general plots, we can also create specific plots directly with different control over them. We summarize these specific plots in Table 15.1.

15.10 INTERACT WITH GENAI

Here are some questions and prompts you can interact with generative AI tools, including ChatGPT.

- Why is Seaborn considered a high-level data visualization library?
- What types of plots are commonly used in Seaborn, and what are their purposes?
- How to customize Seaborn plots with themes like `darkgrid` or `whitegrid`?
- What is the main difference between a Matplotlib plot and a Seaborn plot?
- How do you use the `hue` parameter in Seaborn to add a dimension to your plot?
- Can Seaborn plots be customized further using Matplotlib? If so, how?
- How can you adjust the color palettes in Seaborn for better visual appeal?
- How can you use Seaborn to add confidence intervals to your visualizations?
- Show how to use Seaborn to identify outliers in numerical data.
- What should you do if a Seaborn plot appears difficult to interpret?

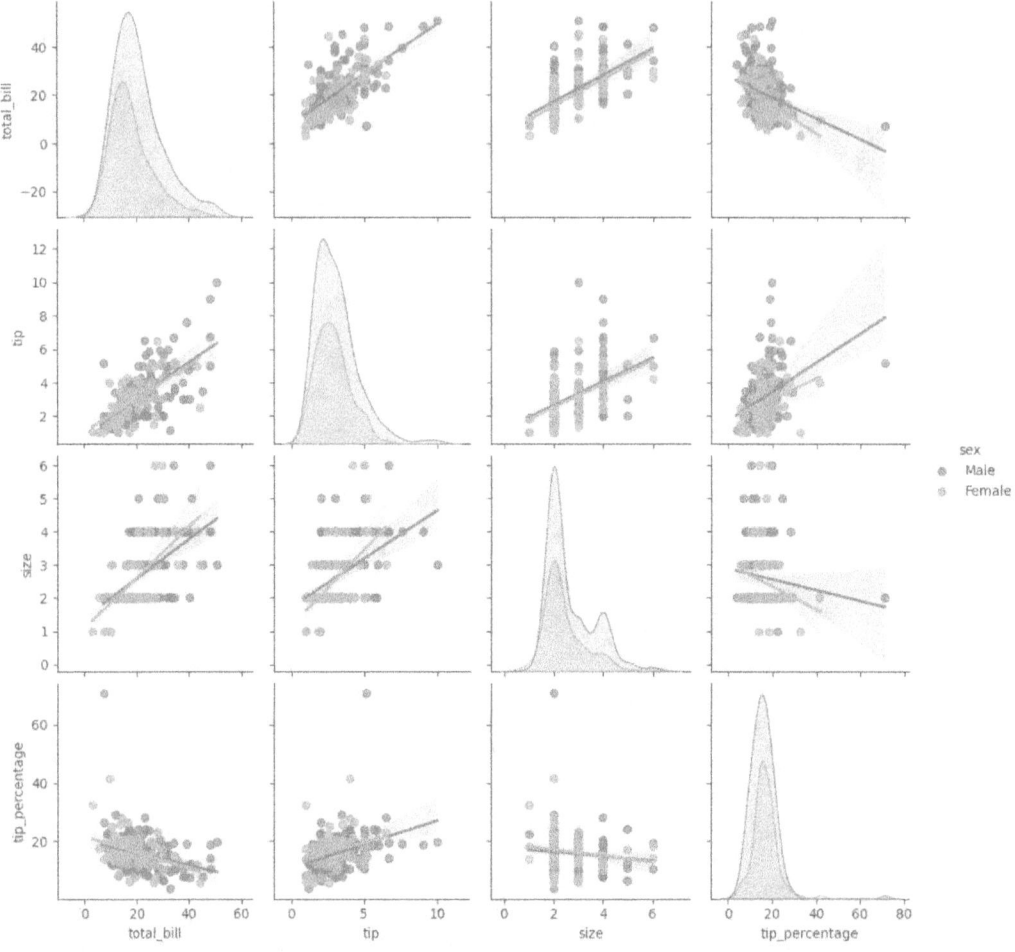

Figure 15.73 A pair plot with regression lines and color differentiating categories by gender.

15.11 EXPLORE MORE SEABORN

Here are the useful documentations you may refer to:

- Overview: https://seaborn.pydata.org/tutorial/function_overview.html
- Statistical relationships: https://seaborn.pydata.org/tutorial/relational.html
- Distributions of data: https://seaborn.pydata.org/tutorial/distributions.html
- Categorical data: https://seaborn.pydata.org/tutorial/categorical.html
- Estimating regression fits: https://seaborn.pydata.org/tutorial/regression.html
- Full API: https://seaborn.pydata.org/api.html

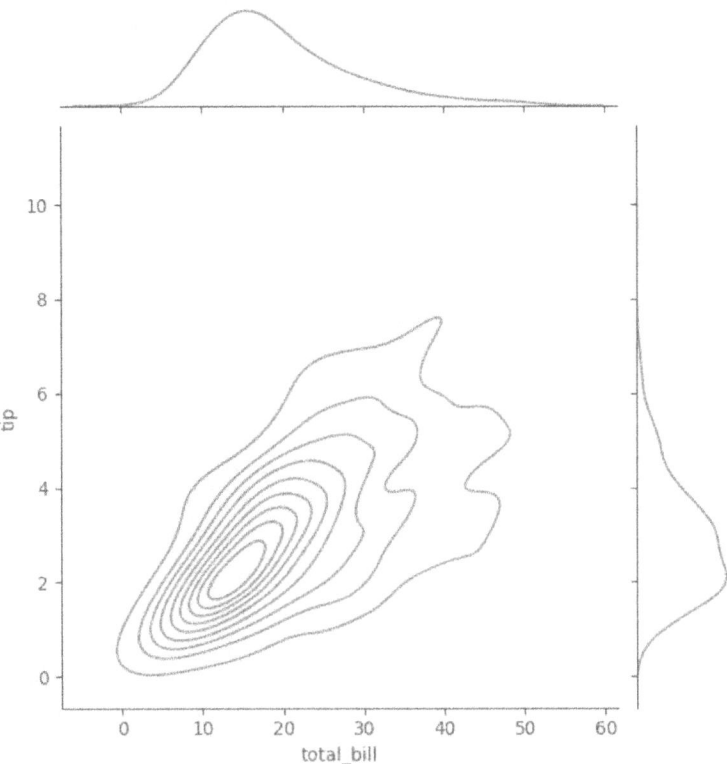

Figure 15.74 A joint plot illustrating the relationship between total bill and tip.

TABLE 15.1 Summary of Seaborn Specific Plot Types

Type	Basic Syntax	Scenario
Scatter	sns.scatterplot()	Shows the relationship between two variables. Example: Analyzing the relationship between advertising budget and sales.
Line	sns.lineplot()	Visualizes trends or changes over time. Example: Tracking monthly revenue over a year.
Bar	sns.barplot()	Compares categorical data with aggregated values. Example: Comparing average customer ratings across product categories.
Count	sns.countplot()	Counts occurrences of categorical data. Example: Counting the number of employees in each department.
Histogram	sns.histplot()	Shows the distribution of a dataset. Example: Visualizing the distribution of exam scores in a class.
KDE	sns.kdeplot()	Estimates the probability density of a continuous variable. Example: Understanding income distribution in a population.
Box	sns.boxplot()	Displays distribution and highlights outliers. Example: Comparing salaries across different job roles.
Violin	sns.violinplot()	Combines box plot and KDE to show distribution and probability. Example: Analyzing height distribution across different age groups.
Heatmap	sns.heatmap()	Visualizes correlation or matrix-like data. Example: Examining the correlation between different financial metrics.
LM	sns.lmplot()	Fits and visualizes linear regression models. Example: Modeling the relationship between study hours and exam scores.

## CHAPTER 16

Plotly

I N THIS CHAPTER, we'll take our data visualization skills to the next level with Plotly, a dynamic library that enables the creation of interactive visualizations. Building on our knowledge of Matplotlib and Seaborn, we'll explore how Plotly makes it easy to create engaging plots that allow users to zoom, pan, hover, and click for deeper insights. We'll cover a variety of plot types, from line and bar plots to more advanced visualizations like 3D plots. Are you ready? Let's get started!

16.1 OVERVIEW

Plotly is a powerful Python library used for creating interactive visualizations. Unlike static visualizations generated by Matplotlib and Seaborn, Plotly produces interactive plots that can be embedded in web applications or displayed in Jupyter notebooks. This interactivity makes it an excellent choice for data exploration and presentation, allowing users to zoom, hover, and click to reveal more details about the data.

Plotly is renowned for its interactive visualizations, which are ideal for dashboards, reports, and exploratory data analysis. Plotly provides a high-level interface for creating complex plots, similar to Seaborn, but with additional interactive capabilities. Plotly supports a broad range of chart types, from basic line and bar charts to more advanced visualizations like 3D surface plots. Plotly plots are based on JavaScript, making them easily embeddable in web applications. They can also be exported to static images if needed. Plotly allows for extensive customization of plots, enabling the creation of highly tailored visualizations.

If you are building dashboards or reports that require user interaction, Plotly is the go-to library. Plotly's interactive features make it ideal for EDA, allowing users to drill down into data points and uncover hidden patterns. When you need to embed plots into a web application, Plotly's JavaScript-based plots are also perfect for seamless integration.

We make a brief comparison for the three packages we learned in Table 16.1.

DOI: 10.1201/9781003624868-16

TABLE 16.1 Comparison of Matplotlib, Seaborn, and Plotly

Feature	Matplotlib	Seaborn	Plotly
Interactivity	Static	Static	Interactive
Ease of Use	Low-level API, more code required	High-level API, easier to create complex plots	High-level API with interactive features
Customization	Extensive	Extensive, built on top of Matplotlib	Extensive, with additional web integration
Range of Plots	Wide	Wide, focused on statistical plots	Very wide, including 3D and map plots
Performance	Good for small to medium datasets	Good for small to medium datasets	Can handle large datasets interactively
Best For	Detailed customization, publication-quality plots	Quick and aesthetically pleasing statistical visualizations	Interactive dashboards, data exploration

16.2 SETUP

Plotly's core plotting module is `plotly.graph_objects`, which provides a low-level API for building complex plots. However, for this chapter, we'll use `plotly.express`, a high-level module that makes it easy to create simple but powerful visualizations with minimal code.

16.2.1 Plotly Express

Plotly Express, commonly imported as `px`, is a module within the Plotly library that simplifies the creation of complete figures with just a single function call. It is a recommended starting point for generating most standard plots due to its ease of use and efficiency.

Plotly Express includes over 30 functions for various types of plots, with a consistent and easy-to-learn API. This consistency allows users to quickly switch between different types of visualizations, such as scatter plots, bar charts, histograms, and sunburst charts, during data exploration.

The key features of the Plotly Express API include:

- **Unified Interface**: By importing `plotly.express as px`, users can access all plotting functions and built-in demo datasets and color scales. Each function generates a `Figure` object that can be customized further.
- **Smart Defaults with Flexibility**: The functions infer sensible defaults but allow for full customization.

- **Versatile Input Formats**: The functions accept various data formats, including lists, dictionaries, DataFrames, numpy arrays, xarrays, and GeoPandas GeoDataFrames.
- **Automated Configuration**: Plotly Express automatically configures traces, layouts, axis labels, legends, and hover labels based on the input data.
- **Styling and Color Control**: The API supports styling through default templates and offers detailed control over categorical variables.
- **Advanced Features**: These include faceting, marginal plots, trendlines, animations, and automatic WebGL rendering for large scatter plots.

```python
import pandas as pd
import numpy as np
import plotly.express as px
```

16.3 SCATTER PLOTS

16.3.1 Demonstration

A scatter plot is used to visualize the relationship between two continuous variables by displaying data points on a two-dimensional graph. Plotly creates interactive plots that allow you to hover over data points, zoom in, and explore the data in dynamic ways. Since the interactive features cannot be captured in a printed format, we have included static screenshots of the plots in this book. To fully appreciate the capabilities of Plotly, we encourage you to run the code provided and experience the interactive features firsthand, as this will give you a deeper understanding of the data and the potential of the package.

Let's start with a simple scatter plot (Figure 16.1) showing the relationship between two variables. we'll use a small sample dataset to demonstrate. This example creates a scatter plot that shows how weight changes with height. The x-axis represents height, and the y-axis represents weight. The `title` parameter sets the plot's title.

```python
# Sample data
data = {
    'Height': [150, 160, 170, 180, 190],
    'Weight': [50, 60, 70, 80, 90]
}

# Creating a basic scatter plot
fig = px.scatter(data, x='Height', y='Weight', title='Height vs. Weight')

# Display the plot
fig.show()
```

Now, we will add more customization, such as setting the size of the markers and adding a trendline to visualize the relationship more clearly. Here, the `size` parameter adjusts the marker sizes based on a list of values, and the `trendline` parameter adds a linear trendline to the scatter plot (Figure 16.2). This helps in understanding the overall trend between height and weight.

Height vs. Weight

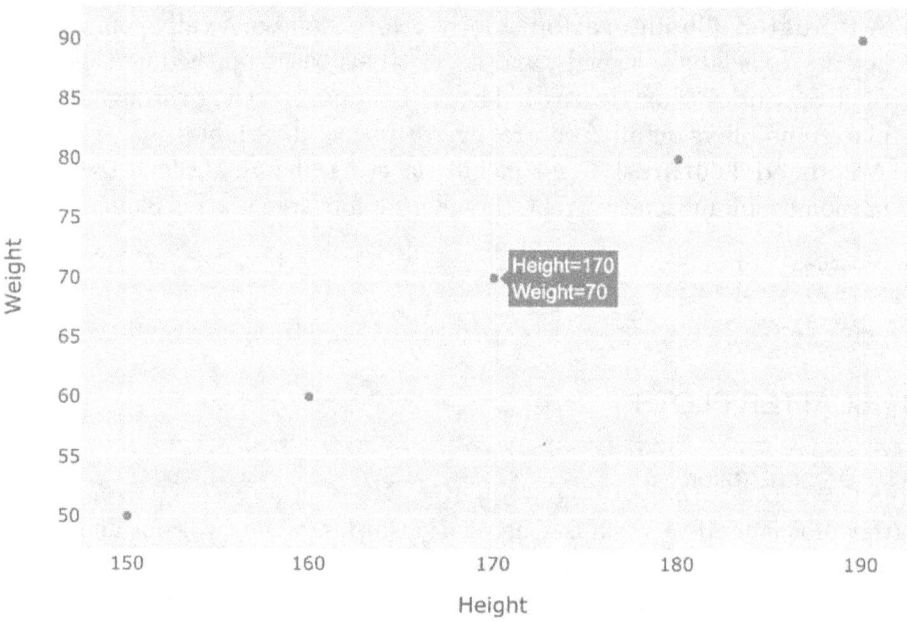

Figure 16.1 A simple scatter plot displaying data points.

```python
# Sample data
data = {
    'Height': [150, 160, 170, 180, 190],
    'Weight': [50, 60, 70, 80, 90]
}

# Creating a scatter plot with customizations
fig = px.scatter(data, x='Height', y='Weight',
            title='Height vs. Weight with Trendline',
            size=[10, 20, 30, 40, 50],  # Adjusting marker size
            trendline='ols')  # Adding a trendline

# Display the plot
fig.show()
```

Let's use color to encode a third variable, making it easier to visualize patterns or groupings in the data. In this example, the `color` parameter is used to differentiate data points based on gender (Figure 16.3). This allows us to see how weight and height distributions vary between males and females.

```python
# Sample data
data = {
    'Height': [150, 160, 170, 180, 190],
    'Weight': [50, 60, 70, 80, 90],
    'Gender': ['Male', 'Female', 'Male', 'Female', 'Male']
```

Height vs. Weight with Trendline

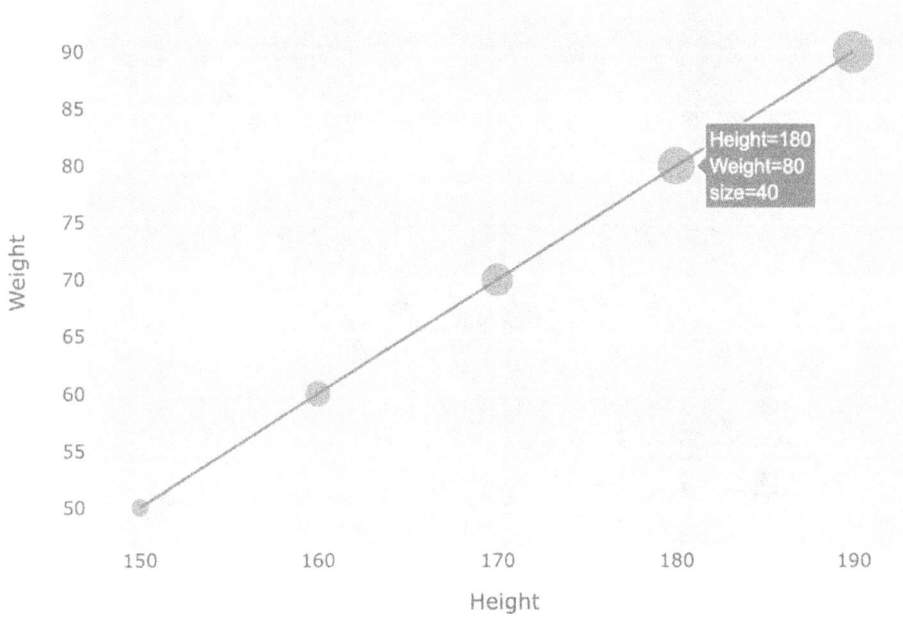

Figure 16.2 A scatter plot with data point size and a trend line.

```
}

# Creating a scatter plot with color encoding
fig = px.scatter(data, x='Height', y='Weight',
                color='Gender',   # Adding color based on gender
                title='Height vs. Weight by Gender')

# Display the plot
fig.show()
```

16.3.2 Practice

We will create a dummy DataFrame `df_dummy` with random data. This dataset
has four numerical features (`feature_1` to `feature_4`) and one categorical feature
`category`.

```
# Set seed for reproducibility
np.random.seed(42)

# Create a dummy dataset
v = np.random.rand(150)
df_dummy = pd.DataFrame({
    'feature_1': v,
    'feature_2': v + np.random.rand(150),
    'feature_3': v**2 + np.random.rand(150),
```

Height vs. Weight by Gender

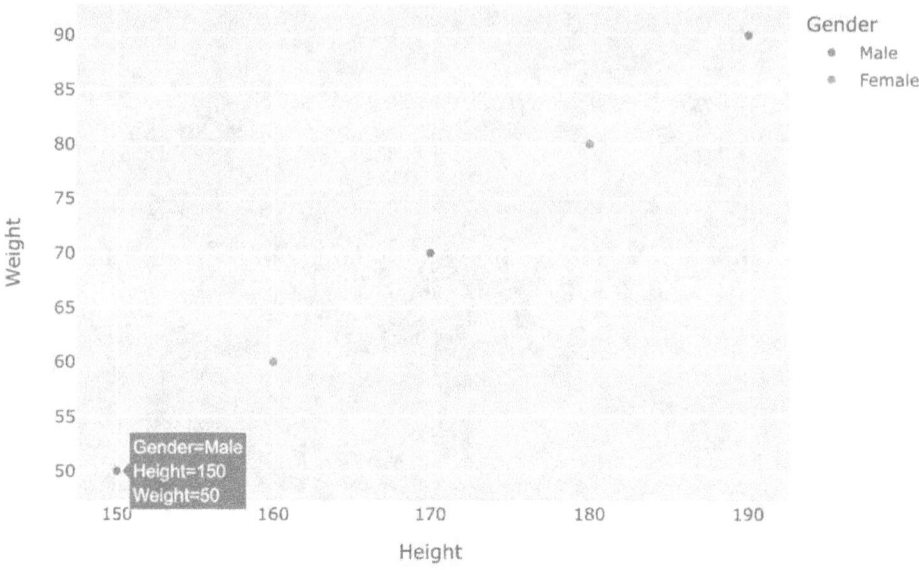

Figure 16.3　A scatter plot using color to encode data values.

```
    'feature_4': v * 7,
    'category': np.random.choice(['A', 'B', 'C'], 150)
})

df_dummy.info()
```

```
<class 'pandas.core.frame.DataFrame'>
RangeIndex: 150 entries, 0 to 149
Data columns (total 5 columns):
 #   Column     Non-Null Count  Dtype
---  ------     --------------  -----
 0   feature_1  150 non-null    float64
 1   feature_2  150 non-null    float64
 2   feature_3  150 non-null    float64
 3   feature_4  150 non-null    float64
 4   category   150 non-null    object
dtypes: float64(4), object(1)
memory usage: 6.0+ KB
```

Task: Create a scatter plot (Figure 16.4) to visualize the relationship between feature_1 and feature_2.

```
# Create scatter plot
fig = px.scatter(df_dummy, x='feature_1', y='feature_2',
                 title='Feature 1 vs. Feature 2')

fig.show()
```

Feature 1 vs. Feature 2

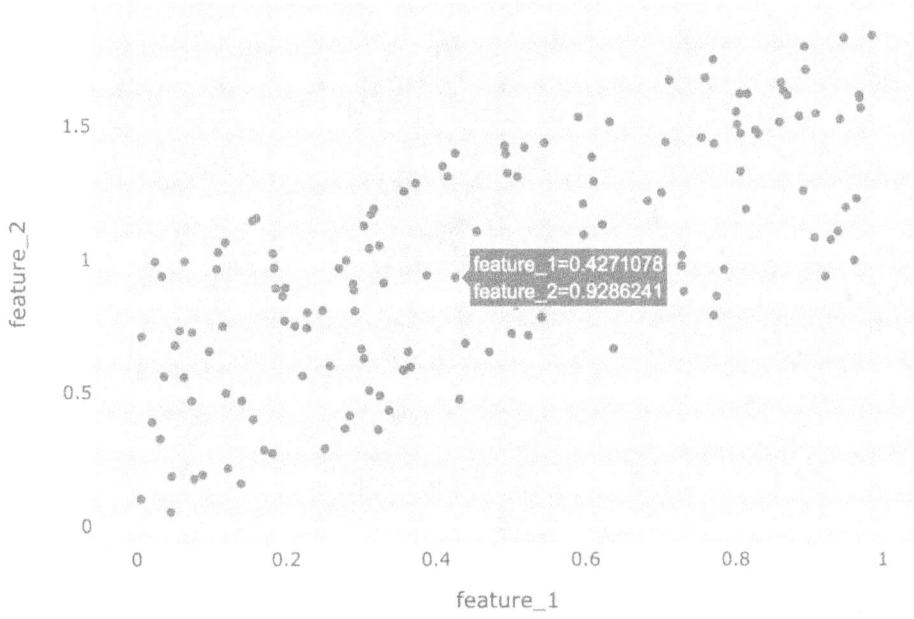

Figure 16.4 A scatter plot showing the relationship between feature 1 and feature 2.

Task: Create a scatter plot (Figure 16.5) to visualize the relationship between `feature_3` and `feature_4`, using `category` as the hue to differentiate the points.

```python
# Create scatter plot with category as hue
fig = px.scatter(df_dummy, x='feature_3', y='feature_4',
                 color='category',
                 title='Feature 3 vs. Feature 4 by Category')

fig.show()
```

Task: Create a scatter plot (Figure 16.6) to visualize the relationship between `feature_1` and `feature_3`. Use the size of the points to represent `feature_4`. Larger points represent higher values of `feature_4`.

```python
# Create scatter plot with size proportional to feature 4
fig = px.scatter(df_dummy, x='feature_1', y='feature_3',
                 size='feature_4',
                 title='Feature 1 vs. Feature 3 with Feature 4 as Size')

fig.show()
```

Task: For previous task, using 'category' as the hue to differentiate the points by categories (Figure 16.7).

Feature 3 vs. Feature 4 by Category

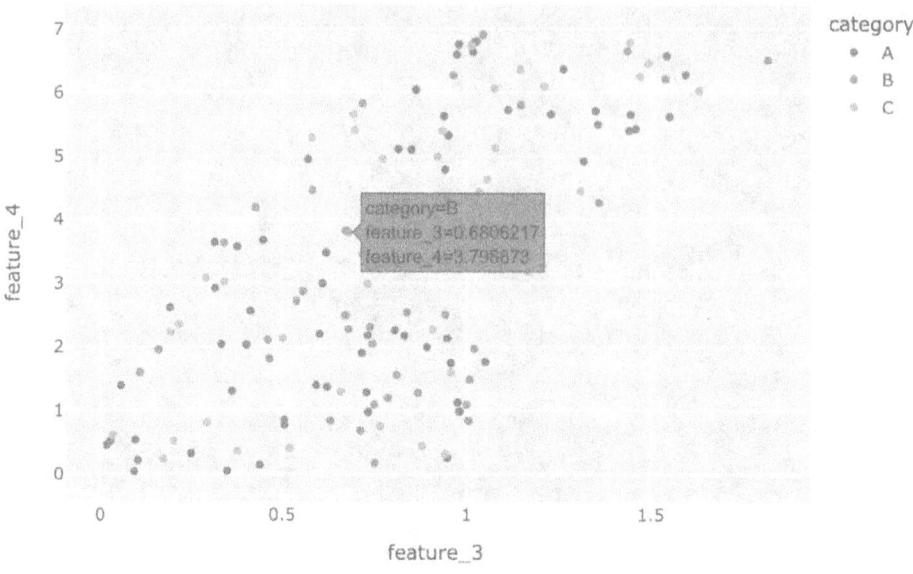

Figure 16.5 A scatter plot of feature 3 and feature 4, with color encoding.

Feature 1 vs. Feature 3 with Feature 4 as Size

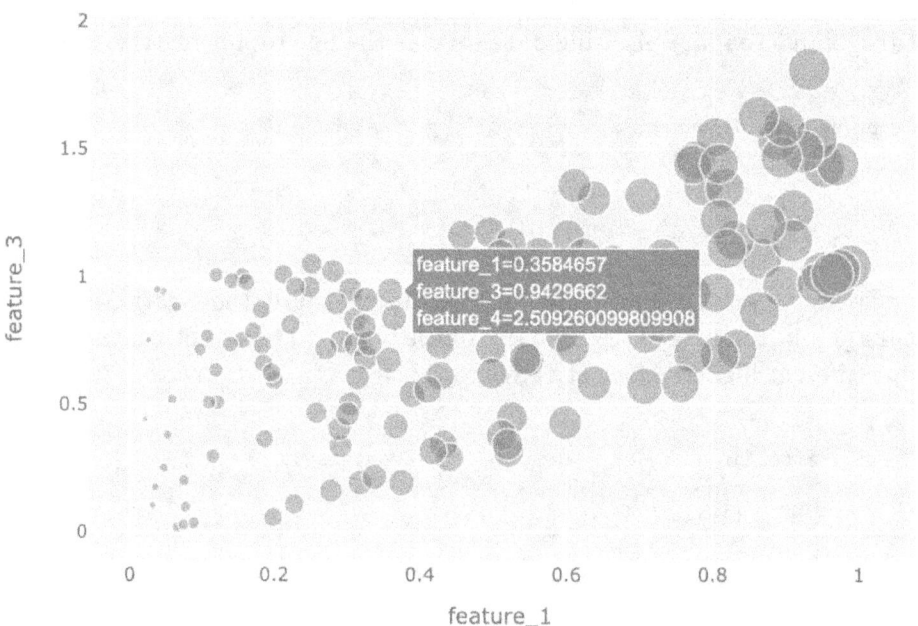

Figure 16.6 A scatter plot of feature 1 and feature 3, with data point size variation.

Feature1 vs. Feature2 with Feature4 as Size

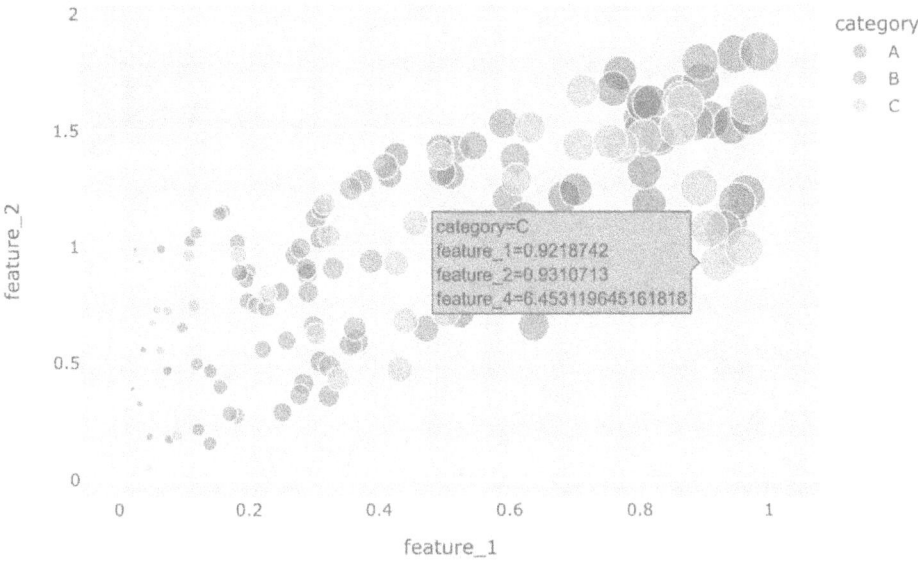

Figure 16.7 A scatter plot of feature 1 and feature 2, using both color and size.

```
# Create scatter plot with size proportional to petal width
fig = px.scatter(df_dummy, x='feature_1', y='feature_2',
                 size='feature_4', color = 'category',
                 title='Feature1 vs. Feature2 with Feature4 as Size')

fig.show()
```

16.4 LINE PLOTS

16.4.1 Demonstration

Line plots are a great way to visualize trends or changes over time. Let's start with a simple line plot (Figure 16.8) that shows how sales have increased over a period of five years. The x-axis represents the years, and the y-axis represents the sales. The `title` parameter is used to set the title of the plot.

```
# Sample data
data = {
    'Year': [2016, 2017, 2018, 2019, 2020],
    'Sales': [100, 120, 230, 250, 200]
}

# Creating a basic line plot
fig = px.line(data, x='Year', y='Sales', title='Sales Over Time')
```

Sales Over Time

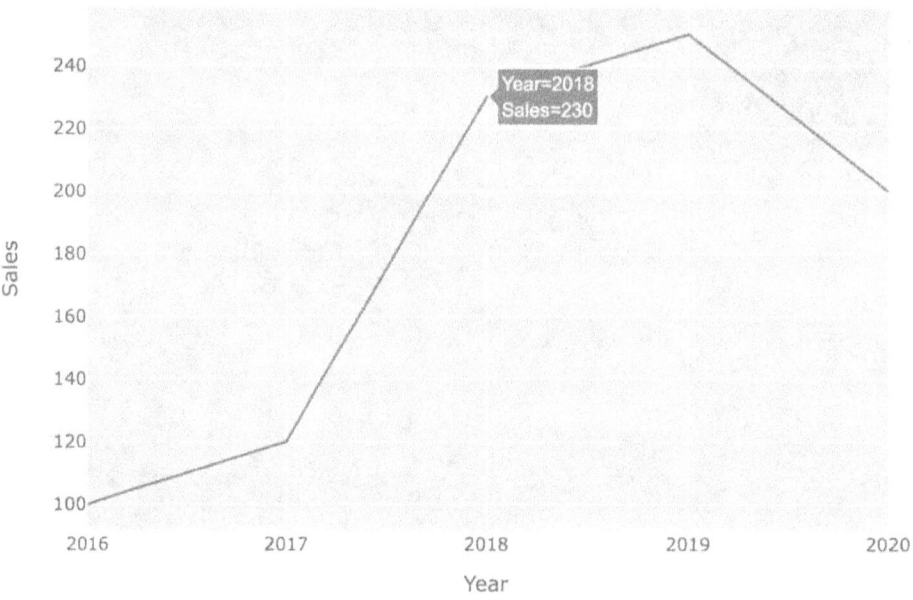

Figure 16.8 A basic line plot showing data trends.

```
# Display the plot
fig.show()
```

You can add multiple lines to the same plot to compare multiple trends (Figure 16.9).

```
# Sample data
data = {
    'Year': [2016, 2017, 2018, 2019, 2020],
    'Sales1': [100, 120, 230, 250, 200],
    'Sales2': [90, 140, 190, 140, 290],
}

# Creating a multi-line plot
fig = px.line(data, x='Year', y=['Sales1', 'Sales2'],
              title='Sales1 and Sales 2 Over Time')

# Display the plot
fig.show()
```

Alternatively, if you have categorical attributes, you can create a multi-line plot (Figure 16.10) to compare the sales of two different products over time. In this example, we use the `color` parameter to differentiate between two products, `Product A` and `Product B`. This creates a multi-line plot where each product's sales are represented by a different line, allowing for easy comparison.

Sales1 and Sales 2 Over Time

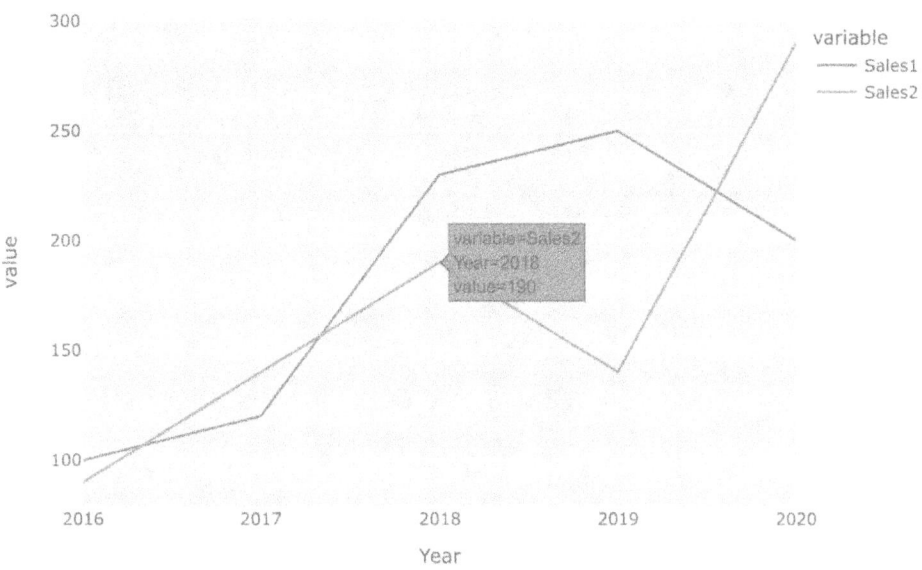

Figure 16.9 A multi-line plot comparing sales1 and sales2 over time.

```
# Sample data
data = {
    'Year': [2016, 2017, 2018, 2019, 2020, 2016, 2017, 2018, 2019, 2020],
    'Sales': [100, 120, 230, 250, 200, 190, 240, 90, 190, 190],
    'Product': ['A','A', 'A', 'A', 'A', 'B', 'B', 'B', 'B', 'B']
}

# Creating a multi-line plot
fig = px.line(data, x='Year', y='Sales', color='Product',
              title='Sales of Product A and Product B Over Time')

# Display the plot
fig.show()
```

You can also add markers to each data point to make the plot more informative. This example (Figure 16.11) adds markers to the line plot, making it easier to see individual data points. The **markers=True** parameter is used to add these markers. This is particularly useful when you want to highlight the exact values at each point.

```
# Sample data
data = {
    'Year': [2016, 2017, 2018, 2019, 2020],
    'Revenue': [90, 140, 190, 140, 290]
}

# Creating a line plot with markers
fig = px.line(data, x='Year', y='Revenue',
              title='Revenue Growth Over Time',
```

Sales of Product A and Product B Over Time

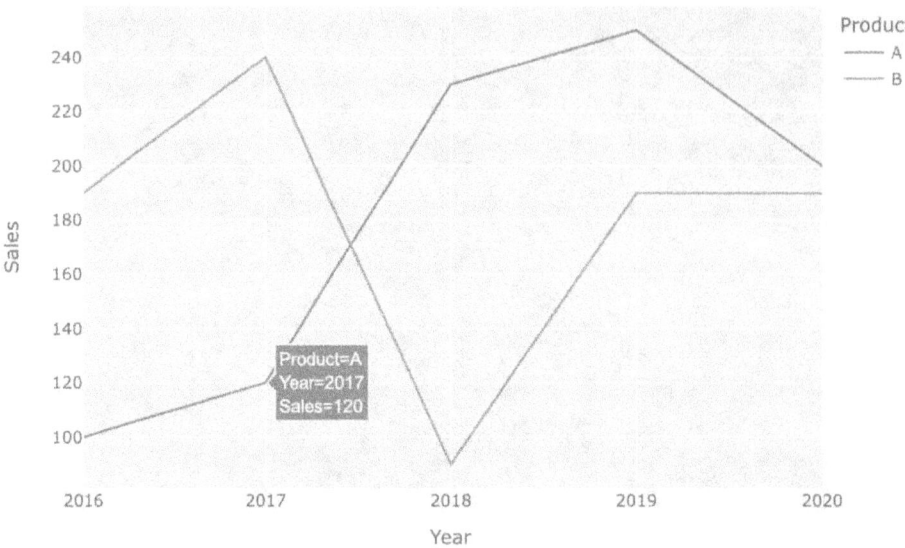

Figure 16.10 A multi-line plot comparing sales of product A and product B over time.

```
                markers=True)  # Adding markers to each data point

# Display the plot
fig.show()
```

We can also customize the line style by adjusting the dash pattern. In this example (Figure 16.12), the `line_dash_sequence` parameter is used to customize the line style. The line is displayed with a dashed pattern, which can be useful for differentiating between different types of trends in a multi-line plot.

```
# Sample data
data = {
    'Month': ['January', 'February', 'March', 'April', 'May'],
    'Temperature': [30, 22, 35, 27, 40]
}

# Creating a line plot with a customized line style
fig = px.line(data, x='Month', y='Temperature',
            title='Monthly Temperature Trend',
            line_dash_sequence=['dash'])  # Customizing line style

# Display the plot
fig.show()
```

16.4.2 Practice

We will continue using the **df_dummy** dataset for these tasks.

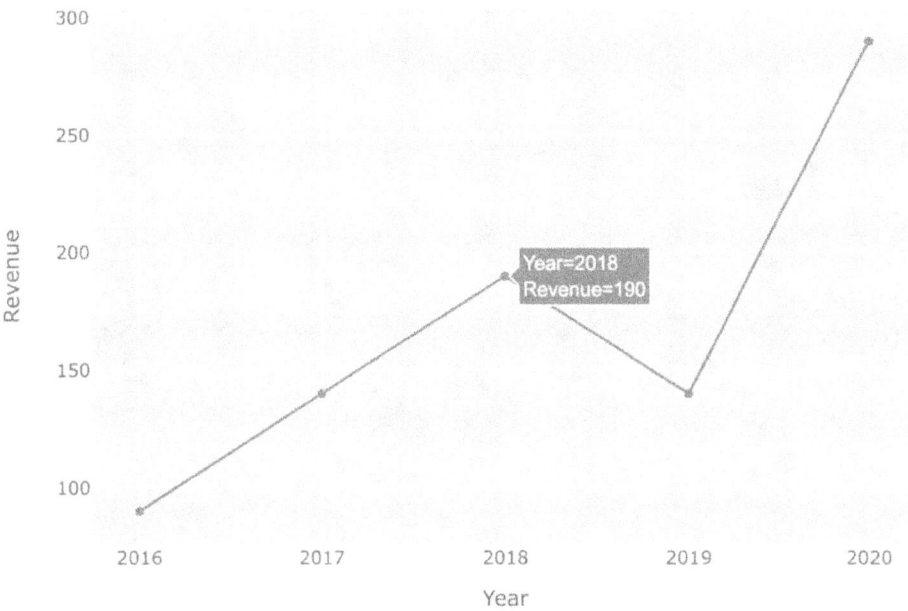

Figure 16.11 A line plot for revenue growth over time with markers indicating data points.

Task: Create a line plot (Figure 16.13) to visualize how **feature_1** changes over the index (row numbers).

```
# Create a line plot of feature_1 over index
fig = px.line(df_dummy, y='feature_1', title='Feature 1 over Index')

fig.show()
```

Task: Create a line plot (Figure 16.14) to visualize how **feature_2** changes over the index. Add markers to the line.

```
# Create a line plot of feature_2 over index with markers
fig = px.line(df_dummy, y='feature_2',
            title='Feature 2 over Index with Markers', markers=True)

fig.show()
```

Task: Create a line plot (Figure 16.15) to compare **feature_1** and **feature_3** on the same plot.

```
# Create a line plot comparing feature_1 and feature_3
fig = px.line(df_dummy, y=['feature_1', 'feature_3'],
            title='Comparison of Feature 1 and Feature 3 over Index')
```

Monthly Temperature Trend

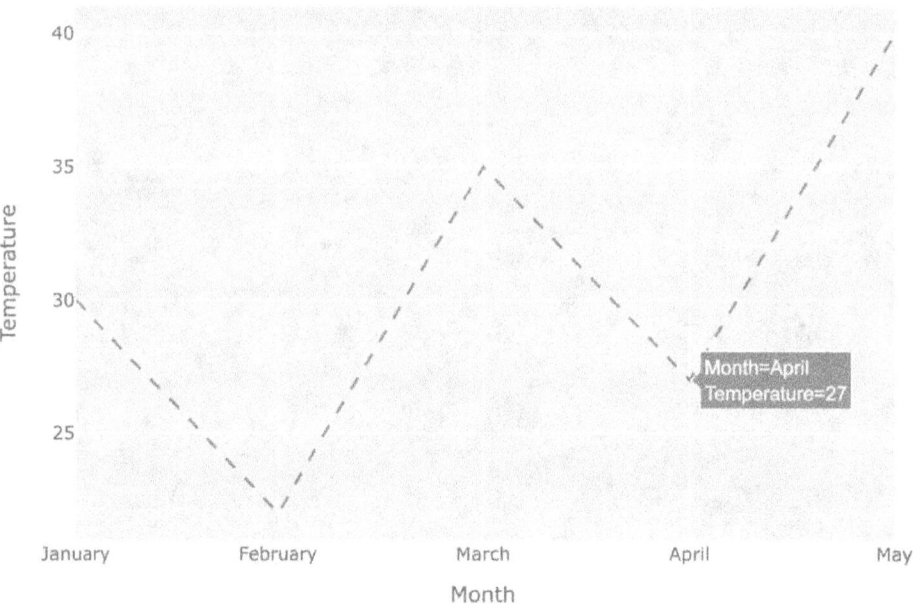

Figure 16.12 A line plot showing monthly temperature trends with different line styles.

```
fig.show()
```

Task: Create a line plot (Figure 16.16) to visualize how **feature_4** changes over the index for each category. Use the **category** column to differentiate the lines by color.

```
# Create a line plot of feature_4 for each category
fig = px.line(df_dummy, y='feature_4', color='category',
              title='Feature 4 over Index by Category')

fig.show()
```

16.5 AREA PLOTS

16.5.1 Demonstration

Area plots are useful for visualizing cumulative data or showing the part-to-whole relationships over time. They are similar to line plots but with the area under the line filled in.

Let's start with a simple area plot (Figure 16.17) that shows how sales accumulate over a period of five years. The x-axis represents the years, and the y-axis represents the cumulative sales. The area under the line is filled, making it easy to see the total sales over time.

Feature 1 over Index

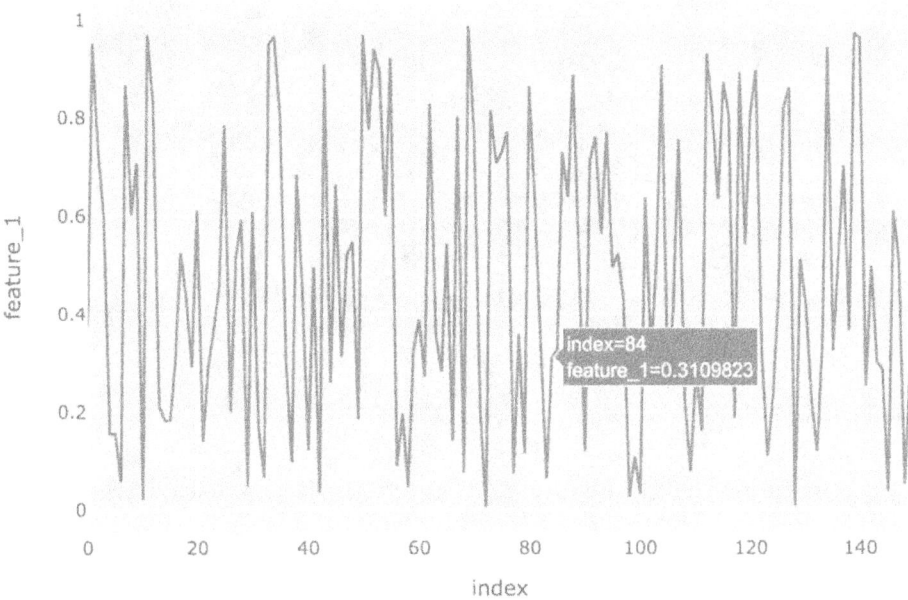

Figure 16.13 A line plot displaying feature 1 over an index.

```
# Sample data
data = {
    'Year': [2016, 2017, 2018, 2019, 2020],
    'Sales': [100, 120, 230, 250, 200]
}

# Creating a basic area plot
fig = px.area(data, x='Year', y='Sales',
              title='Cumulative Sales Over Time')

# Display the plot
fig.show()
```

Next, Let's create a stacked area plot (Figure 16.18) to visualize the cumulative sales of two different products over time. In this stacked area plot, the sales of `Product A` and `Product B` are visualized together. The `color` parameter is used to differentiate between the two products, with the area for each product stacked on top of the other. This allows for a clear comparison of the contribution of each product to the total sales.

```
# Sample data
data = {
    'Year': [2016, 2017, 2018, 2019, 2020] * 2,
    'Sales': [100, 120, 230, 250, 200, 90, 140, 190, 240, 290],
    'Product': ['Product A'] * 5 + ['Product B'] * 5
```

Feature 2 over Index with Markers

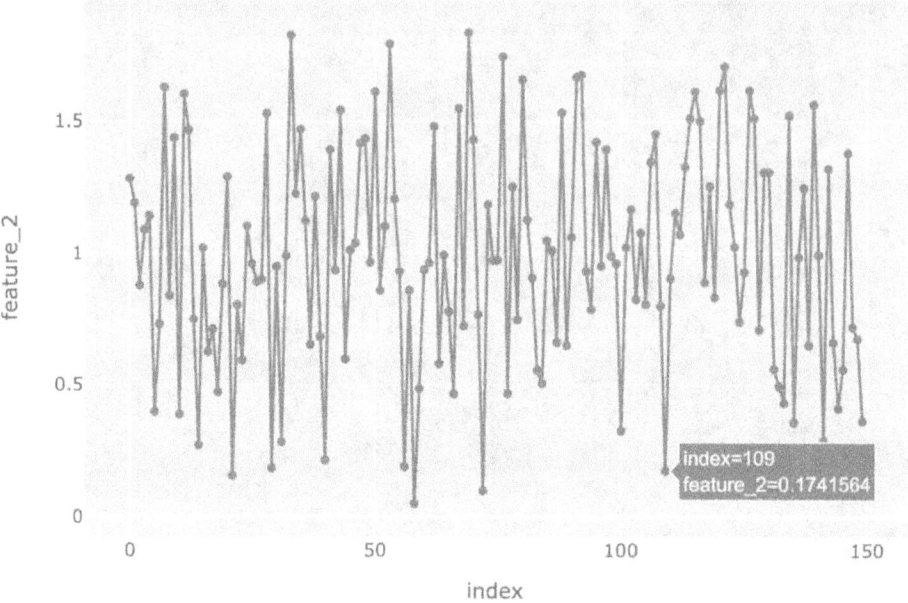

Figure 16.14 A line plot of feature 2 over an index, with markers.

Comparison of Feature 1 and Feature 3 over Index

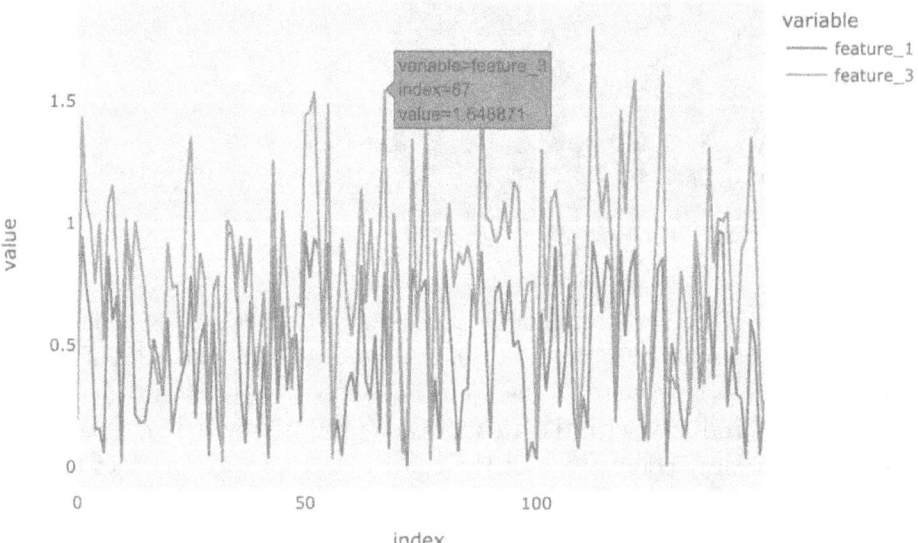

Figure 16.15 A line plot comparing feature 1 and feature 3 over an index.

Feature 4 over Index by Category

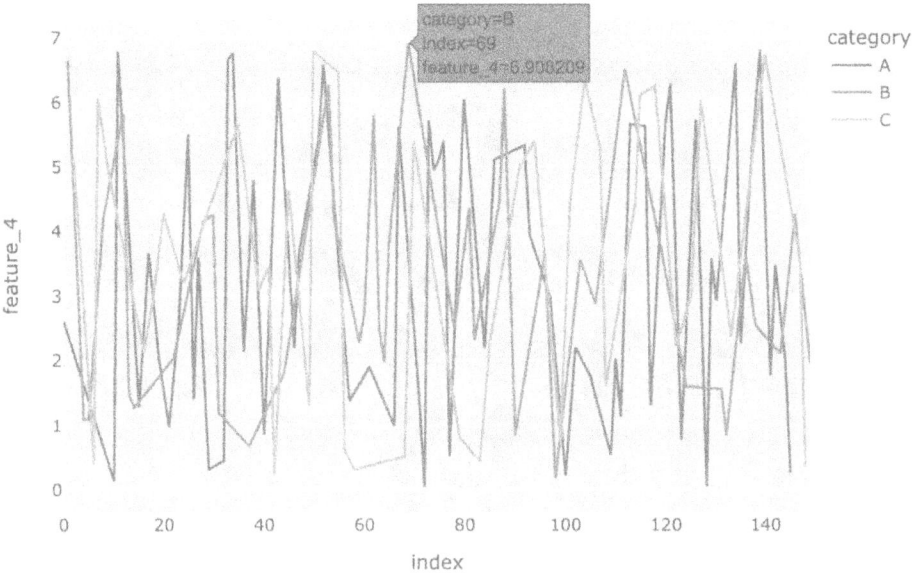

Figure 16.16   A line plot of feature 4 over an index, grouped by category.

Cumulative Sales Over Time

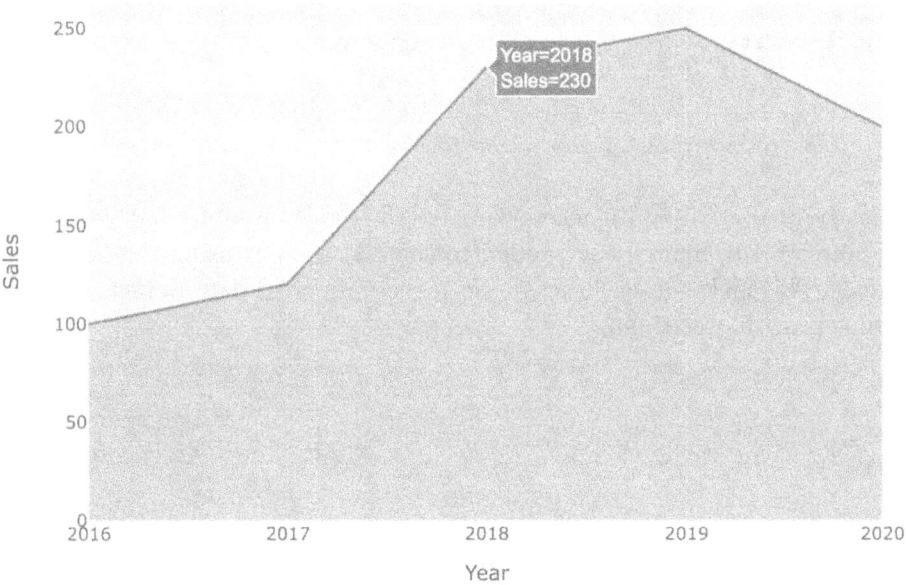

Figure 16.17   A basic area plot showing the magnitude of data over a range.

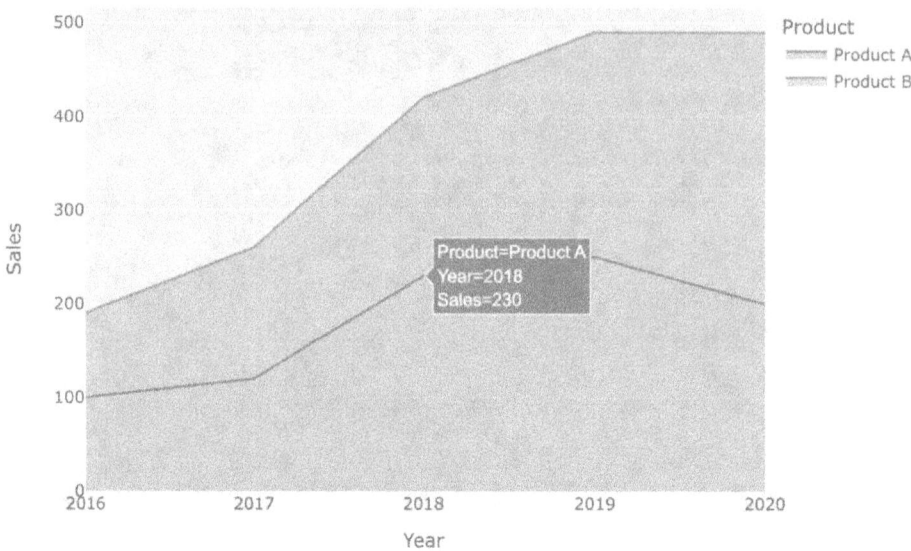

Figure 16.18 A stacked area plot showing cumulative sales of product A and B over time.

```
}
# Creating a stacked area plot
fig = px.area(data, x='Year', y='Sales', color='Product',
         title='Cumulative Sales of Product A and B Over Time')

# Display the plot
fig.show()
```

For this example, we'll add markers to make the plot more informative. In this area plot (Figure 16.19), markers are added to each data point using the `markers=True` parameter. This makes it easier to see both the individual data points and the trend in revenue growth over time.

```
# Sample data
data = {
    'Month': ['January', 'February', 'March', 'April', 'May'],
    'Revenue': [100, 120, 230, 250, 200]
}

# Creating an area plot with markers and customized line style
fig = px.area(data, x='Month', y='Revenue',
         title='Monthly Revenue Growth',
         markers=True)  # Adding markers to each data point)

# Display the plot
fig.show()
```

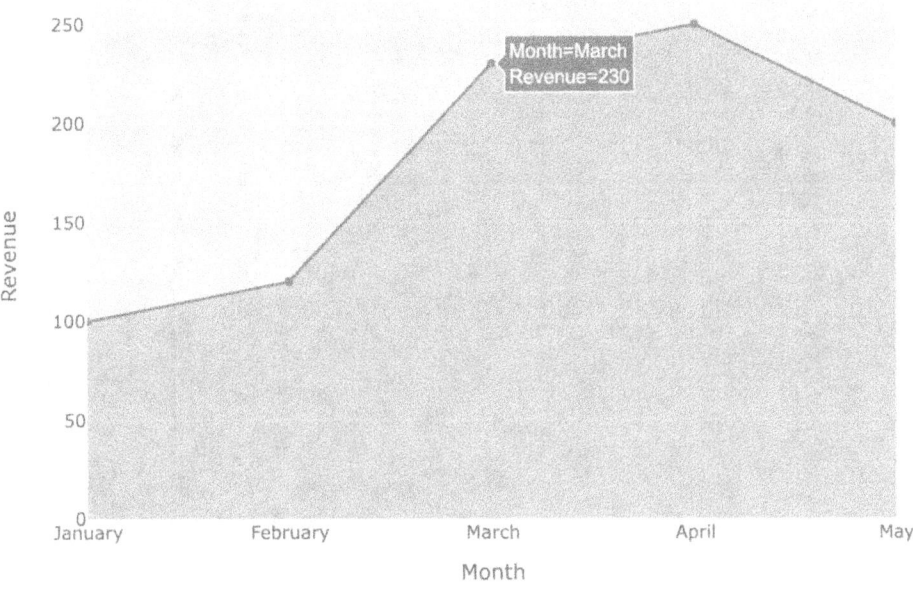

Monthly Revenue Growth

Figure 16.19 An area plot of monthly revenue growth with markers and line style variations.

16.5.2 Practice

We will continue using the **df_dummy** dataset for these tasks.

Task: Create an area plot (Figure 16.20) to visualize how **feature_1** changes over the index.

```
# Create an area plot of feature_1 over index
fig = px.area(df_dummy, y='feature_1',
              title='Area Plot of Feature 1 over Index')

fig.show()
```

Task: Create an area plot (Figure 16.21) that shows **feature_2**, **feature_3** and **feature_4** on the same plot.

```
# Create an area plot of feature_2 with feature_3 overlay
fig = px.area(df_dummy, y=['feature_2', 'feature_3', 'feature_4'],
              title='Area Plot of Feature 2, 3, 4 over Index')

fig.show()
```

Task: Create an area plot (Figure 16.22) to visualize **feature_3** over the index, using **category** as a color to differentiate the areas.

Area Plot of Feature 1 over Index

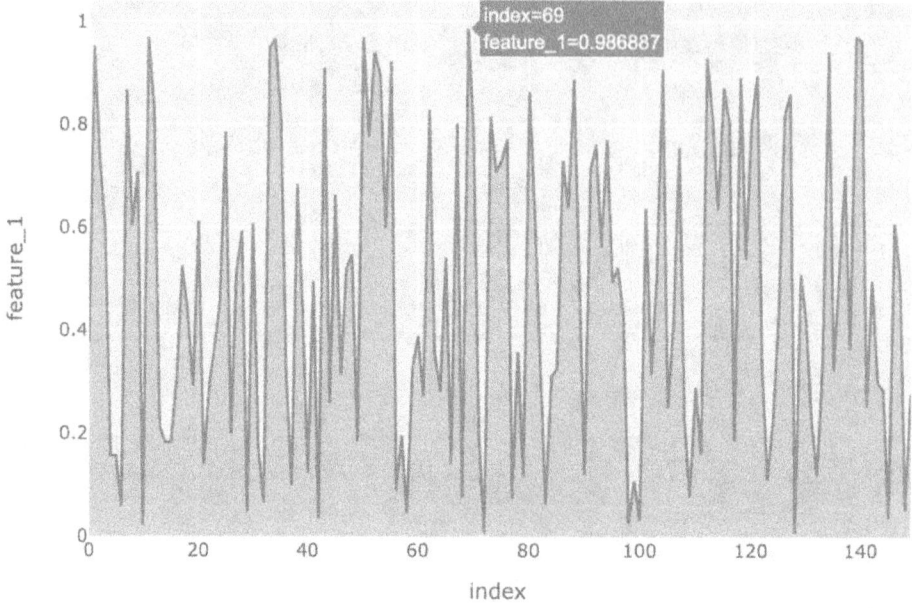

Figure 16.20 An area plot displaying feature 1 over an index.

Area Plot of Feature 2, 3, 4 over Index

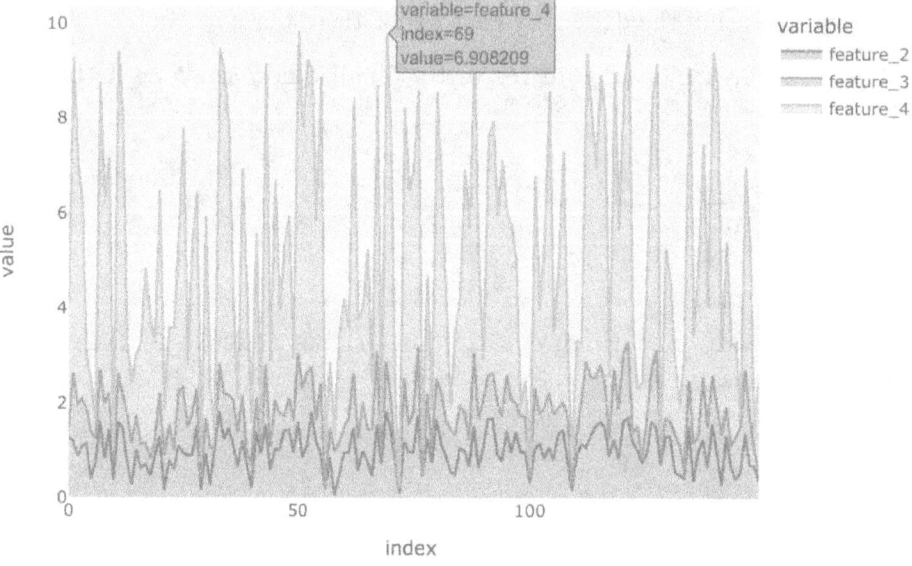

Figure 16.21 A stacked area plot of feature 2, 3, and 4 over an index.

Area Plot of Feature 3 over Index by Category

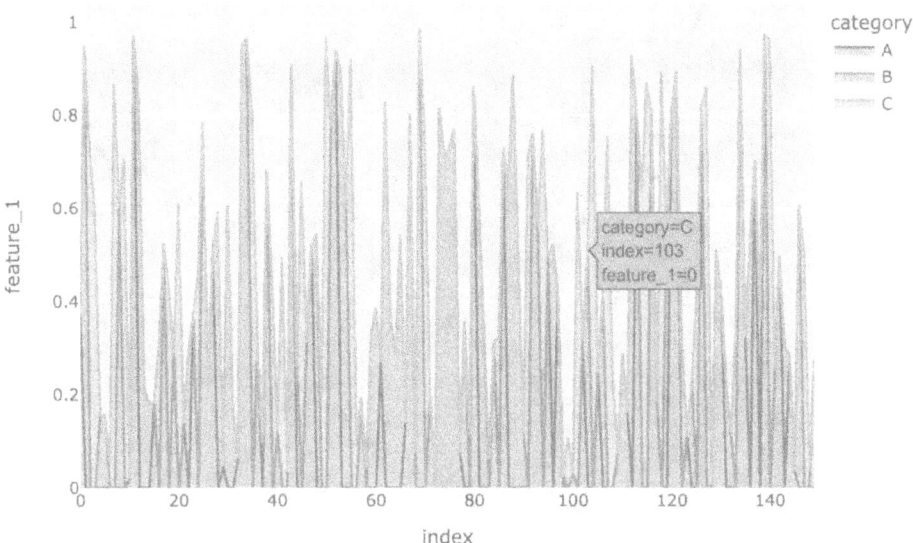

Figure 16.22 An area plot displaying feature 3 over an index, grouped by category.

```
# Create an area plot of feature_3 by category
fig = px.area(df_dummy, x = df_dummy.index, y='feature_1',
            color='category',
            title='Area Plot of Feature 3 over Index by Category')

fig.show()
```

16.6 BAR PLOTS

16.6.1 Demonstration

Bar plots are ideal for comparing quantities across different categories.

Let's start with a simple bar plot (Figure 16.23) to compare the sales figures for four different products. The x-axis represents the product names, and the y-axis represents the sales figures. The height of each bar corresponds to the sales of each product.

```
# Sample data
data = {
    'Product': ['Product A', 'Product B', 'Product C', 'Product D'],
    'Sales': [100, 230, 190, 250]
}

# Creating a basic bar plot
fig = px.bar(data, x='Product', y='Sales', title='Sales by Product')
```

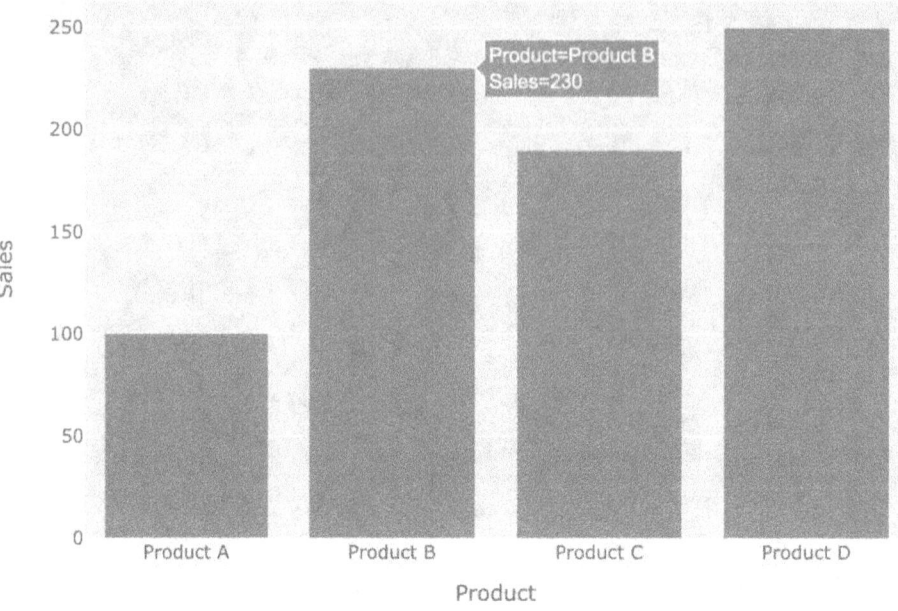

Figure 16.23 A basic bar plot displaying sales by product.

```
# Display the plot
fig.show()
```

Next, Let's create a grouped bar plot (Figure 16.24). In this grouped bar plot, sales for each product are shown for two different years (2019 and 2020). The `color` parameter is used to differentiate the years, and the `barmode='group'` option places the bars for each year side by side within each product category. This allows for easy comparison of sales between years for each product.

```
# Sample data
data = {
    'Product': ['Product A', 'Product A', 'Product B', 'Product B',
                'Product C', 'Product C', 'Product D', 'Product D'],
    'Year': ['2019', '2020', '2019', '2020',
             '2019', '2020', '2019', '2020'],
    'Sales': [100, 120, 150, 140, 190, 200, 250, 230]
}

# Creating a grouped bar plot
fig = px.bar(data, x='Product', y='Sales', color='Year',
             barmode='group', title='Sales by Product and Year')

# Display the plot
fig.show()
```

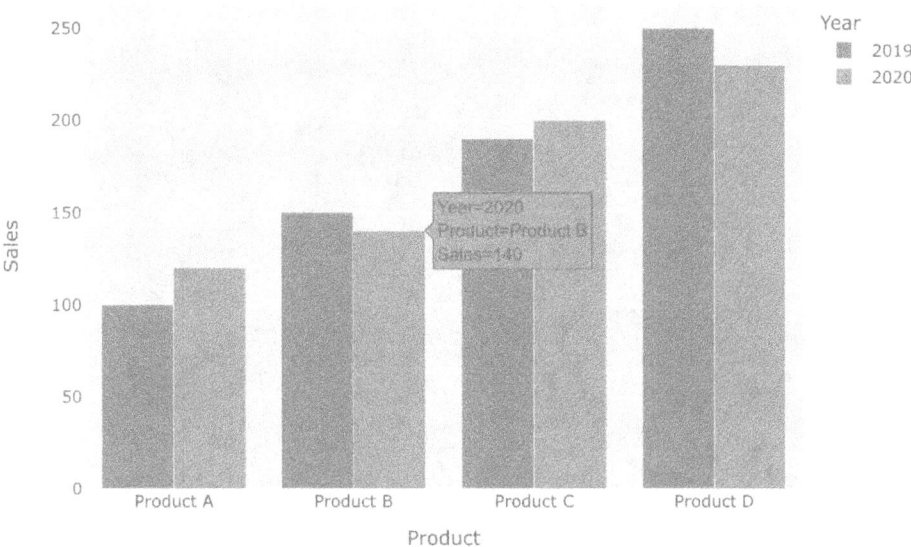

Figure 16.24 A grouped bar plot comparing sales by product and year.

Now, Let's create a stacked bar plot (Figure 16.25) to visualize the cumulative sales contributions of each year within each product category. In this stacked bar plot, the sales figures for each year are stacked on top of each other within each product category. The `barmode='stack'` option is used to create this effect. This visualization helps to see the cumulative sales for each product, along with the contribution of each year to the total sales.

```
# Sample data
data = {
    'Product': ['Product A', 'Product A', 'Product B', 'Product B',
                'Product C', 'Product C', 'Product D', 'Product D'],
    'Year': ['2019', '2020', '2019', '2020',
             '2019', '2020', '2019', '2020'],
    'Sales': [100, 120, 150, 140, 190, 200, 250, 230]
}

# Creating a stacked bar plot
fig = px.bar(data, x='Product', y='Sales', color='Year',
             barmode='stack', title='Stacked Sales by Product and Year')

# Display the plot
fig.show()
```

Bar plots can also be displayed horizontally, which is useful when dealing with long category names or when you prefer a different orientation. This example (Figure 16.26) shows a horizontal bar plot, where the x-axis represents the sales figures and the y-axis represents the products. Horizontal bar plots can be helpful for improving readability, especially when category labels are lengthy.

Stacked Sales by Product and Year

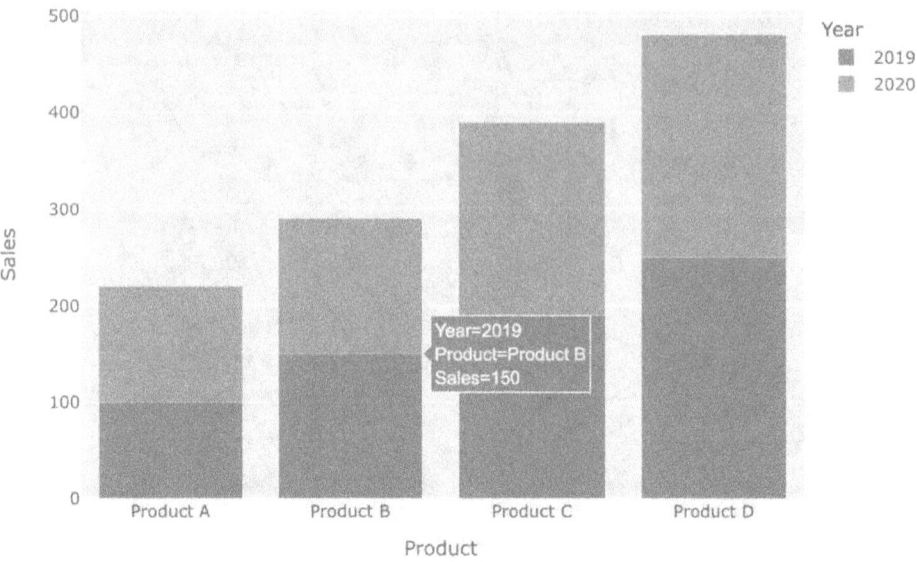

Figure 16.25 A stacked bar plot showing sales by product and year.

```python
# Sample data
data = {
    'Product': ['Product A', 'Product B', 'Product C', 'Product D'],
    'Sales': [100, 120, 150, 140]
}

# Creating a horizontal bar plot
fig = px.bar(data, x='Sales', y='Product',
            title='Sales by Product (Horizontal)')

# Display the plot
fig.show()
```

16.6.2 Practice

Let's create another dummy dataset for this practice.

```python
# Define the data
data = {
    'product': ['Product A', 'Product B', 'Product C', 'Product A',
                'Product D', 'Product B', 'Product B', 'Product C',
                'Product B', 'Product A'],
    'sales': [1500, 2300, 1200, 3400, 2900, 4100, 3200, 1800, 2700, 2200],
    'profit': [400, 800, 300, 1200, 900, 1400, 1100, 500, 700, 600],
    'region': ['North', 'South', 'East', 'West', 'North',
               'South', 'East', 'West', 'North', 'South']
}
```

Sales by Product (Horizontal)

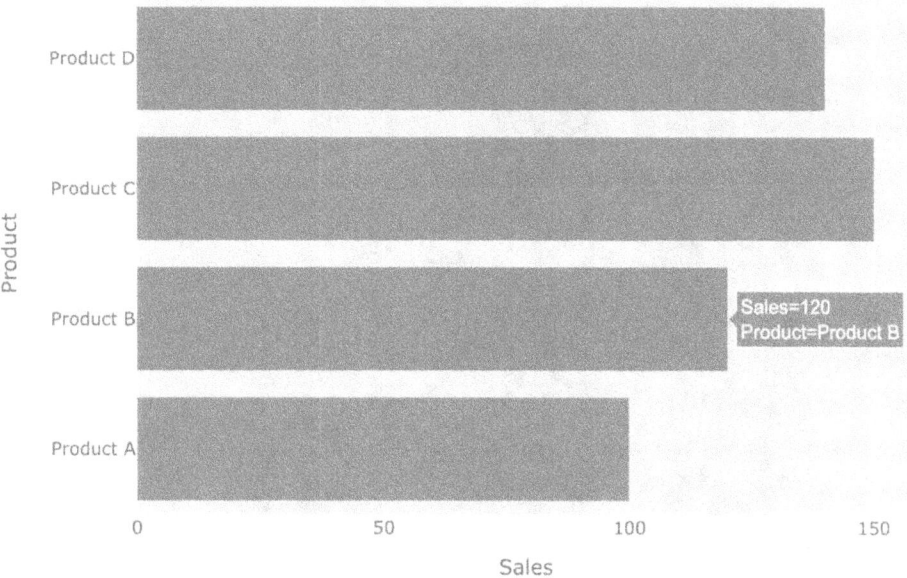

Figure 16.26 A horizontal bar plot showing sales by product.

```
# Create the DataFrame
df_simple = pd.DataFrame(data)
df_simple.head()
```

Task: Create a bar plot (Figure 16.27) to visualize the sales for each product.

```
# Create a simple bar plot of sales by product
fig = px.bar(df_simple, x='product', y='sales', title='Sales by Product')

fig.show()
```

Task: Create a bar plot (Figure 16.28) to visualize the profit for each region.

```
# Create a bar plot of profit by region
fig = px.bar(df_simple, x='region', y='profit', title='Profit by Region')

fig.show()
```

Task: Create a horizontal bar plot (Figure 16.29) to visualize the sales for each product.

```
# Create a horizontal bar plot of sales by product
fig = px.bar(df_simple, x='sales', y='product',
             orientation='h', title='Sales by Product (Horizontal)')

fig.show()
```

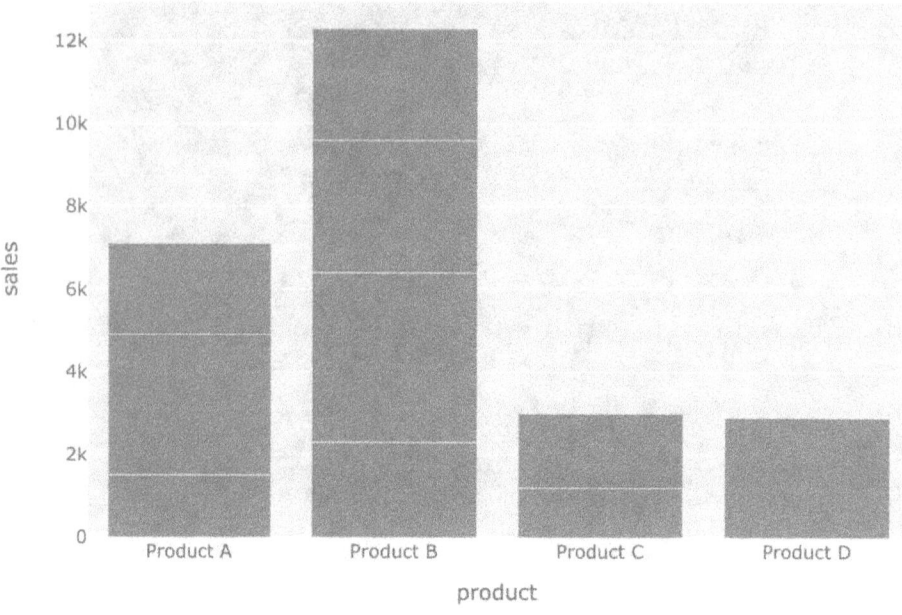

Figure 16.27 A simple bar plot displaying sales by product.

Task: Create a stacked bar plot (Figure 16.30) to visualize the sales for each region, make a color differentiation by product.

```
# Create a stacked bar plot of sales by region
fig = px.bar(df_simple, x='region', y='sales',
             color='product', title='Sales by Region')

fig.show()
```

16.7 TIMELINE PLOTS

16.7.1 Demonstration

Timeline plots are a great way to visualize events or activities over time.

Let's start with a simple timeline plot (Figure 16.31) that shows the duration of different projects. This basic timeline plot visualizes the duration of three different projects. The x-axis represents the timeline, and the y-axis represents the projects. Each bar shows the duration of a project from its start date to its finish date.

```
# Sample data
data = {
    'Project': ['Project A', 'Project B', 'Project C'],
    'Start': ['2023-01-01', '2023-02-01', '2023-03-01'],
```

Profit by Region

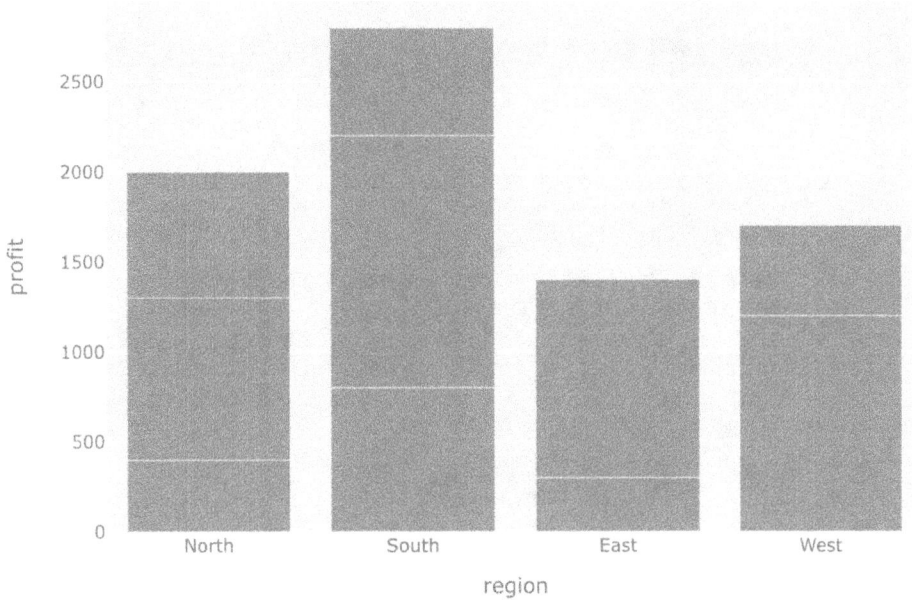

Figure 16.28 A bar plot showing profit by region.

```
    'Finish': ['2023-02-01', '2023-03-15', '2023-04-30']
}

# Creating a basic timeline plot
fig = px.timeline(data, x_start='Start', x_end='Finish',
                y='Project', title='Project Timeline')

# Display the plot
fig.show()
```

Now, Let's add colors to the timeline plot to differentiate between project categories. In this timeline plot (Figure 16.32), the projects are categorized into different groups (e.g., Development, Research, Marketing). The `color` parameter is used to assign different colors to each category, making it easier to identify which project belongs to which category.

```
# Sample data
data = {
    'Project': ['Project A', 'Project B', 'Project C', 'Project D'],
    'Category': ['Research', 'Research', 'Development', 'Marketing'],
    'Start': ['2023-01-01', '2023-02-01', '2023-03-01', '2023-04-01'],
    'Finish': ['2023-02-01', '2023-03-15', '2023-04-30', '2023-05-30']
}

# Creating a timeline plot with colors
fig = px.timeline(data, x_start='Start', x_end='Finish', y='Project',
```

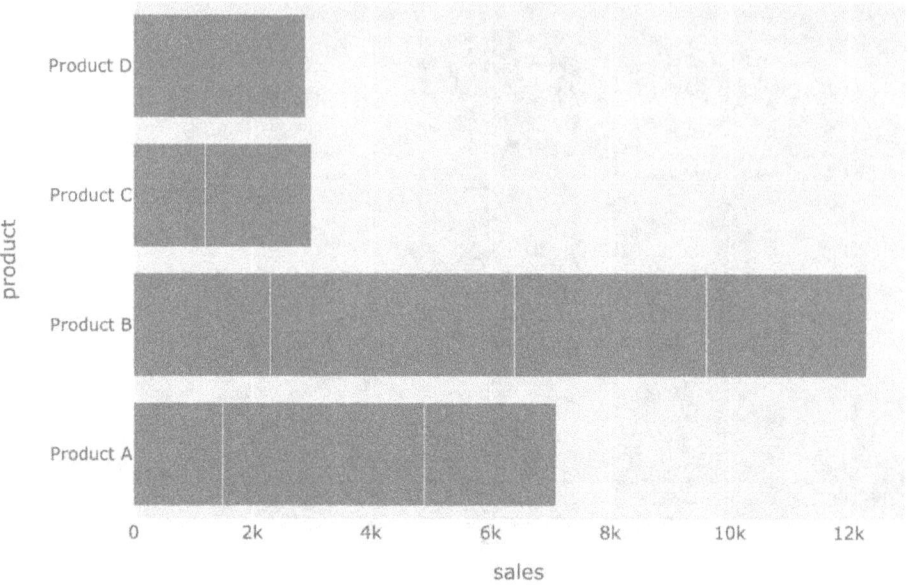

Figure 16.29 A horizontal bar plot displaying sales by product.

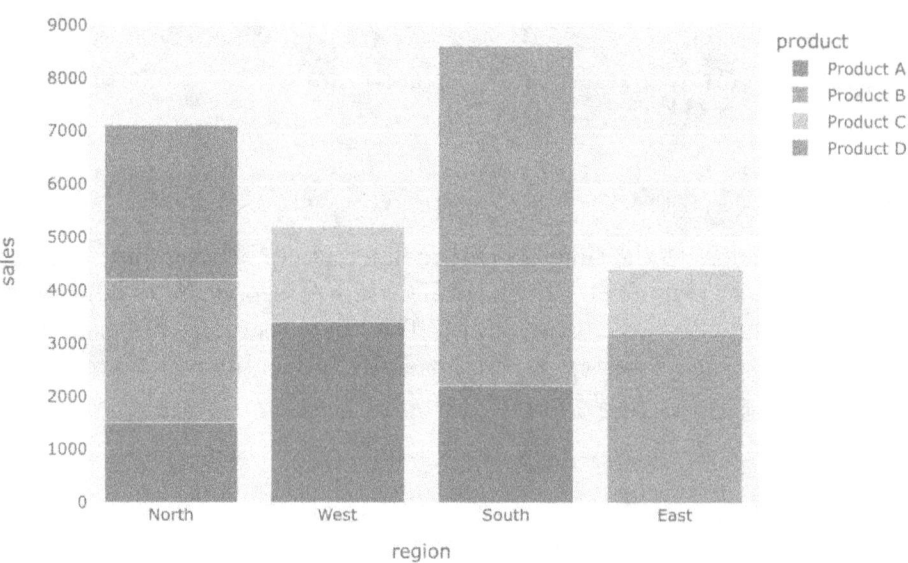

Figure 16.30 A stacked bar plot showing sales by region.

Project Timeline

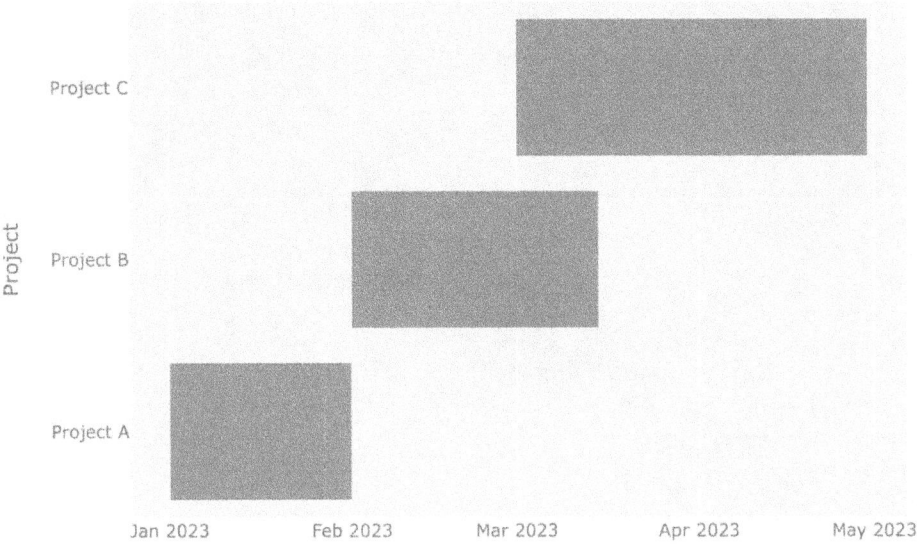

Figure 16.31 A basic timeline plot for projects.

Project Timeline by Category

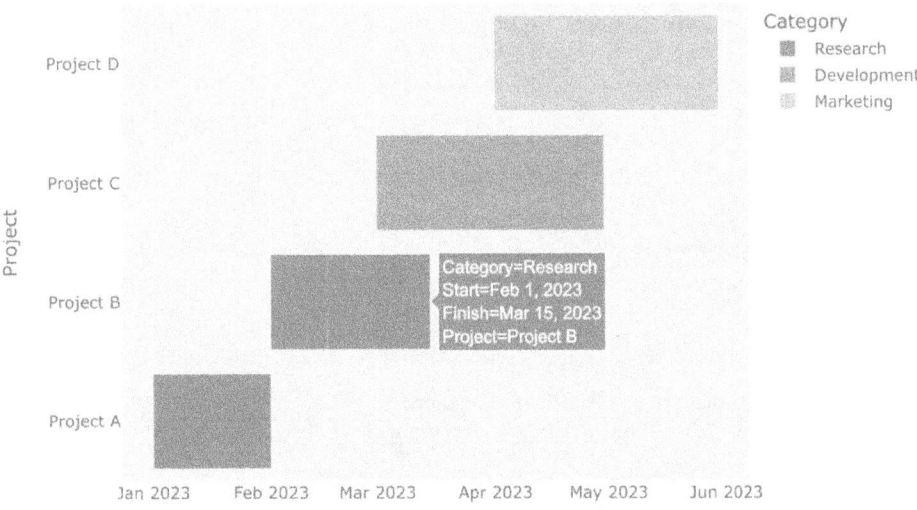

Figure 16.32 A timeline plot for projects, categorized by type.

```
                    color='Category', title='Project Timeline by Category')
# Display the plot
fig.show()
```

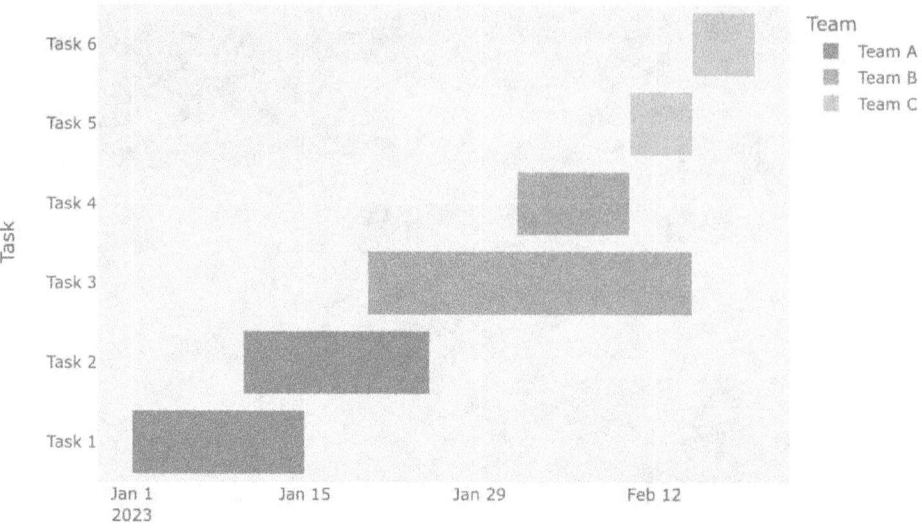

Figure 16.33 A timeline plot for projects, grouped by teams.

In this example (Figure 16.33), we'll create a timeline plot that groups tasks by different teams. In this timeline plot, tasks are grouped by different teams (e.g., Team A, Team B, Team C). The `color` parameter differentiates the teams by color, making it easy to see which tasks belong to which teams.

```python
# Sample data
data = {
    'Task': ['Task 1', 'Task 2', 'Task 3', 'Task 4', 'Task 5', 'Task 6'],
    'Team': ['Team A', 'Team A', 'Team B', 'Team B', 'Team C', 'Team C'],
    'Start': ['2023-01-01', '2023-01-10', '2023-01-20',
              '2023-02-01', '2023-02-10', '2023-02-20'],
    'Finish': ['2023-01-15', '2023-01-25', '2023-02-15',
               '2023-02-10', '2023-02-15', '2023-02-15']
}

# Creating a timeline plot grouped by teams
fig = px.timeline(data, x_start='Start', x_end='Finish', y='Task',
                  color='Team', title='Task Timeline Grouped by Teams')

# Display the plot
fig.show()
```

16.7.2 Practice

To practice timeline plots, we can create a simple dummy dataset that represents events or tasks over time. This DataFrame `df_timeline` with 10 rows representing different projects, their start and end dates, their duration, and the responsible department.

```
# Define the data
data = {
    'event': ['Project A', 'Project B', 'Project C', 'Project D',
              'Project E', 'Project F', 'Project G', 'Project H',
              'Project I', 'Project J'],
    'start_date': ['2024-01-01', '2024-02-01', '2024-03-15',
                                 '2024-04-01', '2024-05-10', '2024-06-20',
                                 '2024-07-15', '2024-08-01', '2024-09-10',
                                 '2024-10-01'],
    'end_date': ['2024-01-15', '2024-03-01', '2024-04-10',
                               '2024-04-20', '2024-06-01', '2024-07-05',
                               '2024-08-01', '2024-09-01', '2024-10-01',
                               '2024-11-01'],
    'department': ['HR', 'Finance', 'Marketing', 'IT', 'HR',
                   'Finance', 'Marketing', 'IT', 'HR', 'Finance']
}

# Create the DataFrame
df_timeline = pd.DataFrame(data)
df_timeline.head()
```

Task: Create a basic timeline plot (Figure 16.34) showing the start and end dates of each event.

```
# Create a basic timeline plot
fig = px.timeline(df_timeline, x_start='start_date', x_end='end_date',
                  y='event', title='Timeline of Events')

fig.show()
```

Task: Create a timeline plot (Figure 16.35) where events are color-coded by the department.

```
# Create a timeline plot with color by department
fig = px.timeline(df_timeline, x_start='start_date', x_end='end_date',
                  y='event', color='department',
                  title='Timeline of Events by Department')

fig.show()
```

Task: Create a timeline plot (Figure 16.36) that includes the department in the hover information.

```
# Create a timeline plot with department in hover information
fig = px.timeline(df_timeline, x_start='start_date', x_end='end_date',
                  y='event', hover_data=['department'],
                  title='Timeline of Events with Department Info')

fig.show()
```

Timeline of Events

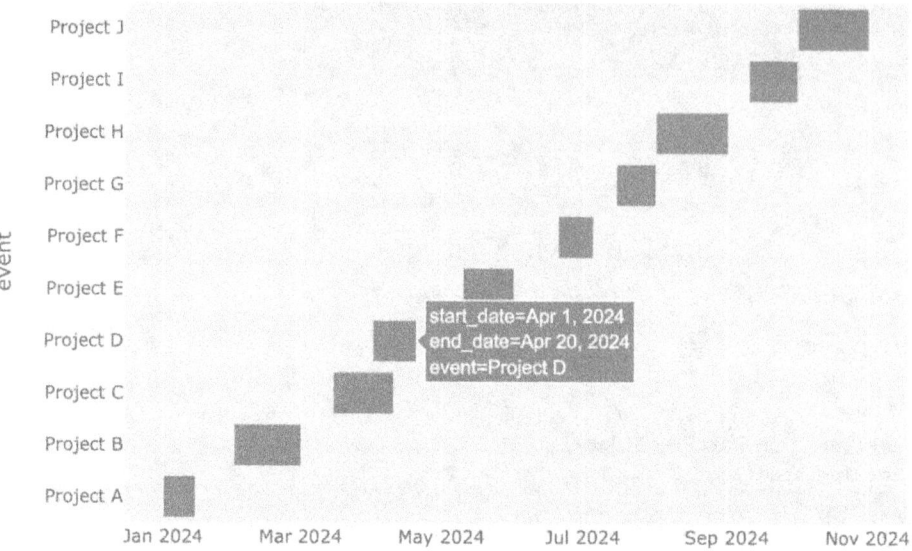

Figure 16.34 A basic timeline plot for events.

Timeline of Events by Department

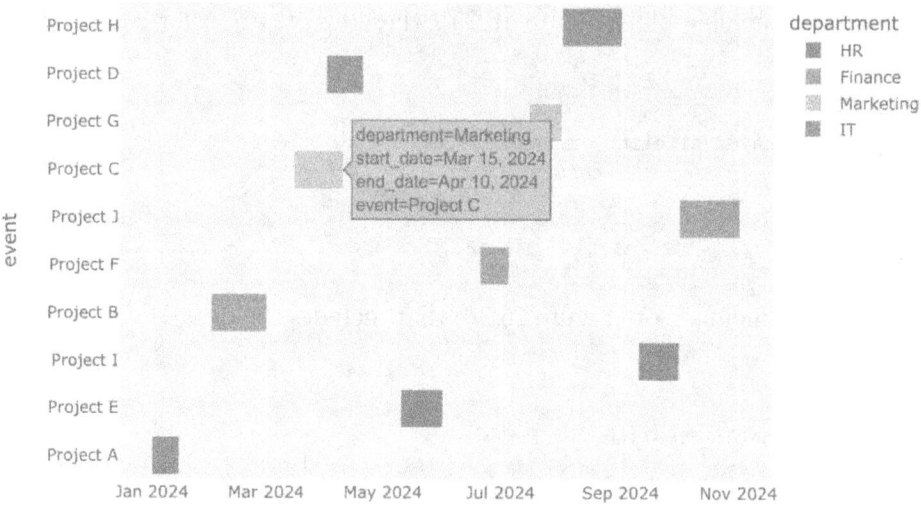

Figure 16.35 A basic timeline plot for events, categorized by department.

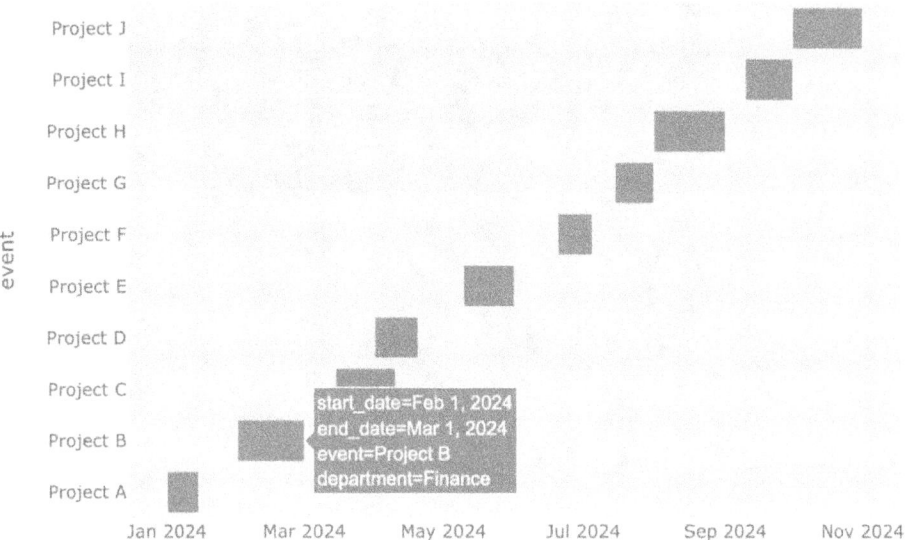

Figure 16.36 A timeline plot for events, with department information.

16.8 FUNNEL PLOTS

16.8.1 Demonstration

Funnel charts are useful for visualizing the progressive reduction of data as it passes through different stages in a process.

Let's start with a simple funnel chart representing the stages of a sales funnel (Figure 16.37). This funnel chart visualizes the number of entities (e.g., potential customers) at each stage of the sales funnel. The x-axis represents the count of entities, while the y-axis represents the stages.

```
# Sample data
data = {
    'Stage': ['Prospects', 'Leads', 'Opportunities',
              'Proposals', 'Closed Deals'],
    'Count': [1000, 500, 400, 200, 50]
}

# Creating a basic funnel chart
fig = px.funnel(data, x='Count', y='Stage', title='Sales Funnel')

# Display the plot
fig.show()
```

Let's add another dimension to the funnel chart by grouping the data by category. In this funnel chart, the data is grouped by region (in this case, "North America")

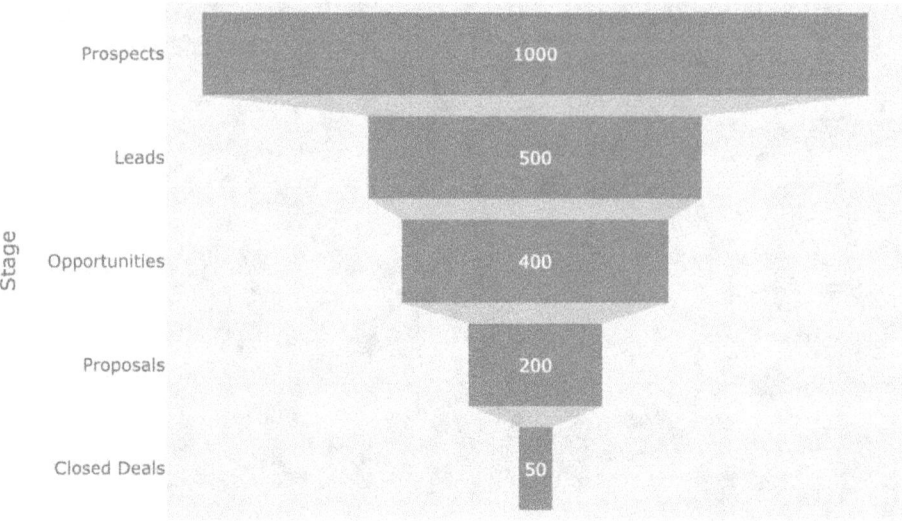

Figure 16.37 A basic funnel plot for sales data.

(Figure 16.38). The `color` parameter is used to differentiate categories, which could be useful for comparing the performance of different regions, products, or segments.

```python
# Sample data
data = {
    'Stage': ['Prospects', 'Leads', 'Opportunities',
              'Proposals', 'Closed Deals'],
    'Count': [1000, 750, 500, 300, 100],
    'Region': ['North America'] * 5
}

# Creating a funnel chart with categories
fig = px.funnel(data, x='Count', y='Stage',
                color='Region', title='Sales Funnel by Region')

# Display the plot
fig.show()
```

In this example, we'll create a funnel chart with data from multiple regions to compare their performance (Figure 16.39). This funnel chart displays sales funnel data for "North America", "Europe" and "Latin America". The chart allows you to compare how the funnel progresses in different regions, showing the differences in the number of entities at each stage.

```python
# Sample data
data = {
    'Stage': ['Prospects', 'Leads', 'Opportunities',
              'Proposals', 'Closed Deals']*3,
```

Sales Funnel by Region

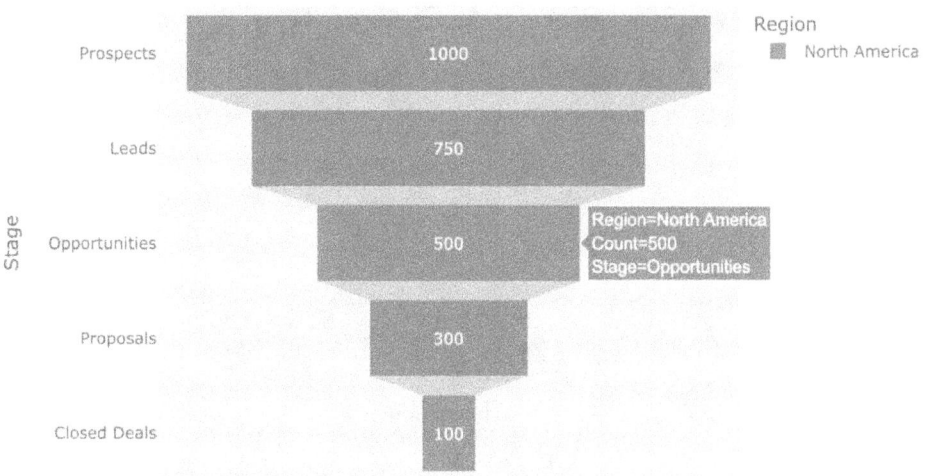

Figure 16.38 A funnel plot showing sales by region.

```
    'Count': [1000, 750, 500, 300, 100,
              1200, 900, 600, 350, 150,
              900, 800, 400, 200, 10],
    'Region': ['North America']*5 + ['Europe']*5 + ['Latin America']*5
}

# Creating a funnel chart with multiple regions
fig = px.funnel(data, x='Count', y='Stage',
                color='Region', title='Sales Funnel by Region')

# Display the plot
fig.show()
```

16.8.2 Practice

To practice funnel plots using Plotly, we can create a dummy dataset that represents a sales or conversion funnel. This DataFrame df_funnel with four rows representing different stages in the funnel and the number of leads at each stage.

```
# Define the data
data = {
    'stage': ['Awareness', 'Interest', 'Consideration', 'Purchase']*2,
    'leads': [1000, 600, 300, 150, 2000, 1800, 800, 200],
    'agent': ['Tom'] * 4 + ['Ron'] * 4
}

# Create the DataFrame
df_funnel = pd.DataFrame(data)
df_funnel.head()
```

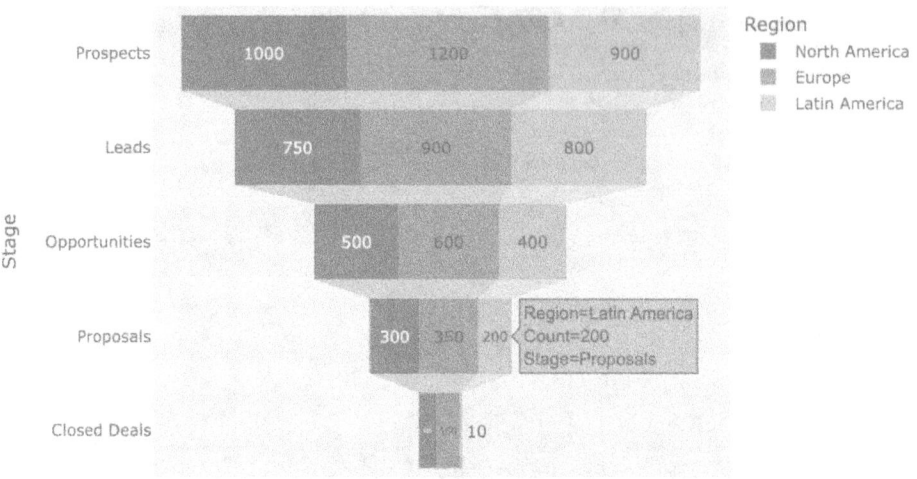

Figure 16.39 A funnel plot displaying sales by region.

Task: Create a funnel plot (Figure 16.40) to visualize the number of leads at each stage of the funnel.

```
# Create a basic funnel plot
fig = px.funnel(df_funnel, x='leads', y='stage',
                title='Basic Sales Funnel')

fig.show()
```

Task: Create a funnel plot (Figure 16.41) to visualize the number of leads at each stage of the funnel, differentiate color by 'agent'.

```
# Create a colored funnel plot
fig = px.funnel(df_funnel, x='leads', y='stage',
                color='agent', title='Basic Sales Funnel')

fig.show()
```

16.9   PIE PLOTS

16.9.1   Demonstration

A pie chart is a circular statistical chart, which is divided into sectors to illustrate percentages.

Let's start by creating a basic pie plot to visualize the proportion sales (Figure 16.42).

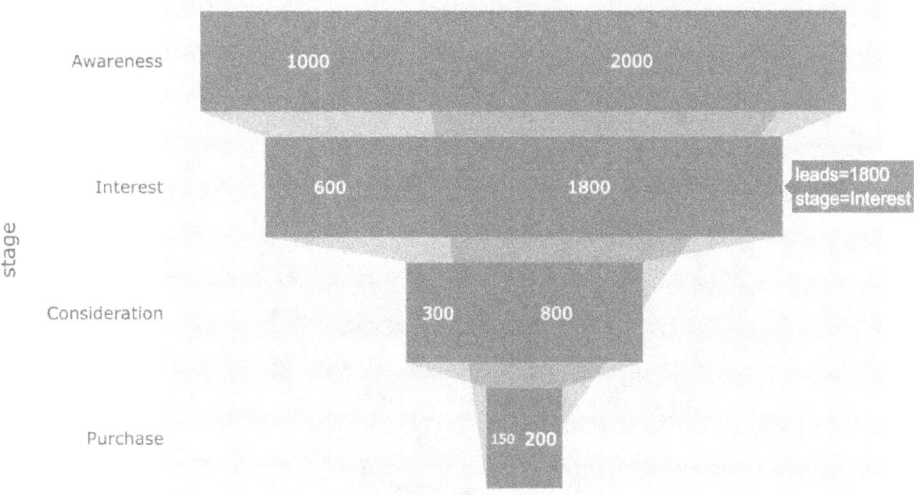

Figure 16.40 A basic funnel plot for sales.

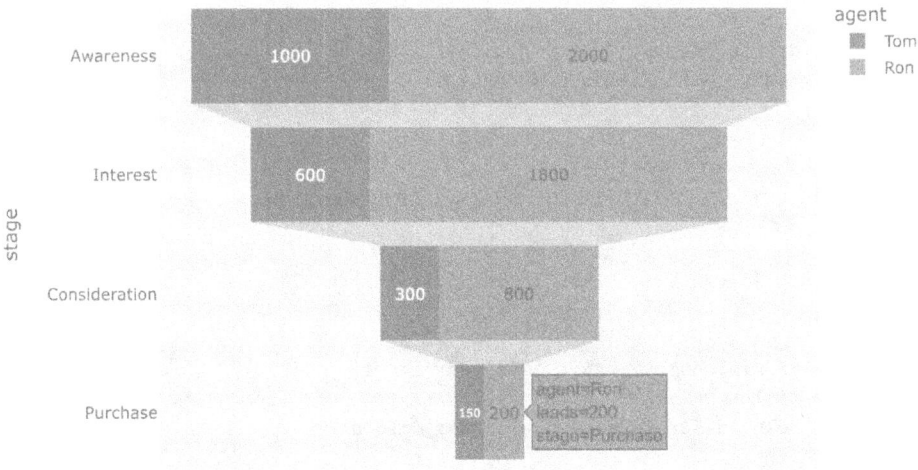

Figure 16.41 A funnel plot showing sales by agent.

```
# Data for the pie chart
data = {
    'stage': ['Awareness', 'Interest', 'Consideration', 'Purchase'],
    'leads': [1000, 600, 300, 150]
}
```

Basic Sales Pie Chart

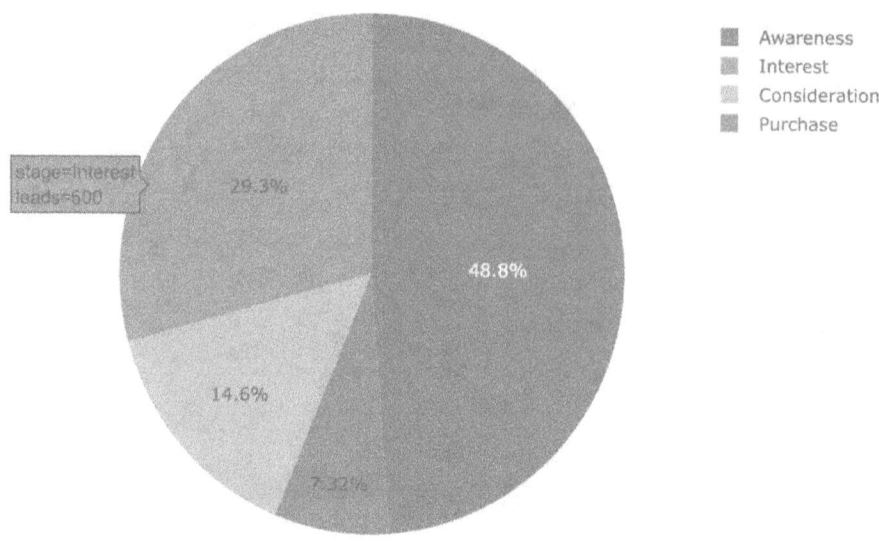

Figure 16.42 A basic pie plot showing sales proportions.

```
df_pie = pd.DataFrame(data)

# Create a basic pie chart
fig = px.pie(df_pie, names='stage', values='leads',
            title='Basic Sales Pie Chart')

fig.show()
```

Let's now add custom colors for the pie plot (Figure 16.43).

```
# Custom colors for the pie chart
custom_colors = ['lightblue', 'lightgreen', 'lightcoral', 'lightpink']

# Create a pie chart with custom colors
fig = px.pie(df_pie, names='stage', values='leads',
            title='Sales Pie with Custom Colors',
            color_discrete_sequence=custom_colors)

fig.show()
```

Let's now show the percentage of sales and add a hole in the center (Figure 16.44).

```
# Create a pie chart showing percentages
fig = px.pie(df_pie, names='stage', values='leads',
            title='Sales Pie with Percentage Display',
            labels={'leads': 'Percentage'},
            hole=0.4)

# Update the trace to show percentages
```

Sales Pie with Custom Colors

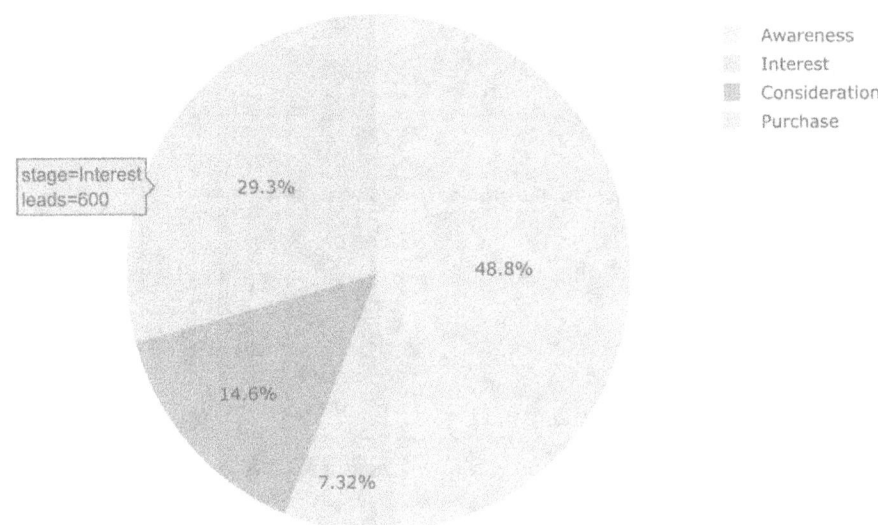

Figure 16.43   A pie plot for sales, with custom colors for each slice.

Sales Pie with Percentage Display

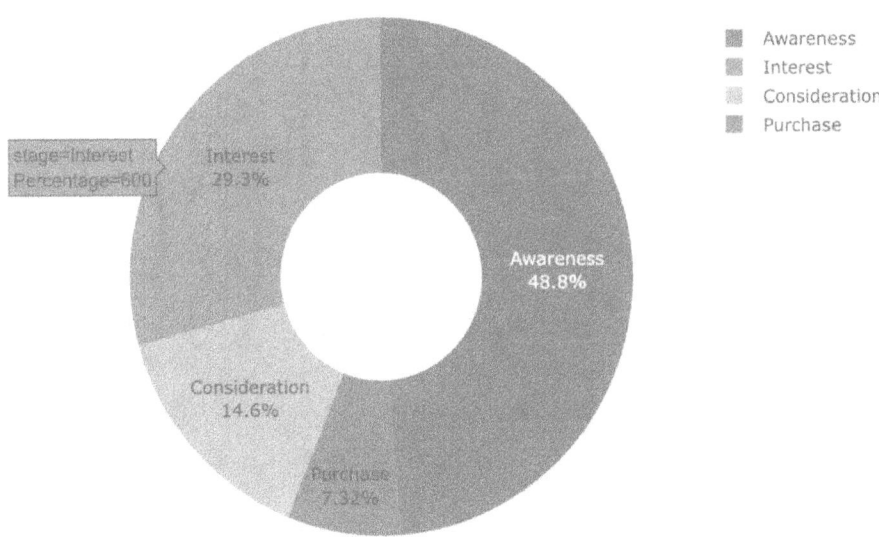

Figure 16.44   A pie plot for sales, displaying percentages for each slice.

```
fig.update_traces(textinfo='percent+label')

fig.show()
```

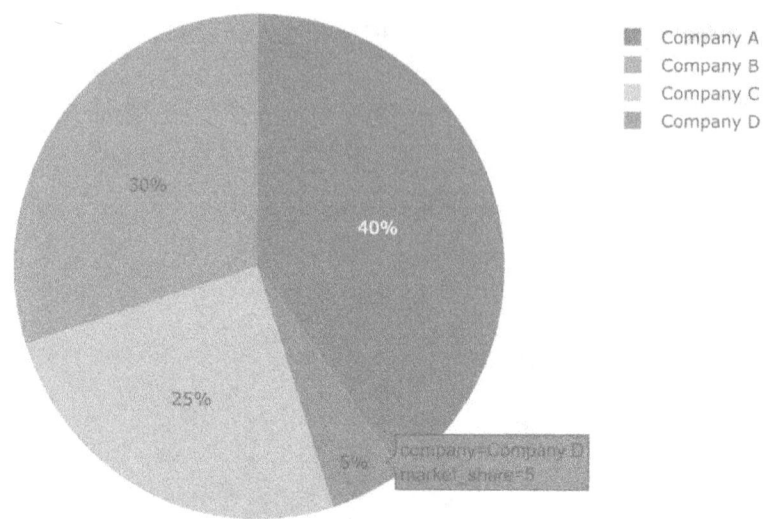

Figure 16.45 A pie plot showing market share distribution.

16.9.2 Practice

Let's create a dummy dataset for practicing pie plots.

```
# Dummy dataset
data = {
    'company': ['Company A', 'Company B', 'Company C', 'Company D'],
    'market_share': [40, 30, 25, 5]
}

df_market = pd.DataFrame(data)
df_market
```

Task: Create a basic pie plot (Figure 16.45) using the following dummy dataset that represents the market share of different companies.

```
# Create the basic pie plot
fig = px.pie(df_market, names='company', values='market_share',
             title='Market Share of Companies')

fig.show()
```

Task: Create a pie plot (Figure 16.46) using the dataset above, assigning custom colors to each company. custom_colors = ['gold', 'lightblue', 'lightgreen', 'lightcoral']

```
# Custom colors for the pie chart
custom_colors = ['gold', 'lightblue', 'lightgreen', 'lightcoral']
```

Market Share with Custom Colors

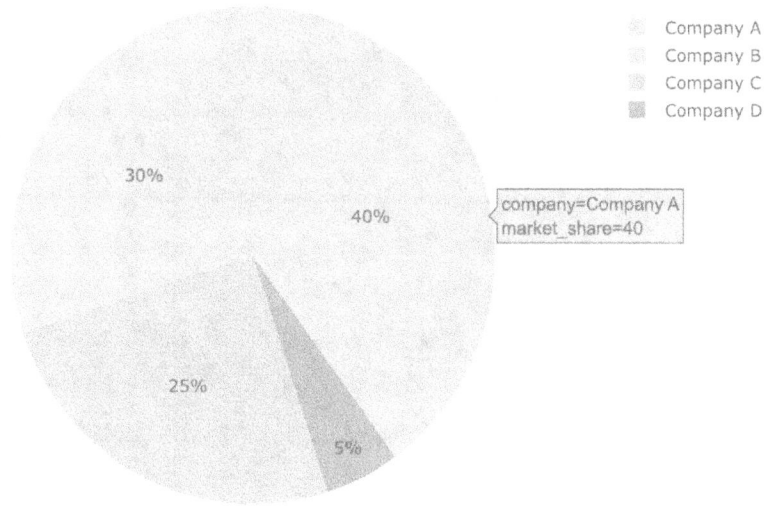

Figure 16.46 A pie plot for market share, with custom colors.

```
# Create the pie plot with custom colors
fig = px.pie(df_market, names='company', values='market_share',
             title='Market Share with Custom Colors',
             color_discrete_sequence=custom_colors)
fig.show()
```

Task: Create a pie plot (Figure 16.47) using the dataset above, displaying the percentage of the total market share for each company.

```
# Create the pie plot showing percentages
fig = px.pie(df_market, names='company', values='market_share',
             title='Market Share by Percentage')

# Update the trace to show percentages
fig.update_traces(textinfo='percent+label')

fig.show()
```

Task: Create a donut chart (Figure 16.48) using the dataset above, with a hole in the center.

```
# Create the donut chart
fig = px.pie(df_market, names='company',
             values='market_share',
             title='Market Share Donut Chart', hole=0.4)

fig.show()
```

Market Share by Percentage

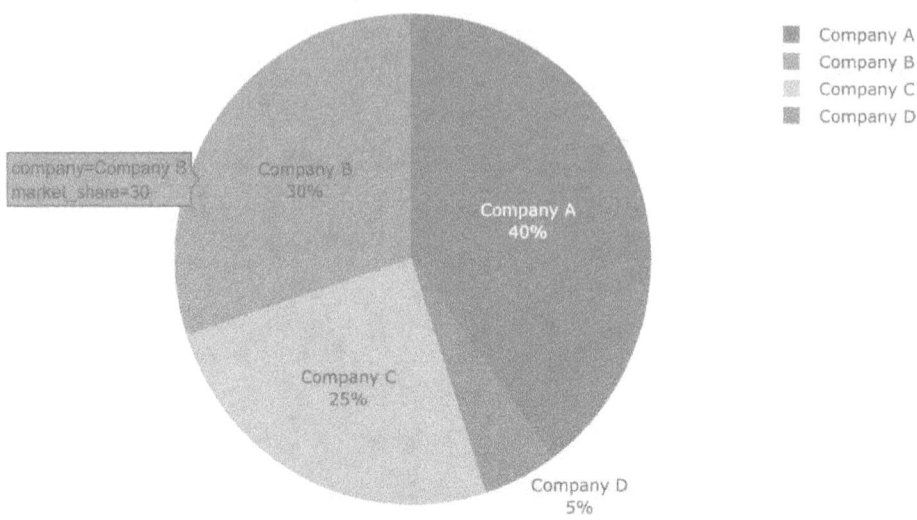

Figure 16.47 A pie plot for market share, displaying percentages.

Market Share Donut Chart

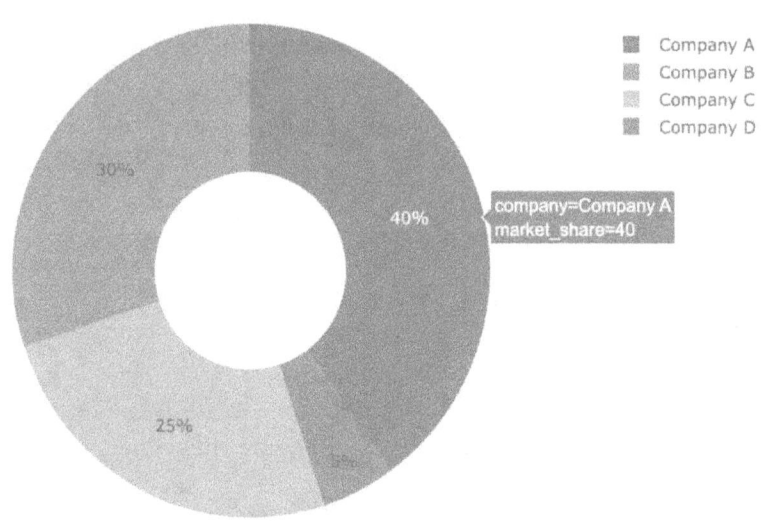

Figure 16.48 A pie plot for market share, with a hollow center.

Basic Histogram of Values

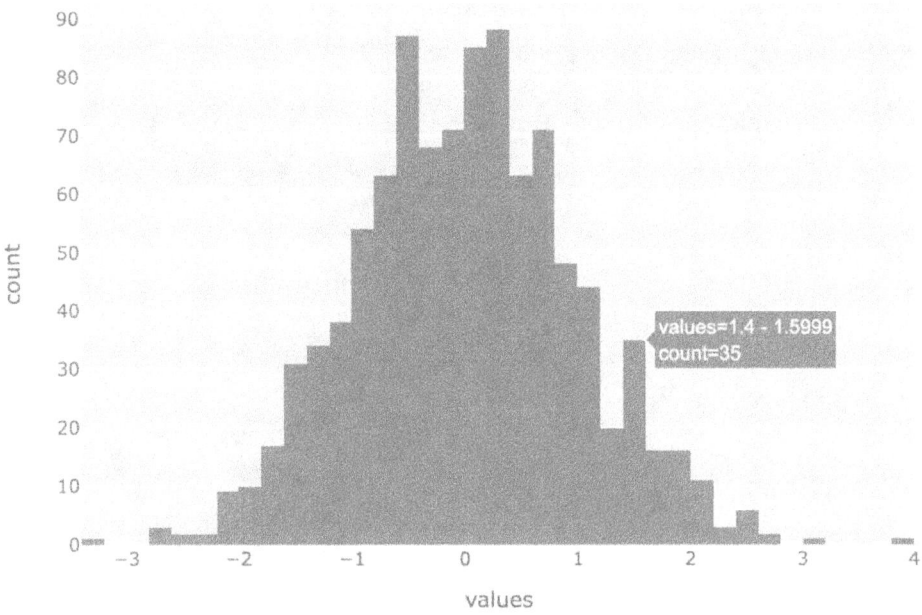

Figure 16.49 A basic histogram displaying data distribution.

16.10 HISTOGRAM PLOTS

16.10.1 Demonstration

Histograms are useful for visualizing the distribution of a dataset. Let's start by creating a histogram to visualize the distribution of a numeric variable (Figure 16.49). This example creates a histogram of a normally distributed dataset. The x parameter specifies the variable to be plotted on the x-axis, and the histogram shows the frequency of data points in each bin.

```
# Creating a dummy dataset
np.random.seed(42)
data = {'values': np.random.normal(0, 1, 1000)}

df_hist = pd.DataFrame(data)

# Create a basic histogram
fig = px.histogram(df_hist, x='values', title='Basic Histogram of Values')
fig.show()
```

Let's make a custom number of bins to better control the granularity of the distribution (Figure 16.50). In this example, we specify `nbins=30` to adjust the granularity of the distribution visualization.

Histogram with 30 Bins

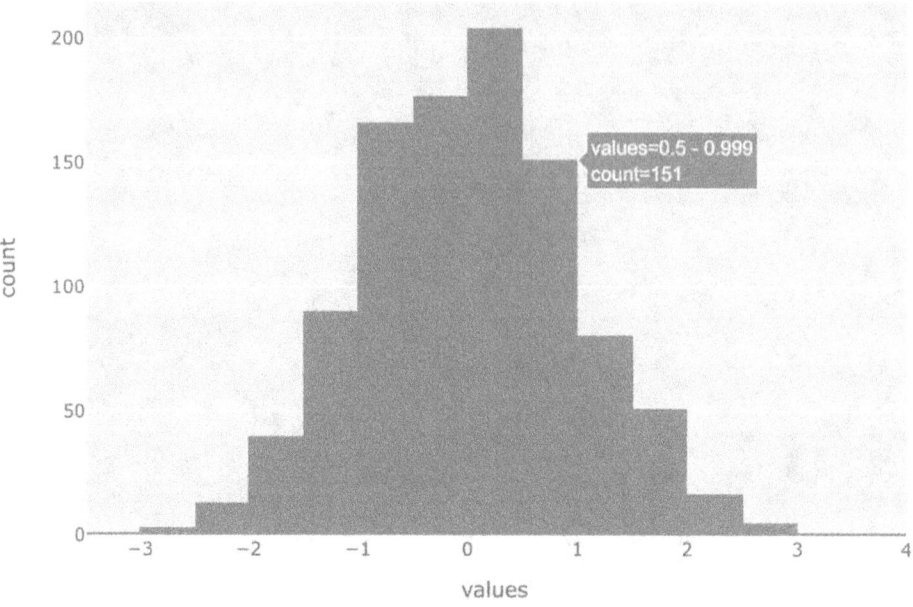

Figure 16.50 A basic histogram with 30 bins for finer data representation.

```
# Create a histogram with 30 bins
fig = px.histogram(df_hist, x='values', nbins=30,
                   title='Histogram with 30 Bins')
fig.show()
```

Let's create a histogram where the bars are colored based on a categorical variable (Figure 16.51). In this example, we add a categorical variable **category** to the dataset. The histogram is colored by this category, allowing us to see how the distribution varies between the two categories.

```
# Adding a categorical variable
df_hist['category'] = np.random.choice(['Category A', 'Category B'],size=1000)

# Create a histogram colored by category
fig = px.histogram(df_hist, x='values', color='category',
                   title='Histogram Colored by Category')
fig.show()
```

16.10.2   Practice

Let's create another dummy dataset for this practice.

```
# Creating a dummy dataset
np.random.seed(0)
data = {
```

Histogram Colored by Category

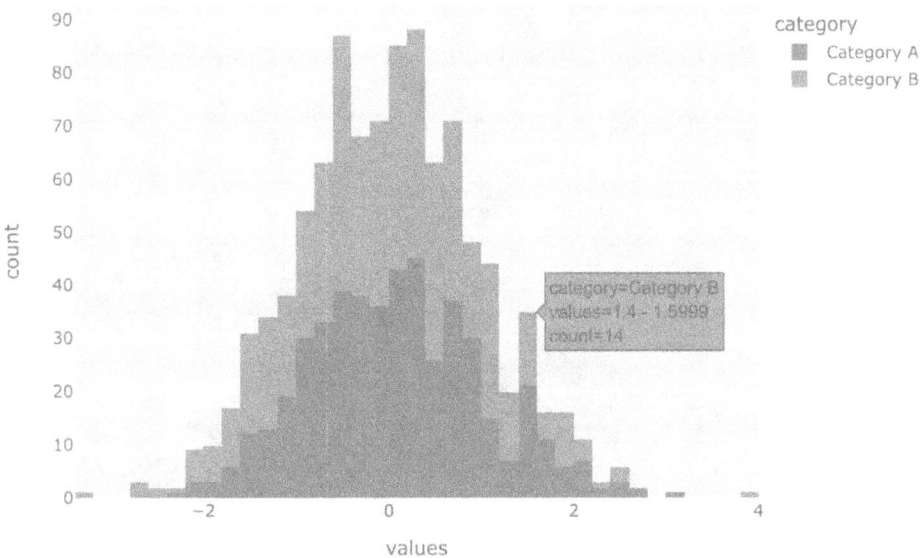

Figure 16.51 A histogram colored by category to show distribution differences.

```
    'test_scores': np.random.normal(75, 10, 500)
}

df_scores = pd.DataFrame(data)
```

Task: Create a histogram (Figure 16.52) to visualize the distribution of a dataset representing the test scores of 500 students. The scores are normally distributed.

```
# Create the histogram
fig = px.histogram(df_scores, x='test_scores',
                   title='Distribution of Test Scores')
fig.show()
```

Task: Create a histogram (Figure 16.53) from the same test scores dataset, but this time, use 20 bins to better observe the distribution.

```
# Create the histogram with 20 bins
fig = px.histogram(df_scores, x='test_scores', nbins=20,
                   title='Test Scores Histogram with 20 Bins')
fig.show()
```

Task: Add a 'gender' column to the test scores dataset, where each student is randomly assigned as 'Male' or 'Female'. Then, create a histogram (Figure 16.54) that shows the distribution of test scores, with bars colored by gender.

```
# Add a 'gender' column
df_scores['gender'] = np.random.choice(['Male', 'Female'], size=500)
```

Distribution of Test Scores

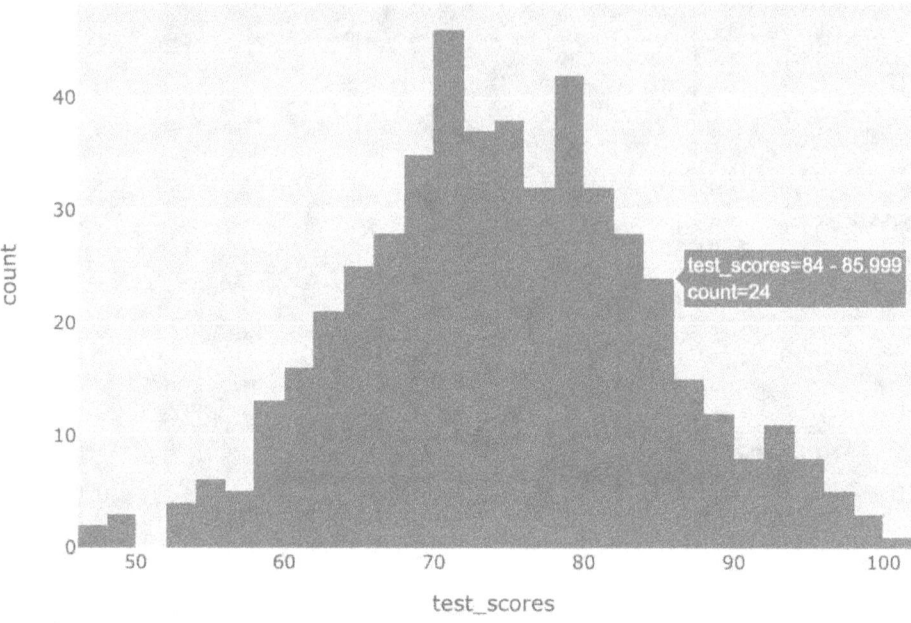

Figure 16.52 A histogram displaying the distribution of test scores.

```
# Create the histogram colored by gender
fig = px.histogram(df_scores, x='test_scores', color='gender',
                   title='Test Scores Histogram by Gender')
fig.show()
```

Task: Create a histogram (Figure 16.55) that shows the cumulative distribution of test scores.

```
# Create the cumulative histogram
fig = px.histogram(df_scores, x='test_scores',
                   cumulative=True,
                   title='Cumulative Distribution of Test Scores')
fig.show()
```

Task: Using the same dataset, create two separate histograms: one for 'Male' and one for 'Female' students. Overlay them on the same plot (Figure 16.56) to compare the distributions.

```
# Create overlaid histograms for male and female students
fig = px.histogram(df_scores, x='test_scores', color='gender',
                   barmode='overlay',
                   title='Overlaid Histograms of Test Scores by Gender')
fig.show()
```

Test Scores Histogram with 20 Bins

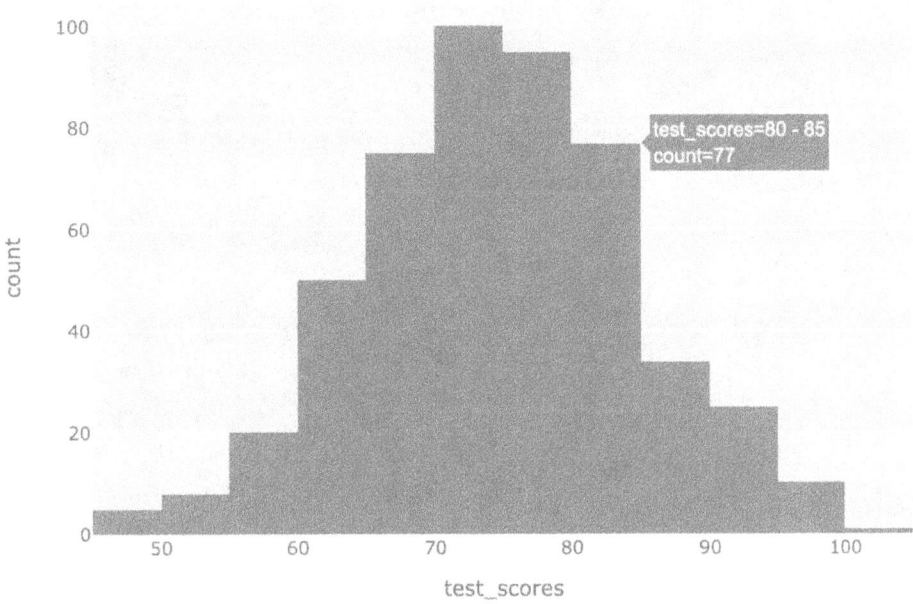

Figure 16.53 A histogram for test scores, with 20 bins.

Test Scores Histogram by Gender

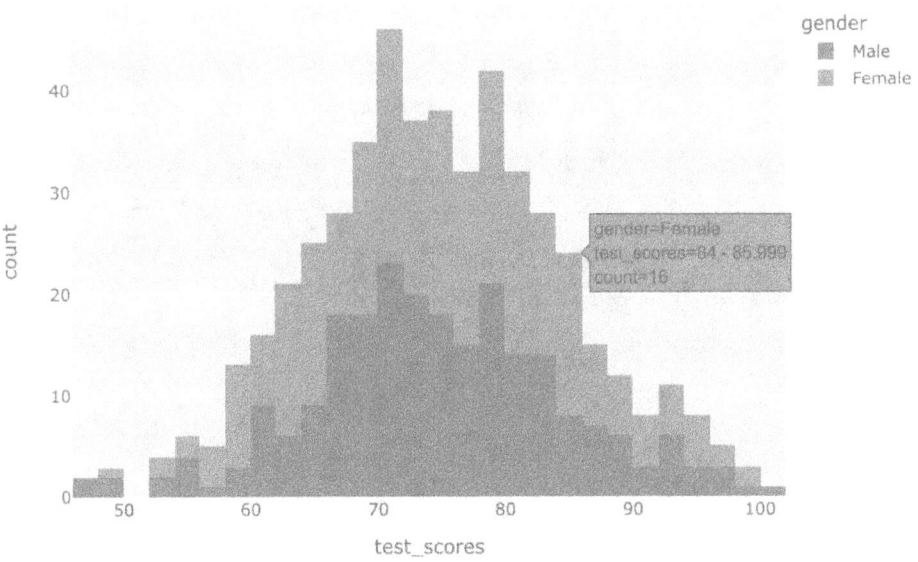

Figure 16.54 A histogram for test scores, grouped by gender.

Cumulative Distribution of Test Scores

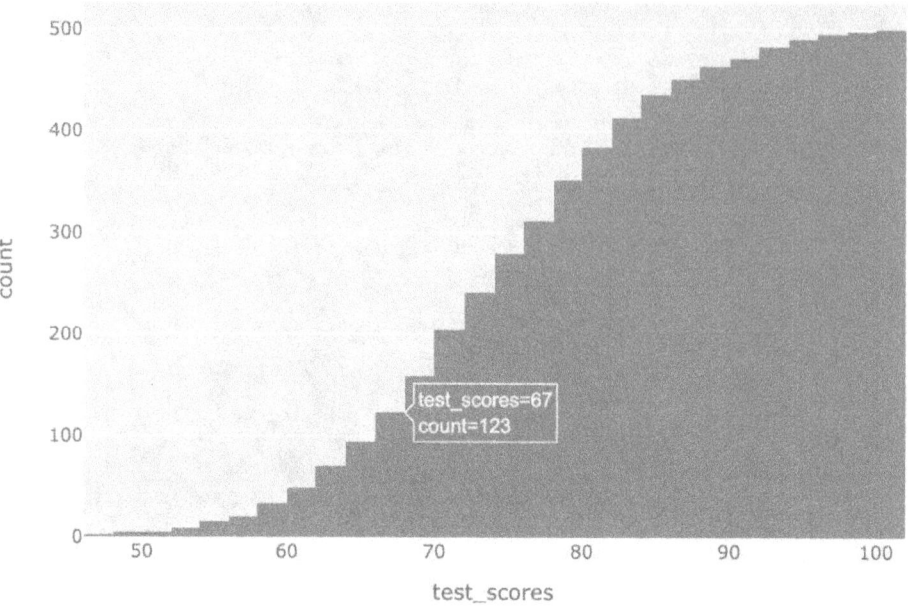

Figure 16.55 A cumulative distribution of test scores.

Overlaid Histograms of Test Scores by Gender

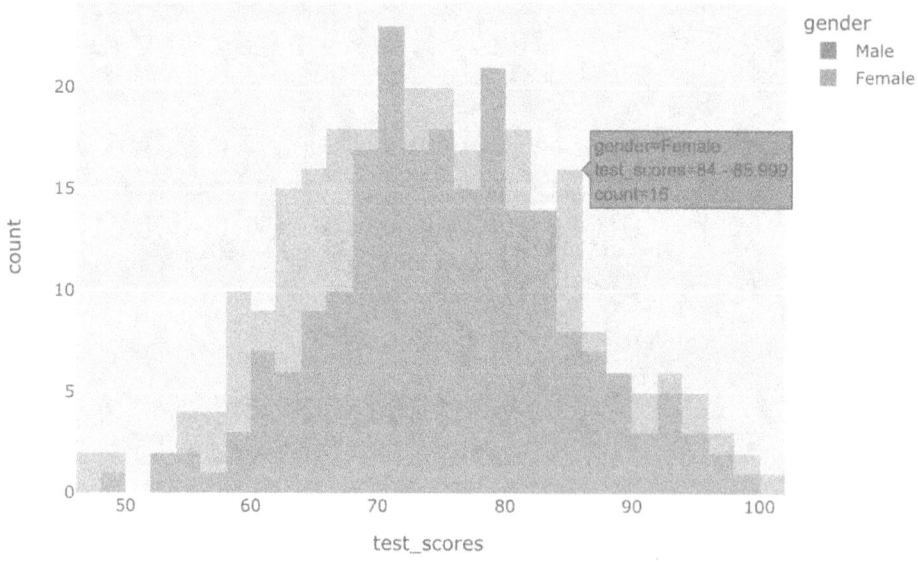

Figure 16.56 An overlaid histogram comparing test scores by gender.

Basic 3D Scatter Plot

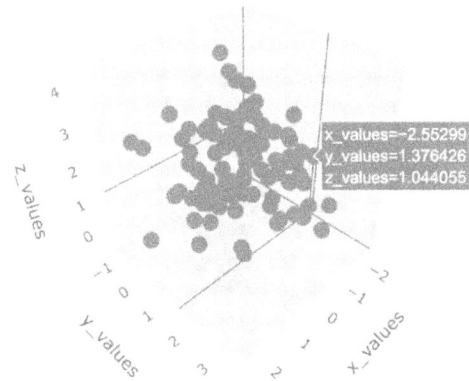

Figure 16.57 A basic 3D scatter plot showing data points in three dimensions.

16.11   3D SCATTER PLOTS

16.11.1   Demonstration

3D scatter plots are useful for visualizing the relationship between three variables in a dataset.

Let's create a basic 3D scatter plot using a dummy dataset with three numeric variables (Figure 16.57). This basic 3D scatter plot shows the relationship between three variables (x_values, y_values, and z_values) in a dummy dataset. The px.scatter_3d function is used to create the plot.

```
# Creating a dummy dataset
np.random.seed(0)
data = {
    'x_values': np.random.normal(0, 1, 100),
    'y_values': np.random.normal(1, 1, 100),
    'z_values': np.random.normal(2, 1, 100)
}

df_3d = pd.DataFrame(data)

# Create a basic 3D scatter plot
fig = px.scatter_3d(df_3d, x='x_values', y='y_values', z='z_values',
                    title='Basic 3D Scatter Plot')
fig.show()
```

Let's create another 3D scatter plot with points colored based on a fourth variable (Figure 16.58). In this example, a categorical variable color_variable is added to the dataset. The points in the 3D scatter plot are colored based on this variable, allowing you to see how the data is grouped.

3D Scatter Plot with Color Mapping

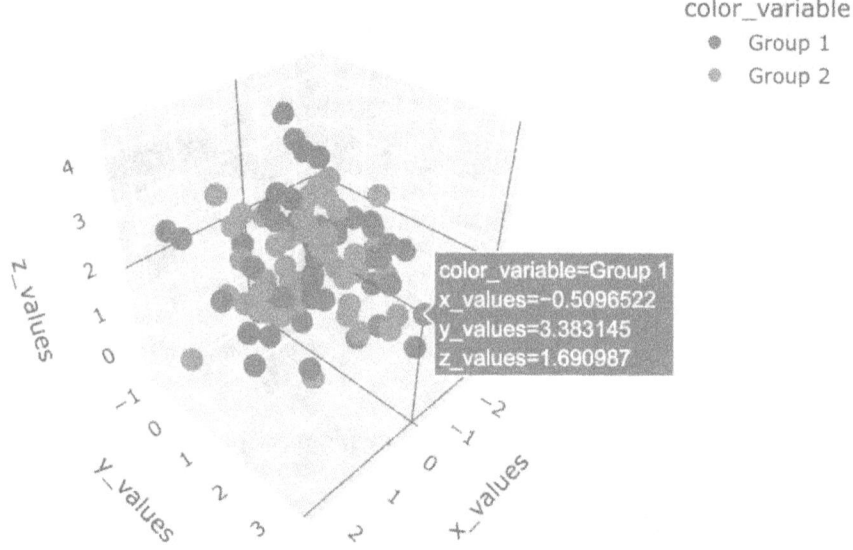

Figure 16.58   A 3D scatter plot with data points colored according to a mapping.

```python
# Adding a fourth variable for color mapping
df_3d['color_variable'] = np.random.choice(['Group 1', 'Group 2'],
                                            size=100)

# Create a 3D scatter plot with color mapping
fig = px.scatter_3d(df_3d, x='x_values', y='y_values', z='z_values',
                color='color_variable',
                title='3D Scatter Plot with Color Mapping')
fig.show()
```

Let's create a 3D scatter plot where the size of the points represents a numeric variable (Figure 16.59). This example introduces a numeric variable `size_variable` that controls the size of the points in the 3D scatter plot. Larger values result in bigger points, making it easier to identify trends related to this variable.

```python
# Adding a variable for size mapping
df_3d['size_variable'] = np.random.uniform(5, 50, size=100)

# Create a 3D scatter plot with size mapping
fig = px.scatter_3d(df_3d, x='x_values', y='y_values', z='z_values',
                size='size_variable', color='color_variable',
                title='3D Scatter Plot with Size Mapping')
fig.show()
```

3D Scatter Plot with Size Mapping

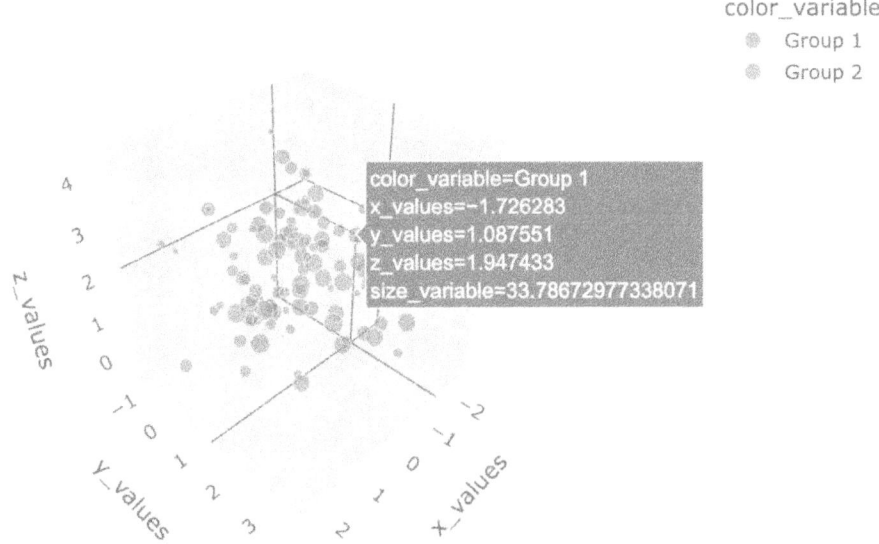

color_variable
◉ Group 1
◉ Group 2

color_variable=Group 1
x_values=-1.726283
y_values=1.087551
z_values=1.947433
size_variable=33.78672977338071

Figure 16.59 A 3D scatter plot with data points sized and colored based on mappings.

16.12 3D LINE PLOTS

16.12.1 Demonstration

3D line plots in Plotly are a powerful way to visualize the relationship between three variables over a sequence or time. They are particularly useful for showing trends in three-dimensional space. You can represent three-dimensional data with additional variables like color or group to make your plots more informative and visually appealing.

Let's create a basic 3D line plot using a dummy dataset with three numeric variables (Figure 16.60). This basic 3D line plot shows the relationship between three variables (x_values, y_values, and z_values) in a dummy dataset. The data represents a helical trajectory, with z_values increasing linearly while x_values and y_values oscillate sinusoidally.

```python
# Creating a dummy dataset
np.random.seed(42)
t = np.linspace(0, 10, 100)
data = {
    'x_values': np.sin(t),
    'y_values': np.cos(t),
    'z_values': t
}

df_line_3d = pd.DataFrame(data)
```

Basic 3D Line Plot

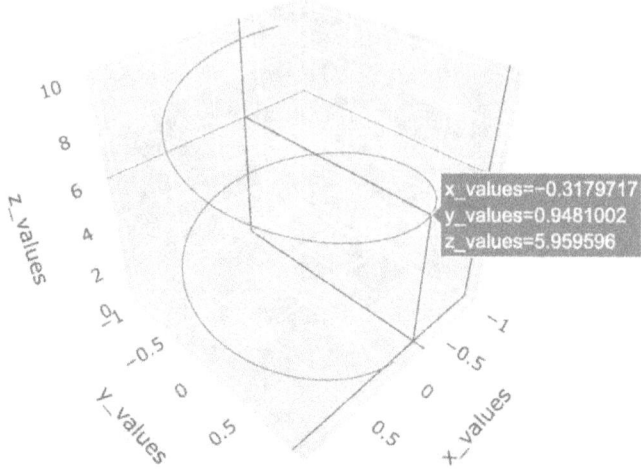

Figure 16.60 A basic 3D line plot showing a line in three dimensions.

```
# Create a basic 3D line plot
fig = px.line_3d(df_line_3d, x='x_values', y='y_values', z='z_values',
                 title='Basic 3D Line Plot')
fig.show()
```

Let's create another 3D line plot with multiple lines, each representing a different group or category (Figure 16.61). This example introduces a categorical variable group, with each line representing a different group. The 3D line plot now shows two trajectories, one for each group, which helps to compare the patterns across different categories.

```
# Creating a dataset with multiple lines
df_line_3d['group'] = np.random.choice(['Group 1', 'Group 2'], size=100)

# Create a 3D line plot with multiple lines
fig = px.line_3d(df_line_3d, x='x_values', y='y_values', z='z_values',
                 color='group',
                 title='3D Line Plot with Multiple Lines')
fig.show()
```

We summarize the plots using Plotly in Table 16.2.

16.13   INTERACT WITH GENAI

Here are some questions and prompts you can interact with generative AI tools, including ChatGPT.

- Why is Plotly preferred for creating interactive visualizations?

3D Line Plot with Multiple Lines

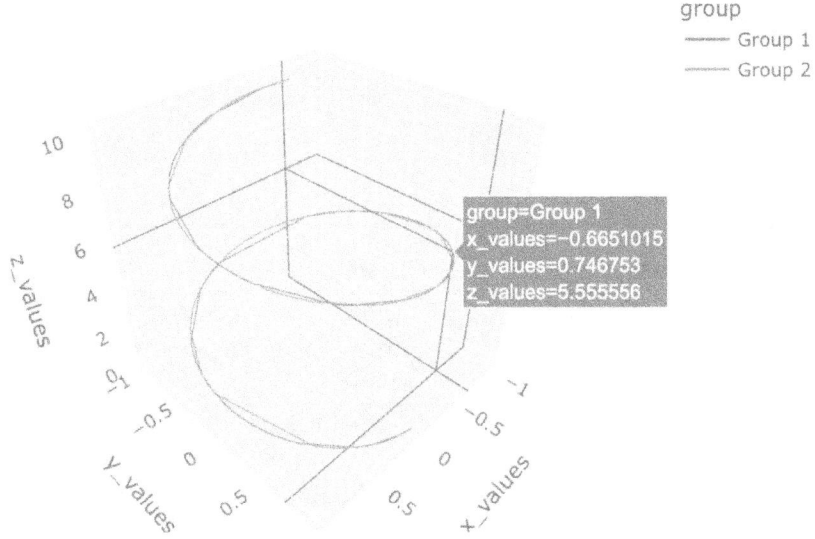

Figure 16.61 A 3D line plot with multiple lines, each representing a different group or category.

- What are the advantages of using Plotly for web-based or presentation-ready visualizations?
- Illustrate how to add a dropdown menu to switch between different views in a Plotly chart.
- How can you create subplots in Plotly and control their layout and size?
- Explain how to use Plotly's `animation` feature to create dynamic visualizations.
- How can you link multiple Plotly charts to interact together, such as zooming or filtering?
- Discuss how to use custom data in Plotly hover tooltips.
- Create a Plotly dashboard combining multiple charts to visualize sales data.
- Demonstrate how to use Plotly's tree map for hierarchical data visualization.
- Why might a Plotly chart not render properly in a Jupyter Notebook, and how can you fix it?

16.14   EXPLORE MORE ABOUT PLOTLY

Here is the Python documentation for Plotly: https://plotly.com/python/

TABLE 16.2 Summary of Plotly Plot Types

Type	Basic Syntax	Scenario
Scatter	`px.scatter()`	Shows the relationship between two variables. Example: Analyzing sales vs. marketing spend.
Line	`px.line()`	Visualizes trends or changes over time. Example: Tracking daily temperature changes.
Area	`px.area()`	Highlights the area under a line plot to show volume. Example: Visualizing cumulative sales over time.
Bar	`px.bar()`	Compares categorical data. Example: Comparing monthly revenue across different product categories.
Timeline	`px.timeline()`	Visualizes events over a timeline. Example: Project management to track task durations.
Funnel	`px.funnel()`	Shows stages in a process and drop-offs at each stage. Example: Visualizing a sales pipeline from leads to conversions.
Pie	`px.pie()`	Displays proportions within a whole. Example: Visualizing market share by product type.
Histogram	`px.histogram()`	Shows the distribution of a single variable. Example: Analyzing the distribution of customer ages.
3D-Scatter	`px.scatter_3d()`	Visualizes relationships among three variables. Example: Mapping geographical data with latitude, longitude, and elevation.
3D-Line	`px.line_3d()`	Tracks movement or trends in three dimensions. Example: Visualizing flight paths with altitude changes over time.

What is Next?

Congratulations! You've become a Python master! You now have a solid understanding of Object-oriented programming, advanced data structures in NumPy and Pandas, and data visualization tools like Matplotlib, Seaborn, and Plotly. That's a huge achievement! You're now able to conduct basic data analysis using Python.

After the celebration, you might want to learn more about the data science pipeline and the tools used in each step. For instance, how do you do data wrangling? This includes data collection, manipulation, understanding, preprocessing, and warehousing. Also, how do you do data analysis? This includes classification, regression, clustering, principal component analysis, association rule mining, outlier detection, and more. We have a book, *Data Mining with Python: Theory, Applications, and Case Studies*, to guide you through each topic with thorough explanations of the theory, applications, and real-life case studies. We hope you'll keep growing and becoming even more proficient in the field of data science!

I'm excited to meet you there and continue our journey together.

Index

For Product Safety Concerns and Information please contact our EU
representative GPSR@taylorandfrancis.com
Taylor & Francis Verlag GmbH, Kaufingerstraße 24, 80331 München, Germany

www.ingramcontent.com/pod-product-compliance
Lightning Source LLC
Chambersburg PA
CBHW080903170526
45158CB00008B/1975